3ds max® 6 Killer Tips

The hottest collection of cool tips and hidden secrets for 3ds max

Jon A. Bell

New Riders

Killer Tips series developed by Scott Kelby

PUBLISHER
Stephanie Wall

PRODUCTION MANAGER
Gina Kanouse

ACQUISITIONS EDITOR
Elise Walter

DEVELOPMENT EDITOR
Chris Zahn

SENIOR PROJECT EDITOR
Kristy Hart

COPY EDITOR
Karen A. Gill

INDEXER
Lisa Stumpf

COMPOSITION
Kim Scott

MANUFACTURING COORDINATOR
Dan Uhrig

COVER DESIGN AND CREATIVE CONCEPTS
Felix Nelson

COVER PRODUCTION
Aren Howell

MARKETING
Scott Cowlin
Tammy Detrich

PUBLICITY MANAGER
Susan Nixon

International Standard Book Number: 0-7357-1386-3

Library of Congress Catalog Card Number: 2003116357

Printed in the United States of America

First printing: February 2004

09 08 07 06 05 04 7 6 5 4 3 2 1

Interpretation of the printing code: The rightmost double-digit number is the year of the book's printing; the rightmost single-digit number is the number of the book's printing. For example, the printing code 04-1 shows that the first printing of the book occurred in 2004.

As always, this book is dedicated to my wife, Joan Gale Frank, my partner in adventure. She's always there for me, with good humor, faith, love, and support.

ACKNOWLEDGMENTS

A lot of people contributed to this book, and it's only fair that they get credit up front. I'd like to thank the following people:

- Elise Walter, Chris Zahn, and Stephanie Wall at New Riders Publishing for their editorial support.
- Andy and Stephanie Reese for their ongoing friendship and legal advice.
- Discreet's Dan Prochazka, David Marks, Nikolai Sander, Darvin Atkinson, Roger Cusson, Jamie Clay, John Stetzer, and the other members of the Discreet 3ds max QE team; Mark Gerhardt from Autodesk, Beau Perschall from TurboSquid, and Scott Kirvan from Splutterfish.
- Book contributors and all-around 3ds max experts Neil Blevins, Chad Copeland, Peter DeLappe, Pete Draper, Aksel Karcher, Ben Lipman, Dan Meblin, Michael Spaw, and The King of MaxScript, Borislav "Bobo" Petrov.
- My friends, Steve Dailey, Tom Hudson, and Kirk Wiseman; Bill George and John Goodson from ILM, and the Intrada gang: Doug, Mary Ann, Regina and Veronica Fake, Jeff Johnson, Roger Feigelson, Fred Sheppard, George Champagne, and Rick Hauserman. (Thanks for the music!)
- And, finally, my parents, Jim and Bonnie Thomas; cousins, Lesa and Lori; my sister, Jeanne; nieces, Amber, Afton, and Ariel; and nephew, Dane, because they all wanted to see their names in a book.

ABOUT THE AUTHOR

Jon A. Bell is a writer, 3D computer graphics artist, and software consultant. After working 10 years as an editor and writer in the computer magazine industry, Jon changed careers in 1991 to concentrate on the computer graphics industry. He has produced Common Gateway Interface (CGI) for television, films, computer games, multimedia, and print.

Jon provided animation for the films *Exorcist III: Legion*, *Terminator 2: Judgment Day*, *Honey, I Blew Up the Kid*, *Soldier*, and *Mighty Joe Young*. His video work includes Autodesk's/Kinetix's 1991, 1994, and 1997 SIGGRAPH reels, their 1993 and 1996 NAB reels, and work for Digital Phenomena and Matte World Digital.

Jon's multimedia and game industry work includes architectural models and animation for the Oracle Systems Athenia CD-ROM, model designs and animation for LucasArts Entertainment's *X-Wing* and *Rebel Assault*, Sega of America's *Jurassic Park* and *Wild Woody* CD-ROMS, and Gametek's *Robotech* and *Wheel of Fortune*. He wrote three *3D Studio MAX f/x and Design* books for Ventana/Coriolis Press (1996–1999), covering the first three releases of 3ds max, and provided 3D artwork for the book *Tripping* by Charles Hayes, published in October 2000 by Penguin USA.

Jon's most recent full-time job was working as Third-party Developer Relations Manager for Discreet, the multimedia division of Autodesk. He also provides 3D graphics and technical writing as a volunteer for Hawkes Ocean Technologies, Pt. Richmond, CA, the builders of the experimental minisub Deep Flight I and the Deep Flight 502 Aviator. (For more information, go to http://www.deepflight.com.)

After living in the San Francisco Bay Area for more than 16 years, Jon and his wife, Joan, moved from California to the red rocks of Sedona, Arizona in May 2003. Currently, Jon is working as a freelance 3D computer graphics artist and writer. His hobbies include 3D computer graphics, scuba diving, hiking, traveling to exotic places, reading, drawing, and writing fiction and essays. Jon and Joan have been married for more than 11 years, love to travel around the world, and are the parents of the world's most spoiled cat, Greystone.

You can reach Jon at jonbell@esedona.net.

ABOUT THE TECHNICAL REVIEWERS

These reviewers contributed their considerable hands-on expertise to the entire development process for *3ds max 6 Killer Tips*. As the book was being written, these dedicated professionals reviewed all the material for technical content, organization, and flow. Their feedback was critical to ensuring that *3ds max 6 Killer Tips* fits our readers' need for the highest-quality technical information.

David Marks is a member of the quality engineering team at Discreet and a veteran user of AutoCAD, 3D Studio, and 3ds max. He lives in the San Francisco Bay area with his wife and two daughters. In his spare time, David enjoys gourmet cooking, listening to progressive rock music, and attempting to play piano. Other hobbies include restoration of vintage arcade games, competitive bowling, and Japanese taiko drumming.

Jon McFarland is the manager of the design department of a national developer/owner/manager of retail, office, residential, and entertainment complexes based in Cleveland, Ohio. His department's responsibilities include the creation of computer graphic stills and animations depicting proposed facilities and the incorporation of 3D models into photographs and videos.

In addition to his primary job, Jon teaches computer animation to graphic arts students at The Virginia Marti College of Fashion and Art, a small, accredited college in Lakewood, Ohio.

Jon spent seven years "blowin' stuff up" as a paratrooper in the U.S. Army. This naturally led to a career in computer graphics and animation that began in early 1990. He has a degree in mechanical engineering technology, but he focuses his energy in the architectural visualization and animation fields.

Jon lives in Sheffield Lake, Ohio and coaches baseball, soccer, and wrestling for his sons, Zachary and Jacob.

TABLE OF CONTENTS

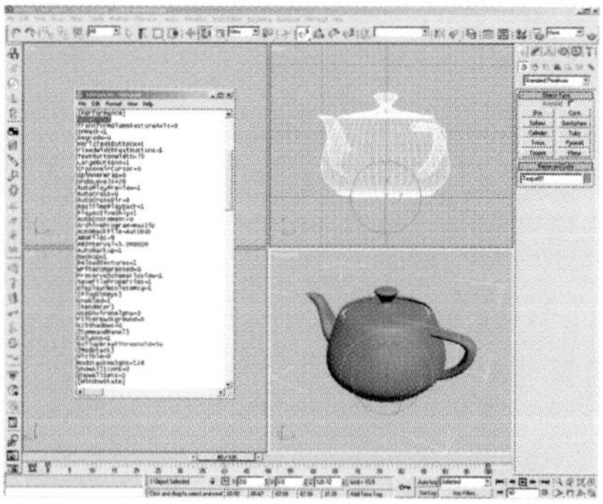

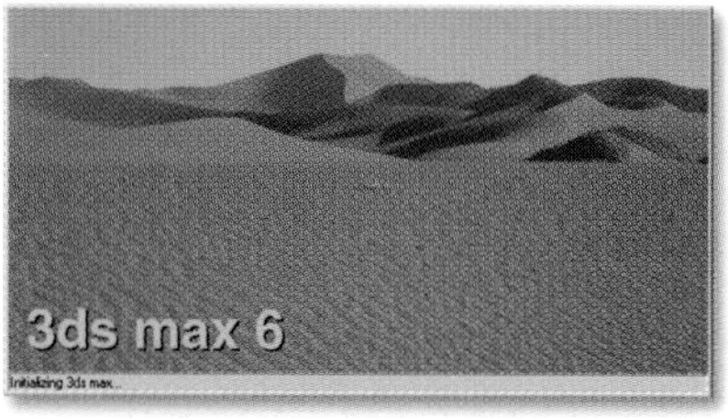

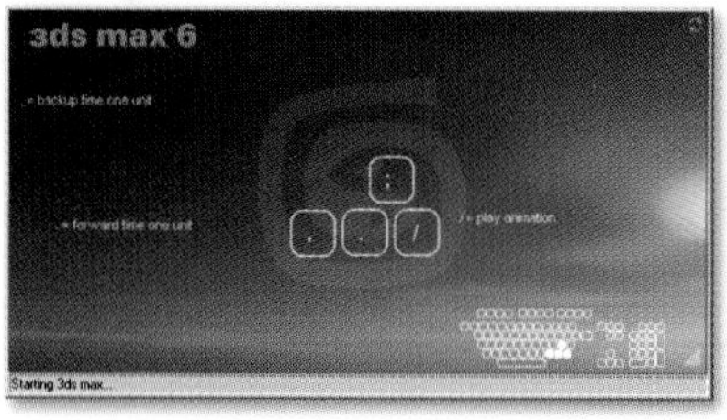

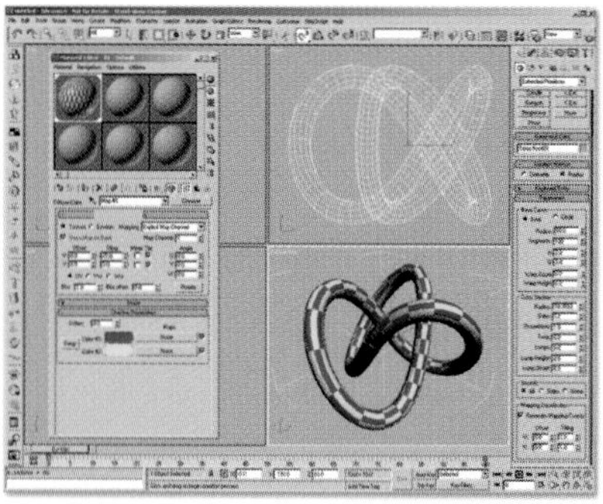

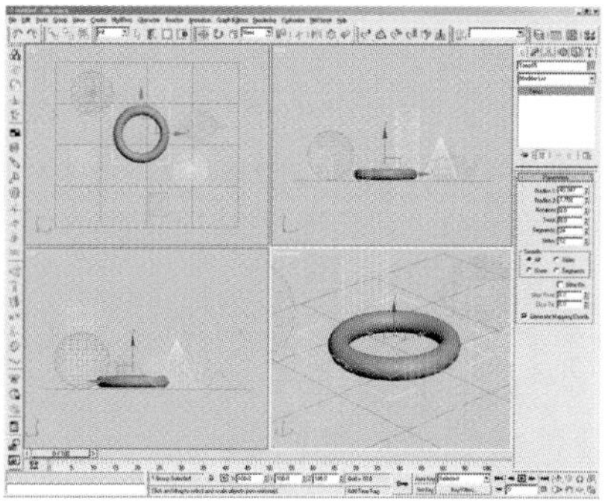

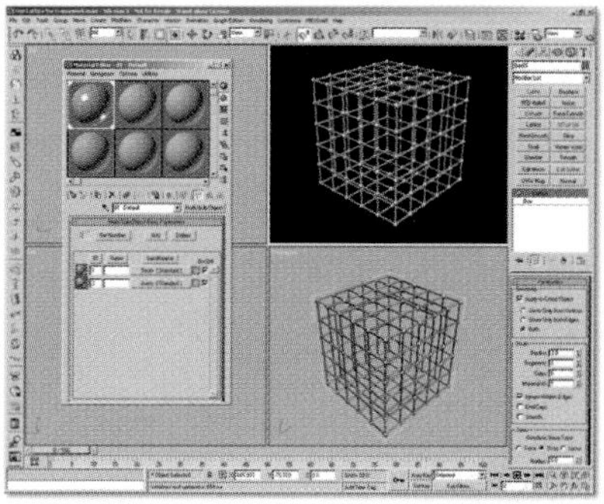

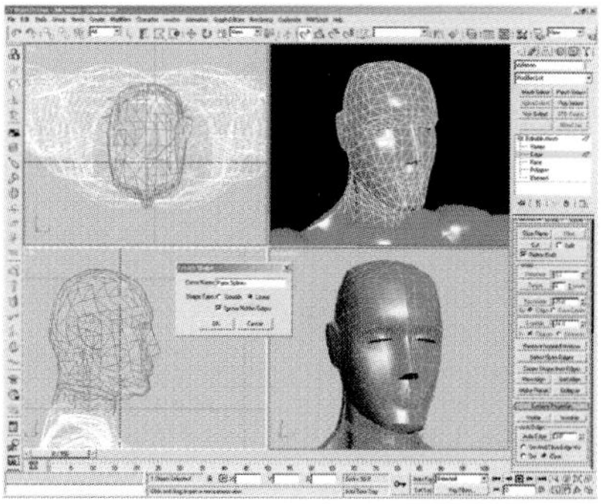

TABLE OF CONTENTS

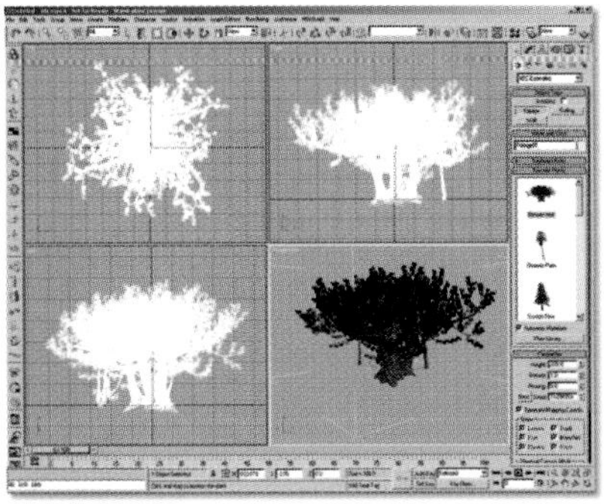

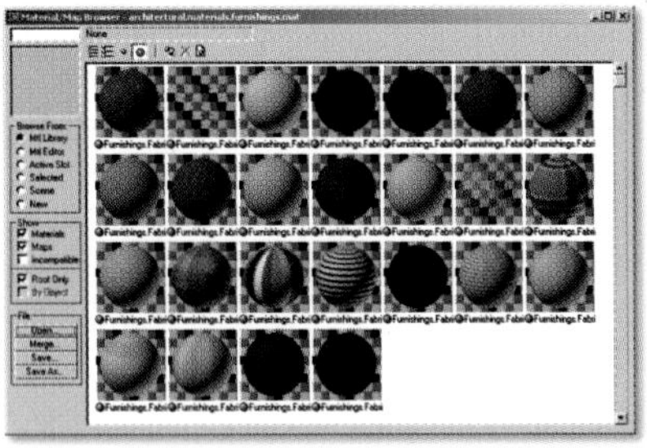

TABLE OF CONTENTS

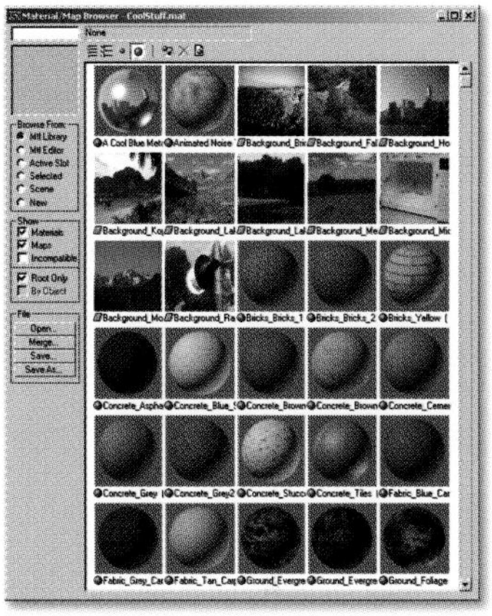

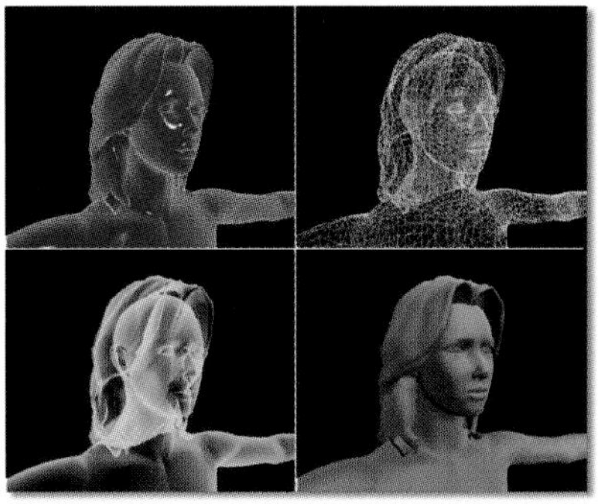

TABLE OF CONTENTS

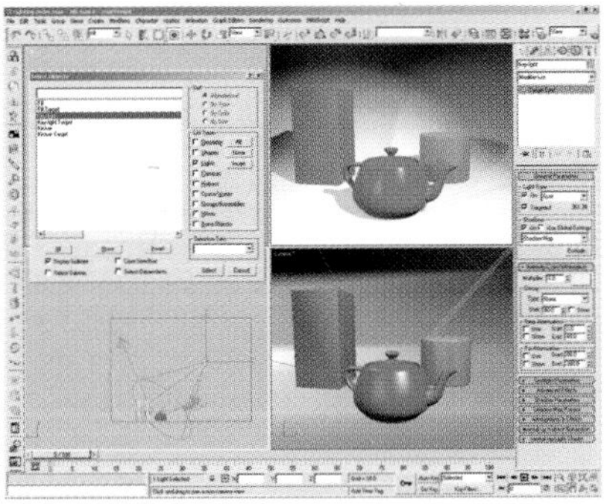

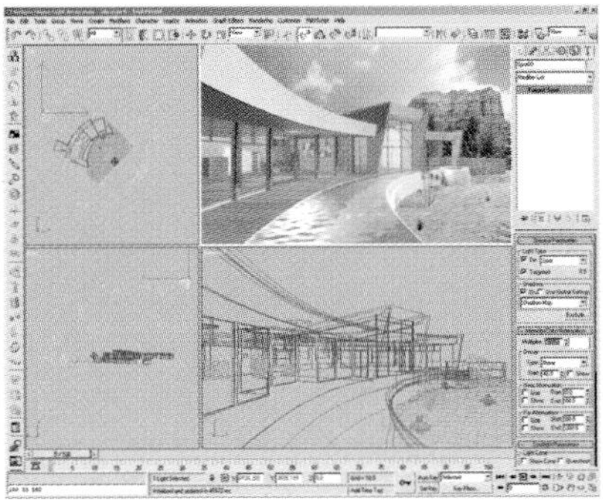

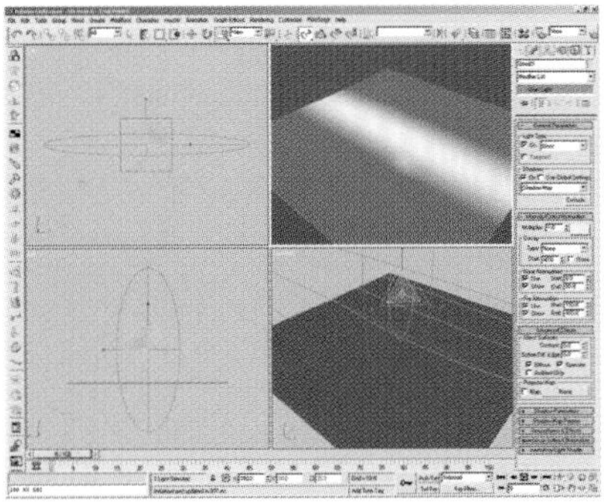

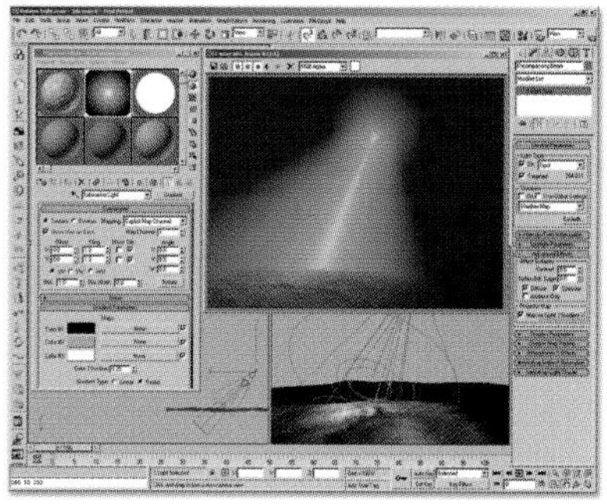

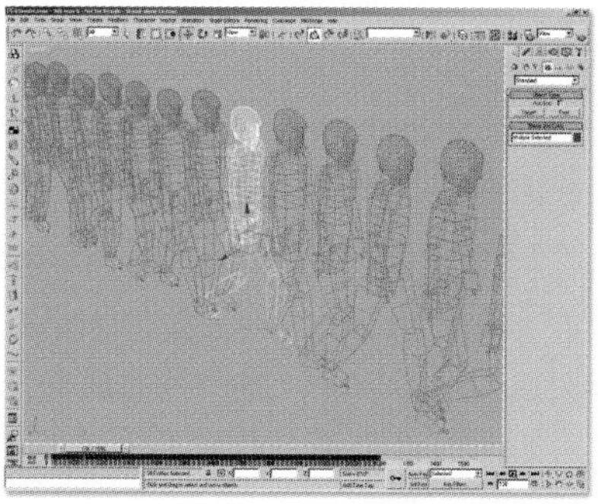

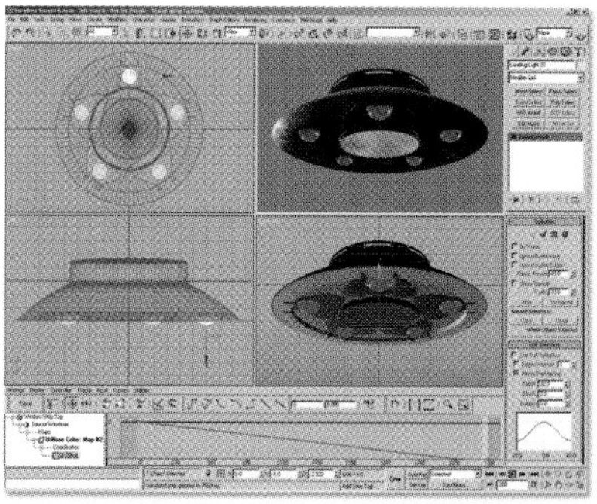

TABLE OF CONTENTS

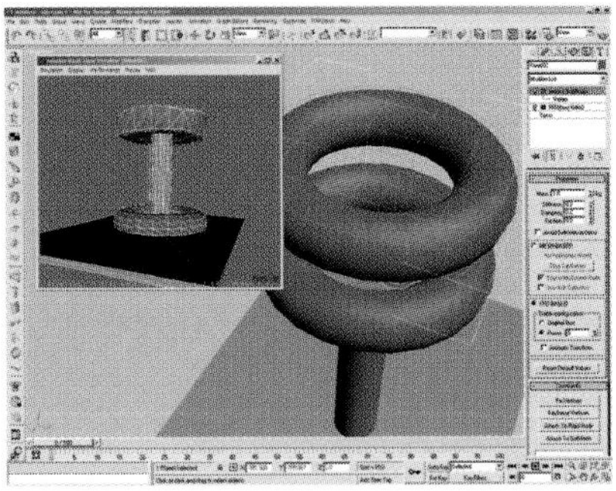

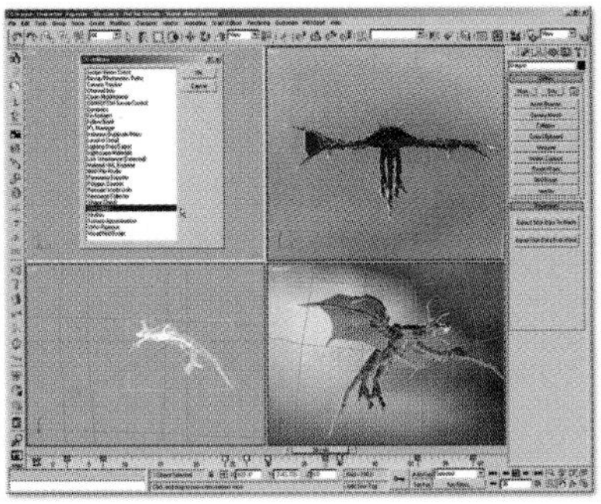

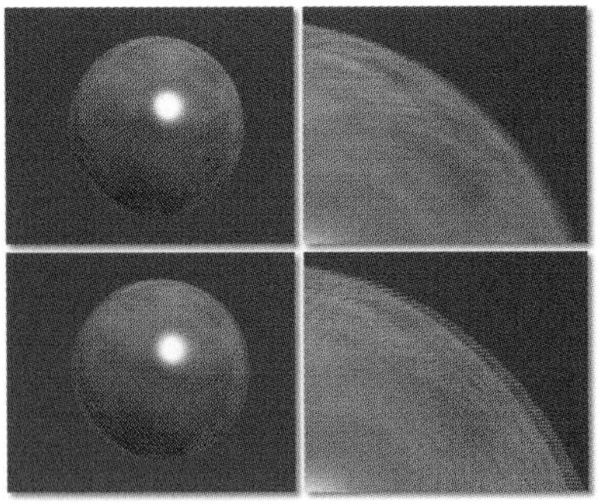

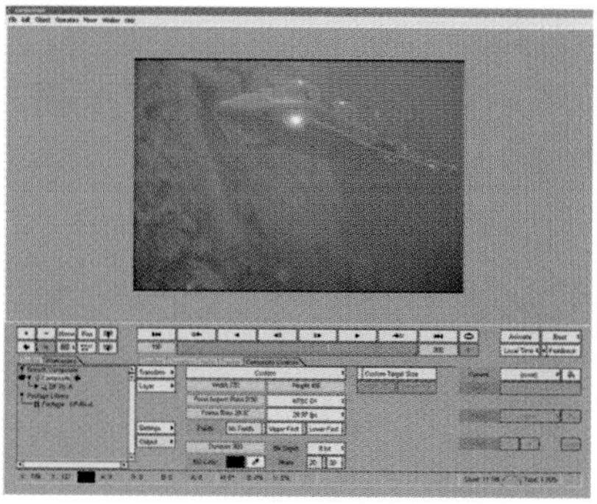

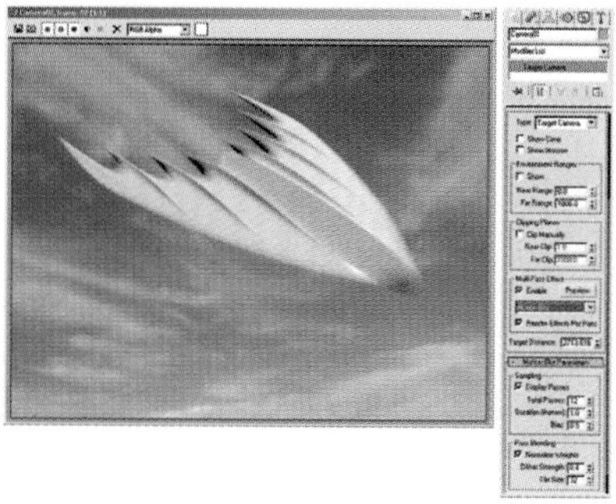

TABLE OF CONTENTS

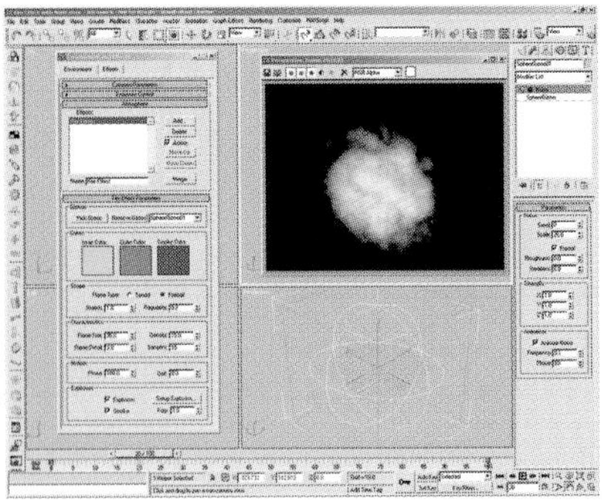

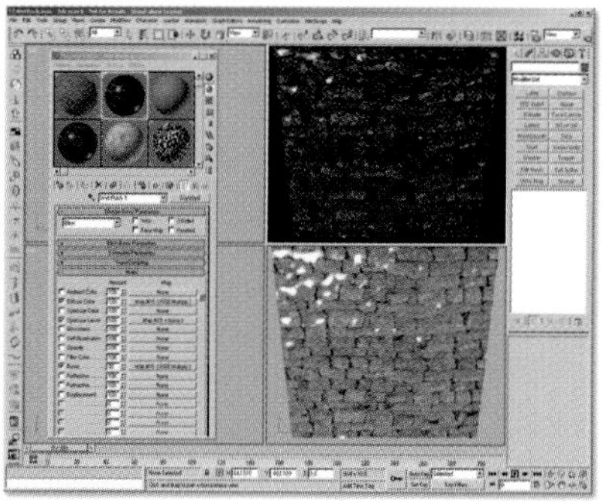

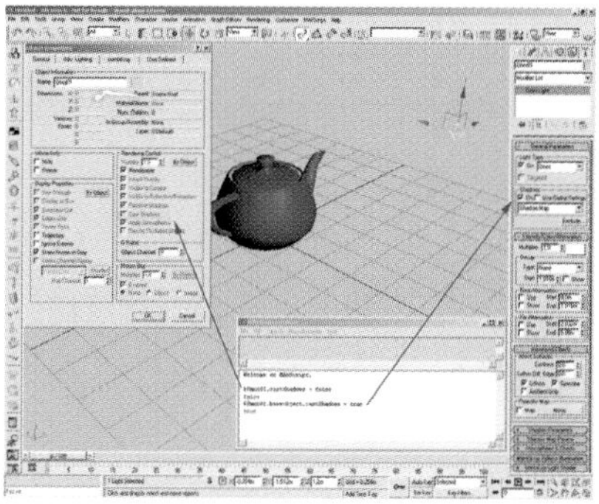

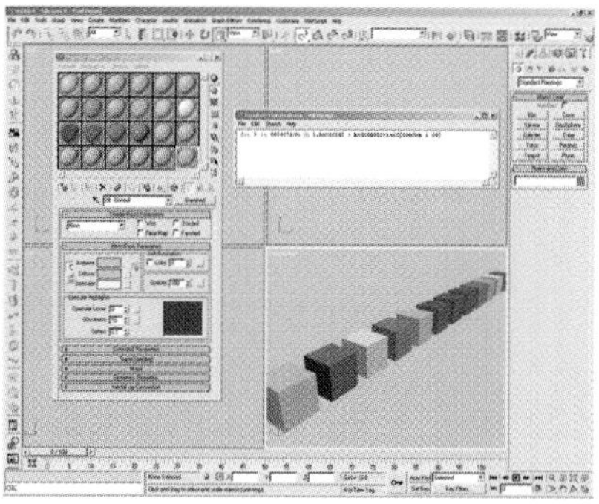

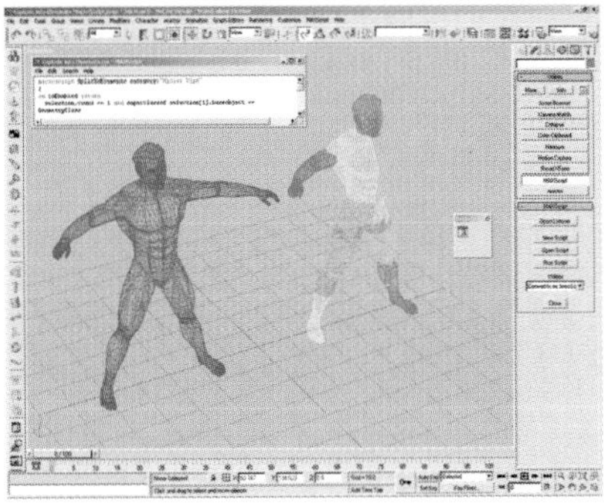

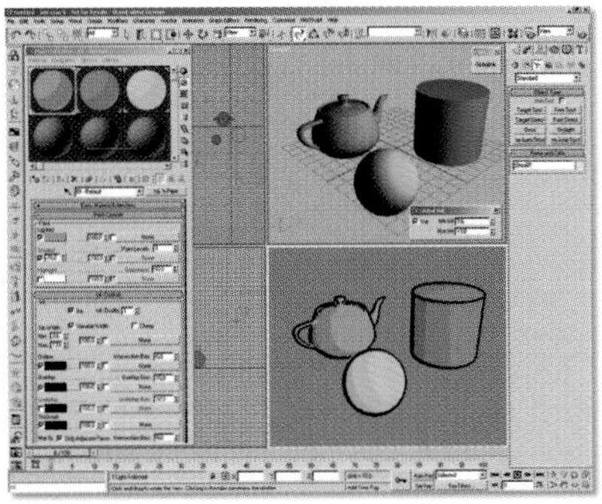

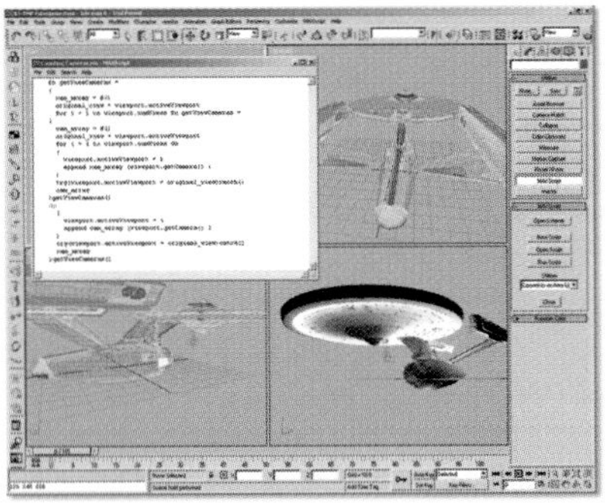

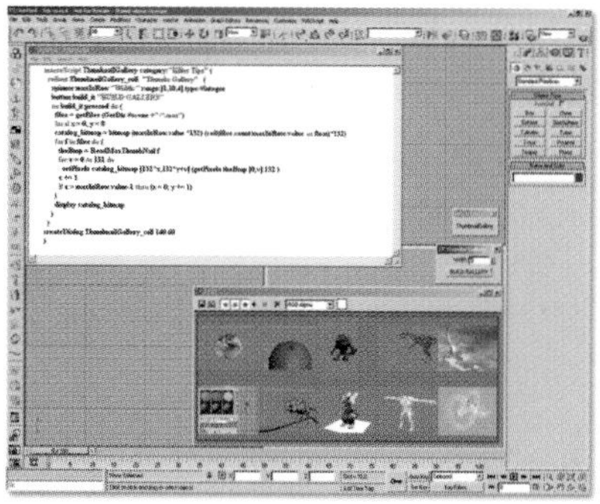

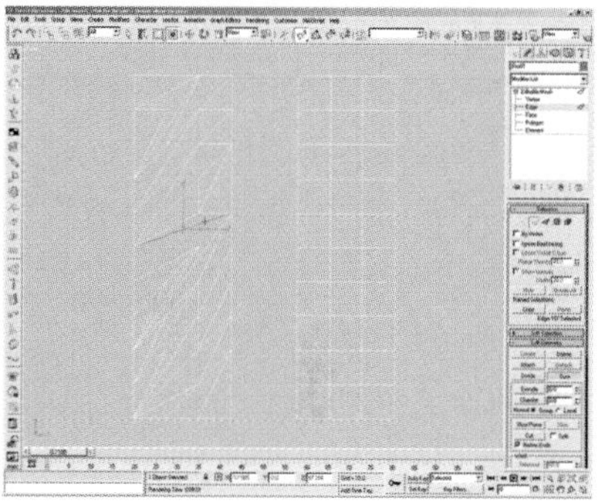

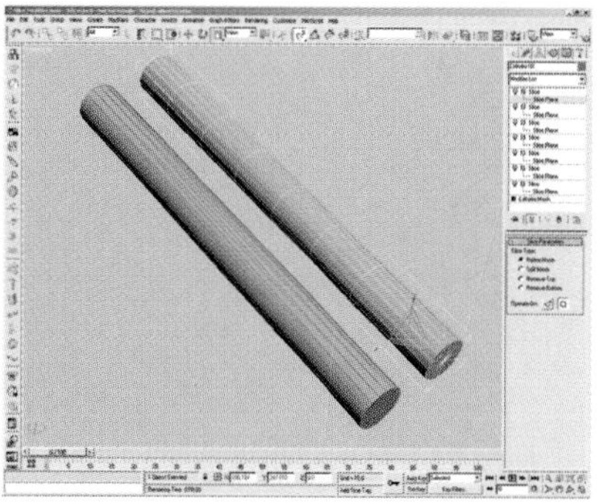

TABLE OF CONTENTS

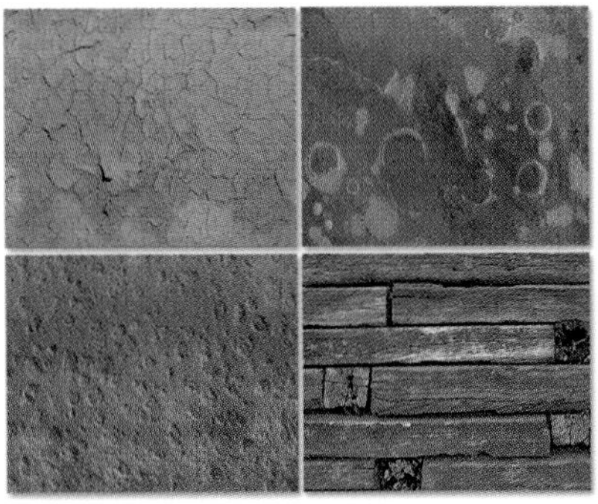

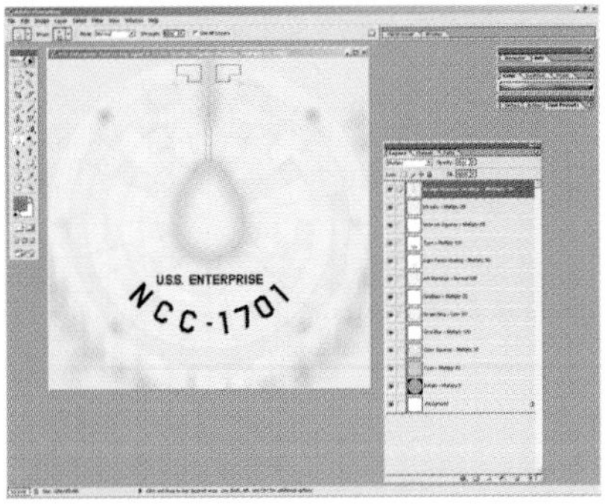

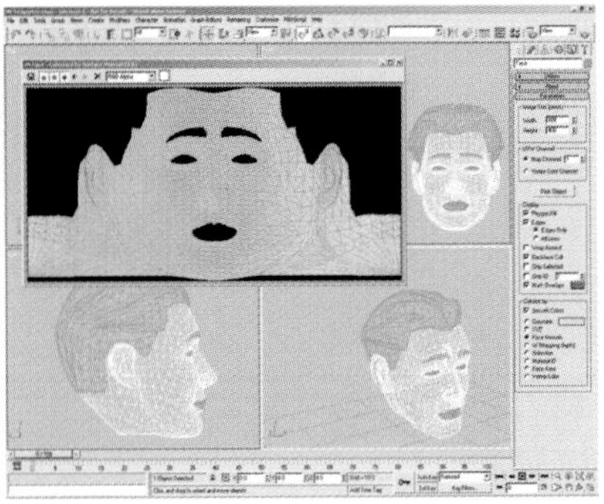

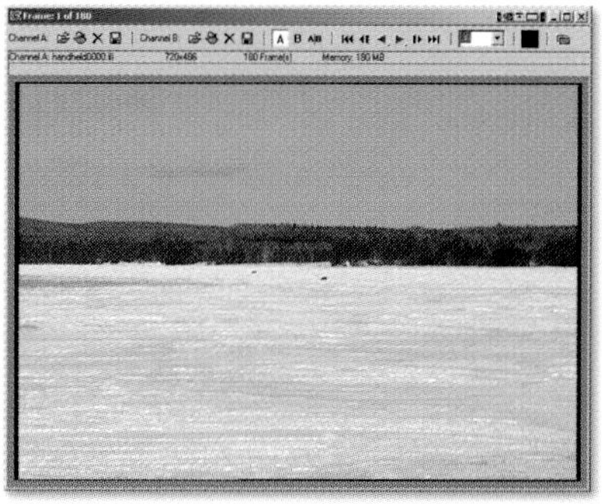

TELL US WHAT YOU THINK

As the reader of this book, you are the most important critic and commentator. We value your opinion and want to know what we're doing right, what we could do better, what areas you'd like to see us publish in, and any other words of wisdom you're willing to pass our way.

As an editor for New Riders Publishing/Peachpit Press, I welcome your comments. You can fax, e-mail, or write me directly to let me know what you did or didn't like about this book—as well as what we can do to make our books stronger. When you write, please be sure to include this book's title, ISBN, and author, as well as your name and phone or fax number. I will carefully review your comments and share them with the author and editors who worked on the book.

Please note that I cannot help you with technical problems related to the topic of this book, and that due to the high volume of e-mail I receive, I might not be able to reply to every message.

Fax: 317-428-3280

E-mail: elise.walter@peachpit.com

Mail: Elise Walter
Acquisitions Editor
New Riders Publishing/Peachpit Press
800 East 96th Street, 3rd Floor
Indianapolis, IN 46240 USA

FOREWORD

3ds max 6 Killer Tips
Edited by Scott Kelby

Welcome to *3ds max 6 Killer Tips*. As Editor for the Killer Tips series, I can't tell you how excited and truly gratified I am to see this concept of creating a book that is cover-to-cover nothing but tips, extend from my original book (*Photoshop Killer Tips*) into *3ds max 6 Killer Tips*.

The idea for this series of books came to me when I was at the bookstore looking through the latest Photoshop books on the shelf. I found myself doing the same thing to every book I picked up: I'd turn the page until I found a paragraph that started with the word "Tip." I'd read the tip, then I'd keep turning until I found another sidebar tip. I soon realized I was hooked on tips, because I knew that if I were writing the book that's where I'd put all my best material. Think about it: If you were writing a book, and you had a really cool tip, an amazing trick, or an inside secret or shortcut, you wouldn't bury it among hundreds of paragraphs of text. No way! You'd make it stand out: You'd put a box around it, maybe put a tint behind it, and if it was really cool (and short and sweet), you'd get everybody's attention by starting with the word "Tip!"

TIP

If you were writing a book, and you had a really cool tip, an amazing trick, or an inside secret or shortcut, you wouldn't bury it among hundreds of paragraphs of text. You'd make it stand out: You'd put a box around it, maybe put a tint behind it, and if it was really cool (and short and sweet), you'd get everybody's attention by starting with the word "Tip!"

That's what got me thinking. Obviously, I'm not the only one who likes these tips, because almost every software book has them. There's only one problem: There's never *enough* of them. And I thought, "Wouldn't it be great if there were a book that was nothing but those cool little tips?" (Of course, the book wouldn't actually have sidebars, since what's in the sidebars would be the focus: nothing but cool shortcuts, inside secrets, slick ways to do the things we do everyday, but faster—and more fun—than ever!) That was the book I really wanted, and thanks to the wonderful people at New Riders, that's the book they let me write (along with my co-author and good friend Felix Nelson). It was called *Photoshop Killer Tips*, and it became an instant bestseller because Felix and I were committed to creating something special: A book where every page included yet another tip that would make you nod your head, smile, and think "Ahhh, so that's how they do it."

If you've ever wondered how the pros get twice the work done in half the time, it's really no secret: They do everything as efficiently as possible. They don't do *anything* the hard way. They know every timesaving shortcut, every workaround, every speed tip, and as such they work at full speed all the time. They'll tell you, when it comes to being efficient, and when it comes to staying ahead of the competition: Speed Kills!

Well, what you're holding in your hand is another Killer Tips book: A book packed cover-to-cover with nothing but those cool little sidebar tips (without the sidebars). Jon A. Bell has captured the spirit and flavor of what a Killer Tips book is all about. I can't wait for you to get into it, so I'll step aside and let him take the wheel, because you're about to get faster, more efficient, and have more fun in 3ds max 6 than you ever thought possible.

Have fun and enjoy the ride!

All my best,

Scott Kelby, Series Editor

INTRODUCTION

In case you've been following my book writing "career…"

It's been a long hiatus since my last 3ds max book, *3D Studio MAX 3 f/x and Design*, published in 2000 by the now-defunct Coriolis Press. Since then, I've worked for Discreet both as a full-time contractor and full-time employee, have done a lot of traveling around the world (Spain, Mexico, the Bahamas), have gotten a chance to pilot the Deep Flight two-man mini-submarine (see the author bio for more info), have moved from the wine country of Sonoma, California to the red rock country of Sedona, Arizona, and have gone on (once again) to being a freelance writer and 3D artist. Whew!

Why I Wrote This Book

And yet here I am again—with a new 3ds max book, but one with a different format from my previous books, which consisted of relatively long, complex, tutorial-based chapters. This book, *3ds max 6 Killer Tips*, is different. It consists of a few hundred short, sweet tips on how to get the most out of 3ds max. Some of the tips are reminders of 3ds max aspects (actually covered in the manual) that newbies need to learn fast and remember forever and that some veterans might actually have forgotten. (When doing research for this book, I realized there were some aspects of 3ds max that I had forgotten about over the years!) Other tips are nifty workarounds for specific production problems, point out little-known features of the program, or give users a leg up on how to use new features in 3ds max 6, including the powerful Mental Ray renderer. If my previous *3ds max f/x* books were a multicourse meal, then *3ds max 6 Killer Tips* is a buffet table of many different canapés and *hors d'oeuvres*; if you don't find one you like, just return to the table and scarf down some different ones.

Is This Book for You?

Absolutely! As noted earlier, 3ds max is big enough and complex enough that everybody needs tips, from the rank beginner (who doesn't yet know all the neat things that 3ds max can do), to the veteran pro who has forgotten about (or maybe never wandered into) some of the nooks and crannies of the program that can lead to techniques helping users become more effective and efficient.

Note that although many of these tips are for 3ds max 6, some of them are applicable to earlier versions of the program, in some cases going back to 3ds max 3.1. Where possible, I've noted certain 3ds max 6-specific tips; other tips might work in earlier versions of the program, but you might have to experiment to see if they work.

Also, you'll notice that most of the screenshots included in this book use a brighter, higher-contrast color palette (similar to the old 3D Studio MAX 3.1 interface) than the current lower-contrast 3ds max default user interface (UI). This is because a.) the higher-contrast images look better when printed, and b.) I'm sometimes a sentimental stick-in-the-mud when it comes to my programs' UI.

Okay, How Do I Get Started?

That's easy—just jump in! There's no set order in which you must move through the book. Just drop in anywhere and start browsing. This is not a step-by-step tutorial book. Pick a tip randomly, or look for chapters of tips on a favorite subject, such as animation or MAXScript. There's no "one way" to approach this book. Just do what will work best for you.

I Get By with a Little Help from My Friends

Finally, please note that almost every author has help when working on a book (both fiction and nonfiction), and this book is no exception. For some tips, I've enlisted the help of some expert contributors, including Discreet's David Marks, Mark Gerhard, Peter DeLappe, and Nikolai Sander; and 3ds max artists, Ben Lipman, Chad Copeland, Aksel Karcher, Pete Draper, Neil Blevins, and MAXScript guru Borislav "Bobo" Petrov. Their expertise will aid your use of 3ds max, just as it aided me in adding useful material to this book.

Okay, let's get started. First up: how to customize 3ds max 6 for your immediate use and gratification.

Nuts and Bolts

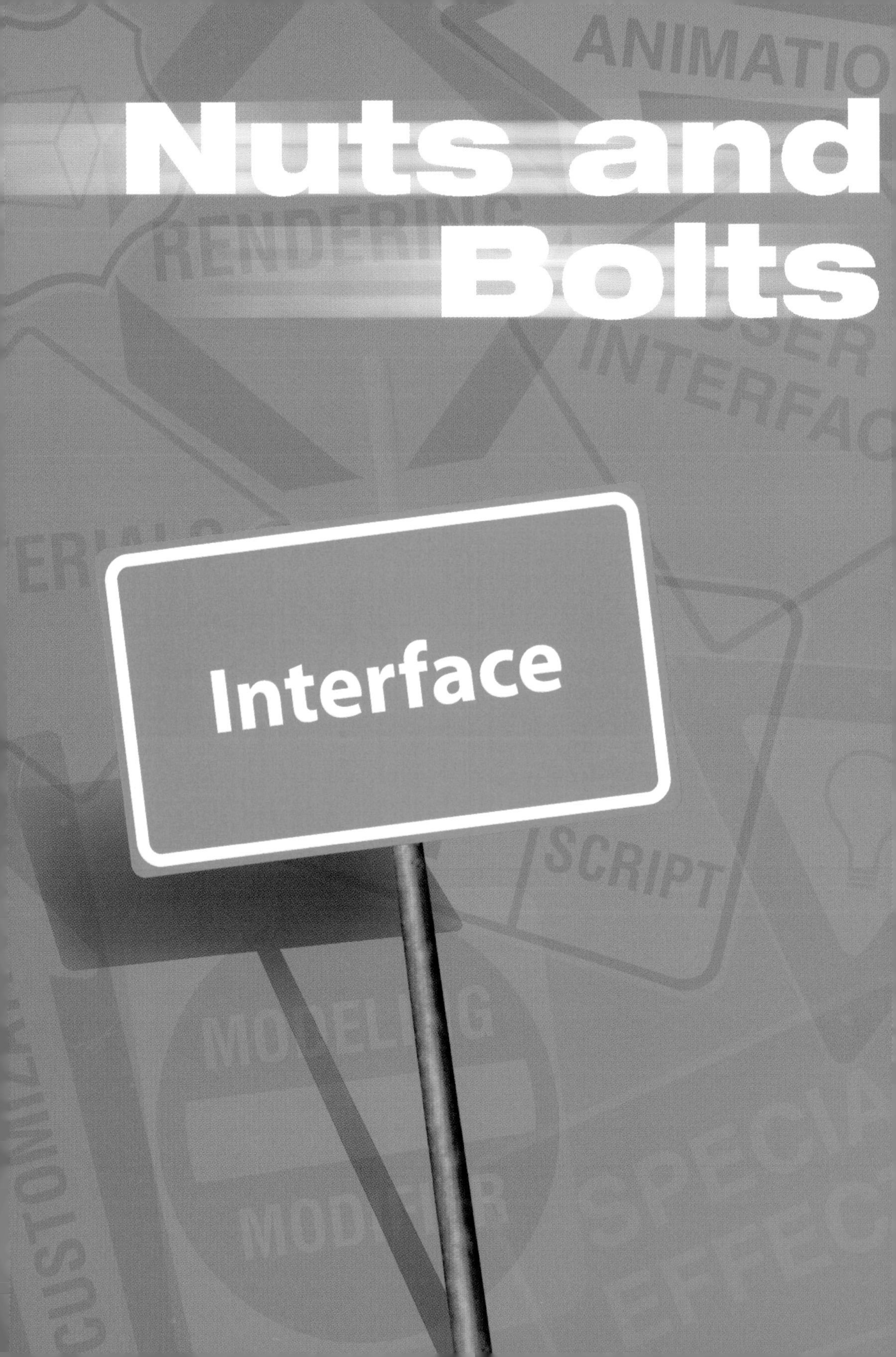

Nuts and Bolts

user interface and customization tips

3ds max is blessed with one of the most customizable user interfaces (UIs) of any program, 3D or otherwise. You can rearrange, recolor, rework, and generally recombobulate (as opposed to discombobulate) a wide variety of UI elements within the program—from icons on your toolbar to the order of rollout elements within a long scrolling menu to creating your own custom floating menus using MAXScript and the Macro Recorder feature.

You can change your icon appearance, create your own icons, or even dispense with icons altogether and create a largely text-based interface. In addition, you can alter the color of the 3ds max UI and screen elements to match your working style, your personality style, or your clothing style—whatever floats your boat.

The first chapter of 3ds max 6 Killer Tips *discusses how you can customize and modify your 3ds max work environment, as well as how you can speed up your most-used tasks in the 3ds max UI. In addition, you'll learn the new features in the 3ds max 6 UI that distinguish it from its earlier incarnations. You'll also read some reminders on how to navigate around the UI more easily.*

BEHOLD: 3DS MAX 6!

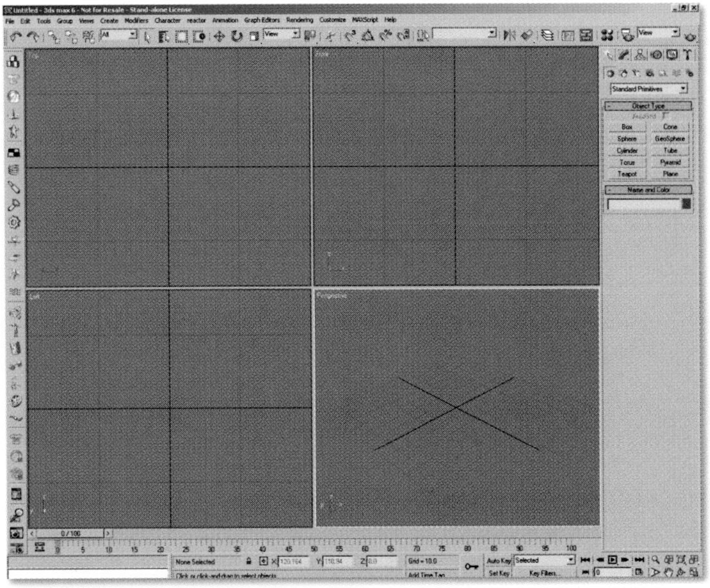

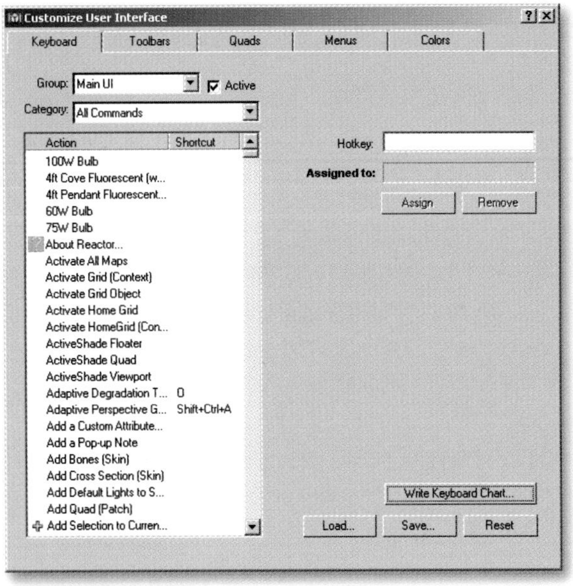

One of the most oft-repeated comments about Hollywood executives is that they'll read a new script and say, "It's perfect! But, we'd like a few changes...." When you first load 3ds max 6, you'll notice that the default UI largely resembles the previous incarnations of 3ds max, but with some changes to the main toolbar and the addition of a dedicated Reactor 2 toolbar on the left side.

If you don't like the default UI look of 3ds max, you can change it easily by going to Customize > Customize User Interface. From this menu, you can alter the UI colors (backgrounds, buttons, borders, and other elements that don't begin with *B*), your keyboard defaults, your Quad menu layouts, and so on. You can then save these settings (which go in the \3ds max6\UI folder), and 3ds max will look exactly as you left it the next time you open it. Alternatively, you can load previously saved settings if you have different UI layouts and preferences for different tasks.

WHAT'S YOUR PREFERENCE?

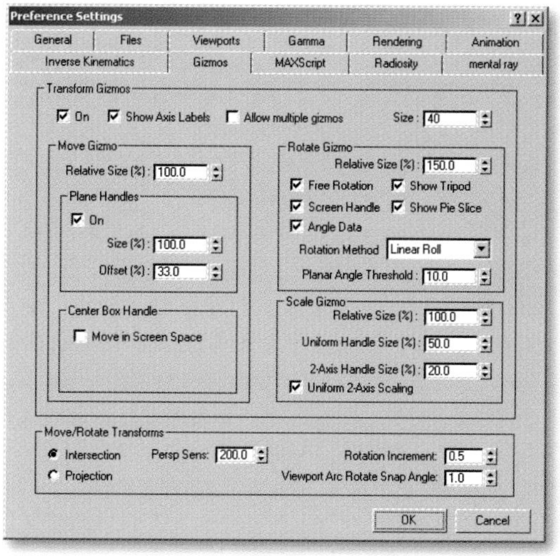

Although you use the Customize > Customize User Interface feature to modify the way 3ds max *looks*, you can use the Customize > Preferences feature to modify how 3ds max *behaves*. In the Preference Settings dialog, you can alter a huge variety of 3ds max defaults, including settings for Rendering, Viewports, Animation parameters, Gamma settings, and so forth. When you finish adjusting these and you close the dialog, these settings are saved in the 3dsmax.ini file, residing in your \3dsmax6 root folder.

Note that this dialog, like several other 3ds max dialogs, consists of two rows of tabs, which reorder themselves depending on which row you click on. Unfortunately, you can't change this behavior, but it's not the 3ds max program's fault; it's a built-in "feature" of the Windows operating system, and every other Windows program that uses tabbed dialogs is stuck with it. (Thanks, Bill!)

ADDING THE GRAPHICS DRIVER SWITCH TO YOUR 3DS MAX SHORTCUT

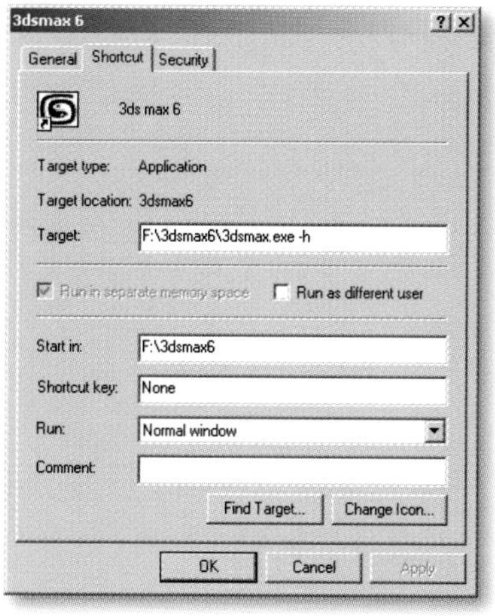

If you want the ability to pick and choose the graphics driver every time you launch 3ds max, you can add the `-h` switch to your 3ds max desktop shortcut icon. Just right-click on the 3ds max desktop shortcut and choose Properties to bring up the 3ds max 6 Properties dialog box. Then add the `-h` switch to the Target command line (for example, `F:\3dsmax6\3dsmax.exe -h`), and click OK. This brings up the Graphics Driver Setup box every time you launch 3ds max from this icon.

This trick is also helpful if you're experiencing stability problems with 3ds max or a third-party plug-in. Many users report that some program bugs go away if they switch to a different graphics driver. Your computer and mileage might vary, but switching to a different graphics driver might be worth trying if you have a persistent bug with the program.

THE NEW WORLD ROLLOUT ORDER

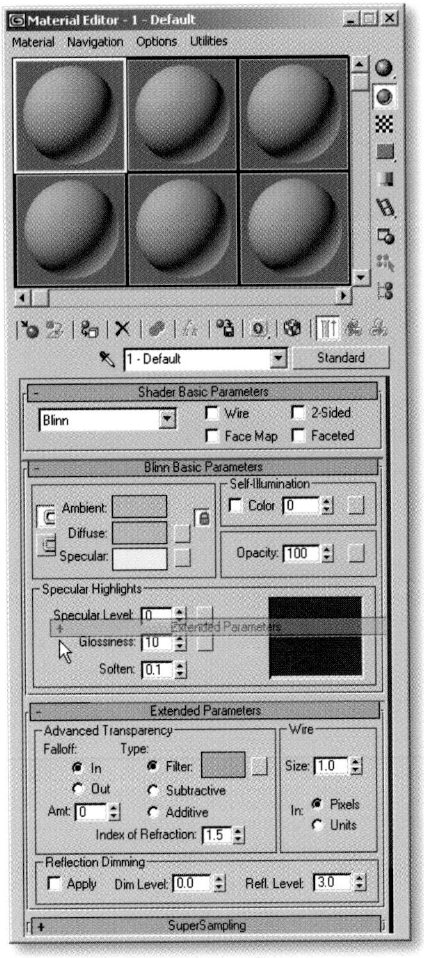

From 3ds max 4 onward, you can reorder the arrangement of rollouts in any window that supports rollouts (such as the Material Editor, the Command Panel, and so on) by simply left-clicking and dragging on the rollout title bar and then dropping the rollout to its new position. (Note that your rollout panels have to be open; you cannot change the order of the rollouts if all of them are closed.) The rollout will be inserted below the blue line that becomes visible as you click-and-drag. (The Material Editor image shows the Extended Parameters section of the rollout in the process of being dragged above the Blinn Basic Parameters section—hence the "ghosted" appearance of the Extended Parameters bar in the middle of the image.)

Note that this new rollout order is stored in a file called RollupOrder.cfg in the 3dsmax6\UI folder. To reset the order of one rollout, right-click on the rollout and select Reset Rollout Order. To reset the order of all rollouts, close 3ds max, delete the RollupOrder.cfg file from the \UI folder, and restart the program.

GENTLEMEN, START YOUR GRAPHICS DRIVERS

When you first launch 3ds max after installing the program, several screens pop up, including the splash screen (more about that in a second), and then a little Graphics Driver Setup dialog box. From there, you can pick one of four different graphics drivers to use with 3ds max: the standard Software driver (formerly called Heidi, and written by Autodesk), OpenGL (developed by SGI), Direct3D (developed by a little-known company named Microsoft), or a Custom driver (seldom used).

Depending on the speed of your graphics card (which is mostly dependent on how much money you've spent on it, and how recently), you should pick the graphics driver that's most suited for your card. Your graphics card should come with drivers included; if you want to get more recent drivers, go to the manufacturer's website and check their drivers, downloads, or support section.

After you choose the graphics driver you want, this screen doesn't reappear when you launch 3ds max. However, what if you want to change to a different driver later? You can do that in two ways. First, within 3ds max, go to Customize > Preference > Viewports > Choose Driver, and modify your settings there. If you want to switch your driver before you start 3ds max, go to the Windows Start, Run menu, browse to your \3dsmax6 root folder, and then pick the 3dsmax.exe file. However, add the command line switch `-h` after this (for example, `C:\3dsmax6\3dsmax.exe -h`). Now when you launch the program, the Graphics Driver Setup box appears, and you can change the driver to whatever you want.

OPENGL IS A GOOD THING—BUT ONLY WITH GOOD SETTINGS

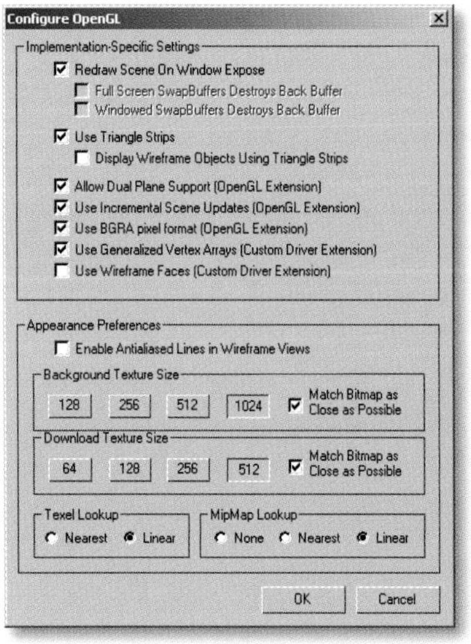

If you've set up 3ds max to use OpenGL, have you then looked at the default settings under Customize > Preferences > Viewport > Configure Driver? These settings are provided for the minimum required features of graphics cards made (gasp) five years ago! Because you're probably running a more modern card today, you should consider refining your display settings. Here are some tips:

- Check Redraw Scene On Window Expose. This makes updates slower when you're moving windows around, but it gets rid of any artifacts behind dialog boxes.
- Bump up both Background and Download Texture Size to their maximum values, especially if you have 64 or 128MB on your graphics card.
- Check both Match Bitmap as Close as Possible options. If you don't, all textures will use the Download Texture Size—even a 32×32 bitmap would load as 512×512! If you do check these options, every texture will use the closest (approximate) resolution, which saves lots of texture memory and makes up for the higher allowed resolution.
- Set both Texel Lookup and MipMap Lookup to Linear. This (effectively) gives you Trilinear Filtering. When you use this mode, modern graphics cards draw as fast (actually faster) as the default Nearest-No MipMapping settings. Texture quality increases to its maximum, too. Never turn off Mipmapping unless you have an old card. (If you do have an old card, you should probably be running in Software Z-Buffer mode anyway.)

WHAT'S YOUR FRAME RATE?

To better measure the performance of your graphics card, you can enable a special feature of 3ds max, which displays the frame rate of your viewports and the overall frame rate in the UI. To enable this feature, first exit 3ds max and locate the file 3dsmax.ini in the 3ds max \root folder. Open the .ini file in a text editor such as Notepad, and locate the header [Performance]. Then add a new line that reads like this:

```
ShowFPS=1
```

Save the file, exit Notepad, and then start 3ds max again. Now, if you look at the status bar at the bottom of your 3ds max UI, you should see five new fields. The first four fields correspond to the frame rate of the (default) four viewports, and the fifth field is the current frame rate.

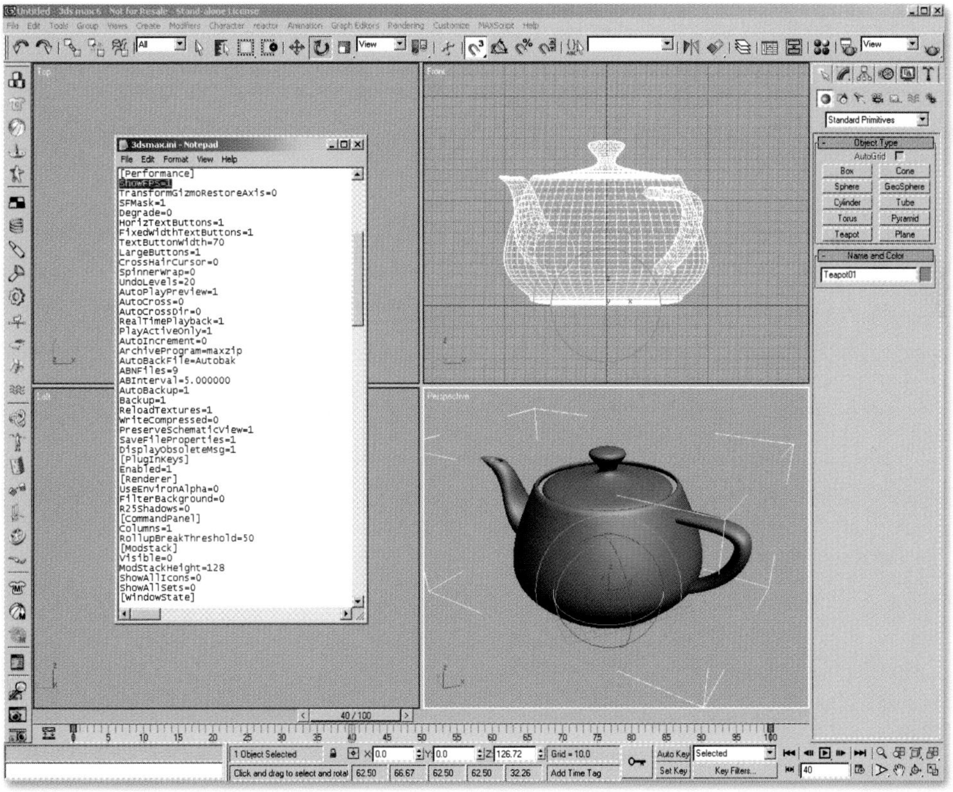

MAKING A SPLASH (SCREEN)

When you load 3ds max 6, the splash screen (or title screen) shows the newest 3ds max logo: a blue, snaky, "Yin/Yang-type" numeral 6. (Hey, don't look at me; I didn't design it!) Then, on top of this image, 3ds max 6 displays the standard program keyboard shortcuts while the various components and plug-ins load. It's a little animated floorshow before the main program UI event; it helps to refresh your memory ("Now, what's the keyboard shortcut for the Min/Max Toggle again?") every time you use the program.

However, if you want to personalize your splash screen on startup, you can add a new image that will appear right when you first start 3ds max. Just drop a .BMP-format image (say, 600 pixels wide × 300 pixels high) into your \3dsmax6 root folder and call it SPLASH.BMP. The next time you launch 3ds max, you'll see your new image first, before the funky blue snake rears its head.

MAKING A BIGGER SPLASH (WITH SHOCKWAVE)

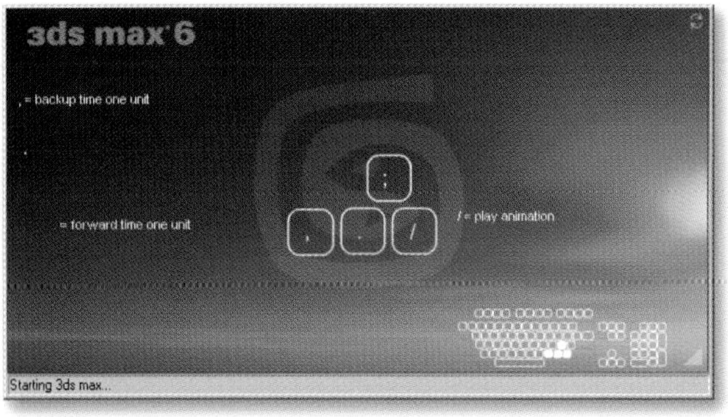

As the previous tip indicates, not only does 3ds max show a static bitmap upon program launch, but right after that, it displays a Shockwave file called Splash.SWF which is programmed to show you random keyboard shortcuts while you're waiting for the application to launch.

If you're familiar with Macromedia Director or Discreet's Plasma program, and you want to create your own funky animated opening as the program loads, then just create a new Shockwave-based Splash.SWF file and place it in the 3dsmax root folder. (Make sure you back up the original .SWF file first.) If you do this, it's probably a good idea to keep the same bitmap dimensions—about 600 × 300 pixels or so.

HELP, I'M ANIMATING AND I CAN'T MOVE!

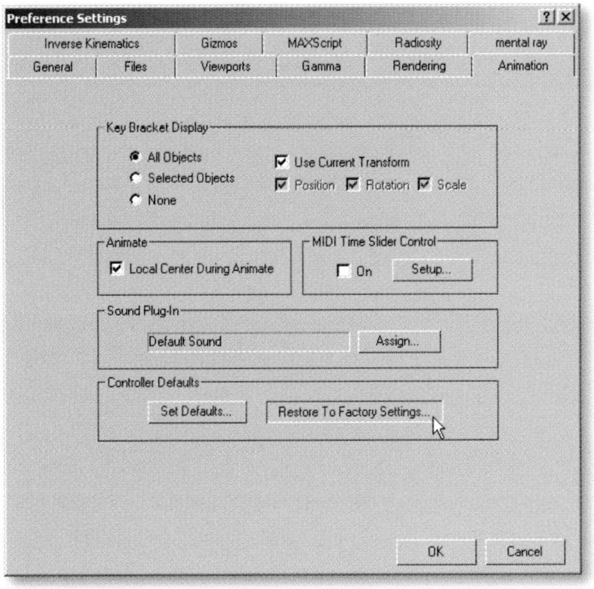

It's happened to almost every newbie using 3ds max: You're trying to animate something, and you can't remember if you hit some weird key combination or you did some weird animation controller assignment, but... you can't move anything on your screen anymore. Anything you've created is fixed in the 3ds max workspace, and if you try to create something new, it gets stuck in the center of the 3ds max universe as if it's been cemented to your monitor with SuperGlue.

What you've done is changed your default animation controllers from their default settings (Position: Position XYZ, Rotation: Euler XYZ, and Scale: Bezier Scale in 3ds max 5/6) to something else. (The Position controller is what's keeping you from moving your stuff around the screen with impunity and insouciance.) You've probably done this by accident from the Assign Controller area of the Command Panel's Motion tab.

To fix this, go back to the handy-dandy Customize > Preferences menu and click on the Animation tab. At the bottom, under Controller Defaults, click the Restore to Factory Settings button; then click OK. Zap! You should be back up and running and animating.

ENLARGE YOUR COMMAND PANEL

Nope, it's not a spam email claim: You can enlarge your Command Panel on the side of your default 3ds max workspace by placing your mouse cursor on the center dividing line (between the Command Panel and your viewports) and click-dragging it to the side. This is especially useful if you want to see all the panels of a particularly long rollout (such as a Particle system). Note that this decreases the amount of viewport space on your screen (unless you have a dual monitor system, and you can afford to sprawl across your electronic real estate), but you can always drag the Command Panel back to its original position if you want.

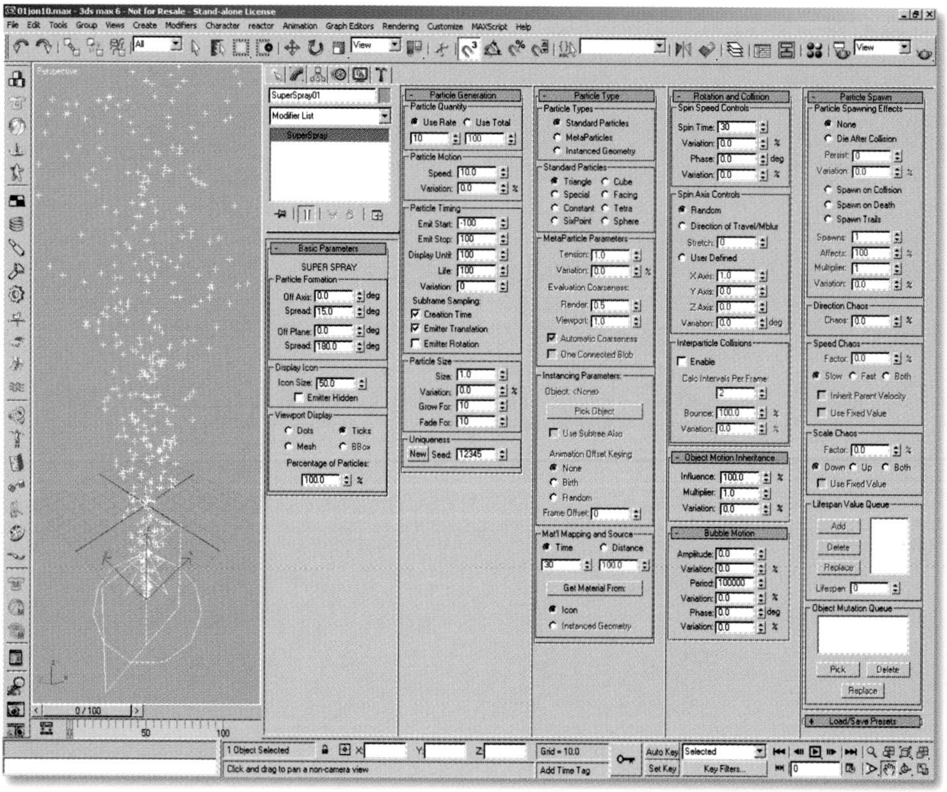

THE COMMAND PANEL: DOCKING AND FLOATING

Hey, did you know that you can undock and "float" the Command Panel from its usual position on the right side of your screen? Just move your mouse cursor to the upper-left corner of the Command Panel (near the Create Tab icon), right-click, and choose Float (or left-click-hold and drag when the cursor changes to an arrow with a rectangle). You can also dock the Command Panel on the left side of your screen. (This is especially helpful if you're a recovering Lightwave user, and that panel position makes you more comfortable.)

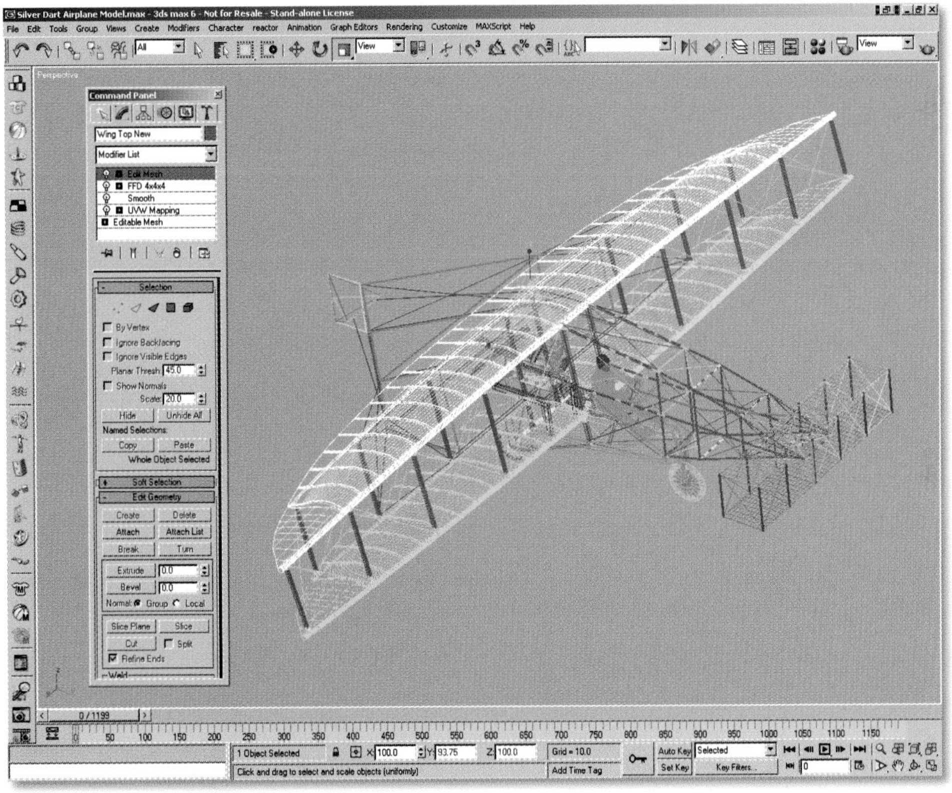

DRAG THE VIEWPORT DIVIDER BARS AROUND

Not only can you drag your Command Panel to the side to widen it, but you can also change the position of the (standard) four viewport divider bars by placing your mouse cursor over them and left-click-dragging them around. To reset the divider bars, place your mouse cursor between any two viewport dividing lines until a directional cursor appears (either a cross or a two-directional arrow); then right-click and click on Reset Layout so that you're four-square again.

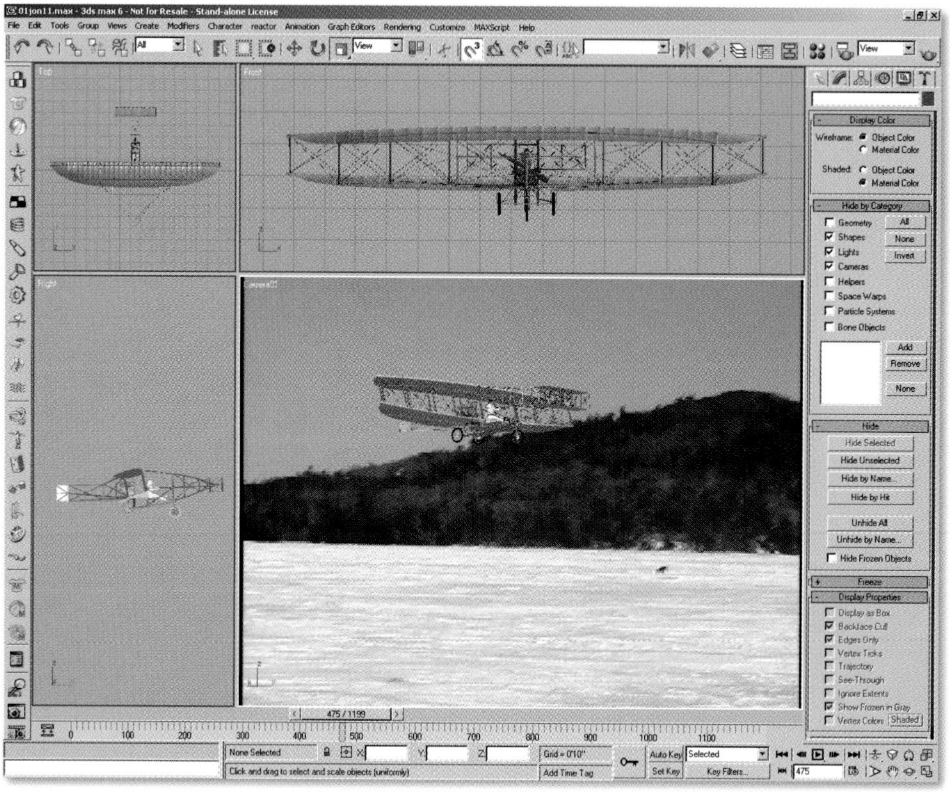

THE MAXSTART.MAX FILE

You already know how to customize your 3ds max UI, but if you want to make some of your settings "sticky" across 3ds max sessions (that is, your UI changes will show up every time you load the program), then do this: Load 3ds max, adjust your UI settings (such as moving the viewport divider bars around, as noted in the previous tip), and then resave this blank scene in your 3dsmax\Scenes folder as maxstart.max. Now whenever you re-start 3ds max, it loads with the UI parameters you just saved.

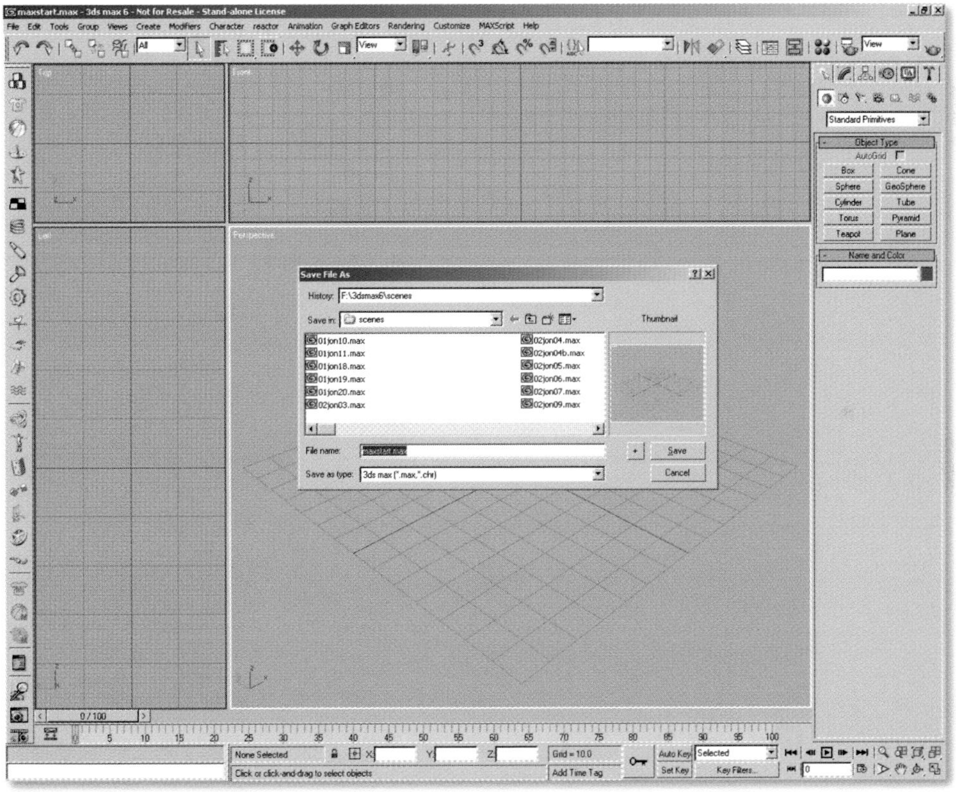

TEAR-OFF TOOLBARS

A reminder: 3ds max allows you to tear off toolbar components from your main 3ds max UI and place them as floating menus anywhere on your workspace. You can tear off some (or all) of your toolbar components and place them anywhere on your screen to help your workflow or to satisfy your craving for rearranging things. (You can also put the components back where you found them, just as your parents told you.) If you're using 3ds max 6, go to Customize > Load Custom UI Scheme, and pick the Modular ToolbarsUI.ui file from your 3dsmax6\UI folder. This loads toolbar components that you can tear off, as shown in the accompanying illustration. To put the components back (in a different order, if you want), just click-hold and drag them back up to the top of the UI.

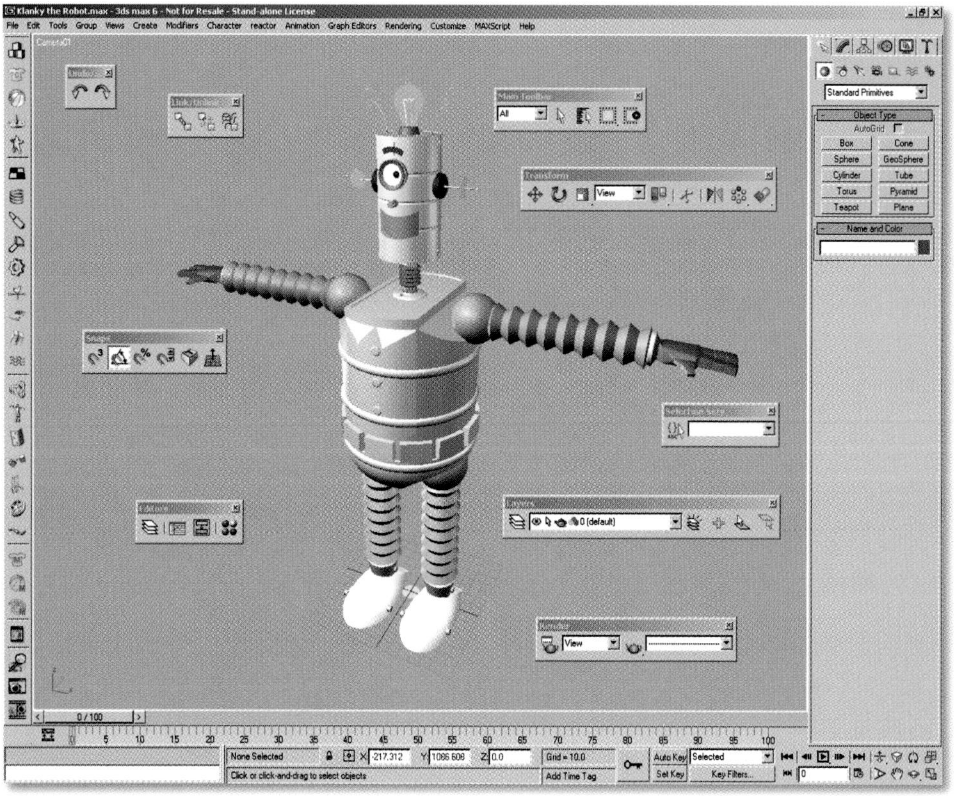

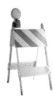

3DS MAX 6 DOES MATH!

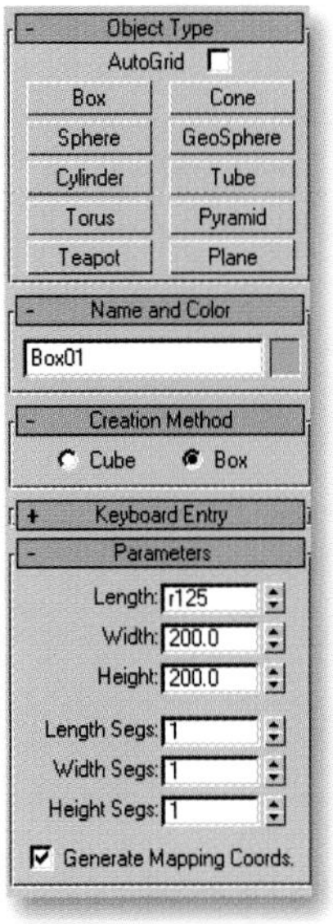

They can't do your algebra homework for you, but did you know that the spinners in 3ds max can do simple math? Simply select the value present in the spinner, type r (for "relative" value), and type the value you want to add to the current value. 3ds max does the math for you. (For subtraction, just enter a negative number.)

To test this, create a simple box of 200 × 200 × 200 units. In the Length setting, select the 200 value, type r125 (so that it replaces the 200), and press Enter. The 3ds max program changes the value to 325.

Now, in the same setting, type r-122.45 and press Enter. The 3ds max program changes the value to 202.55.

This technique works well especially if you're trying to draw connected splines (that are of specific lengths) from keyboard entry. (Also, note that pressing Ctrl+N in any numeric field brings up the Numerical Expression Evaluator.)

INTERACTIVE TRACK BAR/TIMELINE CONFIGURATION

Did you know that you can change the start time and end time of the 3ds max Track Bar interactively? It's easy. All you have to do is hold down the Ctrl and Alt keys simultaneously, and

- Left-click-drag on the Track Bar to move the start time.
- Right-click-drag on the Track Bar to move the end time.
- Middle-click-drag on the Track Bar to scroll the start and end time.

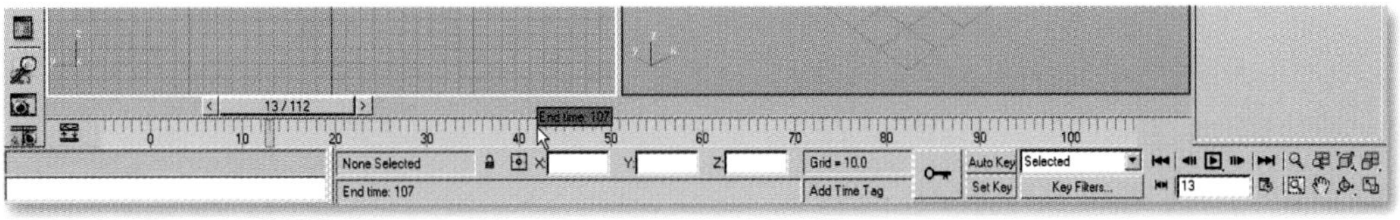

THE WORLD'S SHORTEST 3DS MAX SPINNER TIP

Remember: Right-clicking on a spinner in 3ds max sets it instantly to its smallest absolute value (usually 0).

THE WORLD'S SECOND SHORTEST 3DS MAX SPINNER TIP

Holding down the Ctrl key while adjusting a spinner increments/decrements the spinner values much faster than simply scrolling the spinner alone. (Also, pressing Shift and right-clicking on a spinner sets a keyframe to the spinner's current value, as long as the value isn't 0.)

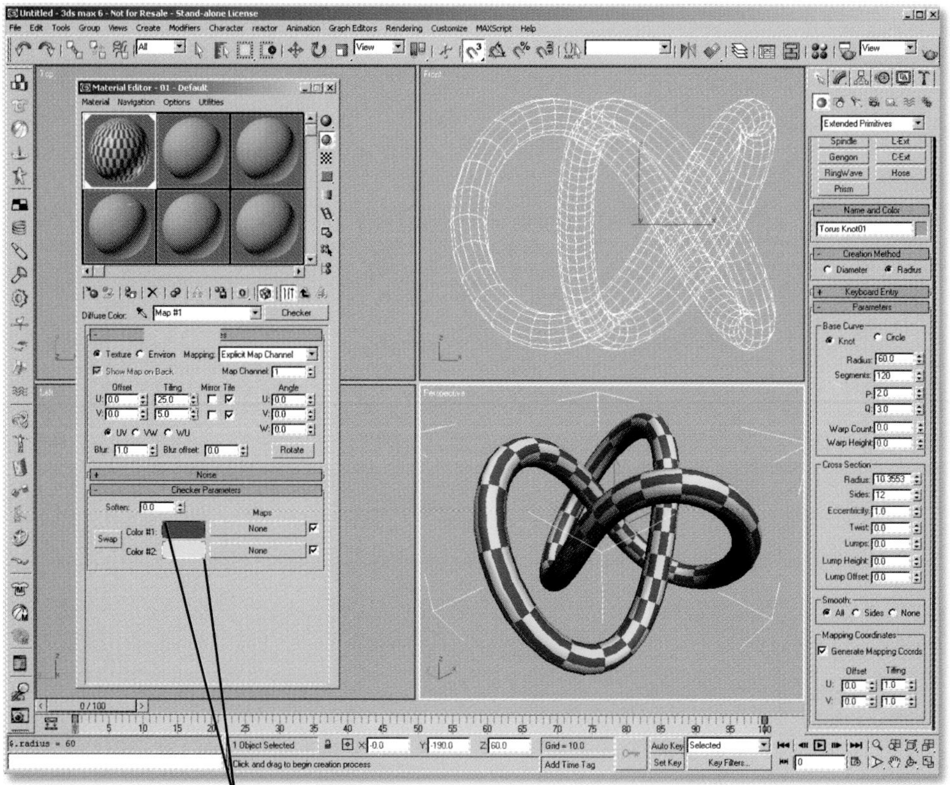

Red brackets appear around spinners and color swatches when keyframes have been set on their values.

SET KEY FOR OLD-TIMERS (THAT IS, 3DS MAX 4.X USERS)

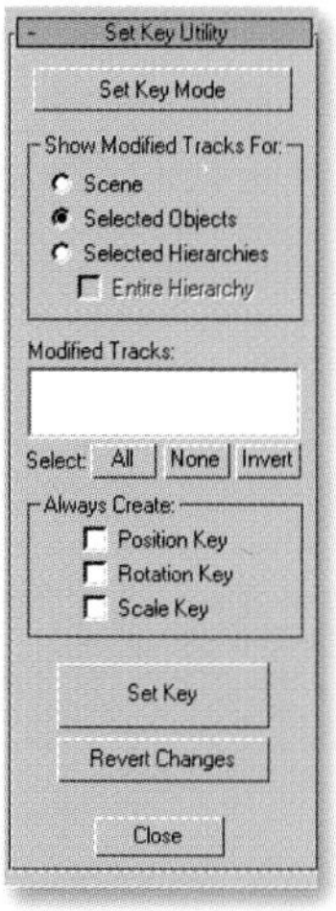

If you're still using 3ds max 4.2 but you want the joy of using the 3ds max 5/3ds max 6 programs' nifty Set Key animation button in your old version of 3ds max, fear not: You can add this feature with a simple .ini update. All you have to do is go to your 3ds max 4.2 \root folder and edit your 3dsmax.ini file.

Look for the heading `[ AnimationPreferences]`. (If it isn't there, just add it after the last setting of another heading.) Then on the line below, type

```
setKeyModeEnabled=1
```

Now when you run 3ds max 4.2, a new utility called Set Key will appear in your Utilities panel; just click the More button to load it. (Note that this is an undocumented—and thus unsupported—feature, so *caveat emptor*.)

ANOTHER .INI TWEAK: RED ALERT!

Here's another interesting 3dsmax.ini tweak: If you want to prevent the Time Slider from turning bright red when you're in Set Key or Auto Key mode, just add the following lines to the bottom of the aforementioned .ini file:

```
[ RedSliderWhenAnimating]
Enabled=0
```

Note: In 3ds max Release 4.x and earlier, this parameter was disabled by default, so setting Enabled=1 was required to turn on the red coloring.

UNDO UNDOES IT

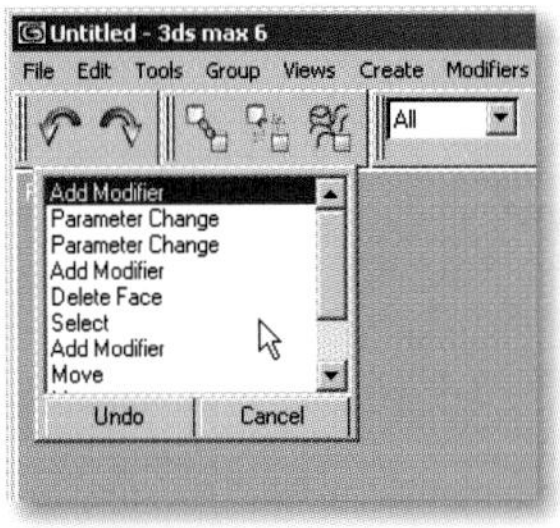

Everyone makes mistakes, but not everyone can go back and fix the consequences of their decisions. Luckily, this isn't really a problem in 3ds max; you can undo your actions by pressing Ctrl+Z on your keyboard, or going up to the Undo/Redo panel on your main toolbar and left-clicking the counterclockwise arrow.

Note that if you've made several mistakes (actually, let's call them "choices you learn from"), you can undo an entire series of operations by right-clicking on the Undo icon to bring up a drop-down list of your previous 20 actions. Just left-click-drag and scroll down to the last good thing that you remember doing; then click the Undo button to delete that history. Now you're back to where you were.

HOW MANY CHANCES DO I GET?

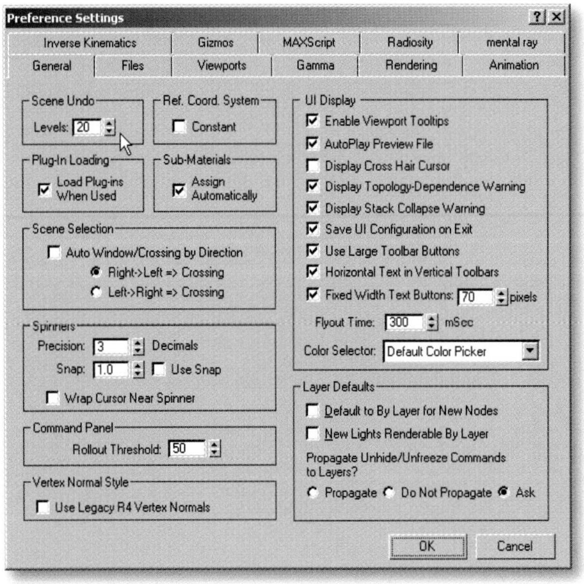

To set the number of Undo operations, just go to Customize > Preferences > General, and under Scene Undo, set the number of levels you want. The default is 20, which should be enough to help you fix any 3ds max scene problem before hitting yourself in the forehead and saying, "Arggh! Why did I do that?!"

SECOND CHANCES (AND THIRD, AND FOURTH, AND FIFTH…)

Although the Undo feature is good for simple blunders (or to revert from scene tweaking "experiments"), you should be in the habit of using other file-saving tools as a way to revert to a known point in your workflow. Following are some of these:

- Using Edit > Hold (Alt+Ctrl+H) to save your current scene state, and Edit > Fetch (Alt+Ctrl+F) to revert to the scene state that you just saved.
- Using File > Save As > + periodically; this increments the name of your file by a numeral 1 and saves it, thus leaving you with a string of files separated by the time between saves.
- Using File > Save > Copy As leaves your file named as is, but saves an incremental numbered copy to disk.
- Going to the Customize > Preferences > Files tab and checking Increment on Save provides similar (but automatic) incremental file naming. (Also, make sure you have Auto Backup checked in this menu, and increase your number of Autobak files to 9.)
- Finally, checking Backup on Save (Customize > Preferences > Files) provides one maxback.bak file in your 3dsmax6\Autobak folder when you save a file.

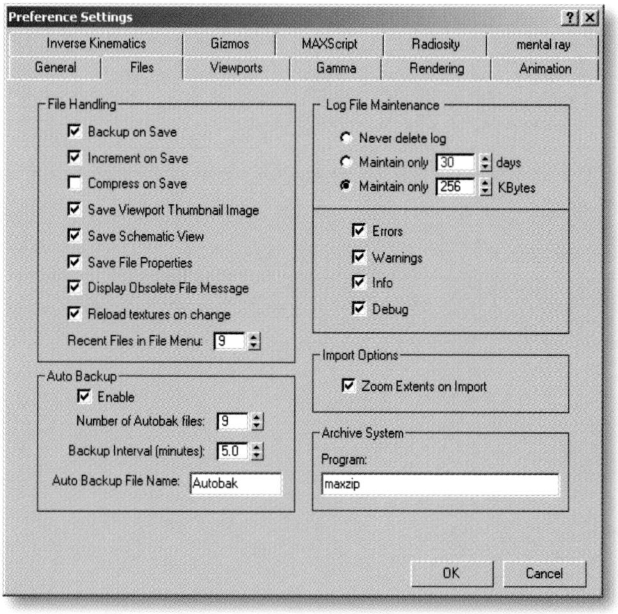

VIEWPORTS: SHADE SELECTED

You can improve your viewport redraw speeds in 3ds max by toggling various features within the program (although it also helps to have a super-fast video card, of course.) If you pick Views > Shade Selected, you'll see a shaded (Smoothed and Highlighted) version of only your selected object(s) in your viewports, even if the viewport's display type is set to apply Wireframe to everything in the scene.

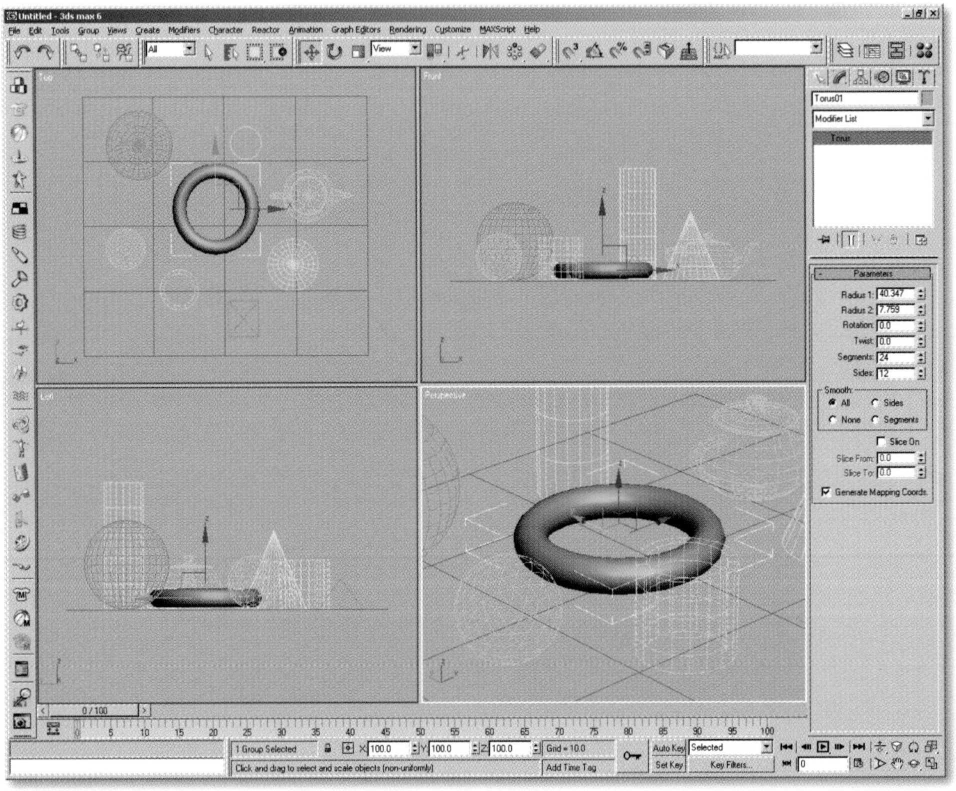

VIEWPORTS: SEE ONLY WHAT YOU WANT TO SEE

Want to isolate objects in your viewport based on their Z-depth from the Perspective or Camera view? Just right-click on the viewport label to bring up the Properties menu, and choose Viewport Clipping. When you do, you'll see a slider bar with two indicators along the side. Sliding either indicator clips (cuts off or hides) objects either closer or nearer to your point of view. You can use this slider bar to hide pieces of your scene interactively, so you can focus only on what you want to see.

EVEN MORE VIEWPORT ADJUSTMENTS

Did you know that…

- Shift+Z undoes your previous viewport adjustment? (This works in the currently active view only. The Undo feature is also available in the Views menu; just right-click on the viewport label.)
- Other viewport control buttons (on the right side of your bottom toolbar, next to your playback controls) have flyouts: Zoom Extents Selected, Zoom Extents All Selected, Arc Rotate Selected, and Arc Rotate SubObject. The latter is useful for modeling; you can select a single vertex on your model and then Arc Rotate around that focal point.
- Finally, you can use Region Zoom in a Perspective viewport (from 3ds max 4.x onward) by holding down the Field-of-View button and choosing Region Zoom from the flyout.

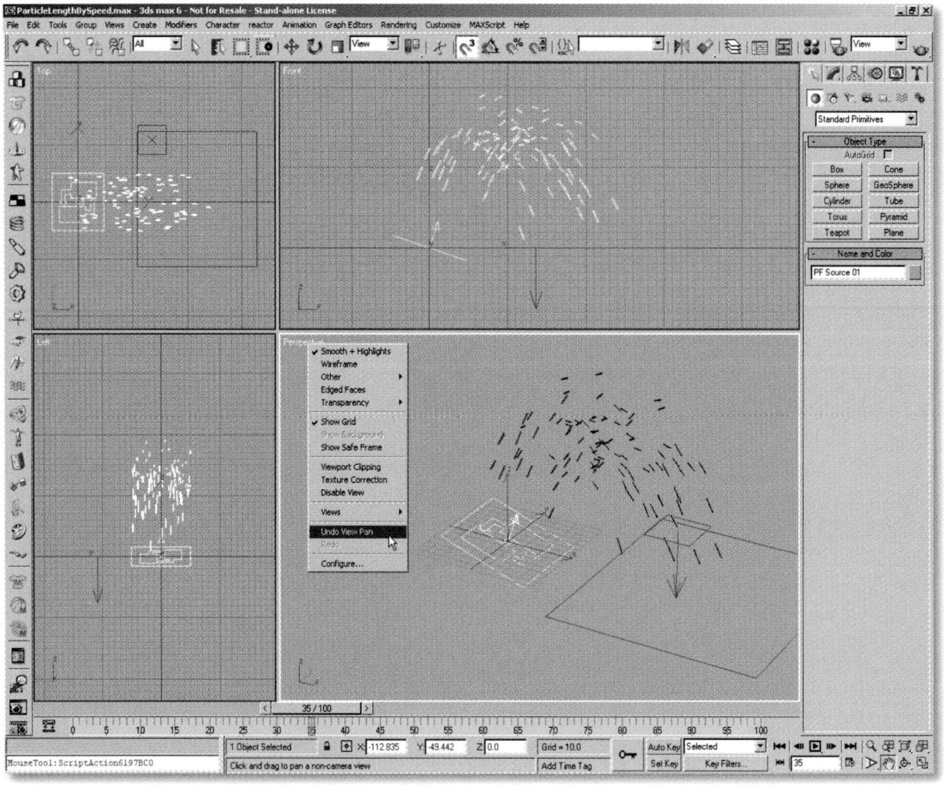

DON'T FORGET THE MIDDLE MOUSE BUTTON!

It's useful to have a mouse that features a wheel as the middle button when you're navigating in 3ds max. You can use the wheel for interactive zoom (or press Ctrl, Alt+the middle mouse button [MMB]), depress the wheel to pan (or Shift+middle mouse button) and hold Ctrl to pan faster. For interactive viewport rotation, use Alt+MMB and spin away. Finally, using Shift+Alt+MMB allows you to arc rotate with quadrant restrictions.

You can also add Shift+Alt+MMB to arc rotate with quadrant restrictions.

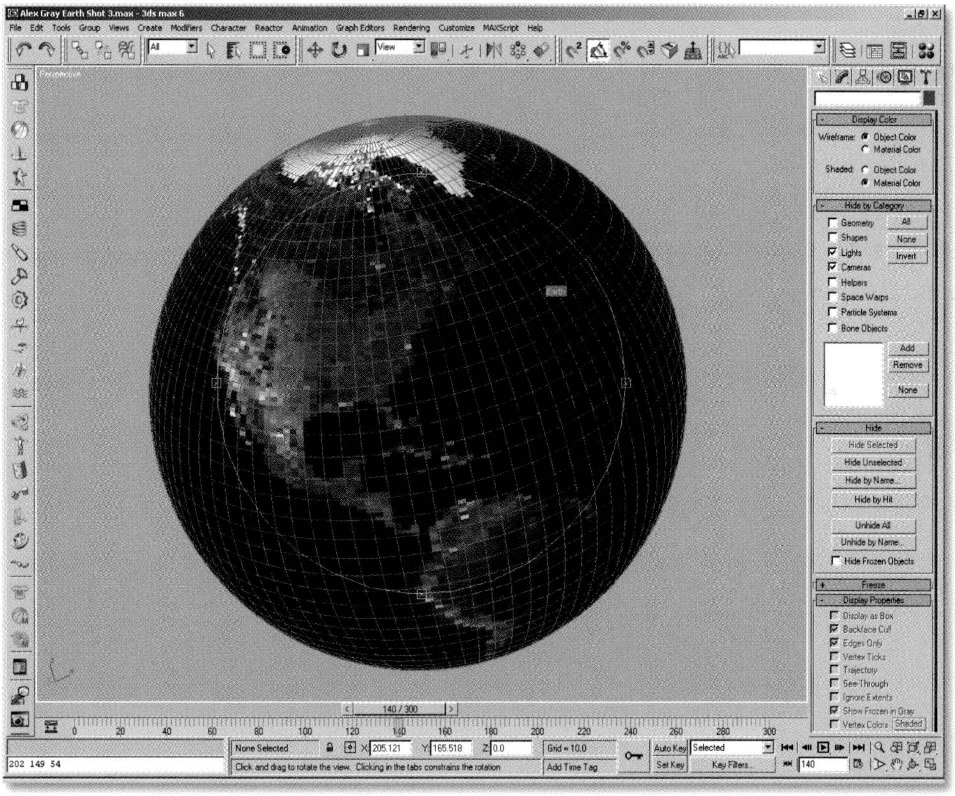

CTRL+ALT+SHIFT+RIGHT-CLICK = BIG FUN

By holding down Ctrl, Alt, or Shift and right-clicking in a viewport, you can quickly select different quad menus that are specialized to the area the mouse cursor is over for the selected item, such as Select Mode, Quick Render, Create Primitive, and so on. Also, selecting Shift+Alt+Right-click in an open area of your viewport opens a Reactor 2 quad menu. Try it!

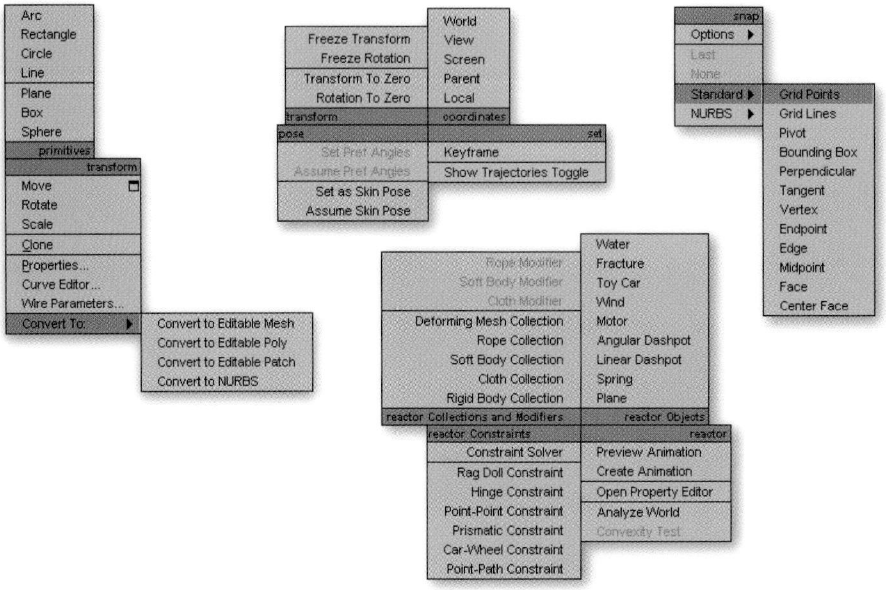

AN OLD FRIEND RETURNS: THE AXIS CONSTRAINTS TOOLBAR

Although you might consider it superfluous (because 3ds max has visible Transform manipulators on selected objects), the good ol' Axis Constraints toolbar is still available for those people who want to see that they're locked into X, Y and/or Z Transform mode. To get the toolbar to reappear, just right-click in any open space in the main 3ds max toolbar and choose Axis Constraints. Poof! It appears!

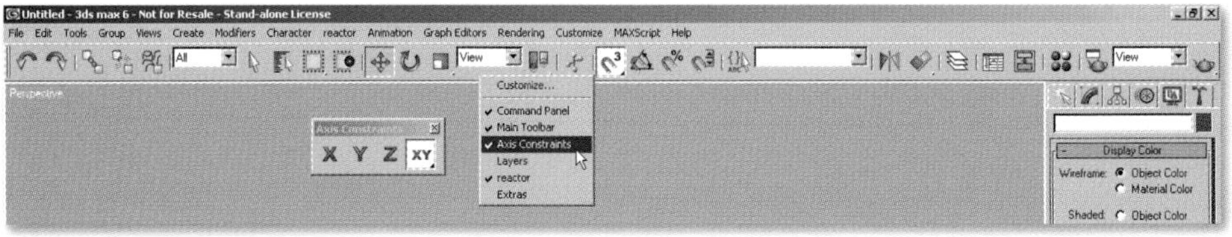

PLUG-INS: LOAD JUST WHAT YOU WANT

Third-party plug-ins can occasionally conflict with other plug-ins. To fix this, you can create multiple, custom 3ds max shortcuts on your desktop, which load specific plug-ins when you double-click the shortcuts. If you want to launch a 3ds max session with only specific modeling plug-ins, for example, and leave out rendering plug-ins, you can do it easily.

First, make sure that each plug-in (or plug-in type, such as Modeling, Rendering, and so on) is in its own folder within your 3dsmax6\plugins folder (for example, 3dsmax6\plugins\exampleplugin). Load the plugin.ini file (located in your root \3dsmax6 directory) into Notepad. Add your new entry to the existing plugin.ini file as such:

```
Standard MAX plug-ins=C:\3dsmax6\StdPlugs\
Additional MAX plug-ins=C:\3dsmax6\Plugins\
New Entry=C:\3dsmax6\Plugins\ExamplePlugin\
```

Save this .ini file in your \3dsmax6 root folder as ExamplePlugin.ini. (Don't resave it as plugin.ini!) If you want to load the Example plug-in only, copy your current 3ds max 6 Desktop shortcut to make a second (duplicate) shortcut; then right–click on it and choose Properties. Go to the Shortcut tab, and enter the following:

```
C:\3dsmax6\3dsmax.exe -p ExamplePlugin.ini
```

Rename the new Shortcut 3ds max 6 - ExamplePlugin. Now, when you double–click on this shortcut, you launch a copy of 3ds max 6 that loads only the Example plug-in, which helps avoid potential conflicts with other plug–ins.

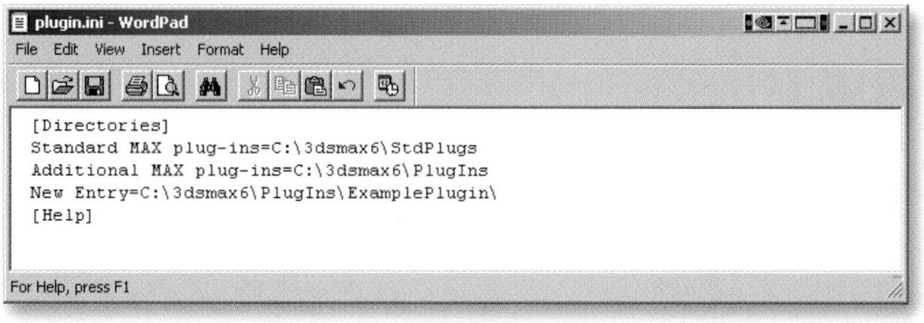

"ZIP IT!"—COMPRESS ON SAVE

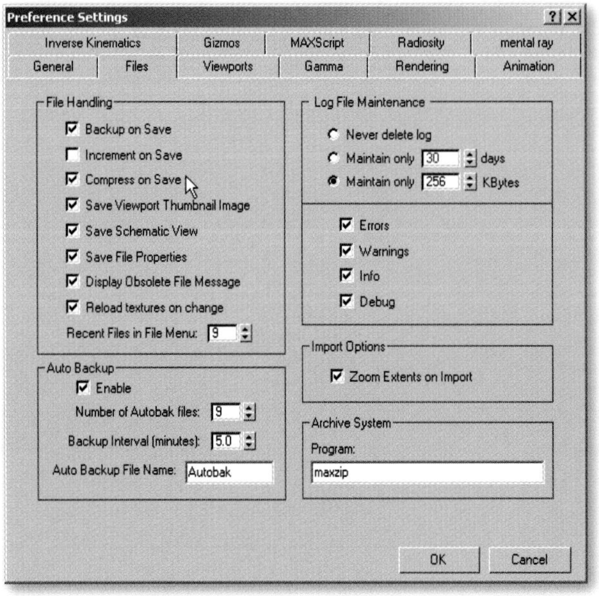

3ds max has a compression algorithm (maxzip, written by Larry Minton) built into its file-saving system. To use it, go to Customize > Preferences > Files and check Compress on Save. Any files you save from then on will be reduced in size; however, file properties and thumbnail data remain uncompressed, so you can access them via Windows Explorer and the 3ds max Asset Manager. (A 3ds max file that contains 100 mesh spheres saved without compression takes up 4.566K. The same file saved *with* file compression takes 1.349K. Note that if you use PK-Zip or WinZip on the uncompressed file, you can reduce it to approximately 1.307K in size.)

And, of course, if you use the File > Archive feature, 3ds max zips up your entire scene, as well as all bitmaps associated with the materials used in the scene. This is handy for moving all scene components from your home office to work, or when sending scene files and all their associated components to friends or co-workers.

FOCUS YOUR INTENTIONS: INTERACTIVE PAN

One extremely quick way of centering a selected or unselected object in an active viewport is to use the Interactive Pan keyboard shortcut. Simply place your mouse cursor over an item or area in an active non-Camera viewport, and then press the I key. The viewport redraws, focusing on the area around the cursor and repositioning it at the center of the viewport.

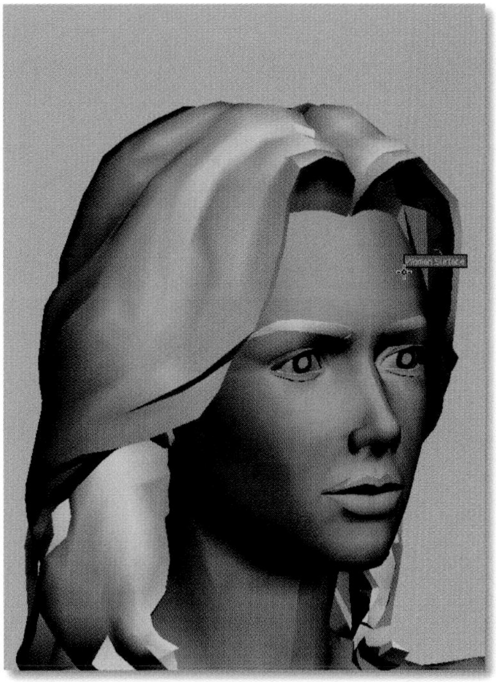

Sculpting the Body

Sculpting the Body

modeling and modifier tips

3ds max has a wide range of modeling tools and methodologies. You can build polygonal models out of pre-existing primitives, sculpt smooth polygonal forms using the MeshSmooth modifier and reference objects, create organic models using splines and Surface Tools, edit patches, or even (if you're brave!) create Non-Uniform Rational B-Spline (NURBS) objects. If you can think of a shape or an object, then you can probably build it in 3ds max and take your pick of varied tools and techniques to get the best results.

This chapter looks at some of 3ds max's modeling tools and how you can augment your modeling work with the vast array of the object- and world-space modifiers that are available at the click of a button (or two.)

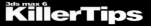

DESIGN YOUR MODELS ON PAPER FIRST!

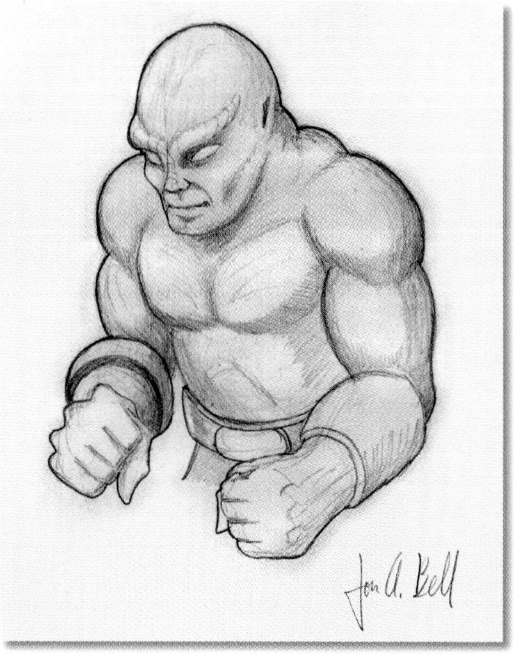

Although it's fun to simply launch 3ds max and start constructing your 3D models from scratch, if you have any 2D artistic skills at all, then I recommend that you create some basic line drawings to work out aesthetic problems beforehand, or just to give you some inspiration for your final 3D design. You don't have to be an industrial engineer, a draftsman, or a professional sketch artist to find the usefulness of committing several ideas to paper before constructing them in 3D. Often, even a simple thumbnail sketch (the proverbial "drawing on the back of a paper napkin") will help you work out object (and especially character) proportions and balance in your 3D scene.

CREATE YOUR OWN CUSTOM MODIFIER MENUS

I'm a traditionalist, at least when it comes to my 3ds max layout—I haven't changed the look and feel of my program very much since the 3D Studio MAX 3 days. So, when the default in 3ds max 4 became *not* to show a list of modifiers, I rebelled and immediately set it back to the way I wanted it. When modeling, I find that having a dozen (or more) of my most commonly used modifiers available, all the time, is extremely helpful, and I don't care if it takes up some additional space on the Modify Panel rollout. (You can drag your Command Panels over, remember?)

To show your Modifier buttons all the time, go to the Modify panel, right-click on the Modifier List drop-down button, choose Show Buttons, and then right-click again and choose Configure Modifier Sets. There, you can create as many button slots as you need (I usually create about 18), drag the specific modifiers to the desired buttons, and then name (and save) these settings. You can then call up this specific modifier set by clicking on the Sets drop-down menu and picking it from the list (which also includes a number of premade modifier sets for animation, free form deformations, mesh editing, and so on).

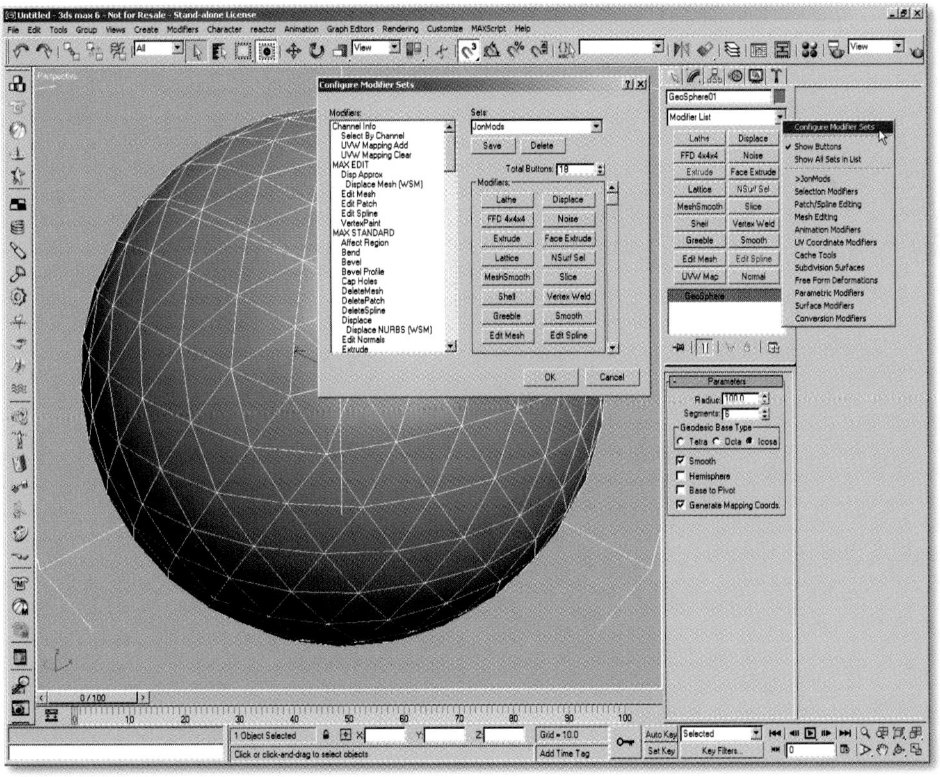

NAMED SELECTION SETS: IT'S NOT JUST FOR OBJECTS

You know that you can group object selections into their own selection sets, using (drum-roll here…) the Named Selection Sets menu from the main toolbar. However, did you also know that you can name (and edit) selections on a sub-object basis as well? If you select a group of faces on an object, you can give that selection a unique name. Deselect the faces and select another group of faces (even within the same Edit Mesh modifier, or on an Editable Mesh basis), and you can name those separately. To go back to your first face selection, just choose it from the Named Selection Sets drop-down menu. It's a fast and easy way to work on specific areas of your mesh and keep all your work straight. (And don't use it just for faces; it works on vertices, edges, polygons, and elements, too.)

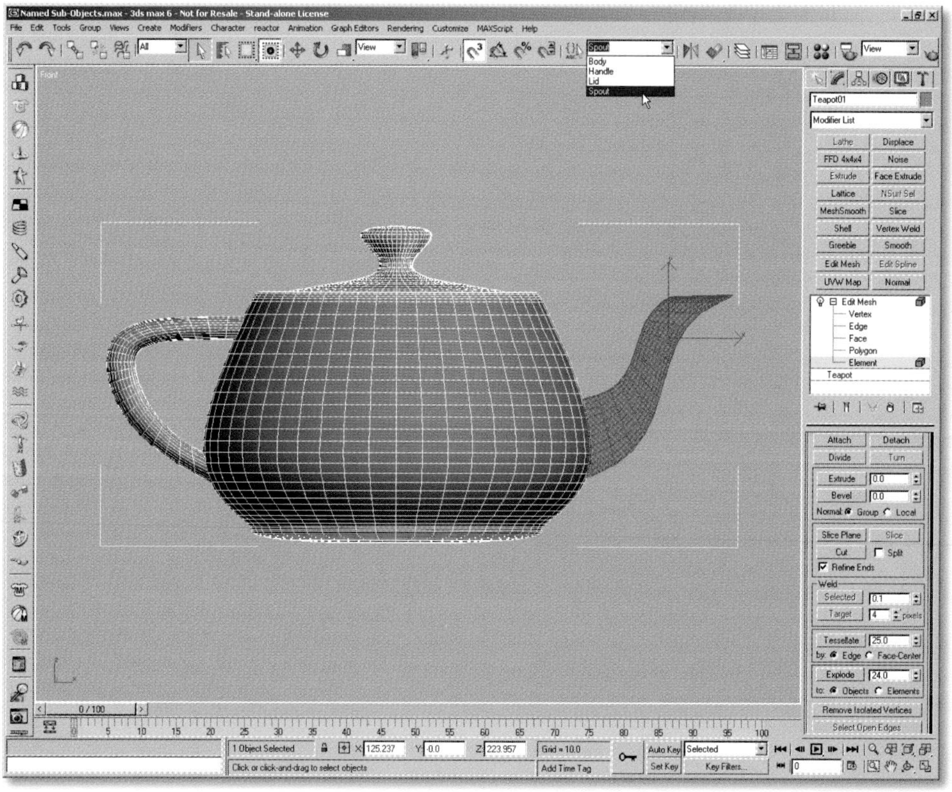

HAVING TROUBLE WITH TAPER OR BEND? USE AN FFD MODIFIER INSTEAD

Sometimes when I create an object and I want to taper or bend all or part of it, I have a heck of a time trying to get it to taper or bend precisely the way I want it to (and in the direction that I want it to) using the forenamed modifiers. When this happens, I apply an FFD modifier (usually an FFD 4 × 4 × 4 will suffice) and then go into Gizmo: Control Points mode. From there, I can simply select the control points I need and move or scale them to get the desired taper or bend that I want.

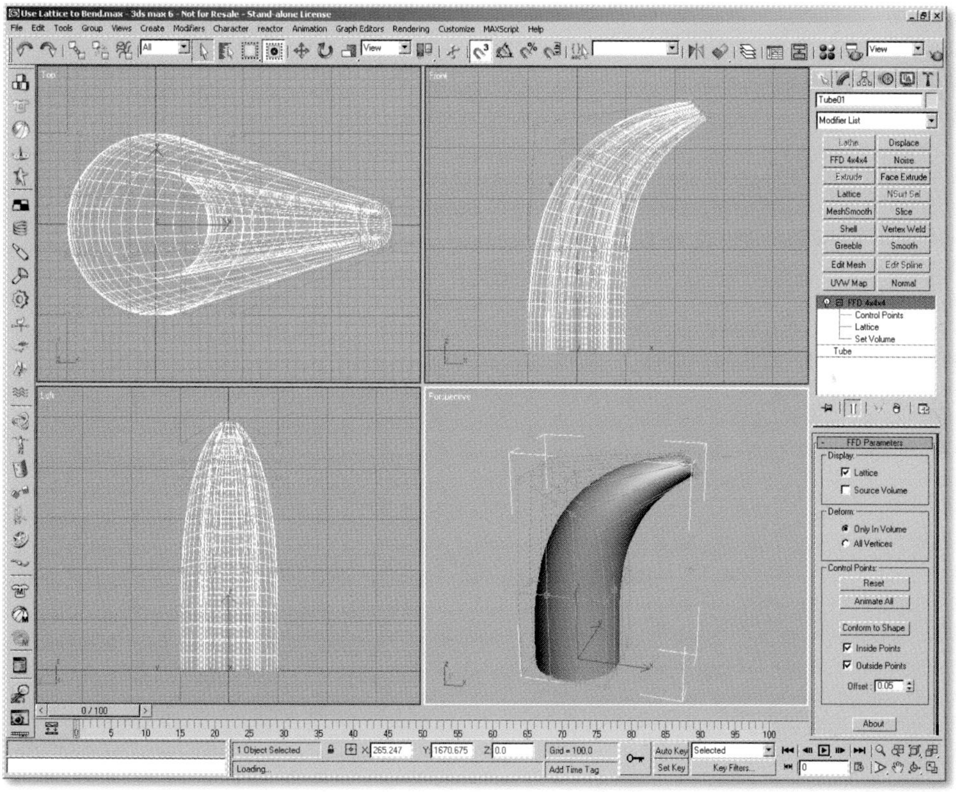

USE LATTICE FOR FRAMEWORK

Faced with creating a framework for an architectural model (such as a building under construction), a rocket gantry, or some other delicate but complex design? The Lattice modifier might be just what you need. Build the general shape that you need—a subdivided box, for instance, with visible edges where you want the framework—and then apply a Lattice modifier to it. You can adjust the struts' radius, their number of sides, their end caps, smoothing, and other parameters after you apply the modifier, and you can turn off the "joints" that appear at each vertex of the original geometry by checking the Struts Only from Edges radio button.

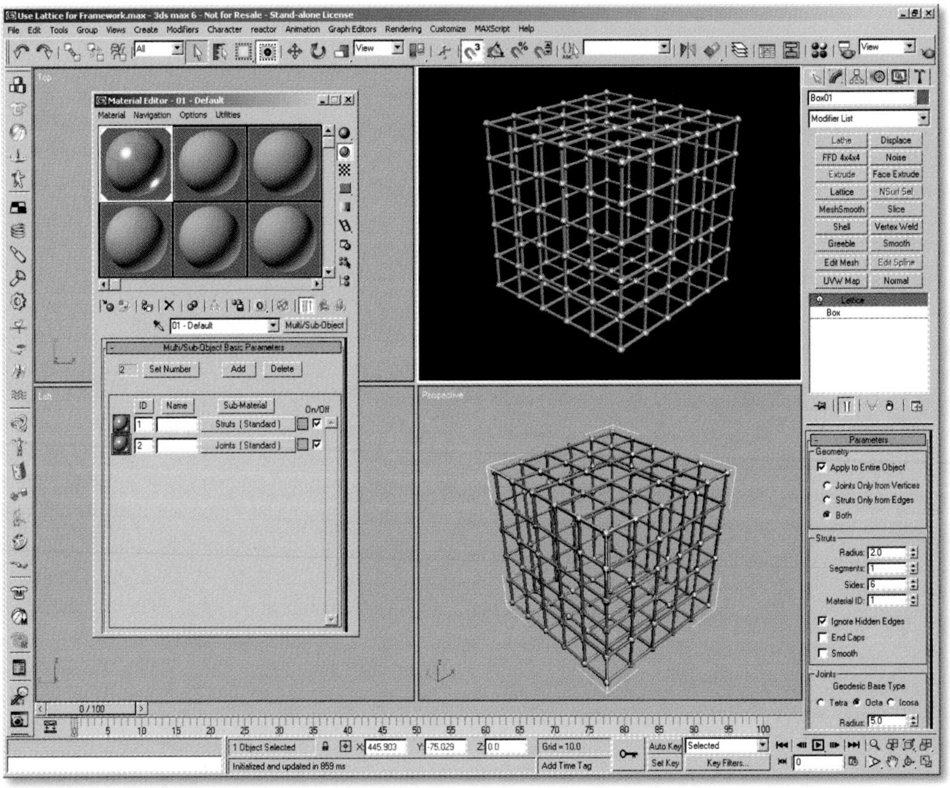

WIREFRAME MODELS, PART I: RETURN OF THE LATTICE MODIFIER

You can use the Lattice modifier to simulate wireframe models for rendering. If you set the radius (thickness) of the individual struts to a small number, you can simulate an extremely lacy, wireframe appearance of your original geometry. If you have two duplicated—and coincident (that is, occupying the same space)—copies of your object, one with the Lattice modifier and one without, you can simulate hidden-line wireframe rendering. Just assign your original, nonlatticed model a different color than the lattice model, or apply a Matte/Shadow material to it, while keeping your lattice version self-illuminated. For best results, link the models together, or parent them to the same dummy object so they don't "pull apart" if you animate them.

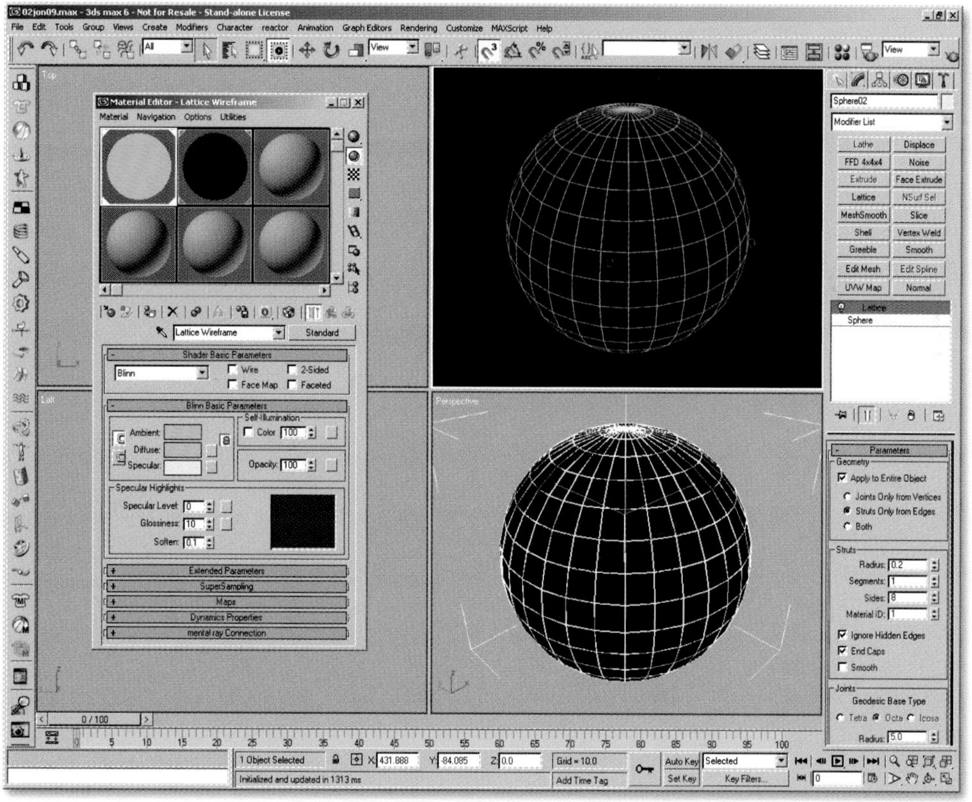

WIREFRAME MODELS, PART II: USE RENDERABLE SPLINES

Can't get enough of that old retro-CG wireframe look? How about a wireframe model made of splines? Just select your model, convert it to an editable mesh (or apply an Edit Mesh modifier to it), and go into Sub-Object/Edge mode. Select the edges of your model you want to show as wireframe; then, at the bottom of the Edit Geometry rollout, click the Create Shape from Edges button. When the Create Shape menu appears, change Shape Type to Linear (so that it follows the original edge contours precisely), make sure Ignore Hidden Edges is checked, name the new shape whatever you want, and click OK. You can then select this new shape object, make it renderable (check the Renderable box in the Modify/Rendering section of the rollout), and assign whatever material you want to it.

Note: Trying to create renderable splines from a large number of selected edges might bog down your system, so be careful when using this technique. Also remember that your original geometry is left, so you can include it in the simulated wireframe rendering or hide it as necessary.

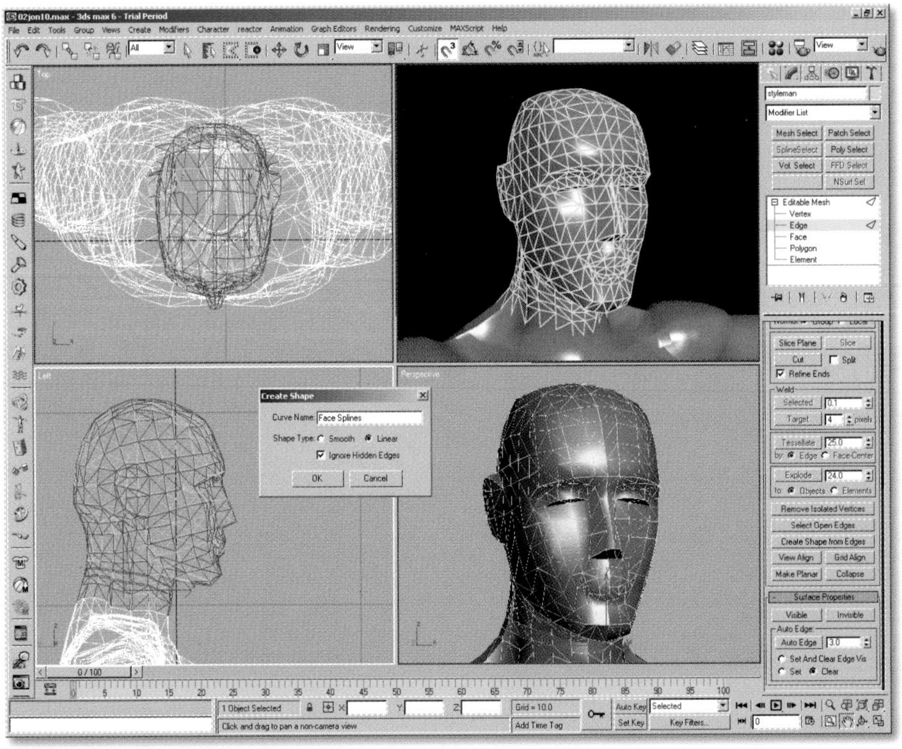

SURFACE TOOLS: SOLID REFERENCES

Surface Tools is a set of two modifiers: CrossSection and Surface. With Surface Tools, you can build smooth, organic patch-based models quickly out of a network of cross-sectional splines and then surface between the splines. Surface Tools are faster than NURBS, almost as powerful, and have fewer calories to boot.

One trick to working with Surface Tools is to create two versions of your model: your original spline cage, and then a cloned reference copy of that spline cage. Apply the CrossSection and Surface modifiers to the Reference object—not the original splines. Then right-click on the Reference object, select Properties > Object Properties > Display Properties, and check the See-Through option for the Reference. When you do, the object becomes translucent in your viewport. (Make sure you are in a Shaded mode by right-clicking on the Viewport label and choosing Smooth + Highlights. Note that this affects the appearance of the object only in the viewport; it does not affect the object's final rendered look.) Now you can manipulate and modify the original spline cage and see the changes propagate immediately on the smooth-shaded, translucent-surface reference model beneath. (Whew, that's a mouthful!)

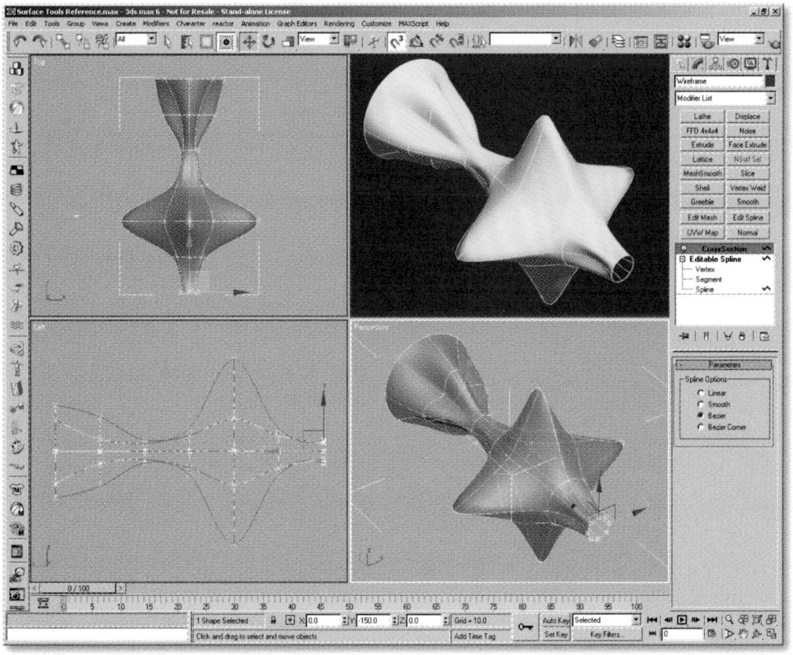

SURFACE TOOLS: WHERE'S MY MODEL?

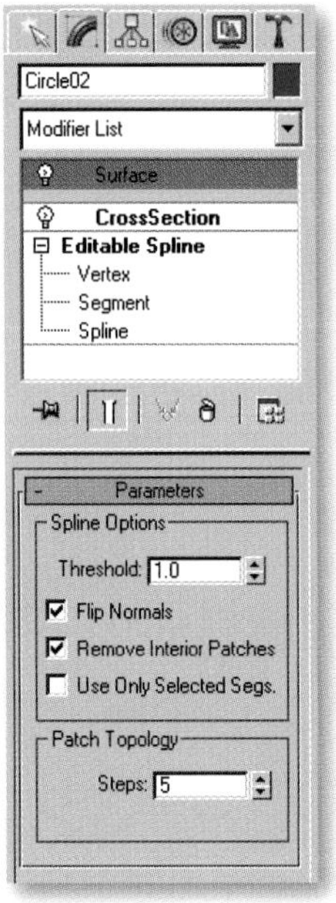

Regarding the tip discussed in "Surface Tools: Solid References": If you're creating new cross-sectional splines for a Surface Tools model, the face normals of the shaded Reference copy might become reversed. Normals for Surface Tools are determined by the direction in which the splines are aligned. You can fix this problem by selecting the solid-shaded Reference model and going to the Surface level in its modifier stack. Then check the Flip Normals box.

SURFACE TOOLS: WAITER, THERE'S A HOLE IN MY (REFERENCE) MODEL

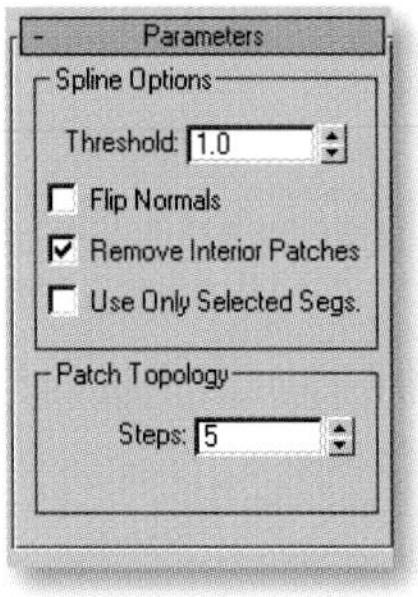

If "holes" appear in your Surface Tools geometry as you're creating it, select your Reference model (again, assuming you're using two techniques discussed in "Surface Tools: Solid References" and "Surface Tools: Where's My Model?") and go to the Surface modifier in its modifier stack. Check to see if the box marked Remove Interior Patches is checked. If not, check it! This should get rid of the holes or ugly interior faces that might have invaded your model.

SURFACE TOOLS: WELL-ORDERED SPLINES

If you work extensively with the 3ds max program's Surface Tools, then you've probably encountered situations where you have to reorder the splines you're creating for your model, or even add splines or subtract existing ones. However, you must have your splines ordered correctly for the CrossSection modifier to work; otherwise, your final surface model will be a jumbled rats' nest of polygons. One way to build your Surface Tools model is to create your splines in any order and then use the Explode command at the bottom of the Edit Spline Modifier panel > Geometry rollout with the To: Objects button checked. This makes every spline its own new object. From there, simply select the spline that you want to be at either end of your CrossSection shape, click on the Attach button, and begin attaching the splines in the order that you want CrossSection to follow.

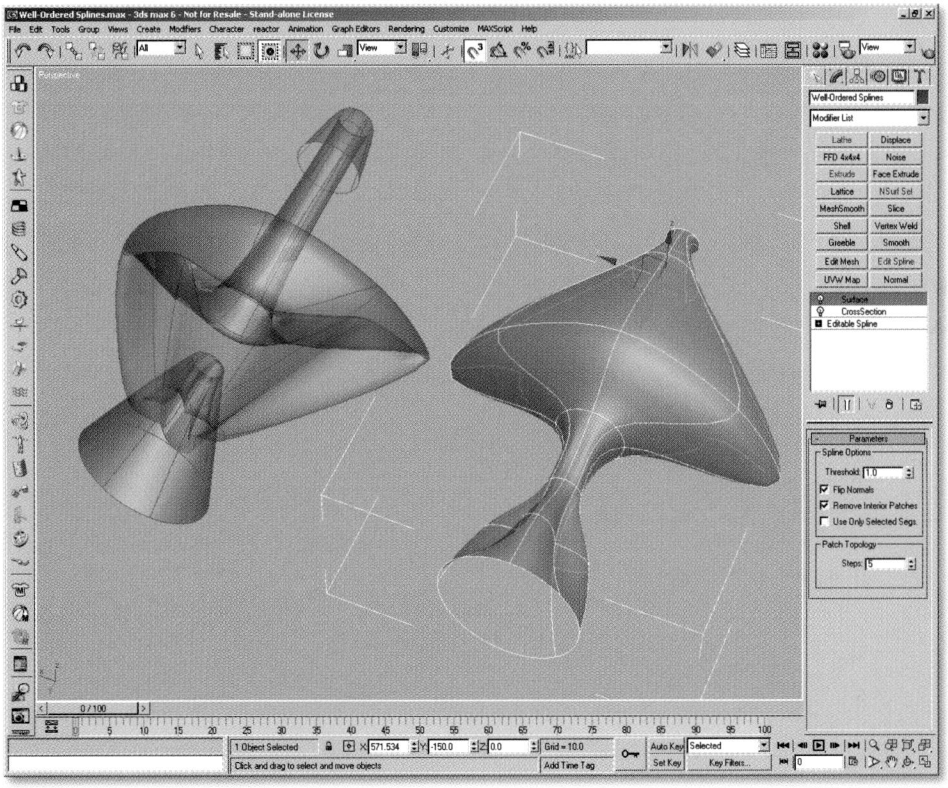

SURFACE TOOLS: NEAR-IMMEDIATE GRATIFICATION

When you're creating new splines in a Surface Tools model, you don't have to have a Sub-Object mode turned on. However, if you do, it will show you the vertices on the existing splines, allowing you to create new lines precisely between existing vertices without guesswork. Any Sub-Object mode can do this, but the Vertex Sub-Object mode lets you create new lines; you can then turn off the Create Line button and immediately adjust your model.

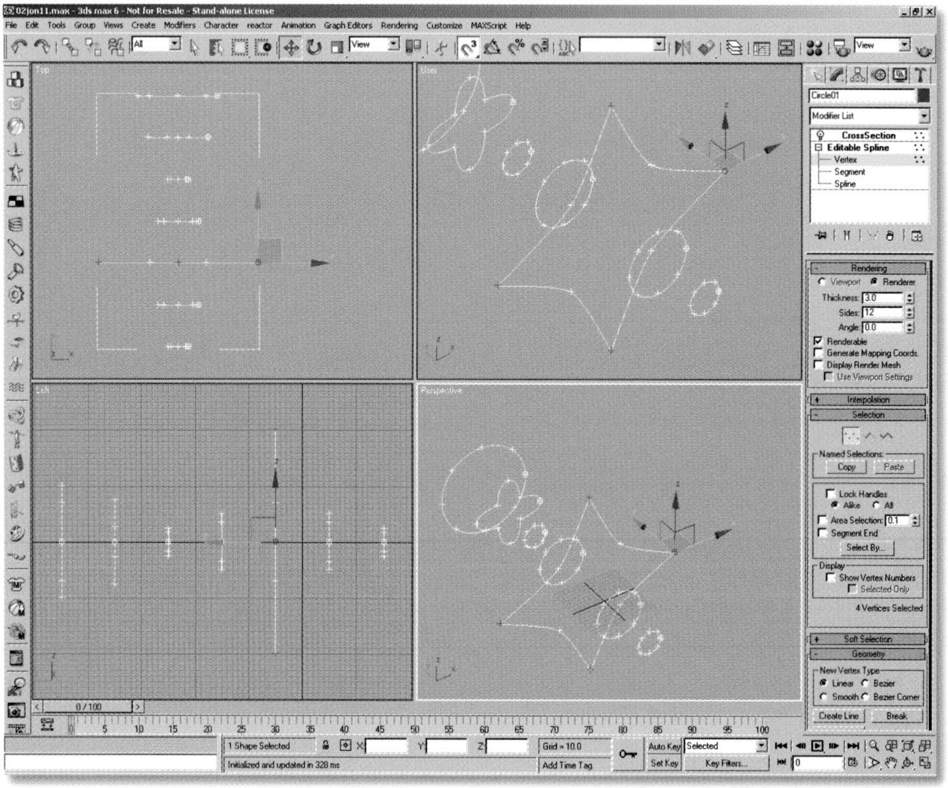

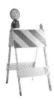

OPEN EDGES: COME OUT AND PLAY! (THE UVW UNWRAP EDITOR)

There is a "hidden" feature of the Edit UVW feature that is accessible through an Action item (which means you could place it on a menu or a toolbar or assign it to a shortcut)—but it's not in the default UI. This feature lets you select open edges in the UVW Unwrap mesh, just as you can do with Editable Polys.

To use this feature, you should do some manual customizations. Go to Customize > Customize UI and select the Menus tab. From the upper-right drop-down list, choose UVW Unwrap—UVW Select. From the Group list, select Unwrap UVW and leave Category set to All Commands. In the Action list, scroll down to Open Edge Select. Click and drag this Action item into the menu to the right. Add a separator if you want, and then save the menu to disk as MaxStartUI.mnu.

Now apply an Unwrap UVW modifier to your desired object, open the Unwrap UVW editor, select a single open edge, and call the action from your new menu. Any open edges that are connected to the one you selected become selected instantly!

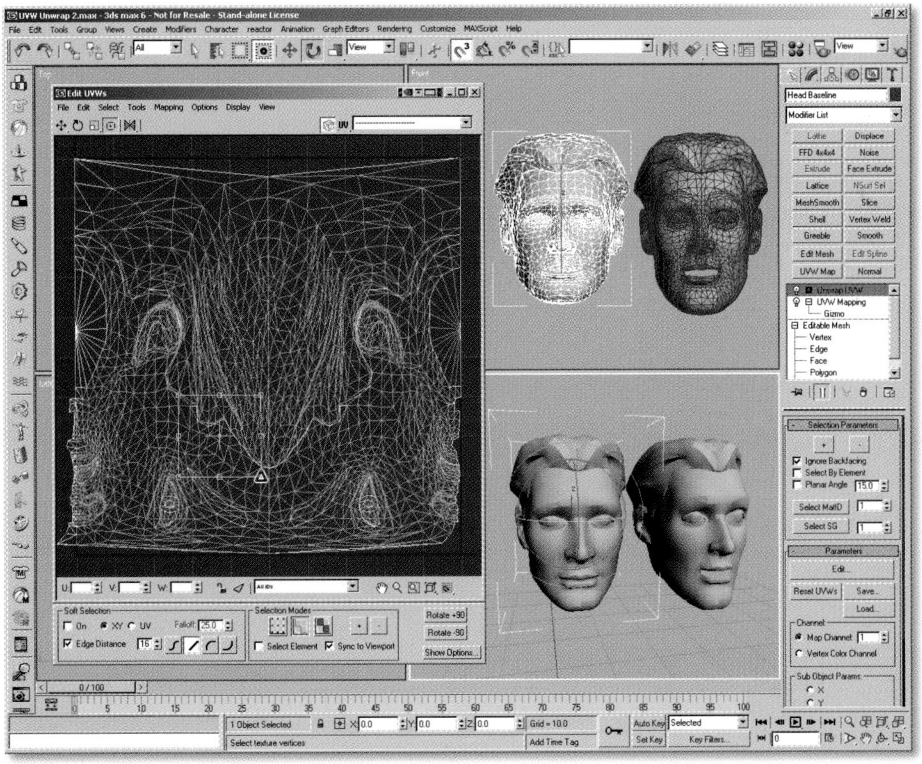

NEW 3DS MAX 6 FEATURES FOR ARCHITECTS: WALLS, RAILINGS, AND PLANTS

3ds max 6 includes some modeling features taken from the Autodesk VIZ program (which is adapted from the original 3ds max code base). These features might be new to some 3ds max users; they were designed especially for architects to make their 3D visualization jobs easier.

To access the Architecture, Engineering, Construction (AEC) features, go to the Command Panel > Create > Geometry tab; then select the AEC Extended entry from the drop-down menu. There you'll see three new features: Foliage, Railing, and Wall. The Foliage feature has a wide variety of procedural trees and smaller plants (with textures) that you can use to make your 3D building sites more realistic. ("Bring me… a shrubbery!") The Railing feature creates procedural railings, which are useful for architectural and industrial visualization (oil rigs, factory floors, and so forth). Finally, the Wall feature allows you to create linked walls simply by pointing, clicking, and moving your mouse where you want the walls to be. With these three features, you could amuse yourself for veritable minutes creating a lush "silicon garden"—an arboretum with plants, walkways with railings, and a security wall surrounding the whole thing.

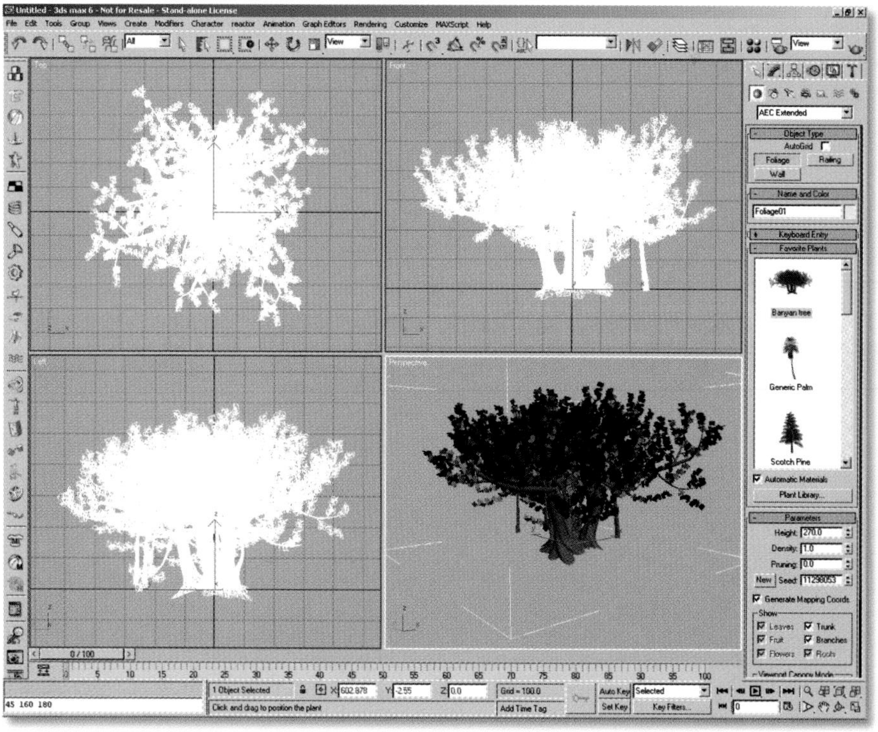

ARCHITECTURAL FEATURES, THE SEQUEL: STAIRS

Here's another nifty architectural modeling feature included with 3ds max 6: stairs! Under the Create > Geometry drop-down menu, pick the Stairs item. You'll then see four different types of stairs: LTypeStair, Straight Stair, Spiral Stair, and UTypeStair. Just click on one of the buttons, and then click-hold and drag, release, move, and continue in one of your viewports to create an ascending or descending set of steps. Want to create that oh-so-modern wide staircase so prominently featured in the living room of *The Brady Bunch* house? Then this is your menu item.

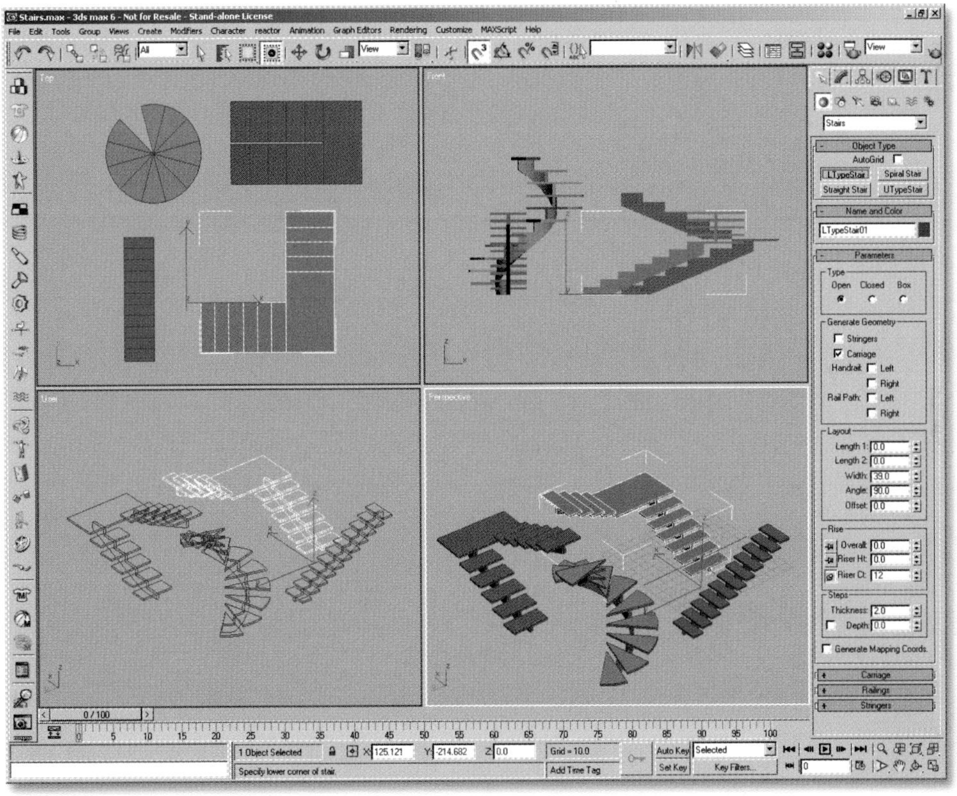

BENEATH THE PLANET OF THE ARCHITECTURAL FEATURES: DOORS AND WINDOWS

It's not much use to create spacious rooms and a roof over the heads of your 3D people unless they can (theoretically) get into and look out of said rooms. That's where the additional 3ds max 6 architectural modeling primitives Doors and Windows come in handy. Like the Stair objects mentioned in the previous tip, you just choose the various Door and Window objects you need (from the Create > Geometry panel) for your 3D dwellings. Each of the three Door object types has parameters allowing you to adjust the door (and door well) height, width, and depth, and even other details, such as the door thickness, edge widths, glass panels, and so on. The six Window objects include Awning, Fixed, Projected, Casement, Pivoted, and Sliding. Note that doors do not include knobs, handles, or knockers. If you want, you can model these pieces separately and then attach them to the Door Leaf surface by using an Attachment controller (Command Panel > Motion tab > Parameters > Assign Controller > Position > Attachment Controller.) Because the entire structure is considered the "door," simple linking won't work to attach the hardware to the door surface.

THE SCATTER COMPOUND OBJECT

The Scatter Compound object (Create > Geometry > Compound Objects) can be useful for adding random detail throughout your scenes, such as plants and rocks on a landscape, or even messy room details, such as Lego blocks strewn about the floor of a child's room. It allows you to scatter copies of a picked object and distribute them across the surface of another object.

Because duplicating (and then scattering) tons of 3D objects in your scene can increase your polygon count dramatically, the Scatter object lets you display the distributed objects as low-resolution proxies (basically, wedge-shaped boxes). This enables the objects to be displayed more quickly in your viewports, but the objects still render with all their original details. However, if you're displaying your scattered objects as proxies and then collapse them into editable mesh objects (or just one big mesh), they collapse into actual wedge-shaped boxes, causing you to lose all the plant, rock, or Lego detail in your scene.

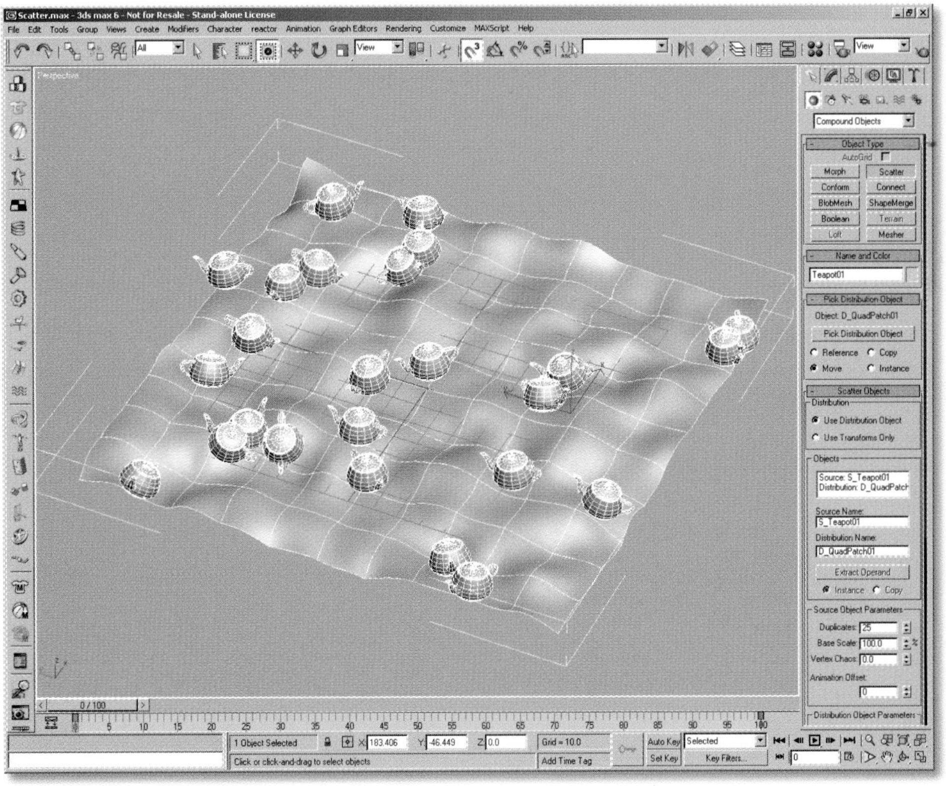

A MATTER OF INTEGRITY: STL CHECK

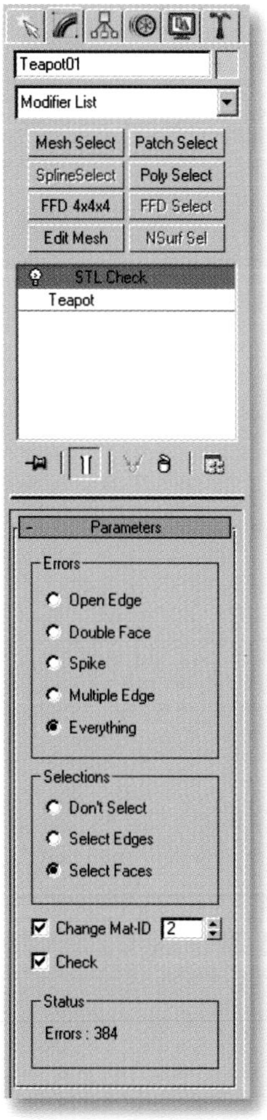

The Stereo Lithography (STL) file format was designed to accommodate the needs of stereo lithography machines—hardware that creates physical resin or acrylic models from 3D object data. Due to the restrictions of this process, the 3D objects have to be as "clean" and unified as possible. They cannot have coincident faces, duplicated vertices, or other spurious modeling information, or they will make the STL machine unhappy.

3ds max can export .STL format data from its 3D scenes. To check the integrity of your models, go to the Modify panel and apply an STL Check modifier to your objects. This modifier checks for errors in your mesh construction before export—but you don't have to be exporting your files to STL format to use this modifier. For example, it's handy for checking your model integrity after doing multiple booleans; it also helps point out face and vertex problems that you might need to correct before rendering.

DIDN'T THINK I COULD GET AWAY WITHOUT MENTIONING THE GREEBLE MODIFIER, DID YOU?

Tom Hudson's Greeble plug-in first appeared in my 1998 book *3D Studio MAX R2.5 f/x and Design*, published by Coriolis Press. (A version for 3ds max 3 appeared in an updated version of this book.) Greeble is an object modifier that builds industrial detail consisting of beveled plates with additional "widget" details on top. These parametric building blocks are excellent for creating quick details to dress up either objects or selected faces in your scene. Properly used, Greeble can give the illusion of complex city landscapes (such as the industrial wasteland seen at the beginning of *Bladerunner*) or spacecraft details similar to vehicles you might have seen in the *Star Wars* or *Star Trek* films and TV series.

Over the years, the Greeble plug-in has achieved almost cult-like status among 3ds max users—and has earned the envy of other 3D software users not blessed with such functionality in their software.

To download the Greeble plug-in (and documentation) for 3ds max versions 3.x, 4, 5 and 6, go to http://www.klanky.com.

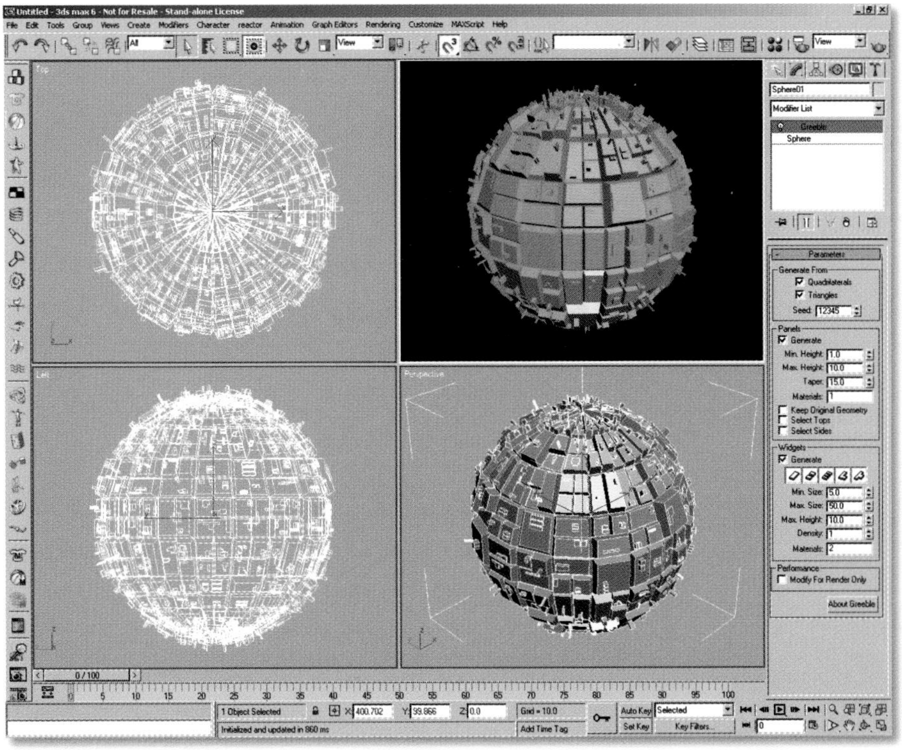

IMPORTING OBJECT FILES

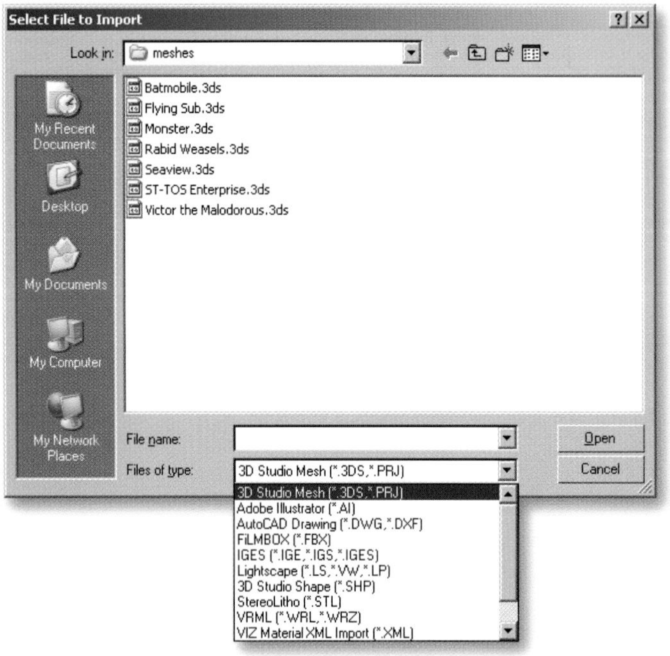

When you're working with 3D artists who are using tools other than 3ds max (sorry!), and you need to import their object files, here are some basic rules of thumb (approved by the Institute of Thumbology):

- AutoCAD's venerable .DXF format is okay for exporting files to 3ds max, but be forewarned: The .DXF format is old and not particularly elegant (it's basically a giant scene text description), and importing large .DXF files can take a long time as 3ds max converts the information. (Also, Macintosh 3D programs are notorious for outputting gnarly .DXF files that PC-based programs can't read.) The AutoCAD .DWG (drawing) file format is also a candidate for file exchange.
- People who are using Lightwave can export their object files by using the old 3D Studio/DOS .3ds file format, which can be imported into 3ds max directly. However, single objects larger than 65,536 faces have to be diced up into separate elements before export; the old .3DS format can't handle objects that exceed the 64K face count.
- One of the most common 3D object file formats is .OBJ, created by Alias. Most 3D programs can export and import .OBJ files, so it's a good format to fall back on for polygonal model exchange. The downside is that you'll have to search on the Internet for a free 3ds max .OBJ importer. The 3ds max 6 program doesn't come with a native .OBJ importer.
- If you need to get NURBS data from another 3D program into 3ds max, a good way to transfer it is to export it in IGES spline format from the original program, and then import that into 3ds max. (Once again, the import might take a long time for a large NURBS model.) You can then collapse the resultant NURBS model into a polygonal mesh, if necessary.

IMPORTING OBJECTS AND ANIMATION

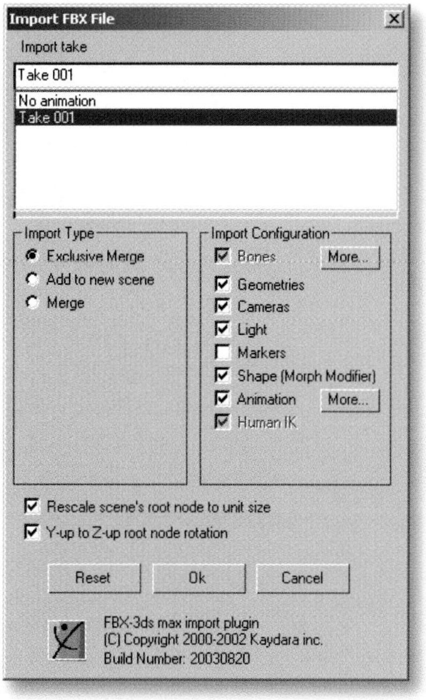

Okay, the previous tip covers basic model import, but what if you need to import both model *and* animation data from another 3D program?

Your best bet is to see if you can get the data from your non-3ds max-using client or co-worker in Kaydara's .FBX (FiLMBOX) format. The .FBX file format is becoming the industry *lingua franca* for 3D programs to share scene and model data, with the animation keys intact. It also handles material assignments.

For more information, go to http://www.kaydara.com.

Waxing the Finish

Waxing the Finish

materials tips

3ds max has one of the most comprehensive material (or surface) editors in the industry. You can create extremely complex, layered materials, maps that reference one another, and materials that will do practically everything but clean your windows and walk your dog.

This chapter presents some cool Material Editor tips on the following:

- *How to customize the Material Editor*
- *How to display larger versions of your sample spheres and create previews of animated materials*
- *How to explore the new mental ray map and shader types*
- *How you can make your materials and maps be all that they can be*

CUSTOMIZE YOUR MATERIAL EDITOR DISPLAY

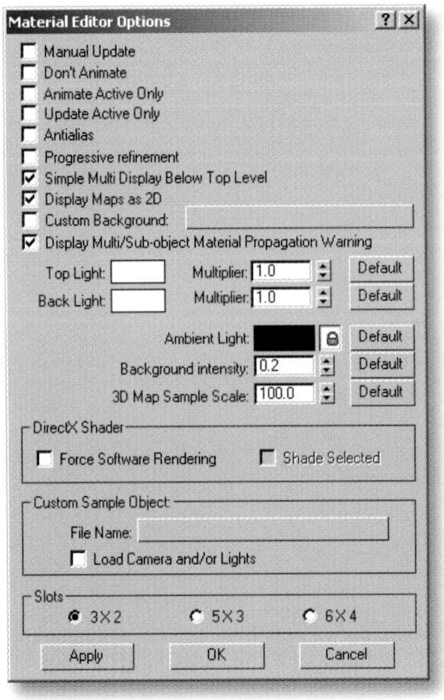

You can change the appearance of the material slots in the Material Editor quite easily by right-clicking on the sample sphere area at the top of the menu. This brings up a basic menu where you can increase the number of visible material sample slots. (You can increase up to 24 at once. If you're displaying the sample spheres at 3 × 2 or 5 × 3, a "hand" icon appearing over the sample spheres lets you click-hold and drag the sample sphere area to see all 24 slots.) In addition, if you choose Options, you get an additional menu allowing you to change the appearance of the sample objects (displaying them with backgrounds, highlights, and so on), change the behavior of animated materials (whether they update or not as you scroll the Time Slider bar), change them from spheres to boxes, and more. The Options menu is also available as an icon on the main Material Editor user interface (UI), on the right side.

MAGNIFY A SAMPLE SPHERE

You can pop up a larger version of a selected sample sphere (or cube) by simply double-clicking on the desired material sample in the Material Editor. When you do, a floating sample sphere menu box appears; click-drag on its corner to make it even larger, if you want. (You can also use the Material Editor Options menu, described in the previous tip, to bring up a magnified sample sphere.) You're not limited to having just one magnified sample sphere open; you can bring up multiple floating windows by double-clicking on additional sample spheres.

HELP, I'VE RUN OUT OF MATERIALS FOR MY SCENE!

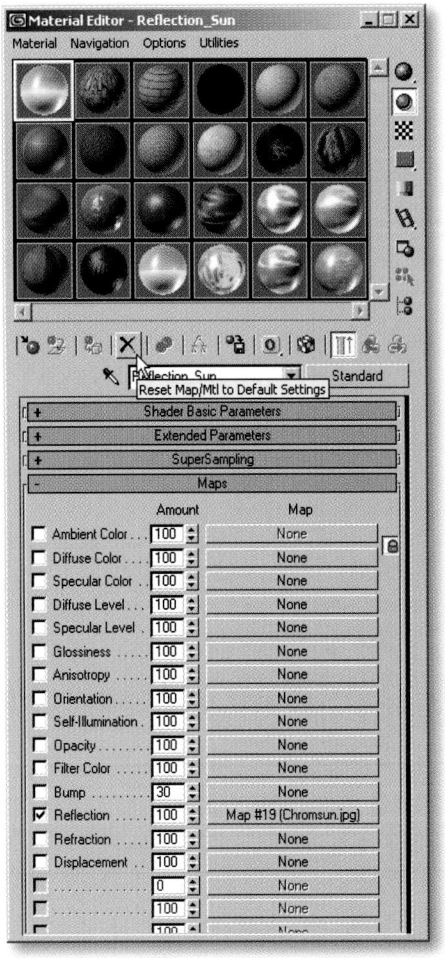

Actually, you haven't. This is a common misconception with 3ds max newcomers. Although you can get the Material Editor to display only 24 different material swatches at the same time, you're not restricted to only 24 materials in your scene.

To create a new material, pick a material slot that's already in use (one that you don't think you'll be modifying soon). Then click on the X icon (the ToolTip actually reads "Reset Map/Mtl to Default Settings"). When the Reset Mtl/Map Params box appears, select Affect Only Mtl/Map in the Editor Slot, and then click OK. When you do, you'll create a new, generic material in the *slot*, but the material you just replaced (in the Material Editor, mind you) is still assigned to the relevant objects in the scene. (That is, if you've already assigned it.)

Another way to do this is to click the Material Type button (Standard, Raytrace, and so on) and pick a new material type from the Material/Map browser. However, if you do this, you'll need to immediately rename the new material. The material retains its original name, and you wouldn't want to accidentally replace your original material in the scene with these new parameters, causing a great disturbance in The Force.

LIKE YOUR NEW MATERIALS? THEN SAVE THEM!

If you're creating new materials or replacing them in a scene (as noted in the previous tip), then it's a good idea to save all your materials in a Material Library. From your Material Editor, open a Material/Map Browser window, drag your materials to a new or existing .MTL library, and then save the library (to your 3dsmax6\Matlibs folder) with the name of your choice.

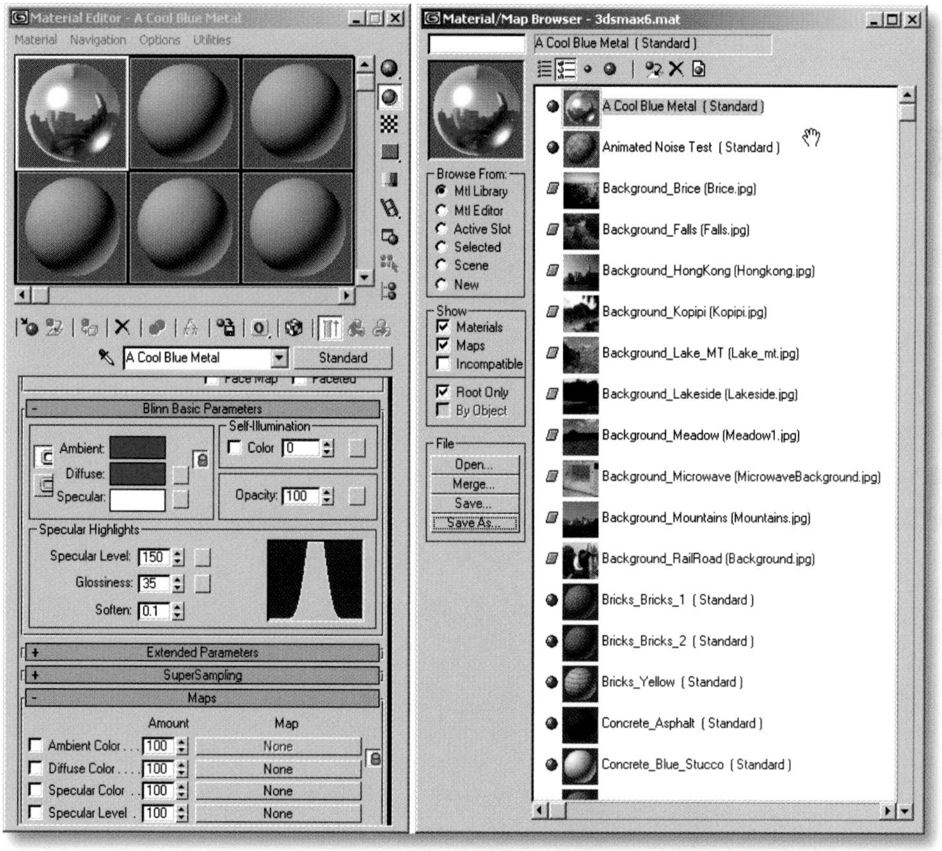

MY MATERIALS ARE "HOT!"

When you assign a material to an object or element in your scene, that material becomes "hot" or active in the scene and in the Material Editor. ("Hot" materials in the Material Editor are noted by the triangles in the corner of their respective sample slots. White triangles indicate materials that are "hot" and selected; gray triangles are just "hot.") Any changes you make to this hot material (replacing maps or adjusting other parameters) are updated automatically on the same-named material in your scene.

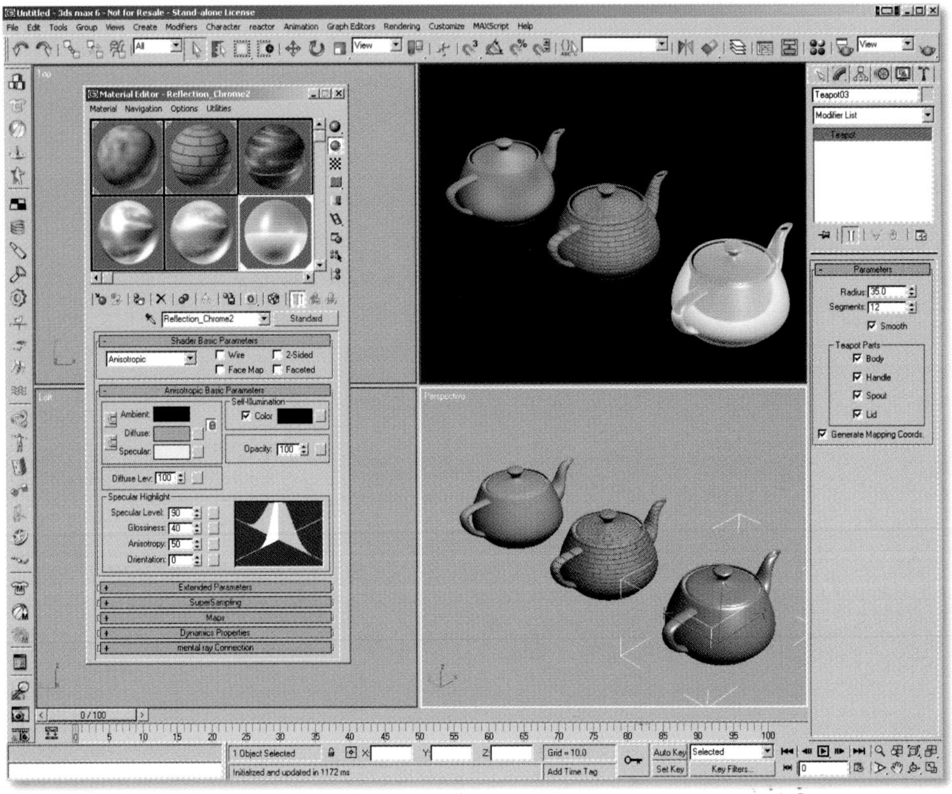

USING IDENTICALLY NAMED MATERIALS

To build off the previous tip: Although it might seem like a pain to keep track of identically named materials in your Material Editor (with only one at a time active, or "hot," in your scene), you can actually use this to your advantage. You can create multiple versions of the same-named material in the Material Editor, each with different parameters, allowing you to test each one in the scene until you get the rendered results you want.

Note that if you create a new material with the same name as one already assigned in your scene, you can use this material to replace the original by clicking on the Put Material to Scene icon. (If you click on the Assign Material to Selection icon, you get a warning that a material with the same name already exists in your scene.)

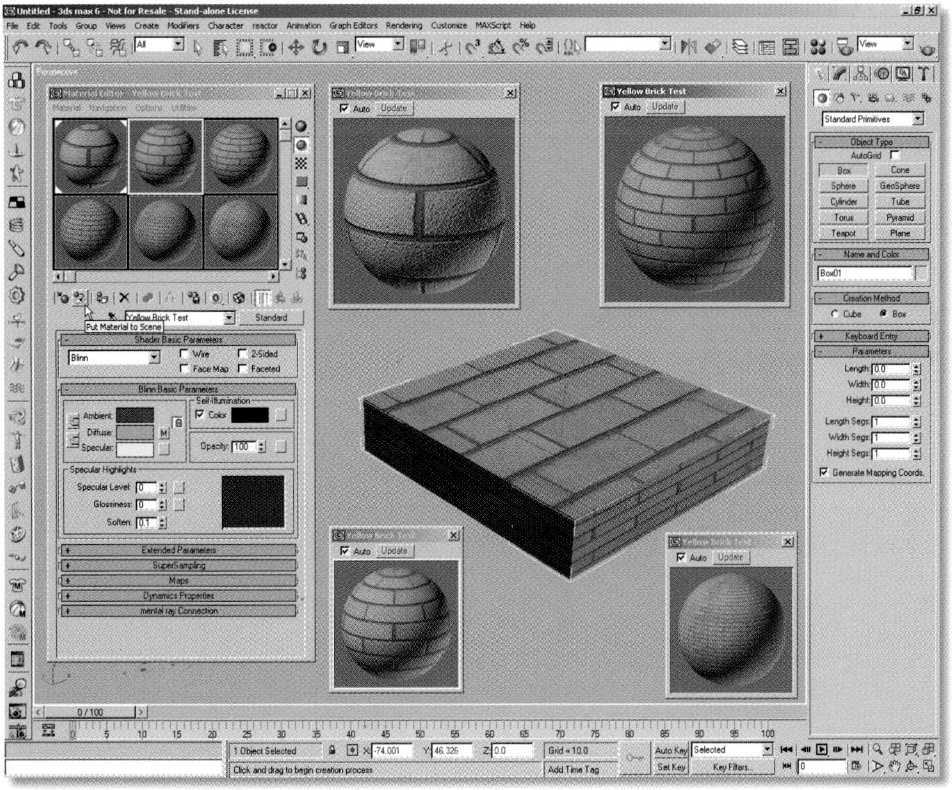

SNEAK PREVIEWS: CHECK OUT YOUR ANIMATED MATERIALS

If any one of your material parameters is animated, you can get a preview of how it will appear in your scene by clicking on the Make Preview icon (the little filmstrip image) in the Material Editor. You'll then get a Create Material Preview dialog box that lets you set the parameters of the preview. When you click OK, 3ds max creates a small, fast animation of your sample sphere, which appears in a Media Player window when it's finished rendering.

Note that if your animated parameters are so subtle as to not be readily noticeable in the Material Editor sample slots as you scrub the Time slider bar in your scene, then making a preview probably won't help you. You should just render a low-resolution animation of your scene, and go out and grab a sandwich.

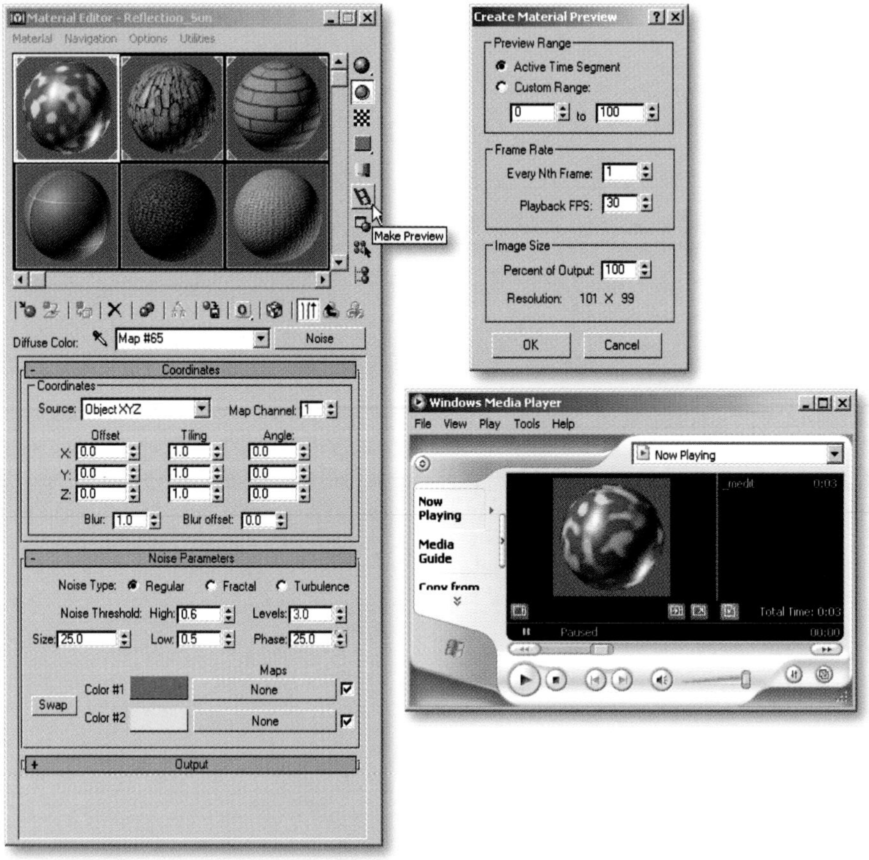

SHOW MENTAL RAY MATERIALS IN THE MATERIAL EDITOR

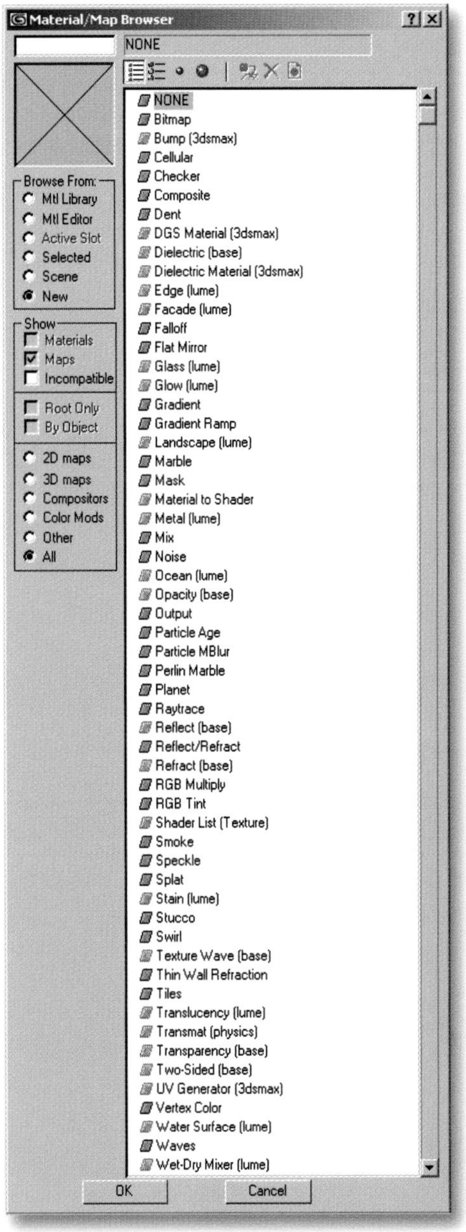

Here's one thing you'll notice in 3ds max 6 when you open the Material Editor: At the bottom of any Standard material, you'll see a new rollout section called "Mental Ray Connection." Open it, and you'll see additional map slots for Basic Shaders, Caustics and Global Illumination (Global Illumination), Extended Shaders, and Advanced Shaders.

To make these additional maps and shaders available for rendering, click the Lock buttons on the far right of the slots to unlock them. However, to see mental ray-specific maps, you have to have mental ray assigned as your production renderer. Click the Render icon to bring up the Render panel, or go to Rendering > Render > Common. Under Assign Renderer, click on the … button to the right of Production and pick Mental Ray Renderer from the list. Now, when you close the Render menu and return to the Material Editor, you'll see a full complement of mental ray maps and shaders if you open the Material/Map Browser. (Note: You can also see the mental ray shaders if you check Incompatible in the Material/Map Browser, before you assign the mental ray renderer.)

THE NEW MENTAL RAY MATERIAL TYPES AND MAPS

The mental ray 3.1 renderer included with 3ds max 6 features a wide variety of maps and several new material types that work exclusively with mental ray to produce striking results that you can't get (or at least, not easily) with the default scanline renderer. Among the new mental ray material types are the DGS material, glass, and the mental ray material itself. The DGS and glass materials have the designation "physics phenomena." "Phenomena" in mental ray are shading types that replicate the look of complex physical object/surface properties, such as reflections, refractions, caustics, diffuse transmission, translucency, and so forth.

The new mental ray maps or materials show up as yellow parallelogram or yellow sphere icons, respectively; 3ds max Standard maps have a green parallelogram, and Standard materials have a blue sphere. The new mental ray map types include Dielectric (to simulate glowing and iridescent materials); the new Lume shaders Glass, Glow, Landscape, Metal, Ocean, Stain, Translucency, and Wet-Dry Mixer (used effectively for the first *Myst* adventure game graphics), and many others. If you can't duplicate certain material looks with the core 3ds max materials and the default scanline renderer, then explore mental ray and the new shaders. You'll be experimenting with them for weeks! (For more information, in 3ds max 6 select Help > New Features Guide to load an Adobe Acrobat .PDF document describing the new features of 3ds max 6, including the mental ray renderer and material types.)

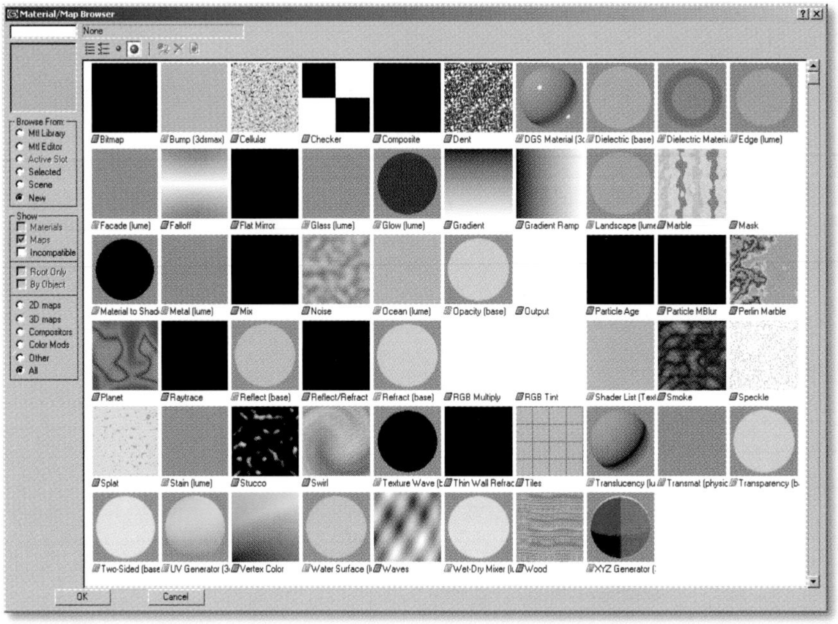

CUSTOM MENTAL RAY ARCHITECTURAL MATERIALS

When you first install 3ds max 6, you get the option of installing Architectural Materials for mental ray. Go ahead and install them and launch 3ds max 6. Then open your Material Editor, click the Get Material icon to bring up the Material/Map Browser, check the Browse From Mtl Library, and click File > Open. When you do, you'll see the various architectural Material Libraries stored in your \Matlibs folder. These include libraries for concrete, doors and windows, furnishings (cloth), masonry, metals, and other build material types. Each library contains custom mental ray materials and bitmap textures. Even if you're not doing architectural visualization, you can use these materials as templates to create more complex textures for your 3ds max scenes. (Just be sure to render them in mental ray, too!)

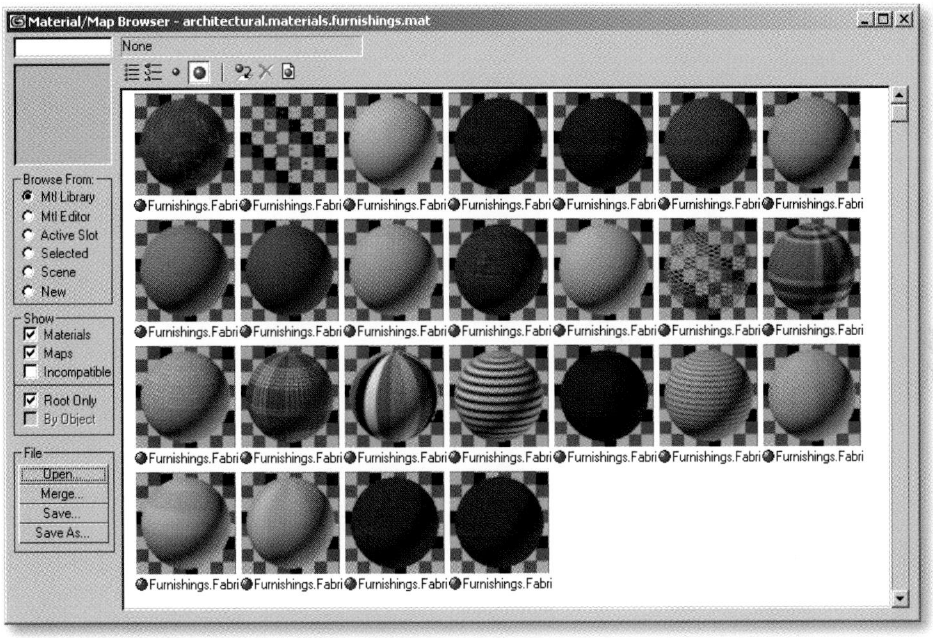

MY, DON'T YOU LOOK ANIMATED TODAY!

If you save animated materials to a 3ds max Material Library (called something like COOL-STUFF.MAT), those materials retain their animated properties if you load the library into any new scene. This is helpful if you're merging files, but make sure you check for any animated materials when you load or merge a new .mat file and you use those previously saved materials in your current scene.

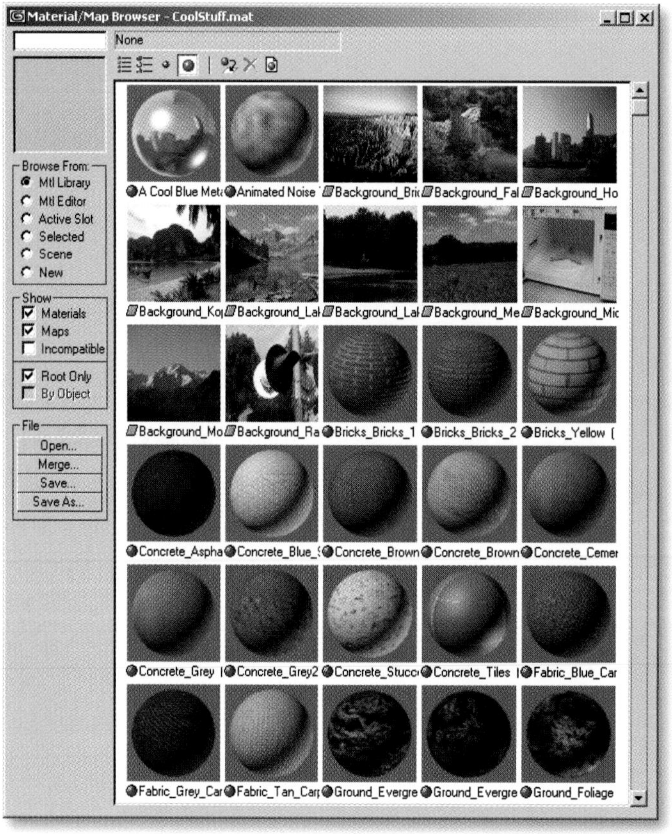

HOW CAN I TELL IF MY MATERIALS ARE ANIMATED?

Whenever you set a keyframe on any spinner in 3ds max, a bright red bracket appears around that spinner, indicating that at least one key has been set on it.

If you don't want to open every menu item on a material (not surprisingly, because there are so many) just to see if animated parameters are set on it, there's a quick way to check. Open the Curve Editor (or Dope Sheet) and then click on the Filters icon. Under Show Only, check Animated Tracks and leave everything else blank. (Or, if you know you have animation keys on a specific object, select that object in your scene and check Selected Objects in the Curve Editor as well.) This will help you find the animated tracks quickly in your scene.

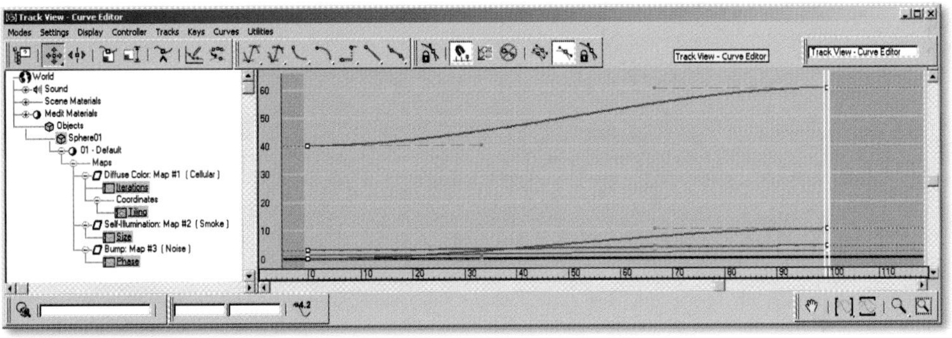

CHECK YOUR MATERIAL ANIMATION TIMINGS!

If you import material keyframes, check your animation timing in both the scene and the merged materials. If the merged animation keys last for only 150 frames but your current animation is 300 frames long, you'll have to adjust (move or scale) the merged animated material keys in the Track View Curve Editor or the Dope Sheet. Otherwise, your new 3D superhero character Dr. Kreinheld, Super-Genius might discover his animated power crystal stops dead, right in the middle of his battle with Victor the Malodorous.

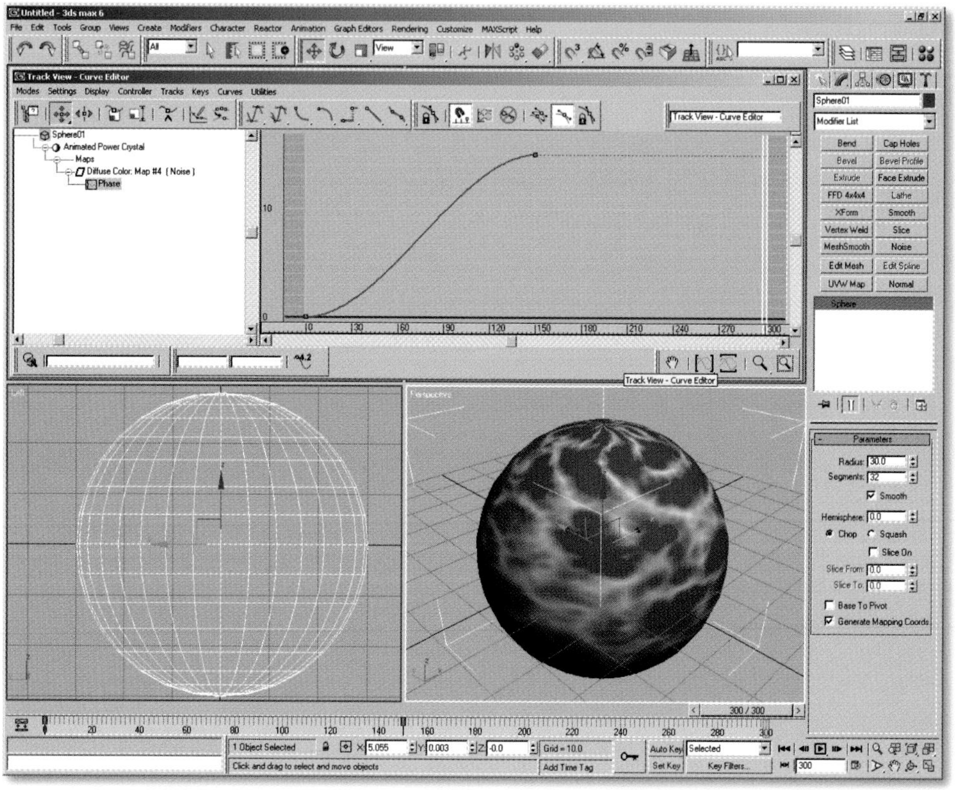

MATERIALS: THEY'VE GIVEN YOU A NUMBER AND TAKEN AWAY YOUR NAME

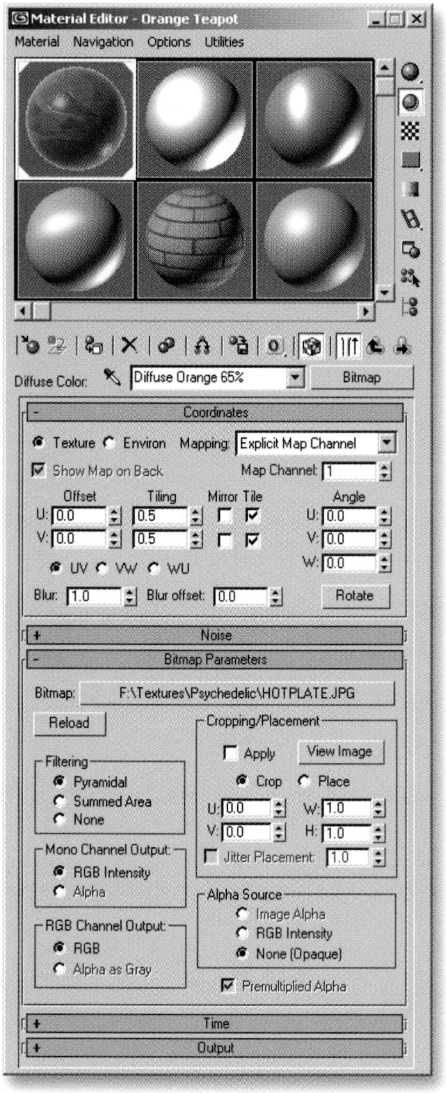

When you're creating complex materials, give the materials and each map within them specific names, rather than just the 3ds max-assigned defaults, such as Map #2 - Bump.jpg. (If you want to be really anal-retentive about it, you could name your materials with the same names as objects in your scene; that way, an object called Chrome Car Bumper gets its own material called—you guessed it—Chrome Car Bumper.) Giving unique names to the materials and map slots in your scene helps you pick them more quickly from the Material/Map Browser. This can be a great timesaver if you want to grab an instance of a Bump map from one material and copy it to another material slot.

EVERYTHING'S BLURRY: USING BLUR OFFSET

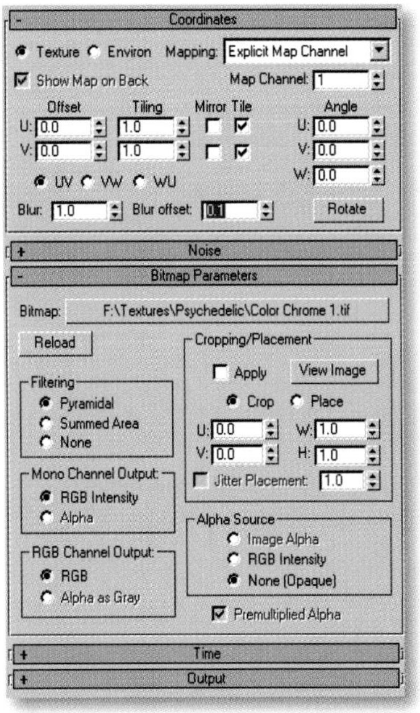

It's usually helpful to use Blur offset (on your bitmaps) to help lessen the effects of aliasing in your final renderings when using the 3ds max scanline renderer. This is especially important for Bump maps and Reflection maps, where the aliasing is most obvious. Try a small setting first, such as 0.01–0.1, and increase as necessary to soften the bitmap. (If you're using the mental ray renderer in 3ds max 6, it's better to adjust your Min/Max sampling rate; you'll hear more about this later in the book.)

LOOK, UP IN THE SKY! IT'S SUPERSAMPLING!

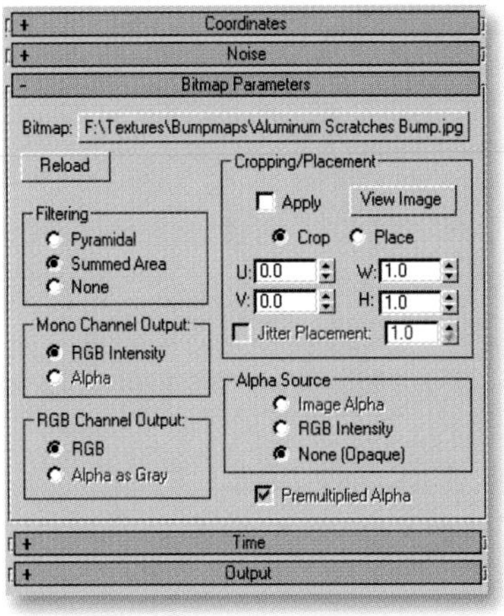

To further decrease aliasing in your 3ds max 6 renders, you can use supersampling on an individual material basis (under the SuperSampling section of a Material rollout), use it on a Global basis (set as the default in the Material Editor, and turned on in the 3ds max scanline renderer Render Scene/Renderer tab), or increase the Minimum/Maximum Samples Per Pixel values in the mental ray renderer. Finally, you can also use the legacy Summed Area filtering in the Bitmap Parameters rollout, again on an individual material basis. Whew! (Note that these sampling techniques *will* increase your scanline rendering times, so have your Game Boy player handy while you're waiting.)

USE NOISE TO BLEND BETWEEN TILING BITMAPS (AND MAKE THEM LAST LONGER!)

Perfectly straight tiles are great if you're refinishing a bathroom, but in a 3D scene, obvious tiling bitmaps scream out, "Bad texturing!" If you want to use tiling bitmaps as textures in a scene, but you don't want them to "repeat" noticeably across a large surface (such as a landscape or a rock wall), here's a trick to hide the seams.

Replace the tiling bitmap in your scene with a Mix map. Keep the existing bitmap as a submaterial, and then drag-copy it down to the second bitmap slot of the Mix material. (Make it a copy, not an instance.) Change this second bitmap's tiling values to be different from the first one; for example, if the first bitmap is tiled 5 on U and 5 on V, then set the second bitmap's tiling to be, say, 9 on U and V. Then use a Noise map in the Mix Amount slot of this material to blend the two. (Adjust the Noise Threshold settings to make the mask either subtle or extreme.)

The odd-numbered second bitmap, blended on top of the first bitmap with the mathematically random Noise map, helps "break up" and hide repeating seams in your maps. (Note: You should use this for organic patterns in your bitmaps, not existing repeating patterns, such as images of bricks.)

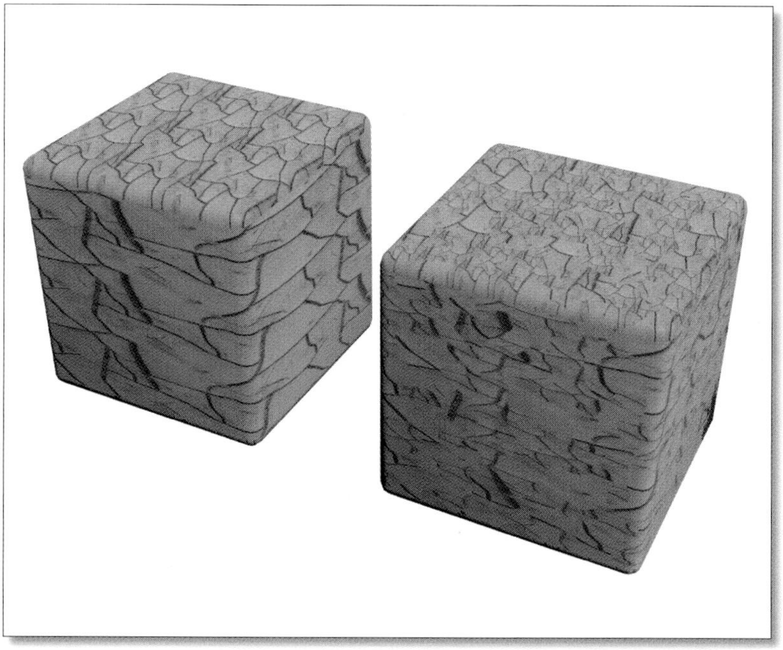

UNLESS YOU'RE THREATENED WITH DIRE BODILY HARM, AVOID MULTI/SUBOBJECT MAPPING

Unless your scene absolutely requires it (because you're exporting to a 3D game engine, for example), don't use Multi/SubObject mapping assignments. I use them less than 1 percent of the time. They're cumbersome, and I'm amazed when I see 3ds max newbies struggling with selecting faces, applying material IDs, assigning subobject materials (lathering, rinsing, repeating...).

If you're going to go to the trouble of selecting those faces and assigning materials to them, then do this: Treat your objects as if they were pieces of a plastic model kit. Select your object faces, detach them, name them something logical, and assign separate mapping coordinates and materials to each detached object element. Then parent them to a Dummy object, Group them, or reattach them, but without welding the vertices of the final model together (again, unless you have to). To eliminate the appearance of seams between the pieces, apply a Smooth modifier to the selected model pieces for the entire model. If you've attached all the pieces, 3ds max requires you to make a decision regarding how you want the (inevitable) new Multi/SubObject material to be created and encompass the resultant model. If you have to detach the pieces again from the now-unified model, you can select the pieces by going into Subobject: Element mode and clicking on the piece you want.

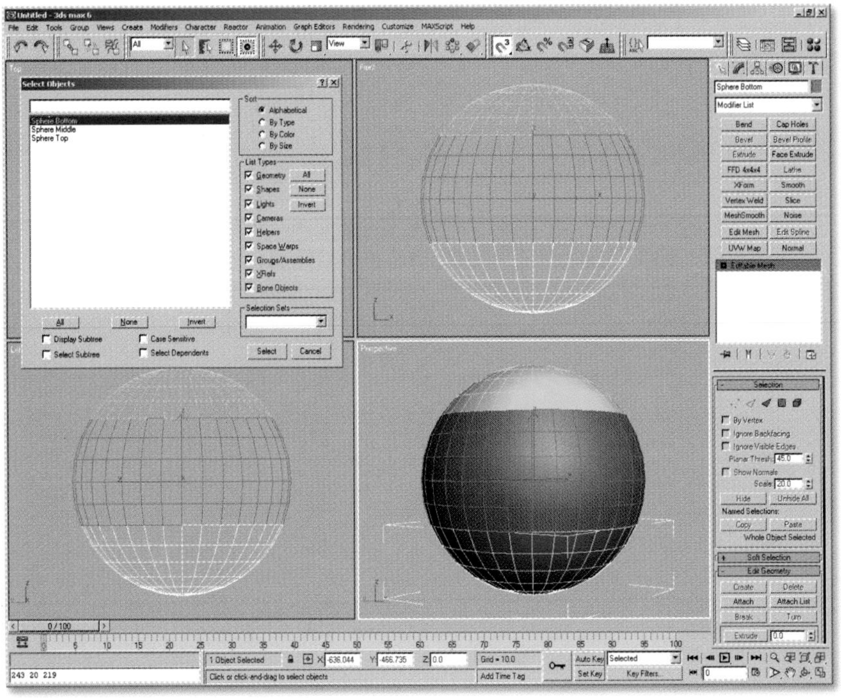

BACKGROUND CHECK: INSTANCE YOUR ENVIRONMENT MAPS

If you're loading any kind of map (especially bitmaps) into your background via the Rendering/Environment menu, when you finish browsing for and picking the map, open the Material Editor and click-drag the map name to an open slot and choose Instance. You'll see the entire map occupy the slot, and the material sample sphere will go away. Having an instance of this map in your Material Editor makes it easier to modify or change the background image as necessary, and you get immediate visual feedback in the Material Editor on how the map should behave in the scene.

INSTANCE YOUR PROJECTOR LIGHT MAPS, TOO

Okay, did you read everything in the previous tip? Then do the same thing with maps (especially procedurals) that you load into the Projector Map button of your lights (typically spot or directional lights.) Click-drag the map name to an open slot in the Material Editor and choose Instance. There, you can manipulate the map's parameters visibly, and the changes translate instantly to the affected light. (It's a "hot" map in your scene, remember?) This trick works especially well if you're using bitmap sequences or animated procedural maps in your projector lights.

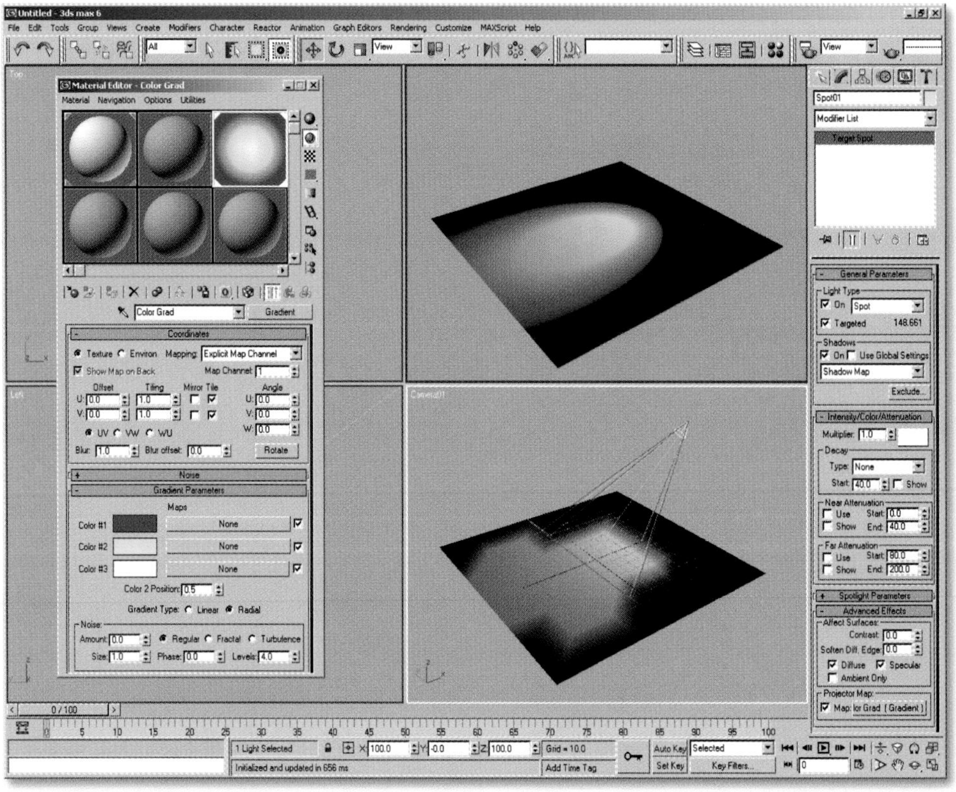

RAYTRACING: USE THE MATERIAL, NOT THE MAP

The 3ds max core Raytrace material and Raytrace map were written originally by programming whizzes Scott Kirvan and Steve Blackmon, when they worked at Blur Studio, a noted 3ds max-using special effects house in Santa Monica, California. (Scott and Steve have gone on to found Splutterfish, the company behind the acclaimed Brazil Rendering System for 3ds max. You can find out more about Brazil by going to http://www.splutterfish.com.) The Raytrace map is convenient; you can load it into any slot—usually Reflection—of your existing 3ds max Standard materials. However, the Raytrace material actually has more features than the 3ds max Standard material (such as the Diffusion option, discussed in the next tip), renders faster than the standalone Raytrace map (especially for reflections/refractions), and can give better rendered results overall if you're rendering with the default scanline renderer. This is true even if you're not using it for raytraced reflections and refractions in your scene.

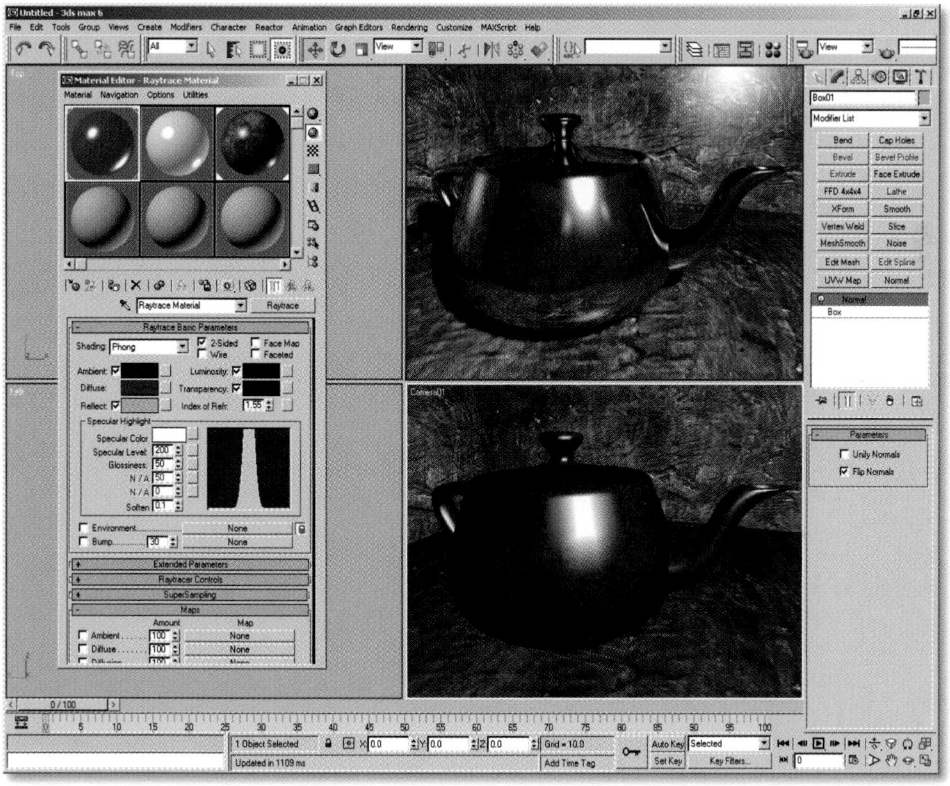

OKAY, SO JUST WHAT IS THIS RAYTRACE: DIFFUSION MAP?

The Diffusion map slot in the Raytrace material works similarly to the RGB Multiply map. Basically, the Diffusion map converts a map to grayscale components (so you might as well just use a grayscale bitmap in that slot) and then applies those values on top of the standard Diffuse (or Color) map. The Diffusion map affects the way light hits your Diffuse surfaces; the grayscale values either darken or lighten the underlying RGB values of the Diffuse map. You can also use the Diffusion map, along with subtle procedural maps (such as Noise) or a bitmap, to suggest dirt and weathering on top of a "clean," unretouched Diffuse map.

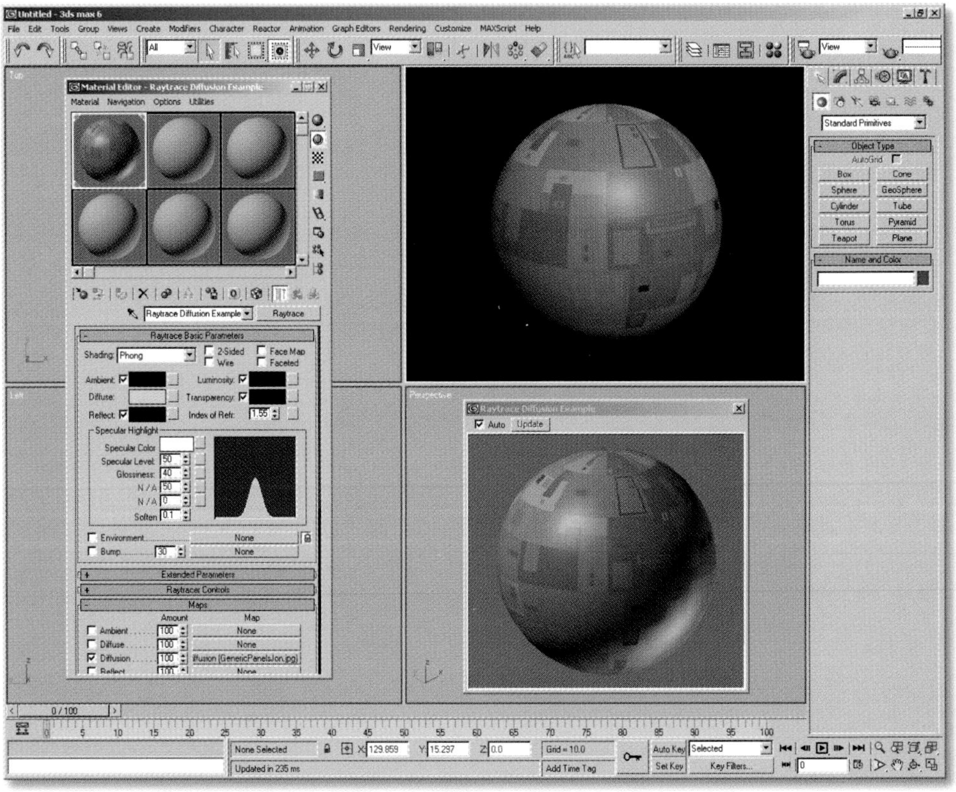

RAYTRACING: ENVIRONMENTAL REFLECTIONS

Although a Raytrace map or material can reflect your existing scene environment (usually a bitmap), for more control, you can use a different bitmap (such as a pre-rendered version of your existing scene) as a reflection map, and still get the other benefits of the Raytrace material over the 3ds max Standard material. Just load the bitmap (or procedural texture) of your choice in the Raytrace material's Environment slot, and then crank up the amount of reflection in the Reflection color swatch. Pure black (RGB 0, 0, 0) doesn't show the bitmap at all; pure white (RGB 255, 255, 255) puts the reflected map at 100 percent.

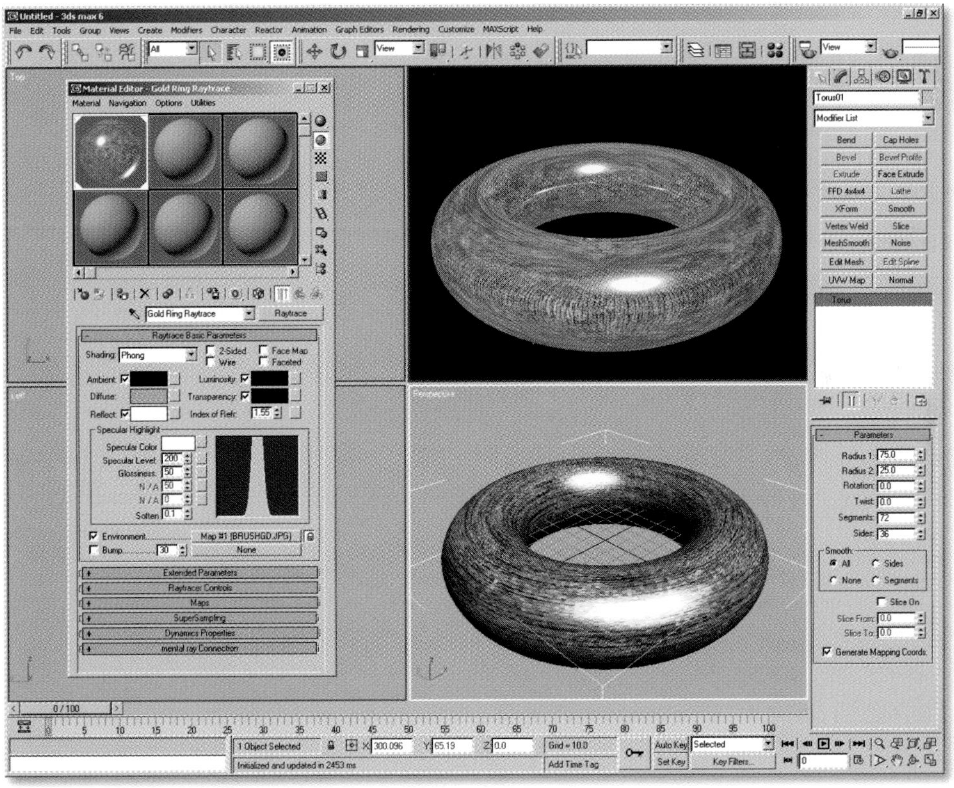

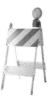

RAYTRACING: JUST WHAT YOU SEE, PAL

As mentioned in the previous tip, the Raytrace material allows you to place any map in its Environment slot, which acts much like a 3ds max Standard material's Reflection map, instead of a physically correct, raytraced reflection of your scene. However, you can also have your Raytrace material reflect physical objects in your scene, while making those objects invisible to the camera. To do this, you can surround the specific objects you want raytraced with a giant sphere. (Make sure the sphere encompasses your camera and the objects you want raytraced.) Make sure the sphere's normals are inverted, and assign this sphere a Matte/Shadow material, with Opaque Alpha and Receive Shadows unchecked. (If your camera or raytraced objects are moving, parent the sphere to the camera, and make sure your objects don't penetrate the faces of the sphere during the course of your animation.) In the Rendering/Raytrace Global Include/Exclude list, pick the sphere and exclude it. (Also, right-click on the sphere, select Properties, and uncheck Cast Shadows.)

The result is that your Environment background (if you have one loaded) and objects outside the encompassing sphere will be reflected in your raytraced objects, but only the raytraced objects and Environment background will be visible to the camera; the objects outside the sphere will not be visible in the final rendering.

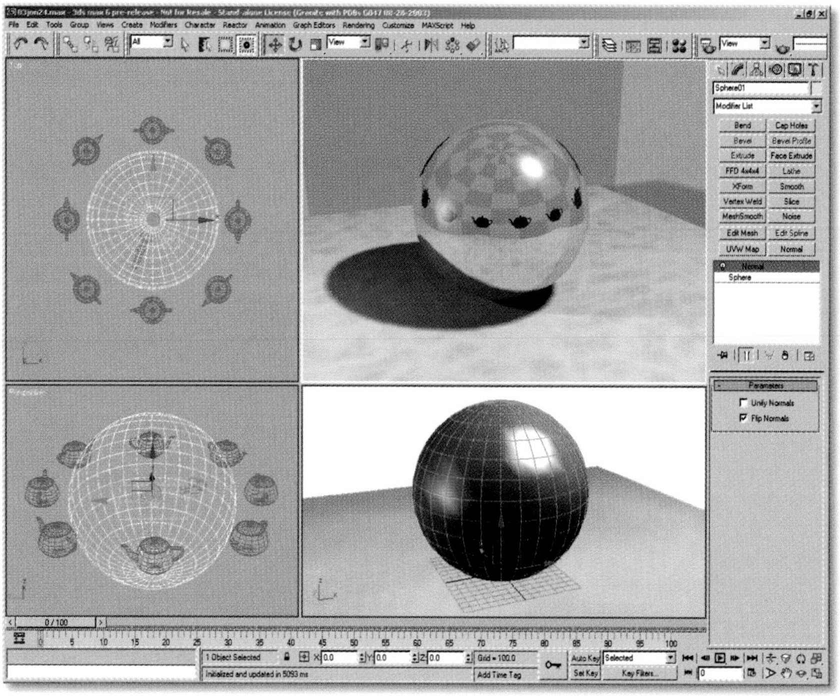

THE RAYTRACE MATERIAL: WHERE THE RUBBER MEETS THE ROAD

You're not limited to using the Raytrace material only for super-glossy chrome and glass surfaces. You can also use it to create more subtle materials, such as soft, "rubbery" surfaces. Unlike the Standard material, the Raytrace material's Soften parameter (in the Specular Highlight section) goes beyond 1.0; it actually goes up to 10.0. (Why does this sound like a scene from *Spinal Tap*?) Anyway, the Soften parameter blurs out the specular highlights on your objects—so much that it can produce a rubber-like look, like a child's bounce ball or balloon. To test this, load a Raytrace material in an empty material slot in the Material Editor; then change Specular Level to 200, Glossiness to 5, and Soften to 2.5. Apply this material to any object in a test scene (one with decent lighting), and then render it. You'll see a soft, diffused specular highlight on the surface of your test object. To get a similar (although not identical) effect using a Standard material, pick the Oren-Nayer-Blinn shader, set Specular Level to 125 and Glossiness to 0, and then crank its Soften setting up to 1.0 (the maximum).

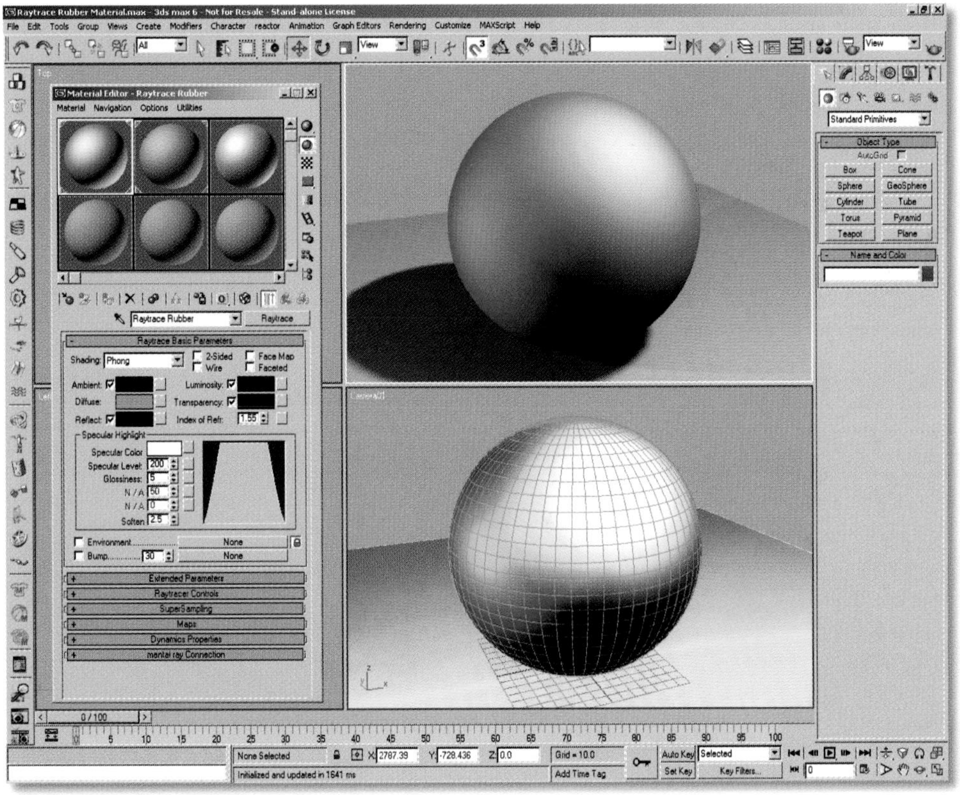

ALWAYS USE FALLOFF WITH REFLECTIONS

One of the problems with using Reflection maps for your materials is that the reflections often make it look as if the material is self-illuminated, even if you're in a "dark" scene. (Note that a pure raytraced reflection won't do this, but a Reflection map renders a lot faster. You win some, you lose some….) The best way to mitigate this is to always use a Falloff map in your Reflection map slot, with your actual Reflection bitmap (or procedural map) in one of the Falloff slots. The Falloff map allows you to adjust your reflected map to appear primarily on object surfaces that are either perpendicular or parallel to the camera's point of view, on surfaces that are illuminated by lights in your scene, and so on. Also, remember that the more reflective your objects, the more shiny they should be, so crank up your material's Specular Level and Glossiness settings. (Note that the 3ds max Standard material Strauss shader uses Glossiness and Metalness settings instead.)

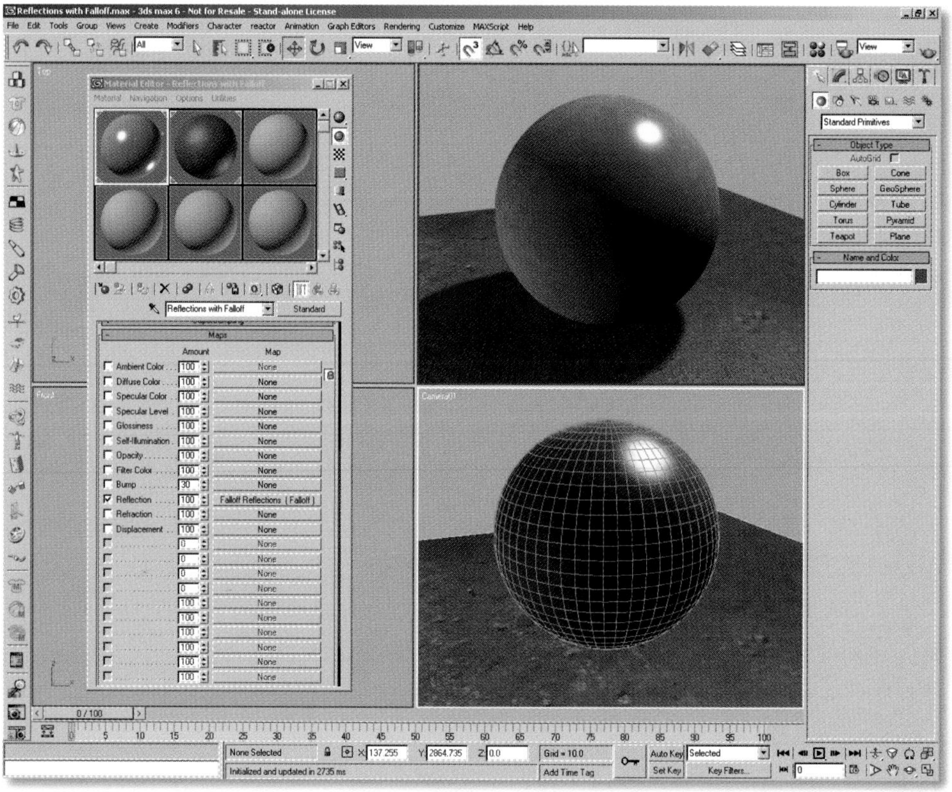

MORE FUN WITH FALLOFF

The Falloff map is extremely useful in making (nonraytraced) reflections appear more realistic in your scene. The Falloff map has many other uses as well. You can use it for any of the following:

- Put the Falloff map in the Diffuse slot of a material and change its color slots (such as putting in complementary colors) to create iridescent effects based on your 3D model's polygon angles relative to your camera.
- Put the Falloff map in the Opacity map slot of your material to create "x-ray" effects. (For best results, make this material self-illuminated and, under Extended Parameters, check Additive under Advanced Transparency Type.)
- Use the Falloff map as a mask between two wildly different submaterial types in a Blend material.

The possibilities are almost endless, so what are you waiting for? Experiment with Falloff today!

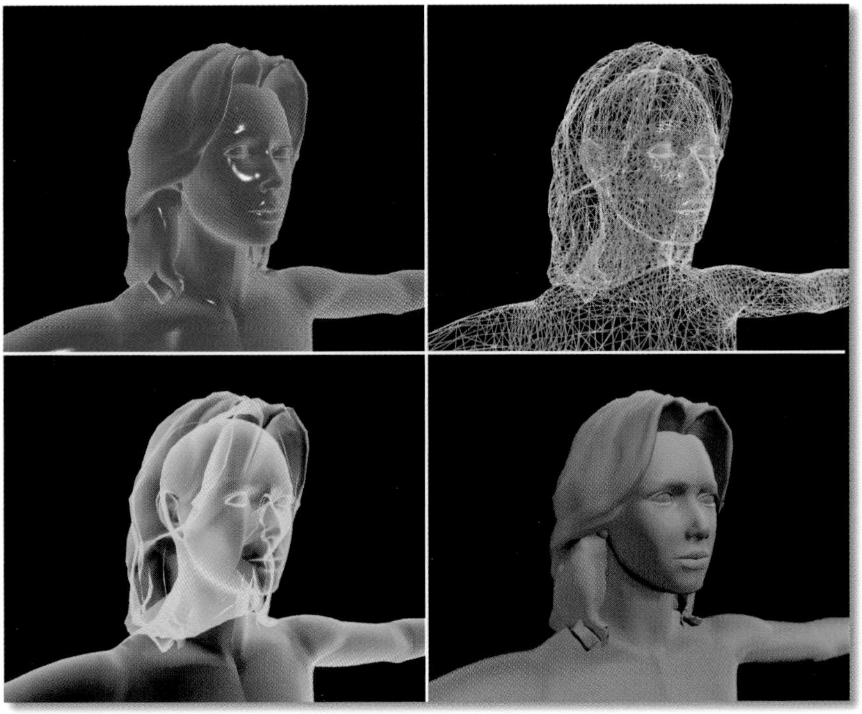

ADDING "OOMPH" TO FLAT REFLECTED SURFACES (SUCH AS WINDOW GLASS)

One problem with rendering completely flat, reflective surfaces (such as flat "window glass" geometry in an architectural scene) is that the reflections often don't show up well in the final render. (The problem is more noticeable when you're using Reflection maps rather than Raytracing, but still….) Reflections on curved or other complex surfaces are simply more noticeable. To fix this, add a slight Bump map to the reflective material(s) you're applying to the flat objects in your scene. The procedural Noise map, applied with a Bump map Amount value of 5 or less and a large Size setting, tends to help break up the Reflection map, making it more "wavy" and noticeable. (In addition, it helps subtly distort specular highlights.) This might be just enough to make your flat reflective materials appear more "alive" in your renders.

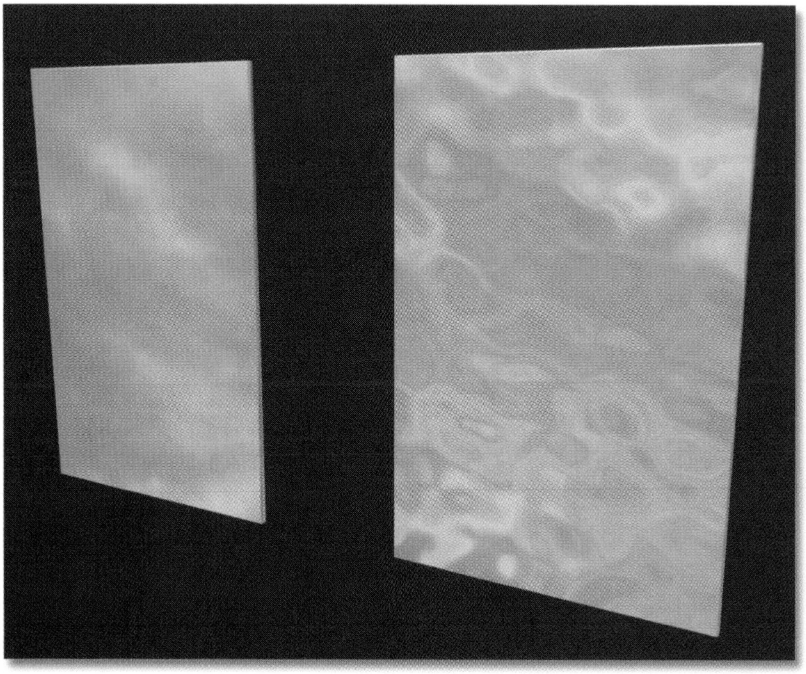

RECEIVING SHADOWS ON 100 PERCENT SELF-ILLUMINATED MATERIALS

Ordinarily, you can't cast shadows on materials that are 100 percent self-illuminated. (That sounds reasonable; a self-illuminated object should wash away any shadows cast on it from another source, right?) However, if you want to confound the rules of nature, then a trick is to create a Blend material with your 100 percent self-illuminated material in the Material #2 (bottom) slot, and a less-illuminated copy of this material in the first (Material #1, or top) slot. Then, in the Mask slot, place a Falloff map with Shadow/Light selected as the Falloff Type. To darken the shadow, decrease the illumination value of the "darker" material.

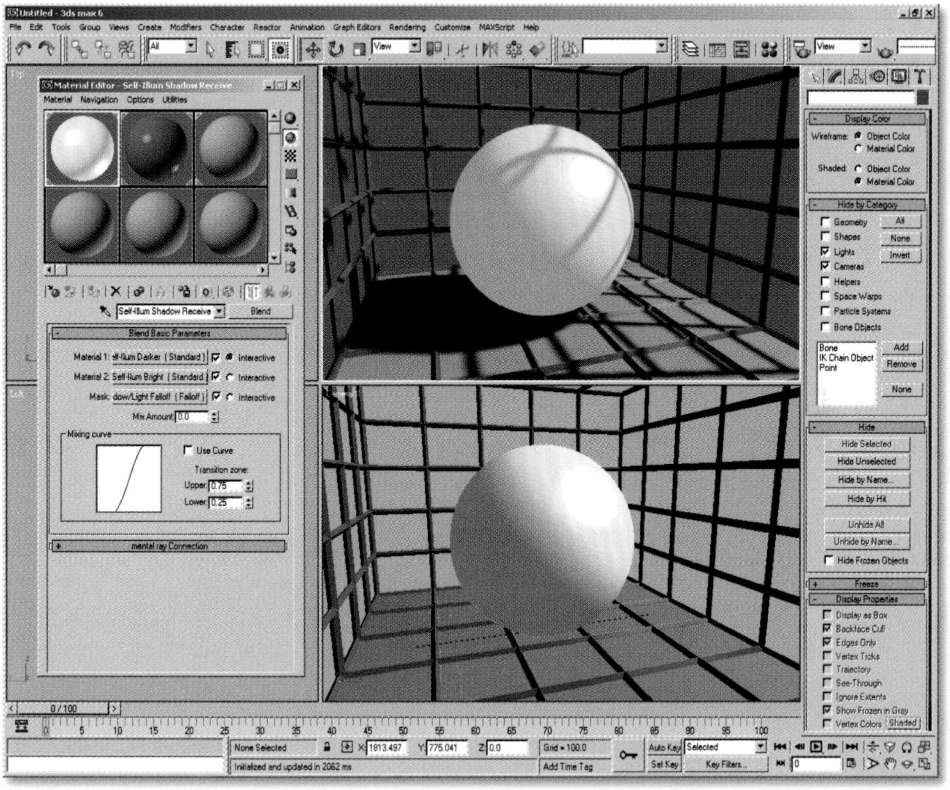

THE MULTI-LAYER SHADER: CREATING LACQUERED FINISHES

The 3ds max Standard material Multi-Layer shader is quite versatile (especially if you don't have 3ds max 6 and its new Mental Ray material and map types). The Multi-Layer shader is especially useful for creating shiny materials that have depth, such as lacquered paint surfaces.

To produce, say, a red lacquered paint finish, open your Material Editor, pick an empty material slot (with a Standard 3ds max material), and from the Shading drop-down, change your default shading type from Blinn to Multi-Layer. Under Basic Parameters, change your Diffuse color to pure red, or RGB 255, 0, 0, and the Diffuse level to 40. For the first specular layer, change the color to pure white (RGB 255, 255, 255), with the Level set to 150 and the Glossiness set to 75. For the second specular layer, set the color to the same red as the Diffuse color. (You can click-hold and drag the Diffuse color swatch down to the second specular layer color swatch, and make it a copy.) Then change Level to 75 and Glossiness to 35 (or, roughly half of the first specular level settings.)

Finally, under Maps, add a Reflection map—preferably a Falloff map, with Falloff Type set to either Perpendicular/Parallel, or Fresnel. Then add a bitmap to the second Falloff map slot. The result, when applied to a model in your scene, should look like an extremely glossy texture that has "depth."

THE MULTI-LAYER SHADER, PART II: CANDY FLAKE CAR PAINT

Okay, let's say that you've created a glossy material using the techniques in the previous tip, but you want to go further. What if you want to create a metallic "candy flake" material for a 3D sports car model? (The "candy flake" effect on finishes like this is actually caused by tiny flakes of metal suspended in the paint.)

To create this "candy flake" material, just copy the instructions in the previous tip, changing your Diffuse and Specular Color 2 levels to whatever you need. (As you know, shiny red cars tend to get pulled over by the police, so change your colors to, say, purple or midnight blue.) Then go to the Maps rollout, and under Specular Level 2, click the Map slot. Then from the Material/Map Browser, pick the Noise map. Change the Noise size to 1.0 (or less, depending on the scale of your scene). Next, apply the material to the relevant objects in your scene, and do a test rendering. The Noise map in the Specular Level 2 slot will help to "break up" the softer specular highlight "under" the primary highlight and help produce the "candy flake" finish you're looking for. (If you don't want to use the Noise map, try other procedurals or custom bitmaps to get the metallic appearance you want.)

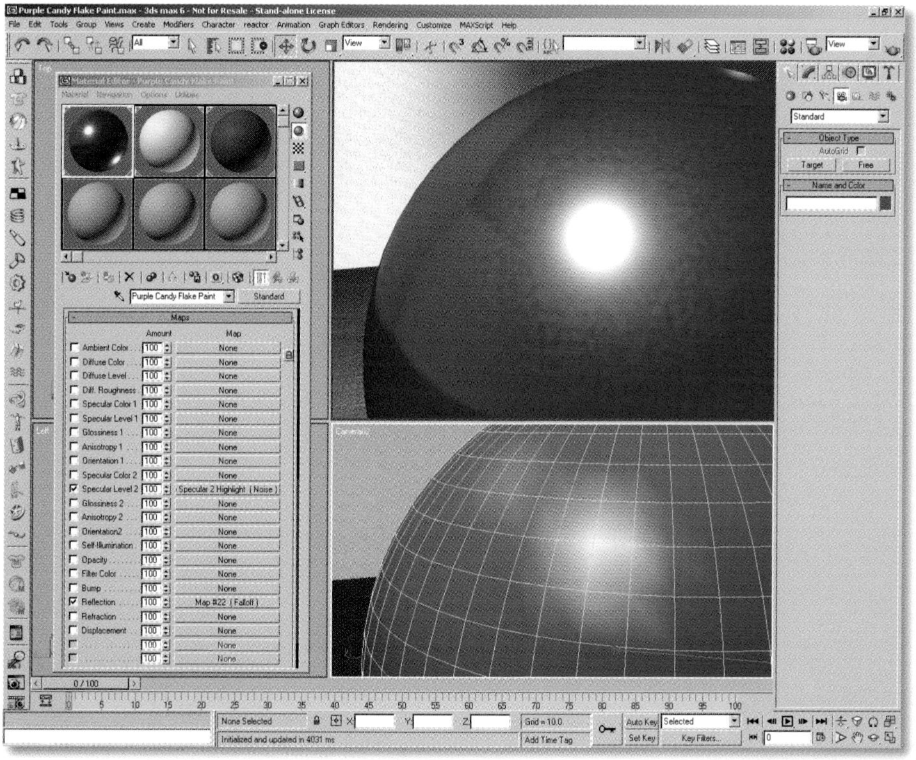

Highlighting the Chrome

Okay, so you've built your models and textured them. What comes next?

Let there be light!

Highlighting the Chrome

lighting tips

In fact, let there be Omnis, Spots, Directs (okay, so that sounds weird), Skylights, Global Illumination, Radiosity, and a host of other 3D options to, well, shed light on your scene. 3ds max allows you to create and modify a wide variety of lights to produce almost any kind of effect—from soft-shadowed skylight effects to harsh deep space lighting.

In this chapter, I present some lighting basics (such as dos and don'ts of good scene lighting) and talk about some of the 3ds max 6 program's advanced lighting features including Light Tracer and Radiosity. Then Aksel Karcher (http://www.akselkarcher.com) addresses some of the finer points of using mental ray's lighting features.

LIGHTING: ORDER OF OPERATIONS

A good method of setting up lights in your 3D scene is creating and modifying them in the order of least importance or brightness. When you first start, you might want to create a main "key" light, but before you get too comfortable with it, turn it off and decide which of the lights you're creating will have the most subtle influence. By doing so, you can clearly see the individual contributions of the various "fill" lights in your scene. This backward process can also help reduce the amount of time you'll spend going back and forth tweaking lights when you don't really know how they contribute to the final effect.

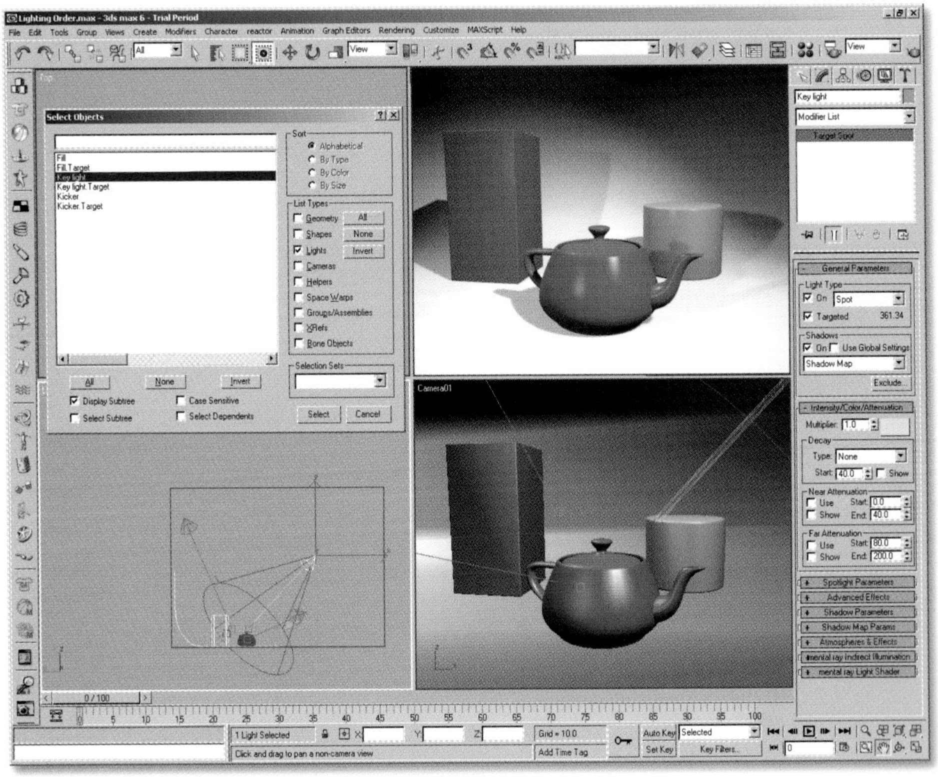

BACKLIGHTING ADDS REALISM

Bill George, Academy Award-winning visual effects supervisor at Industrial Light + Magic, recommends that CG artists remember a lighting rule for shooting miniature sets: When appropriate, try to backlight your miniature or the models in your 3D scene. Backlighting tends to make the models look larger or more imposing, and it can heighten their realism. The 3ds max program's volumetric lighting effects (Rendering > Environment > Atmosphere > Effects), when projected from above or behind the central model in your scene, can particularly enhance your rendering.

COMPLIMENTARY OR COMPLEMENTARY?

Complimentary means flattering; complementary means balancing. Both concepts are useful when you're lighting a 3D scene. If you have foreground elements that you want to differentiate from the background (especially if the scene or composition seems "cluttered" and confusing), see if you can use complementary lighting on the edges of the foreground objects to make them "pop" against your background. Your local art store (or even a painting store) should have books of colors showing complementary shades.

PLACE YOUR LIGHTS AWAY FROM THE CAMERA!

One mistake 3D artists sometimes make is to place their lights right behind their camera. Although this provides more even lighting, it also tends to flatten the rendering. The object of lighting is not only to illuminate your scene, but also to "sculpt" the objects with both light and shadow. Move your lights off to the sides or, better yet, buy a book on cinematography and studio photography to get some professional lighting tips. (See Appendix, "3ds max Resources" for a list of URLs and books that can help you.)

Note: Placing a light right next to the camera, though, is actually an old Hollywood cinematographer's trick to help wash out wrinkles and other imperfections on aging actors and actresses, so if you've got a vain 3D character who's concerned about his looks, you can disregard the previous advice.

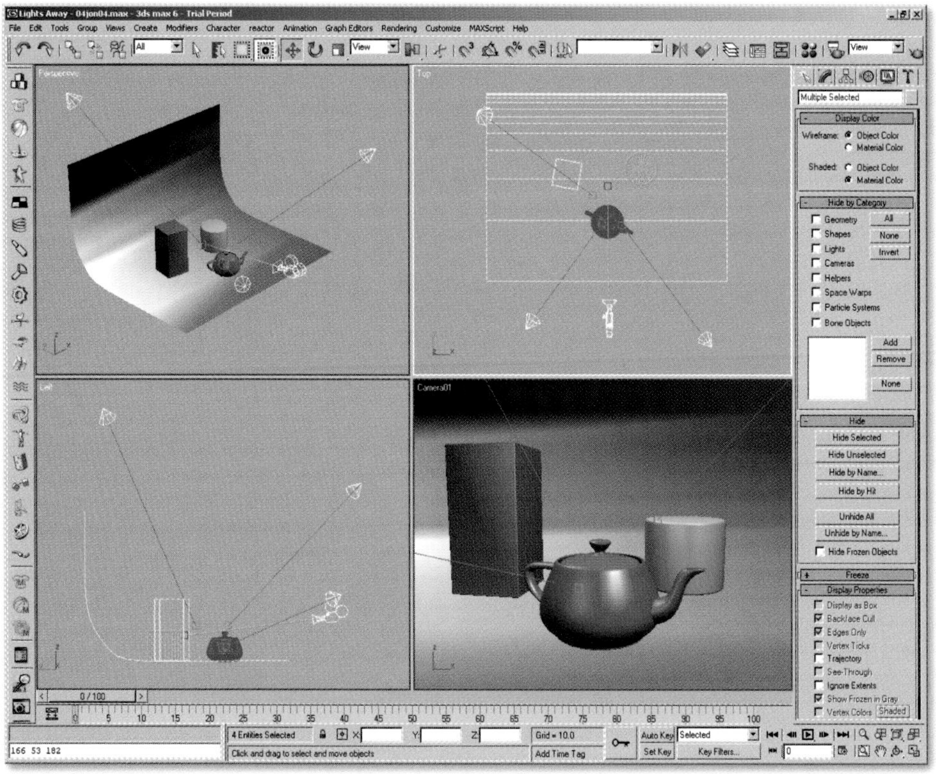

AVOID AMBIENT LIGHTING (USUALLY)

John Knoll, one of the original developers of Adobe Photoshop and a renowned visual effects supervisor at Industrial Light + Magic, suggests that, for optimum realism, 3D artists should use no ambient light in their scenes whatsoever. Ambient light tends to flatten your 3D renderings and make them look less realistic. Although doing so might increase your rendering times, Knoll suggests you use shadow-casting lights for all aspects of your scene—including fill lighting. Luckily, 3ds max has, for the past several versions, had its Rendering > Environment > Common Parameters > Ambient light setting set to black—RGB 0, 0, 0—so this has become less of a concern. Keep your hands off that Ambient Color swatch unless you're going for a specific lighting effect, as outlined in the next tip.

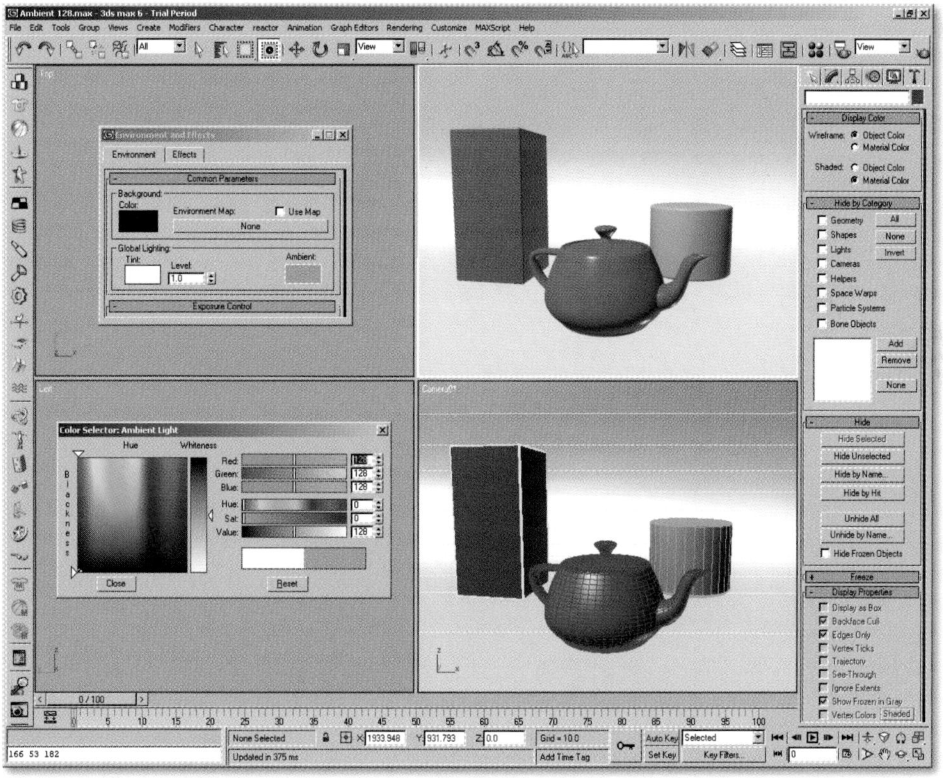

OKAY, IF YOU *HAVE* TO USE AMBIENT LIGHTING...

Ordinarily, using ambient lighting in your scene makes the scene look washed out, or as if the entire scene has self-illuminated materials. However, you can still use ambient lighting for certain effects in your scene. For instance, you can create Omni lights, check the Ambient Only box (under Advanced Effects), check Use and Show under Near and Far Attenuation, and then play with the Decay > Type settings. This enables you to use ambient lighting to enhance your entire scene but still produce custom light effects (and color tinting) in specific areas. (You can even use negative Multiplier values—see the next tip!)

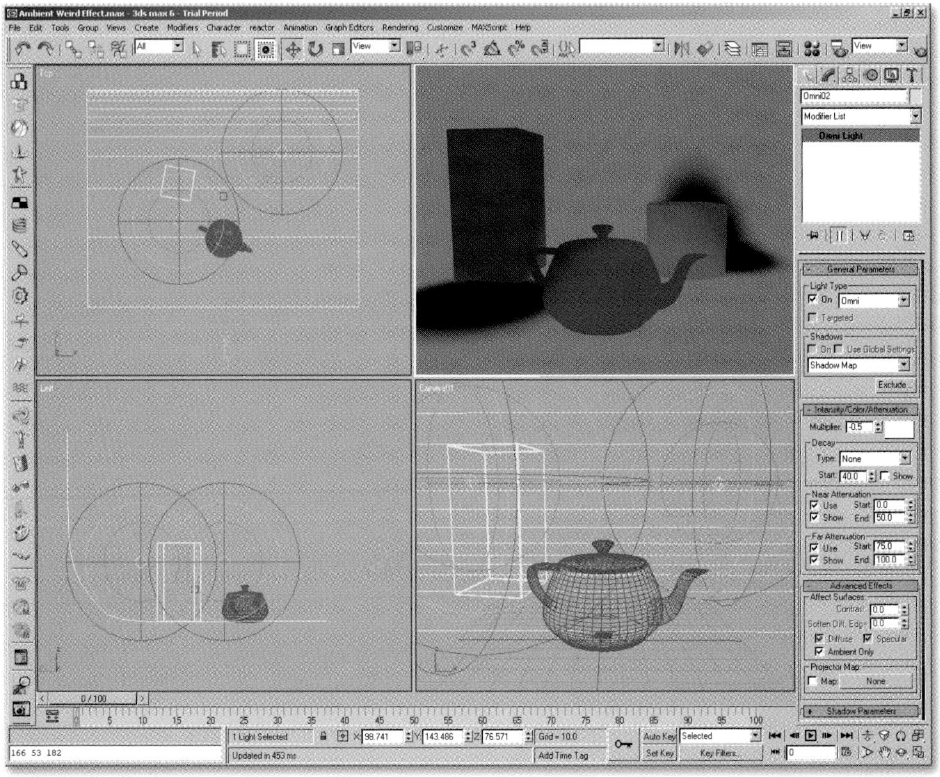

I'M GONNA WASH THAT LIGHT RIGHT OUTTA MY SCENE...

Here's something that a lot of 3ds max users don't realize: You can have "negative" lights in your scene. That's right—by creating a light and giving it a negative Multiplier value (such as –1.0), you can actually use this to pull light right out of your scene. By careful negative light placement and by adjusting the Decay or Attenuation controls, you can control how much light gets pulled away from specific areas. Use this to enhance existing shadows, create scary pools of darkness, or simply tone down the effects of other (positive) lights in your scene.

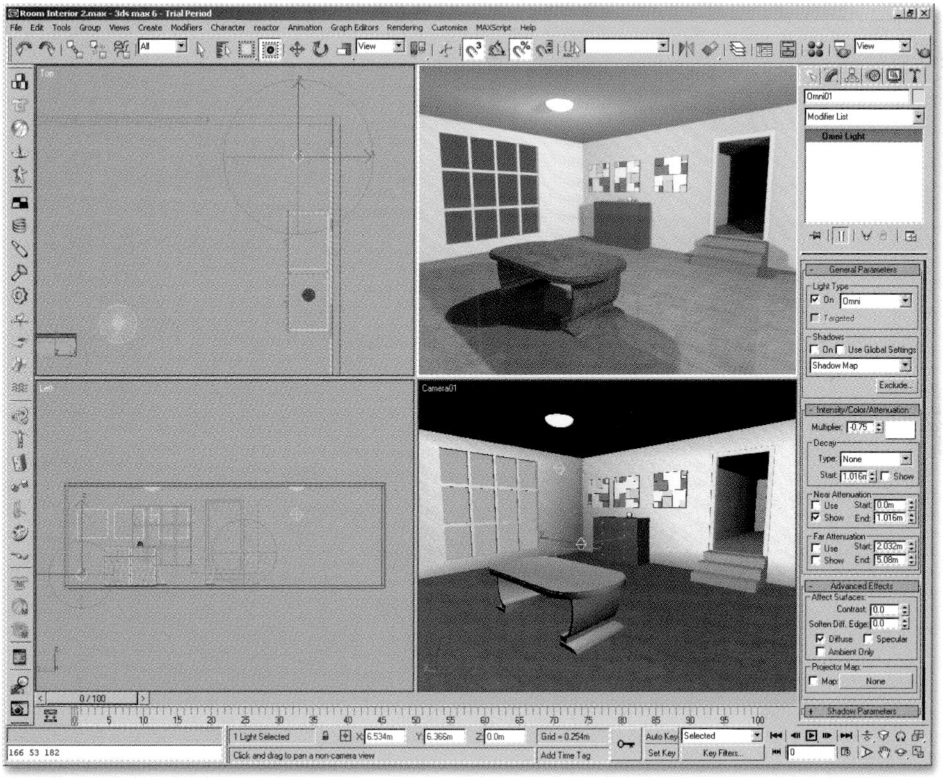

ADDITIONAL LIGHTING CONTROLS: SEPARATE SPECULAR AND DIFFUSE

Remember that 3ds max gives you the capability to control your lights so that they don't affect the diffuse or specular components of the objects they illuminate. You can use this additional control to increase the realism of your scenes. If you're using Omni lights to provide all the ambient light in a scene (as an earlier tip admonished you to do!), you can turn off the Affect Surfaces > Specular option for all of those specific fill lights, so they don't affect the specular component. Because ambient light generally originates from a large source area, it typically doesn't display a specular highlight on the receiving objects. This can allow you to apply light from a variety of locations without quickly betraying the light's location. The Affect Surfaces > Specular option is also useful if you need to place a specular highlight on the surface of an object (especially at a specific location) but not illuminate the rest of the object.

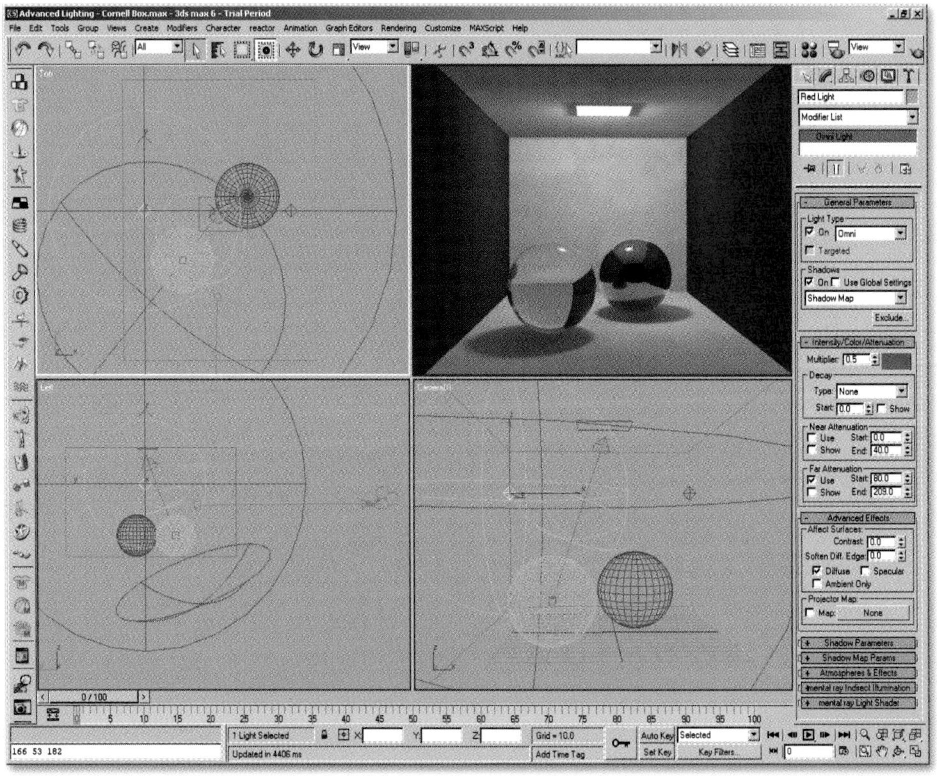

TINT YOUR LIGHTS!

Here's something else to remember: Lights are almost never white. Both natural and artificial lights generally have some colorcast to them. We typically think of sunlight as being pure white light, but even it changes color with the time of day and the environment. Artificial lighting is also notorious for having a tint to it. Fluorescent lights generally have a green cast to them; halogen bulbs give off a blue-white light. Because truly color-corrected lighting environments are rare, use this fact to your advantage when you're trying to reproduce specific lighting. You can add depth and richness to otherwise sterile-looking environments by giving slight variations to the color of lights in a scene. Tinting lights for artistic purposes can also be effective for conveying a specific mood or atmosphere. In most cases, subtlety is best, although dramatic light colors can lead to striking effects.

"ROTATE THE SHADOW MAP, PLEASE, HAL..."

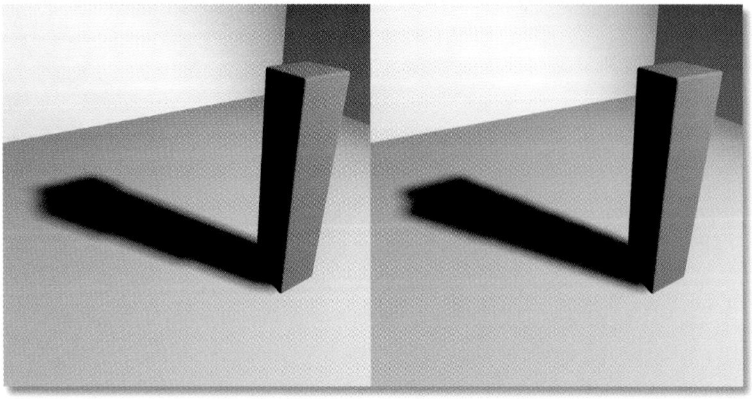

3ds max shadow maps are basically made up of a "grid" of square pixels, which are projected by objects in your scene onto other objects by shadow-mapped lights. If you have a problem with "jaggies" showing up in your renderings when you use shadow maps, try this nifty trick: Just rotate the light (if it's a Spotlight, rotate it along its local Z-axis) around 30–45 degrees and do another test rendering. Rotating the light can cause the cast shadow pixels to better align with your geometry and save you from having to either increase your shadow map size (which eats memory), or use Ray Traced Shadows (which increases your rendering times).

AVOID USING SOFTEN DIFFUSE EDGE

Older versions of 3ds max (say, pre-3ds max 5) used to have the "Soften Diffuse Edge" Light parameter (under the Advanced Effects roll-out) checked on by default and set to 0.5. Luckily, this setting has been changed in later versions of 3ds max (the check box is gone; now there's simply a Value field and a spinner). When you increase the value of the Soften Diffuse Edge setting, the affected light tends to smear across the surface of the objects in your scene and produce a less realistic effect. Unless you specifically need this effect for some reason, you should avoid changing the setting, and keep it at 0.0.

USE RAYTRACED SHADOWS SPARINGLY

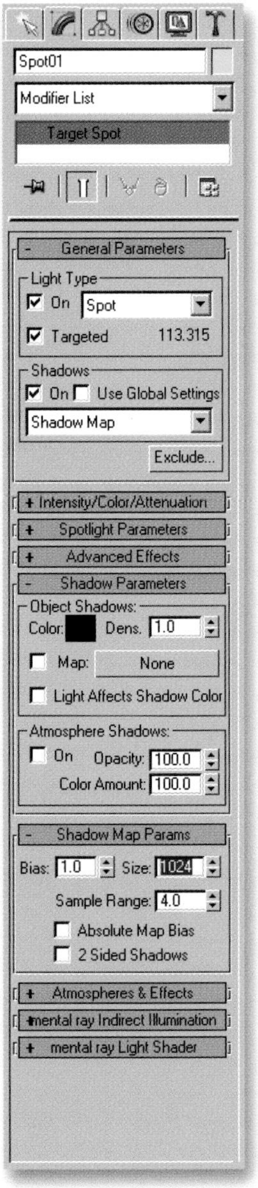

Although raytraced shadows can look crisp in your scenes, they can really add to your scanline rendering times, especially if your scene consists of many fine details, such as framework created with the Lattice modifier. (If your scene consists of shadow-casting transparent or translucent objects, you should use ray-traced shadows to create realistic translucent shadows on other geometry in your scene.)

If you *don't* have to use Ray Traced Shadow lights, consider cranking up your Shadow Map Size instead until you get the sharp edges that you want. The 3ds max program's Shadow Map default sets the Map Size to 512; increase this to 1024 or even 2048, if necessary. (See the Shadow Map Params rollout of the Modify panel.) You can usually duplicate the look of raytraced shadows with properly adjusted shadow-mapped lights, and your scene will render more quickly.

USING A LIGHT ARRAY: QUICK AND DIRTY SOFT SHADOWS

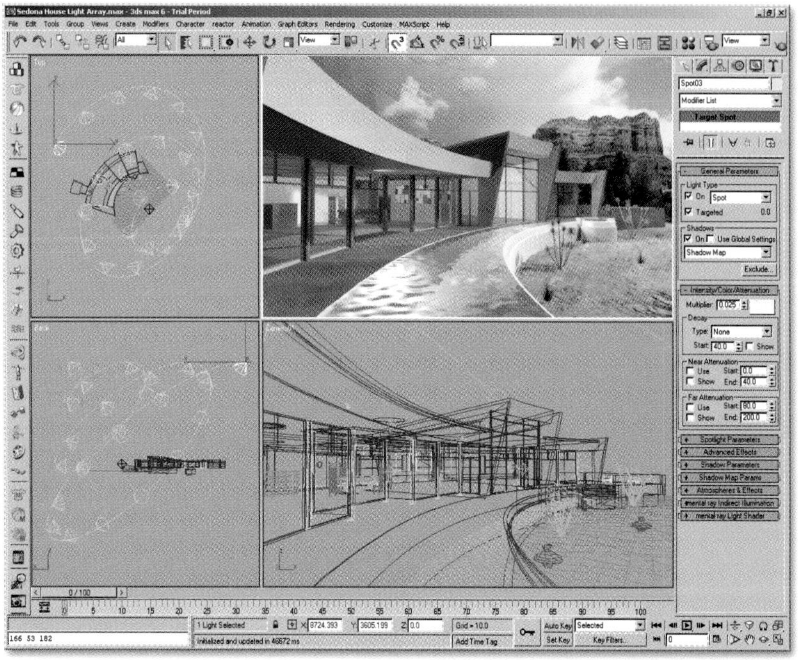

Although advanced rendering tools (such as the 3ds max 6 Light Tracer, Radiosity, and mental ray Global Illumination features) have taken scene lighting to another level, the core tools— basic lights and the scanline renderer—still have a lot of life left in them.

Here's an old lighting trick to produce the illusion of global illumination or raytraced soft shadows: Use an array of instanced lights for your scene. Create one Target Spotlight or Target Direct light, check the Shadows > On box, and then duplicate the light as a series of Instanced lights. Array the Instanced lights in a grid pattern, a series of concentric circles, or even along a Helix spline path. (You can apply a Path Constraint controller to the light by going to the Assign Controller rollout in the Command Panel > Motion tab and selecting the spline path as the target. You can then go to Tools > Snapshot, select Range, set the number of copies, and set the Clone Method to Instance to snapshot your light along the path.) When finished, pick the original light, delete it, and then choose any one of the new Instanced lights and adjust its Multiplier and Shadow Map parameters (Size, Bias, Sample Range, and so on).

Because you're using an array of lights, you should probably adjust the Multiplier value below 1.0; otherwise, you'll just be blasting your scene with intense light. If you've created an array of 50 lights, say, set the Multiplier value to 0.02 (one-fiftieth of the original 1.0 value), and then do a test render. Keep adjusting the light parameters until you get the effect you need. In many cases, this trick lets you produce the effect of raytraced soft shadows or global illumination in your scene, but with a fraction of the rendering time of these effects.

USE DIRECT LIGHTS INSTEAD OF SPOTLIGHTS

Target spotlights are useful when you need a distinctive "cone" of light (especially when you're using projection maps or volumetric lighting effects). However, if you need "parallel" light, try to get into the habit of using Target Direct lights instead of Spots. Direct lights are particularly good for simulating sunlight (either on Earth or for outer space scenes), and are also useful for creating parallel rays of volumetric light (such as shafts of sunlight filtering through water).

And remember: You can switch your light type on-the-fly just by selecting your light, going to the Modify panel, and changing the light type in the General Parameters rollout. That way, you don't have to delete a Spotlight, for instance, and create a Direct light in its place.

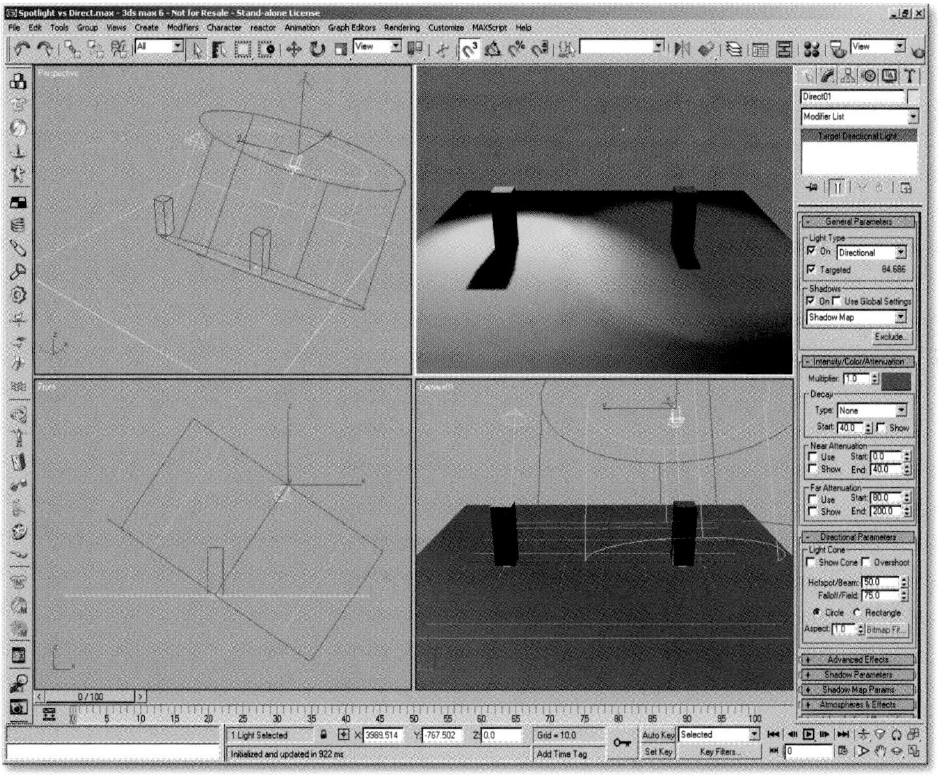

TOTALLY TUBULAR, MAN: USE NON-UNIFORM SCALE ON OMNI LIGHTS

Did you know that you can apply a Non-uniform scale to an Omni light, and "stretch" the light out along one axis? Yep, it's true. Just create an Omni light, and check Use and Show under Near and Far Attenuation, in the Intensity/Color/Attenuation rollout. (This helps you see the effects of the light scaling; you can uncheck these settings after you've scaled the light.) Then select the Omni light, right-click and choose Scale from the Quad menu, and then left-click-hold and drag on one axis of the Transform: Scale gizmo. By stretching the light along one axis, you can create the effect of "tube" lighting in your scene.

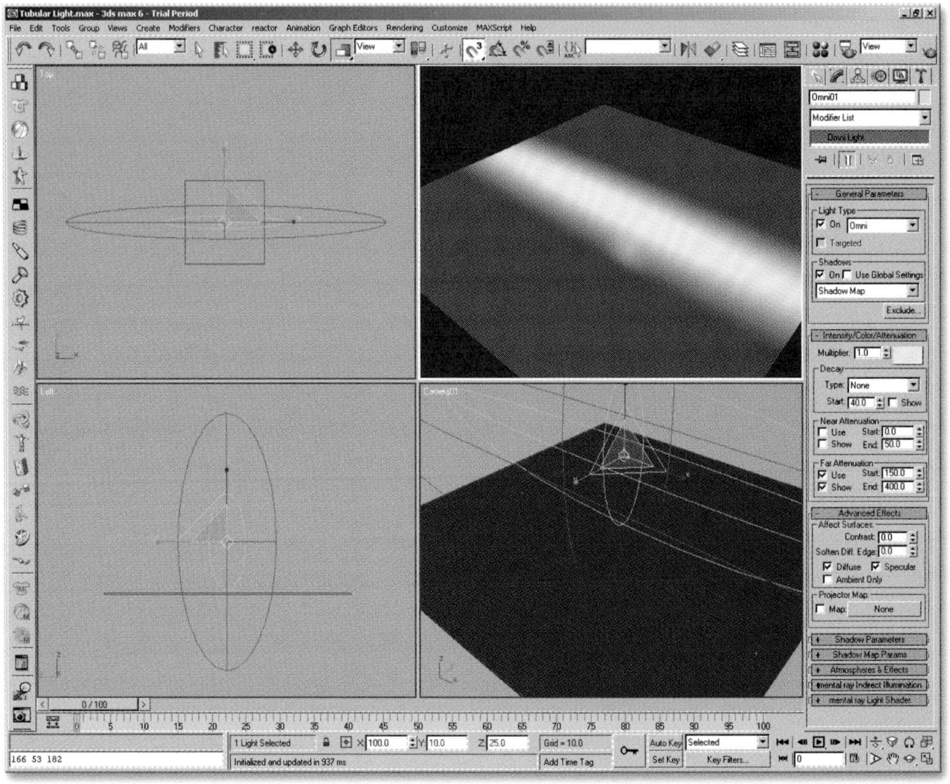

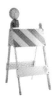

HERE COMES THE SUN, AND IT'S ALL RIGHT...

If you're doing an architectural rendering for a client, remind your client that you can show the effects of the sun on both the interior and exterior of his building—and have the rendering show exactly how the lighting will appear at a particular time of day, relative to the building's actual position on Planet Earth.

The 3ds max Sunlight and Daylight features (found in Create > Systems > Sunlight or Daylight) allow you to create a light that duplicates the effects of the sun as seen from a specified geographic location and time. You can choose the building site location, date, time, and compass orientation, and also animate the date and time (to produce a "time-lapse" effect showing how the light will appear throughout the day, or even the year.) This way, you can indicate to your client that he should orient a proposed house in a particular way on the property so that early morning sunlight does (or doesn't!) come streaming through the master bedroom's windows. (This feature is also useful for planning passive solar gain on eco-friendly homes.)

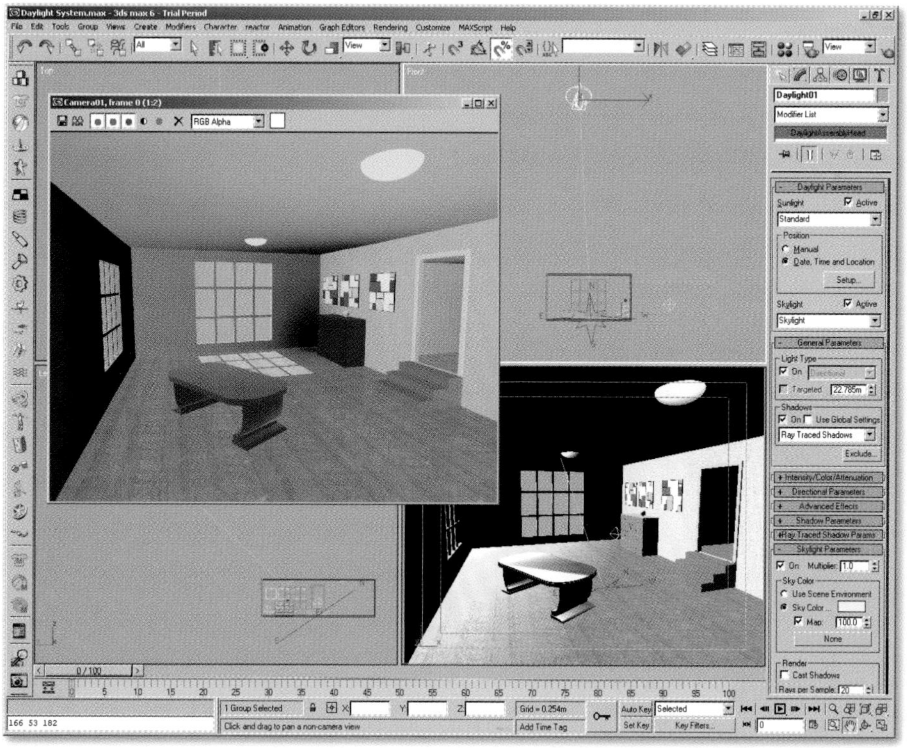

BAD LIGHTING USING SUNLIGHT

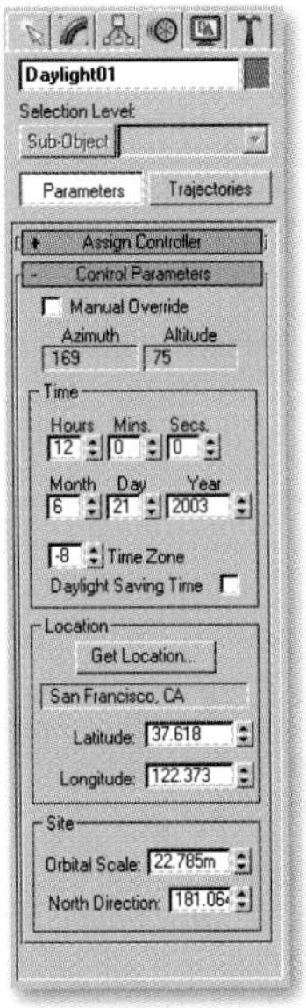

If you see artifacts in your architectural scenes when using the 3ds max Sunlight system, it might be because the Direct light is too close to the objects in the scene. Select the Direct light and change its Orbital Scale in the Motion tab so that it's at a greater distance from your scene objects. A good rule of thumb: Make the Orbital Scale value about three times the height of the tallest object in your scene.

WHEN IN ROME… USE MENTAL RAY'S SHADOWS

The mental ray renderer included with 3ds max 6 has its own Shadow Map type; pick this type for greater control if you're using mental ray as your renderer. Note that if you have lights in your scene that *should* be casting shadows but aren't, and you're rendering with the default scan-line renderer, check to make sure that a.) you have Shadows turned on (duh!) and b.) you're not using mental ray shadows on your lights.

LIGHTING FOR ARCHITECTS: PHOTOMETRIC LIGHTING

3ds max 6 includes a new category of lights: Photometric lights, which you can access through the Command Panel Create > Lights panel, and then choose Photometric from the drop-down list. Photometric lights (which sounds like a *Star Trek* piece of techno-babble) enable you to set real-world light energy values: distribution, intensity, color temperature (to differentiate between fluorescent and incandescent lighting), and so on. Real-world lighting manufacturers also sometimes provide photometric files that you can load and apply to your 3ds max lights to duplicate the effects of commercially available light fixtures.

The new Photometric light types include Target Point, Target Linear, Target Area, Free Point, Free Linear, Free Area, and Illuminating Engineering Society (IES) Sun and IES Sky lights. Note: IES lights must be computed using the 3ds max 6 Radiosity feature. To use this, go to Rendering > Advanced Lighting > Radiosity. In addition, for any advanced lighting simulation, you need to apply exposure control settings to adjust the dynamic range of the rendered solution. When you choose the Radiosity option, its UI macroscript prompts you to immediately set up exposure control.

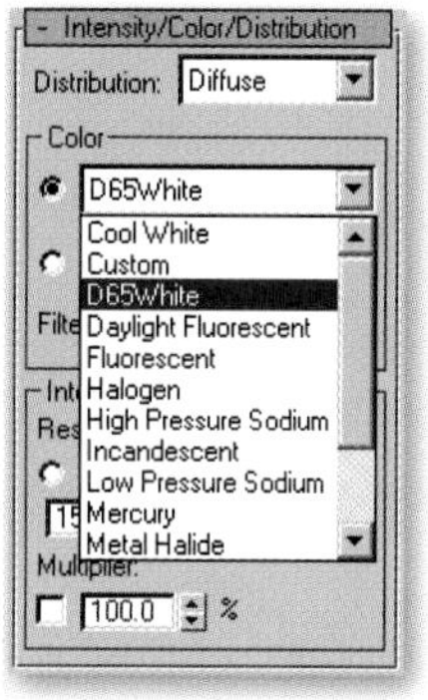

GEOMETRIC LIGHTS AND MENTAL RAY

Although you might have used light-emitting geometry with the 3ds max Light Tracer and Radiosity features, you can also light your entire scene with geometry by using the mental ray renderer.

Here's how. Turn off all the lights in your scene. (You must have some lights in the scene, even if they're all turned off; otherwise, 3ds max reverts to default lighting, which washes out the mental ray effect.) Choose the geometry you want to emit light (such as ceiling light panels in a 3D office model), and assign a Self-Illuminated material to this geometry. Then in your Rendering > Environment menu, set Exposure Control to Logarithmic Exposure Control. Now in mental ray's Render Scene > Indirect Illumination tab, enable Final Gather, and then render. Your geometry lights the scene. To adjust your scene brightness, just tweak the Logarithmic Exposure Control parameters, and render away.

FOR GLOBAL ILLUMINATION AND CAUSTICS, IT'S GOOD BOTH TO GIVE… AND TO RECEIVE

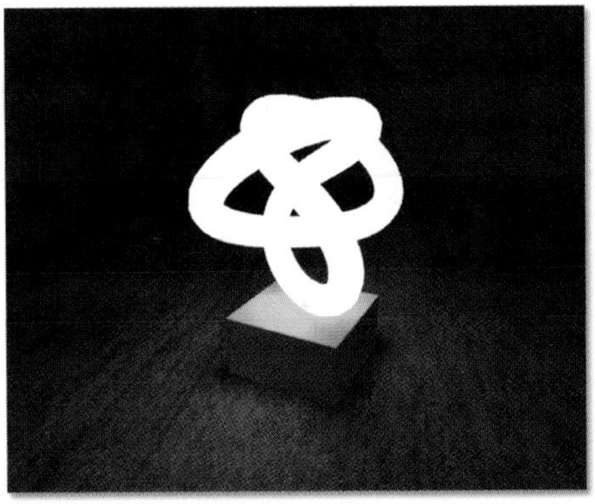

When you're using global illumination (GI) in mental ray, you have to set your object properties (using the Object Properties > Mental Ray menu) to generate (give) or receive global illumination (and caustic reflection/refraction effects) in your scene.

If you fail to modify your object properties (either existing ones or ones you merge into your scene) and try to render with GI, mental ray informs you (politely) that there are no caustic "generators" or "receivers" set in your scene, so the effect isn't going to work. To make your life easier, go to the mental ray Rendering > Render > Indirect Illumination menu and check the box marked All Objects Generate and Receive Caustics & GI. (Note that you must enable Caustics to allow this.) This solves your problem, and you can render your scene immediately; this setting just ignores and walks right over your Object Properties settings.

However, because GI is a computationally intensive effect, be careful when using this brute-force technique. It's always better to set up your individual Object Properties to generate and receive GI or caustics as necessary for your scene.

ROME WASN'T REBUILT IN A DAY

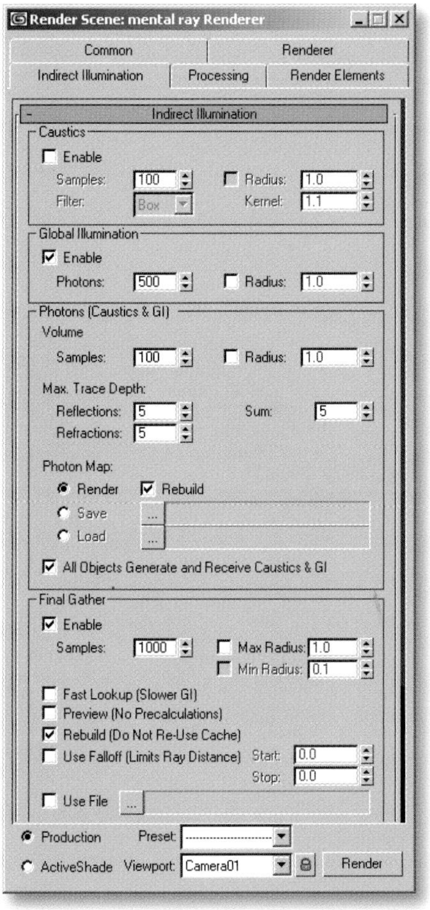

In mental ray's Rendering > Render > Indirect Illumination tab, watch out for two check boxes called Rebuild (under Photon Map and Final Gather, when the latter is active). These are checked on by default and calculate GI from scratch each time you render, so that any animated changes in your scene are rendered properly.

However, for test renderings, you should probably disable these. This ensures that mental ray uses the GI cache (yep, it's stored) of your last rendering and speeds up subsequent renderings greatly. This even works progressively with changing camera angles in your scene—only the newly needed areas are processed!

USING LIGHT TRACER: EVERYTHING'S KINDA BLURRY...

If you're using the 3ds max Light Tracer feature (Rendering > Advanced Lighting > Light Tracer), here's a quick way to speed up your renderings if you're using a bitmap in your Skylight: Blur it. Blur it a lot, actually.

Click-drag the bitmap to an open material slot in the Material Editor, make it an instance, and then adjust the Blur and Blur Offset parameters. The more you blur the map, the fewer rays that Light Tracer will have to use to calculate the lighting in your scene.

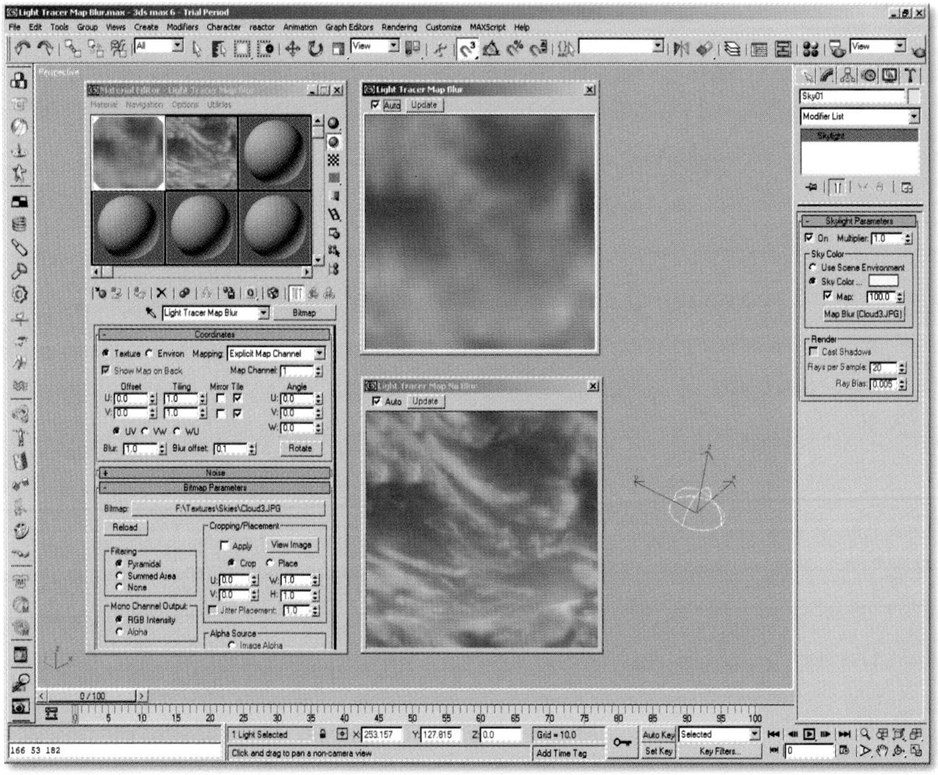

BUST IT UP: VOLUMETRIC LIGHT TIPS

You already know that you can use maps—both bitmaps and procedurals—as Projection maps in your lights. (You add the maps using the Modify > Advanced Effects > Projector Map feature.) As a reminder, you can use Projector maps in lights that have Volume Light effects applied as well (Rendering > Environment > Atmosphere > Add > Volume Light). This enables you to produce vivid color or distinct shading effects in the Volume Light that is seemingly illuminated by your light.

Here's a helpful trick: Place a Gradient map in the Projector Map slot, click-drag the gradient map to an open material slot in the Material Editor, make it an Instance, and change Gradient Type to Radial. By adjusting the Gradient Color #2 swatch and Color 2 Position value, you can create a Volumetric Light with sharply defined edges (or soft and fuzzy ones), and you can vary the "core" intensity and edge color as well. By adding noise to the Radial Gradient map (or additional maps in the Color Map slots), you can break up the edges of the Volumetric light even more so that it doesn't look like a solid band of color emanating from the light.

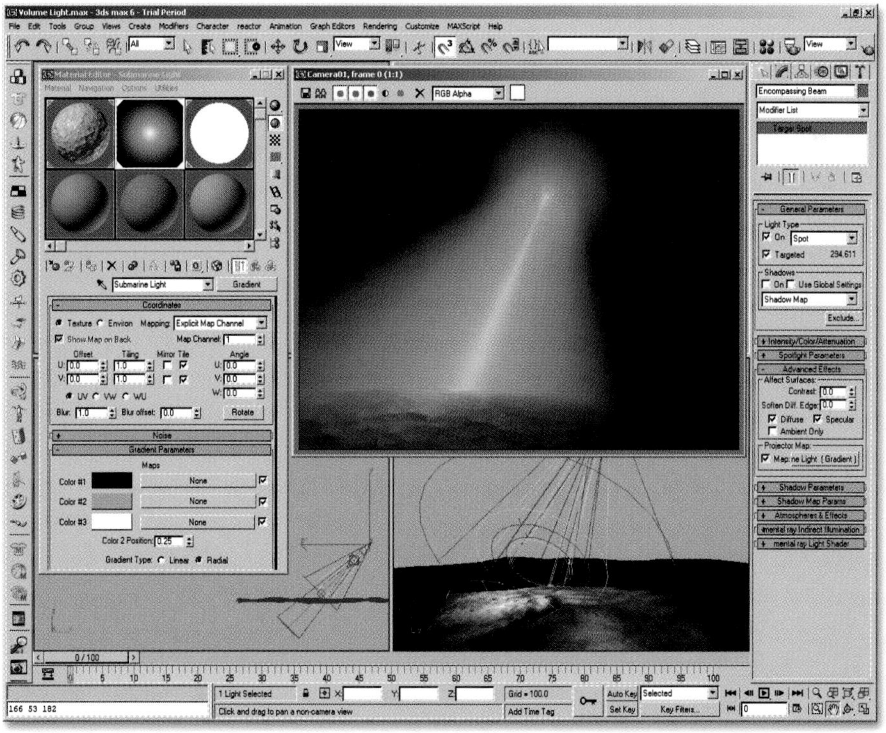

Making It Move

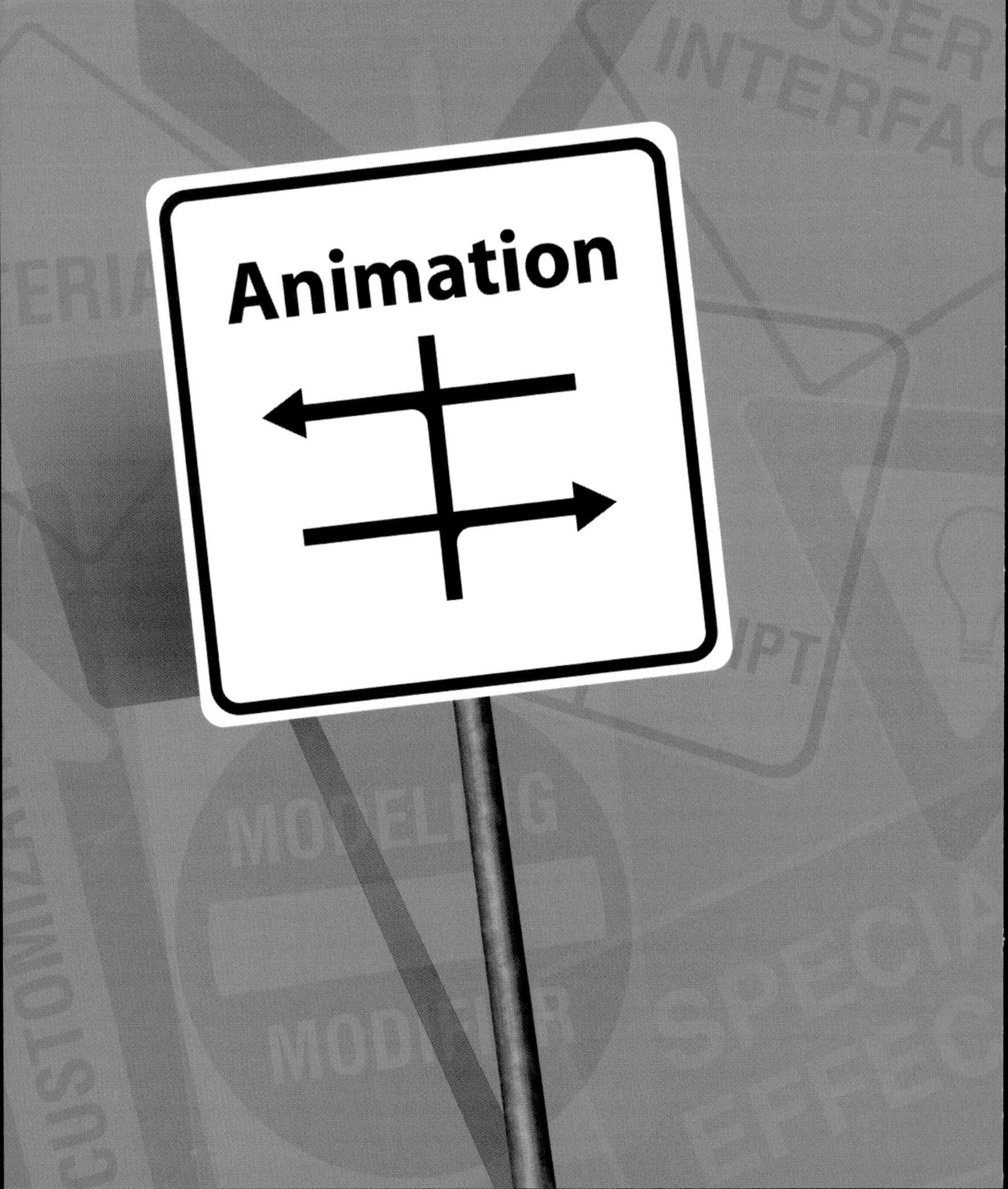

Making It Move

animation tips

Still life paintings can be wonderful… a bowl of fruit, sitting on a table, in a quiet country kitchen… a shaft of sunlight streaming through an open window, curtains hanging down, and motes of dust frozen in mid-air….

But this is the 3D world we're talking about, and there's no reason you can't make things move.

Give those apples and bananas in that bowl animated faces, and make them jump up and dance around. Turn that shaft of sunlight into a multicolored disco light, and make rainbows fly across that table. Have the curtains wave and thrash in a breeze. (And, because I know what most 3D artists are like, have a squad of animated robots kick down the door, blast the table with laser rifles, and eat the fruit to power their fusion reactors.)

In this chapter, contributor Pete Draper (http://www.xenomorphic.co.uk) and I present some useful general tips on animating in 3ds max. Then Paco Vidal of Havok, Inc. (http://www.havok.com—makers of the reactor 2 real-world physics engine included with 3ds max 5 and 3ds max 6) offers some helpful tips on using reactor 2's rigid body and soft-body dynamics. Finally, 3D artist Peter DeLappe offers some tips on using Inverse Kinematics (IK) and Bones in 3ds max 6.

QUICK PATH ANIMATION

With the Trajectories feature (Command Panel > Motion tab > Trajectories button), you can quickly assign a spline path to a selected object by clicking on the Convert From button, and then clicking on the desired spline path or shape. The keys are displayed at intervals defined in the Sample Range settings. (Note: Be sure to verify the Sample Range settings for start time and end time so that the movement covers the correct time in your animation. If the movement doesn't match the path, adjust the Samples setting and repeat these steps.)

You can also reverse this process by converting the animated trajectory of an object to a new spline with one quick click. (Try saying that three times fast!) Make sure the object is selected, and then click the Convert To button. A new spline path is created along the original trajectory of the object. If the subsequent trajectory isn't as close to the original spline path as you would like, try increasing the number of samples.

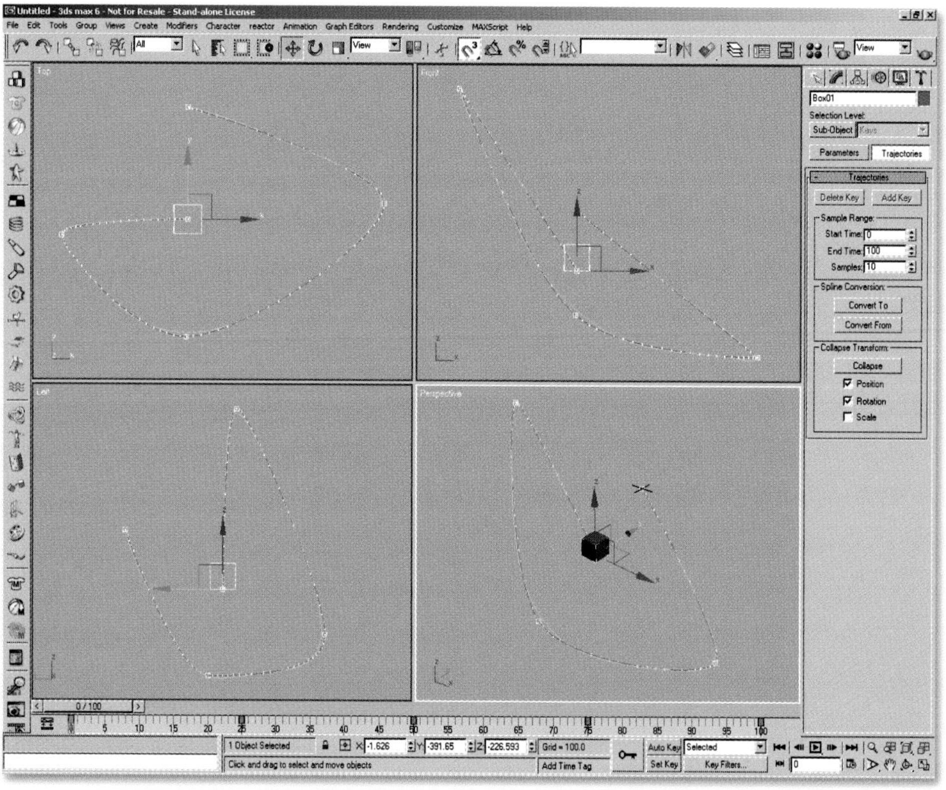

STAY ON THE PATH

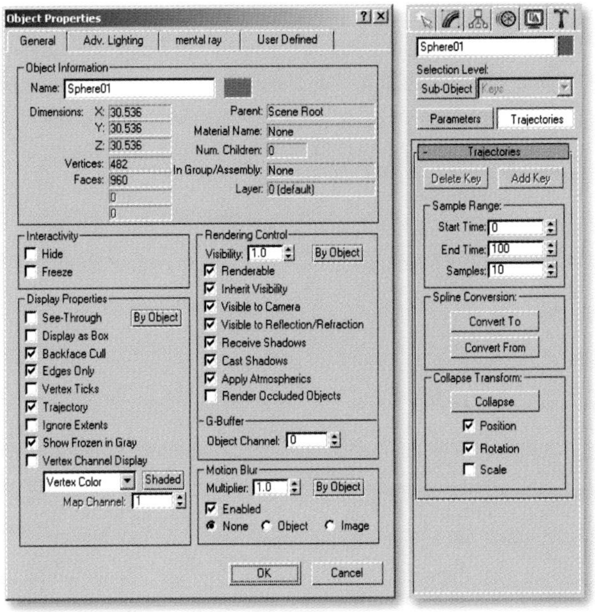

As a corollary to the previous tip: Remember that you can always display an animated object's trajectory in your scene not just by clicking the Trajectories button (Command Panel > Motion tab > Trajectories), but by right-clicking on the object, selecting Properties, and checking the Trajectories button under Display Properties.

I'M ABOUT TO COLLAPSE: GENERATE KEYFRAMES

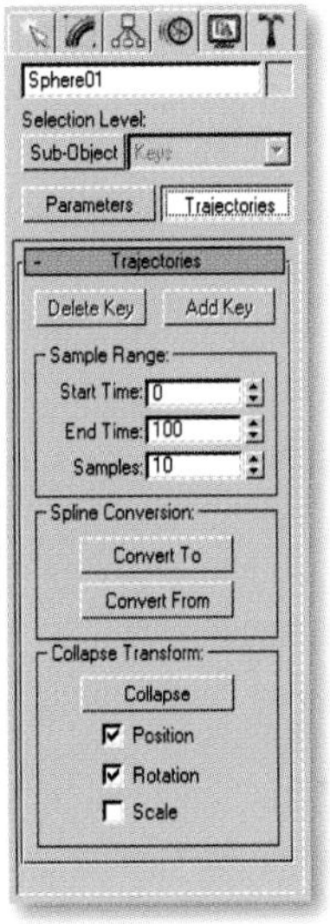

You can convert keys based on any object transformation that's been generated from parametric controllers (such as a Path Constraint or Noise controller) to editable transformation keys by clicking on the Command Panel > Motion tab > Trajectories rollout > Collapse button. The motion might be altered (slightly) from the original, but increasing the number of samples results in a more accurate conversion.

SMOOTHING OUT YOUR MOTION

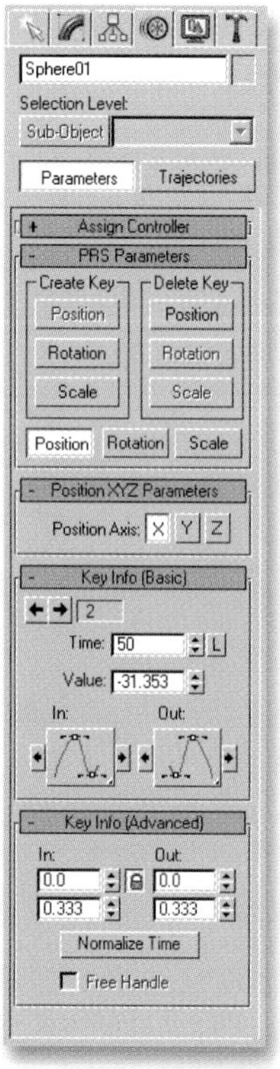

In the Command Panel > Motion tab > Parameters > Key Info (Advanced) rollout, you can quickly modify keyframes for your selected object if you want to "even out" the motion. Just drag the Time Slider bar to the desired keyframe, and click on the Normalize Time button. This is useful if you have an object that speeds up or slows down too much during the course of its movement across your scene.

A caveat: The Normalize Time feature occasionally creates wonky sub-frame keys if a key "falls off" of (previously) evenly numbered frames; this can alter the motion of the object, as well as the animation time. So, be careful when using this feature; you might want to do an Edit > Hold before checking Normalize Time. If you don't like the results, then an Edit > Fetch returns you to solid ground.

A GAME OF TAG

To keep track of key events in your animations, insert time tags at relevant keys or at specific instances along the timeline when an important event occurs. (You can insert Time Tags by simply going to the desired frame and clicking on the Add Time Tag button at the bottom of your 3ds max desktop.) Time Tags act like Post-It notes to label important actions occurring on specific keys, and they pop up whenever you go to a frame that's had one assigned. Time Tags also act as markers, letting you jump to a specific frame where a keyframe might not necessarily exist.

I'VE SEEN A GHOST!

Actually, in 3ds max, you can see many ghosts, if you know where to look. If you go to Views > Show Ghosting, the Ghosting command allows you to see wireframe copies of an animated object for a specified number of frames before or after the current frame. You can use this to analyze your object motion in your scene; tighter "ghosting" indicates slower motion, whereas wider-spaced ghosted objects indicate faster motion. (I guess you could call the latter "spaced ghosts.") You can modify the Ghosting preferences by going to the Customize > Preferences > Viewports dialog.

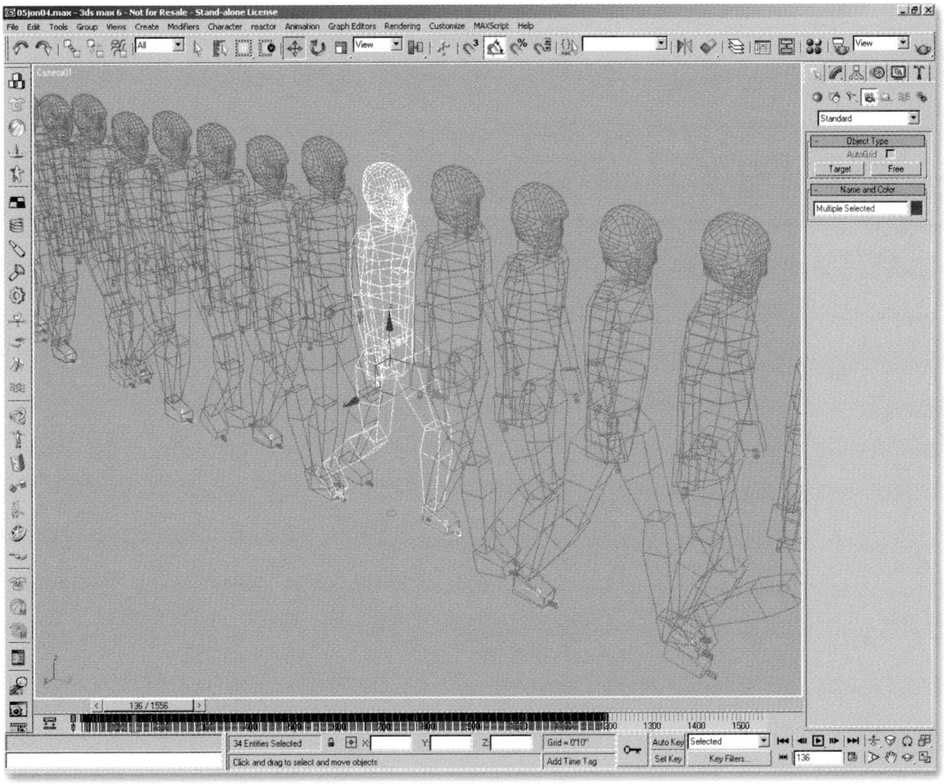

JUMP FEET-FIRST INTO KEY MODE

For a quick way to jump to a frame with a key assigned to it, turn on Key mode. (Click the small Key Mode Toggle button to the left of the frame counter, under your frame Playback controls.) This enables the Time Slider to jump to the next or previous keyframe (for any keyframed parameter) for the current item if you simply click on one of the Increment arrows on the Time Slider, or click on Next Key or Previous Key in the Time Control Buttons panel.

Note: People who are still using 3ds max 4 or earlier versions will note a button with an actual "key" icon for the Key Mode toggle; 3ds max versions 5 and 6 have changed this icon to arrowheads between two vertical bars, and repurposed the "key" icon to the large Set Key button.

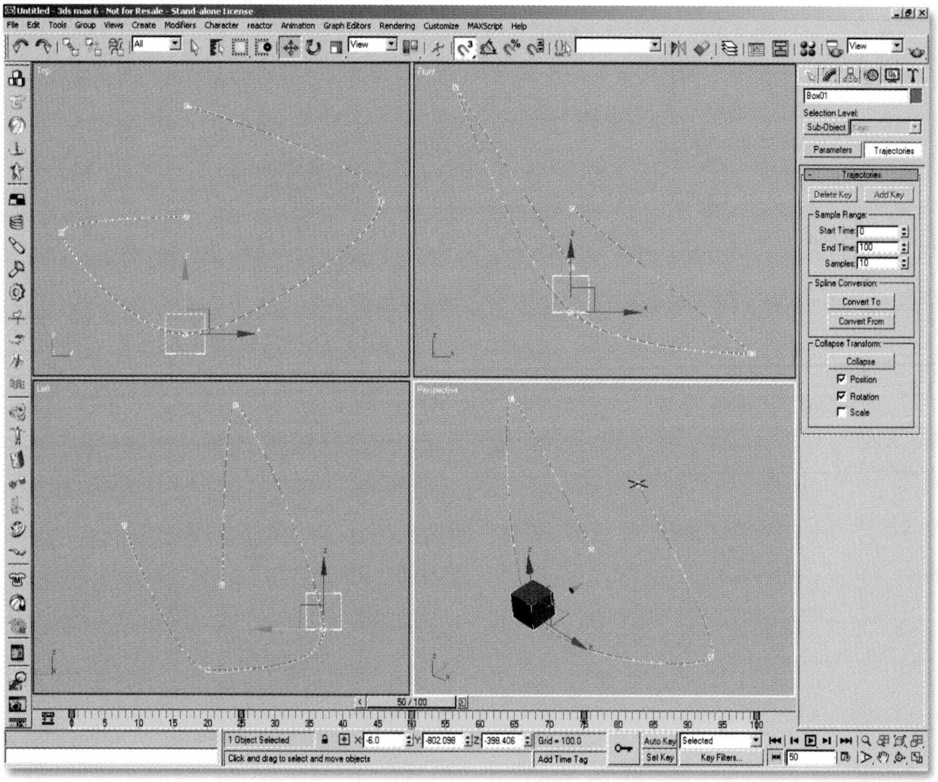

MOTION CAPTURE CONTROLLER AND UTILITY

The Motion Capture Utility (Command Panel > Utilities) is ideal for helping you create a more natural, hand-held feel to animated elements within your scene. To use Motion Capture, you first need to assign a Motion Capture controller to the relevant objects in your scene. Select the objects, and then go to the Curve Editor, select a track (Position, Rotation or Scale), and assign a controller through the Controller menu. (The Motion Capture dialog lets you choose your input device, such as keyboard, joystick, mouse, and so on.) You can then go to the Utilities panel, open the Motion Capture menu, select the desired track in the Tracks drop-down menu, and record your object transformations as you manipulate your animated element in real-time. This is particularly useful for hand-animating objects throughout your entire animation—from limb motion to blinking eyelids for characters or to duplicate a hand-held camera feel.

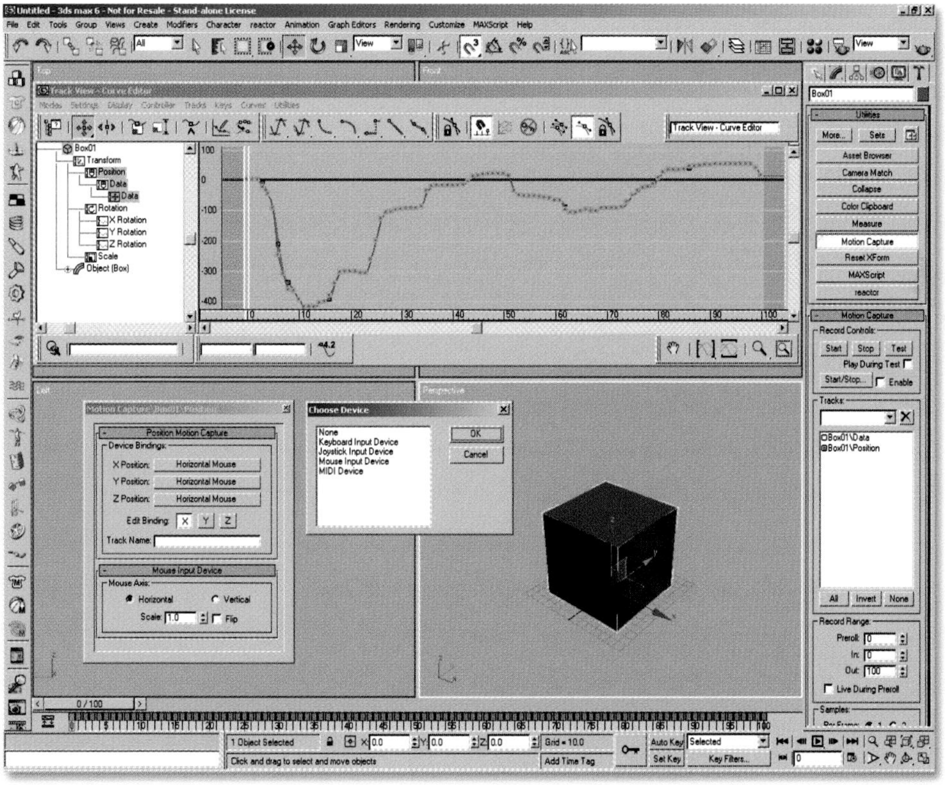

SPEAKING OF HAND-HELD CAMERAS...

The spline-based interpolation between animation keys helps smooth out movements in your 3D scene; indeed, it's an inherent feature of 3D animation. The problem is, it can be *too* smooth; it betrays the inherent mathematical precision of the process. Sometimes you want your animation to be jerky and choppy or your camera movement to feel hand-held.

To "mess up" the precision of your existing animation keys, make friends with the Randomize Keys utility in the Curve Editor or Dope Sheet. By selecting a range of keys (Position, Rotation, or Scale) and then applying the Track View – Curve Editor > Utilities > Track View Utilities > Randomize Keys feature, you can randomize the parameters of both time (frames) and the Position/Rotation/Scale values. This takes some of the digital precision out of your animation and adds some (realistic) analog human imperfection to your work.

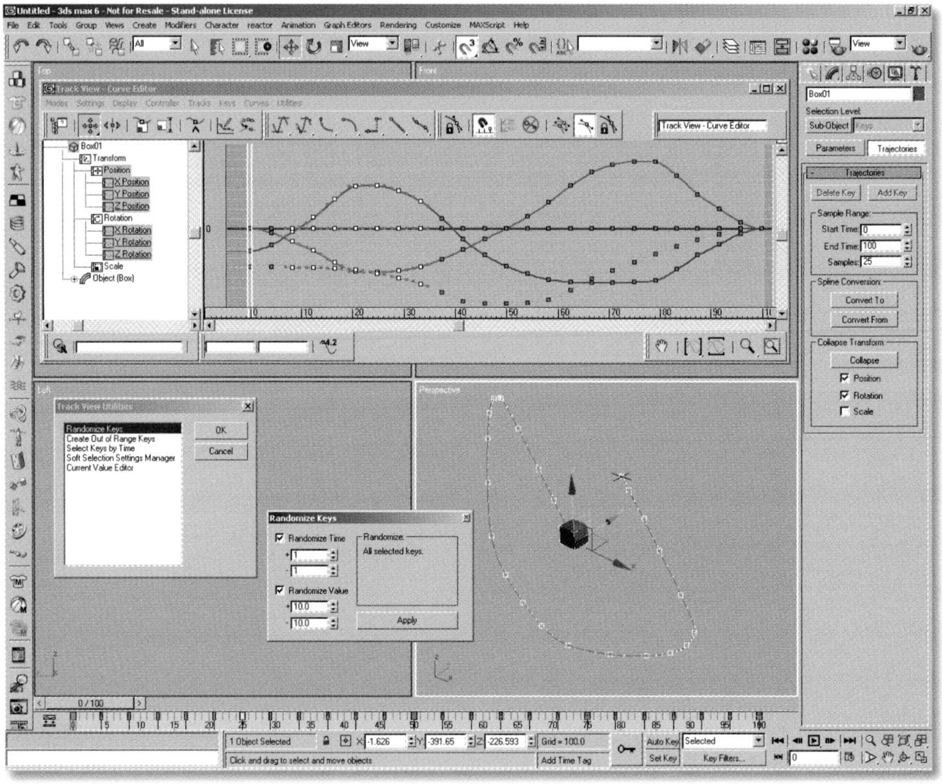

SPEAKING OF THE CURVE EDITOR…

When you create animations in 3ds max, the program assigns its default animation controllers to your keys: Bezier Float for Position and Rotation, and Bezier Scale for Scale. (You can change the default animation controllers by going to the Customize > Preferences > Animation menu. This sets the default values for the controllers; you can change the controllers using the Track View - Curve Editor > Select Track > Controller > Assign > Make Default feature. However, this isn't advisable unless you know exactly what you're doing.) The Bezier curves that are applied to your animation keys produce an automatic ease-out and ease-in on the keys, but sometimes that's not what you want. These controllers can make an object begin to move slowly, speed up, and then end slowly.

To create a more linear transformation from one key to the next, select the objects you want to modify, open your Curve Editor, click the Filters button, and under Show Only, check Animated Tracks to show only animated objects. Then look at your object's animation curves. If you want, you can select the object keys and simply move the corresponding Bezier handle(s) for the curve up or down to create a flat line from one key to the next. Or you can select the first key you want to modify, right-click to bring up the keyframe properties menu, and then change the In and Out curves to the desired type to flatten the Bezier curves for the keys.

Important note: If you're using the Tools > Snapshot feature to array objects across an animation, you'll probably want to use the previous technique to change the current animation path; otherwise, the objects appear to "clump up" at the beginning and end of the original animation path.

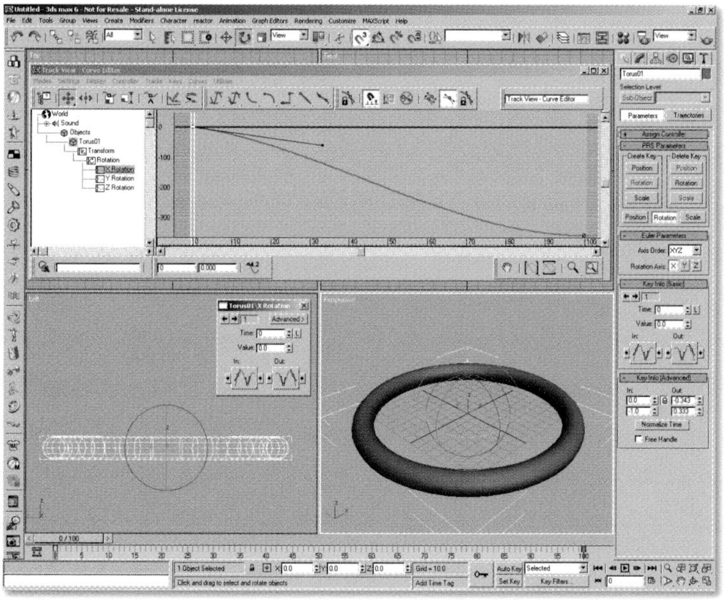

SON OF CURVE EDITOR

The 3ds max Curve Editor is a powerful tool for adjusting every aspect of your animation. However, what if you just want to tweak a few animated elements, and you don't need a large floating menu on your 3ds max desktop?

If that's the case, then don't forget the Mini Curve Editor. You open it with a quick click on the button at the far left of your Track Bar, at the bottom of your screen. When you do, a "Mini-Me" version of the floating Curve Editor appears as a window across the bottom of your 3ds max workspace, enabling you to make ongoing minor changes to your animation. What could be more convenient?

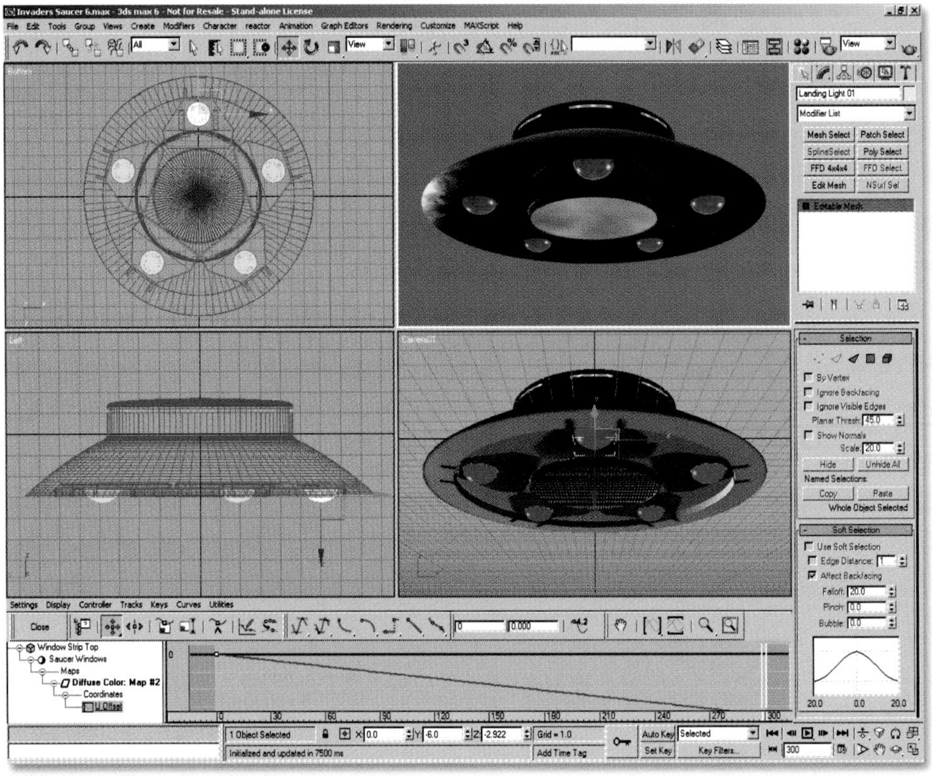

COLLECT YOUR WELL-DESERVED INHERITANCE

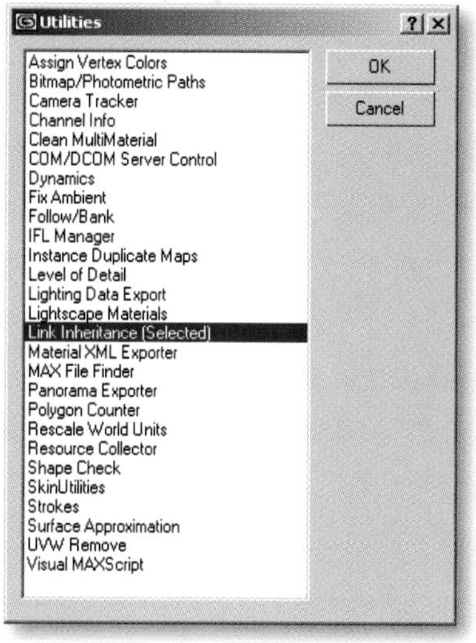

Instead of modifying the Link Inheritance information for each item in the Link Info rollout in the Command Panel > Hierarchy > Link Info tab, select a number of objects and use the Link Inheritance (Selected) Utility (Command Panel > Utilities > More) to perform the operation on all items at once.

LET'S GET THINGS STRAIGHT: THE ALIGN TOOL

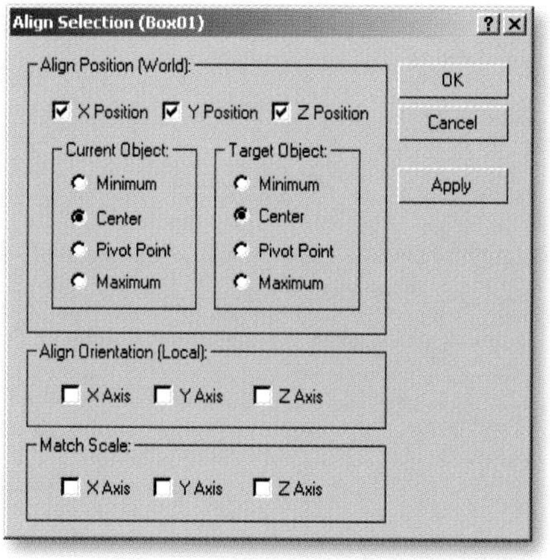

Another handy but oft-neglected feature in the 3ds max toolkit is the Align tool. You can use this on sub-object selections and pivot points, as well as on the entire object you select. You can also animate with the Align tool to create keyframes. Just select a frame, turn the Auto Key button on, and use the Align tool to "snap" your current object to another object in the scene.

READY, SET, MATCH: POSITIONING CAMERAS

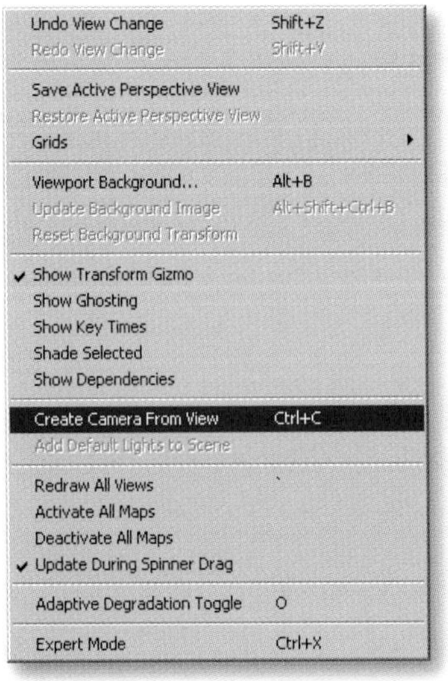

It's often easier to set up and position a Perspective viewport than a camera, but when your scene requires an actual Camera viewport (which is, well, almost always), then set up the desired view in Perspective, select the camera you want matched to the Perspective view, and then select Views > Create Camera From View. Again, you can also animate with this feature; just click on Auto Key, go to a different frame, reposition your Perspective viewport, and then redo the camera match.

REANIMATOR: RESETTING DIFFERENT ASPECTS OF A SCENE

This is an obvious (that is, in-your-face) option, but many 3ds max users don't realize it's there. Every time you select File > New, you are prompted with Keep Objects and Hierarchy, Keep Objects only, or New All.

The first two options mean that you can purge all *animation* from your scene without having to delete a single track or key by hand, and you can do the same with the addition of unlinking all children from their parents. With this, you can blow away all the animation keys from a complex animated scene, but keep all your existing geometry to reanimate.

SLIP SLIDING AWAY: USE LOOKAT CONSTRAINTS FOR MECHANICAL MOVEMENTS

For industrial animations of mechanical parts, it's often useful to depict the actions of levers and pistons moving in concert with other parts. However, setting up IK rigs for these parts can be tedious, so here's a simpler solution: Use LookAt constraints for simple sliding joints. The LookAt constraint works by "pointing" an object toward the pivot point of another object. If you have two piston rods, with one positioned to slide inside the other, and each of them parented to hinged arm pieces, then the pivot points on each rod should (logically) be their anchor points (or else they will rotate around their parents' pivot points). So, to make this work properly, go to Animation > Rotation Controllers > LookAt Constraint, and assign a Rotation LookAt controller to both piston rods, with each LookAt target being the other piston rod (or its parent.) The result is that each rod should pivot about its anchor point, while simultaneously pointing toward the other piston's anchor point, thus creating sliding pistons. (You can adjust the LookAt constraint parameters after the assignment by going to the Command Panel > Motion tab > Parameters rollout.)

Note: Unfortunately, this technique won't work if you do a multi-axis rotation on the pistons' parents; it breaks the piston link and the pistons will more than likely "twist" apart in opposite directions. However, for one-axis rotations, this technique can work well, and it's quick and easy to set up.

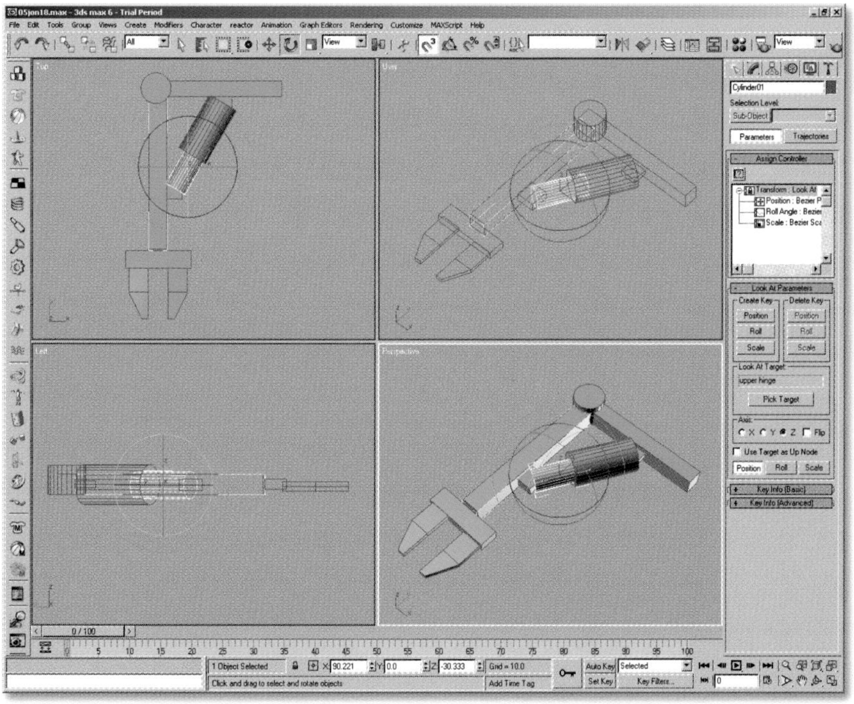

REACTOR: USE TCB CONTROLLERS AS ROTATION CONTROLLERS FOR RIGID BODIES

During a simulation, a reactor sends "snapshots" of the rigid bodies' positions and rotations to 3ds max; those snapshots are then converted into keyframes. The job of the Position and Rotation controllers is to calculate (interpolate) the positions and rotations between those keyframes.

The default Rotation controller in 3ds max 6, Euler XYZ, can sometimes produce non-smooth rotations between keyframes, and create visible artifacts; this is due to the limitations of using Euler angles to specify arbitrary rotations. The TCB controller, based on quaternions, does a much better job at interpolating rotations.

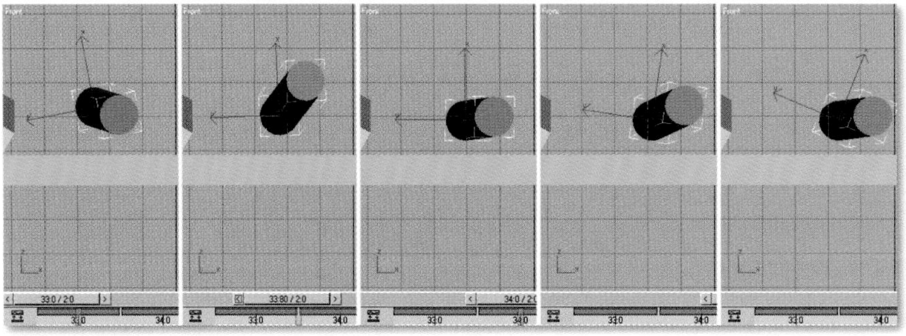

Euler XYZ Rotation

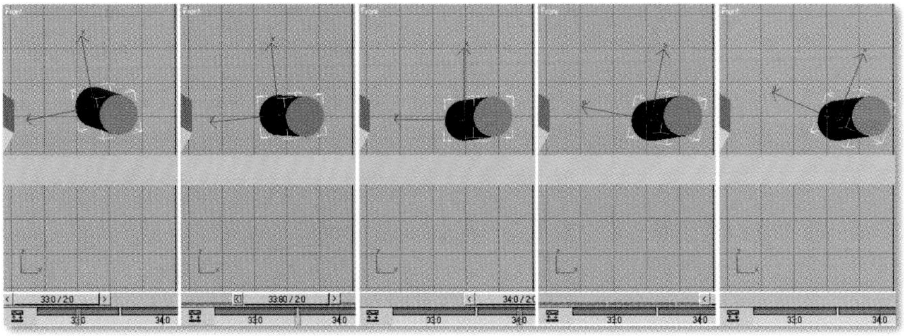

TCB (quaternion) Rotation

To address this problem, you need a piece of code—MAXScript code, that is:

```
bodies = $selection as array
for body in bodies do
(
body.rotation.controller = tcb_rotation ()
)
```

This MAXScript snippet switches all original Euler rotation controllers to TCB for the selected nodes in the scene.

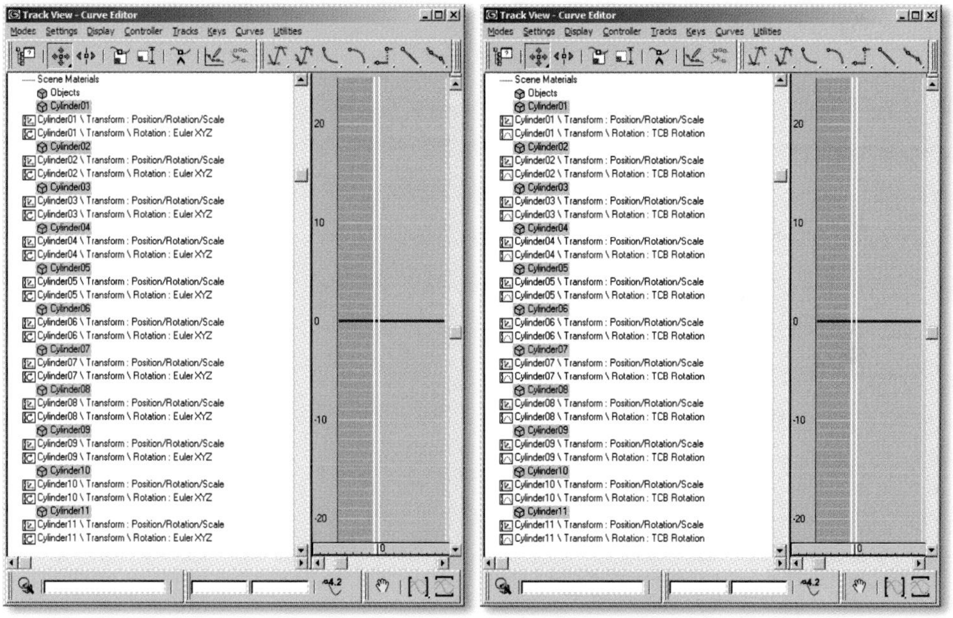

REACTOR: USE MESHSMOOTH MODIFIERS WITH REACTOR CLOTH AND SOFT BODIES

Usually, you don't need to simulate cloth or soft bodies using a highly tessellated mesh. Using a coarse mesh can often produce good results with increased speed and stability. You can then apply a MeshSmooth modifier *on top* of the reactor modifier to smooth out the result. The MeshSmooth modifier usually produces realistic results and allows control over the final look (smoothness, creases, and so on) of the animation without having to run the reactor simulation again.

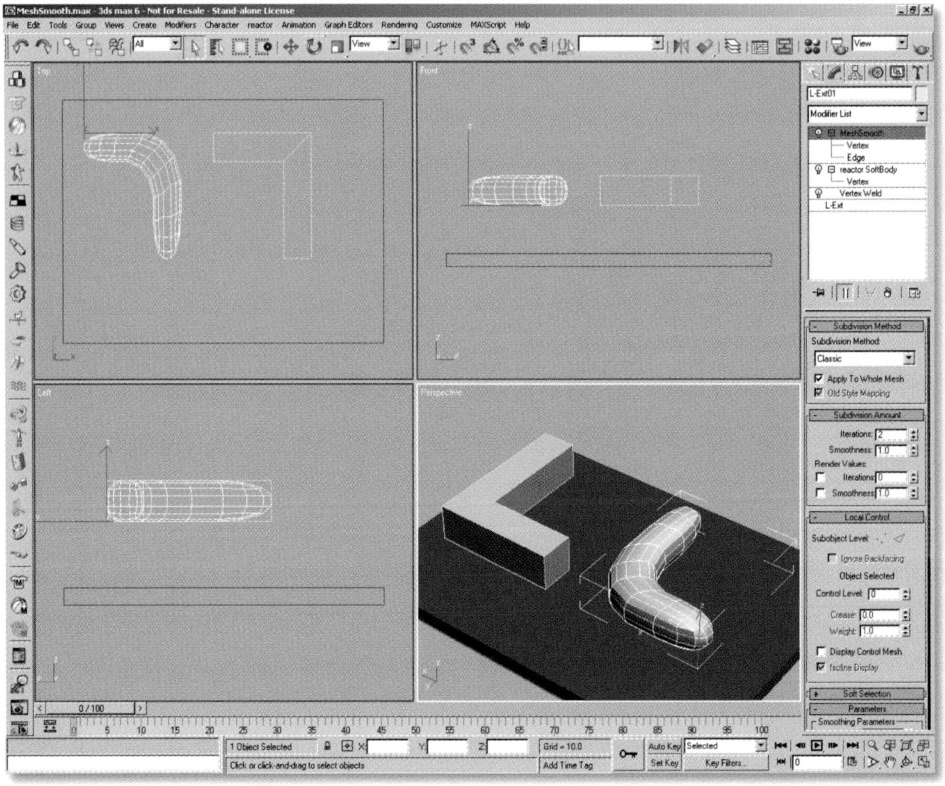

USE "CONFORM TO SHAPE" IN FFD-BASED SOFT BODIES IN THE REACTOR

When using FFD-based soft bodies, the reactor uses the FFD modifier lattice instead of the mesh of the object for the simulation. It's sometimes desirable to modify the FFD lattice to better match the shape of the original mesh. To do this, click the Conform to Shape button in the FFD modifier.

(Note: 3ds max has a bug in which the Conform to Shape button remains disabled when the soft body is part of a soft body collection. Delete the soft body from the soft body collection to enable the button, click on it, and then add the soft body again to the collection.)

Now switch the Stable Configuration radio button in the reactor Soft Body modifier from Original Box to Frame. Set the frame to the start frame of your animation (usually 0). This step prevents the reactor from trying to reset the FFD lattice to its original shape (a box or cylinder) at the beginning of the animation.

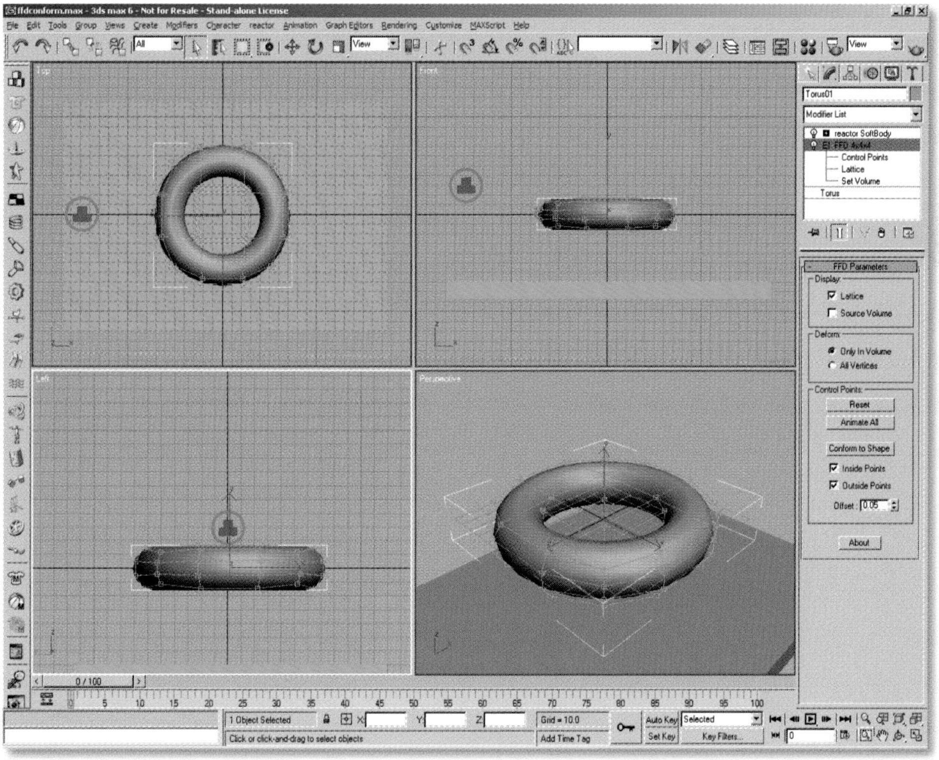

REACTOR: ALWAYS USE A SPECIFIC CAMERA FOR YOUR REACTOR PREVIEW

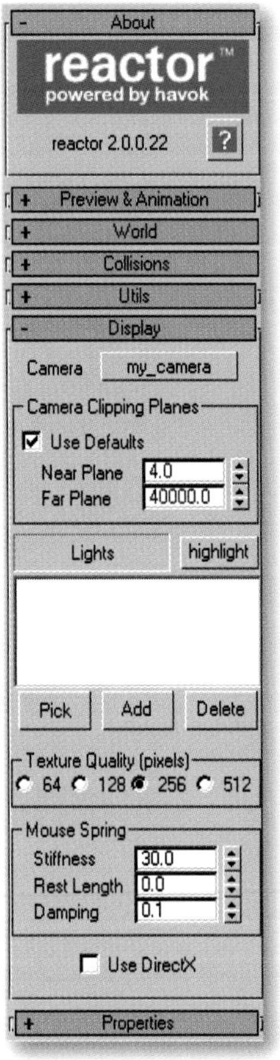

When you're previewing an animation, the reactor creates a default camera based on one current Perspective or Camera viewport in 3ds max. If this default camera doesn't match your desired view for the reactor preview, you're forced to manipulate the camera every time you preview the simulation. It's usually handy to create a camera in the scene to be used by the reactor preview. You can tell the reactor to use a specific camera by selecting a camera in the Display rollout in the reactor utility.

REACTOR: REDUCE THE NUMBER OF KEYS AFTER A RIGID-BODY SIMULATION

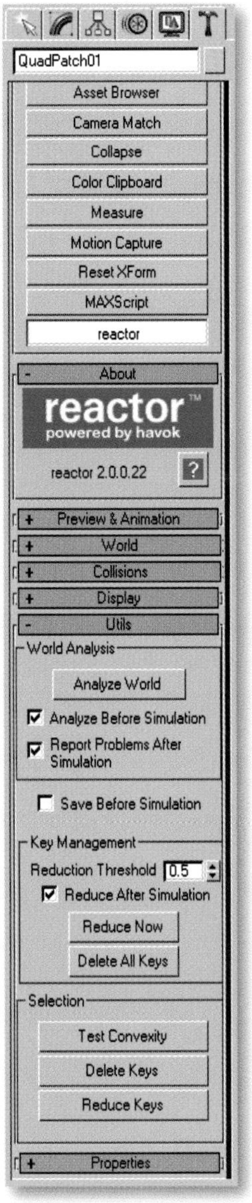

For rigid body simulation, the reactor usually creates a keyframe for every object at every frame. This can dramatically increase the file size if many rigid bodies are involved, as thousands of keyframes are created. The reactor provides functionality to reduce the number of keyframes. This functionality is available from the menu Reactor > Utilities (and also in the Reactor utility > Utils rollout). You can either reduce/delete keys for all rigid bodies in simulation or for only the selected objects.

REACTOR: REDUCE THE NUMBER OF KEYS AFTER AN FFD-BASED SOFT BODY SIMULATION

FFD-based soft body simulation can create many keys (one key for every control point for every frame). You can reduce the number of keys in the FFD modifiers by using the Reduce Keys functionality in the 3ds max Track View Curve Editor or Dope Sheet. Notice that the default threshold (0.5) is usually too high and can delete too many keys; therefore, it can result in a different animation from your original. A threshold of 0.01 is likely to produce good results. Decrease the threshold if too many keys are deleted and the animation is affected; increase the threshold if not enough keys are deleted.

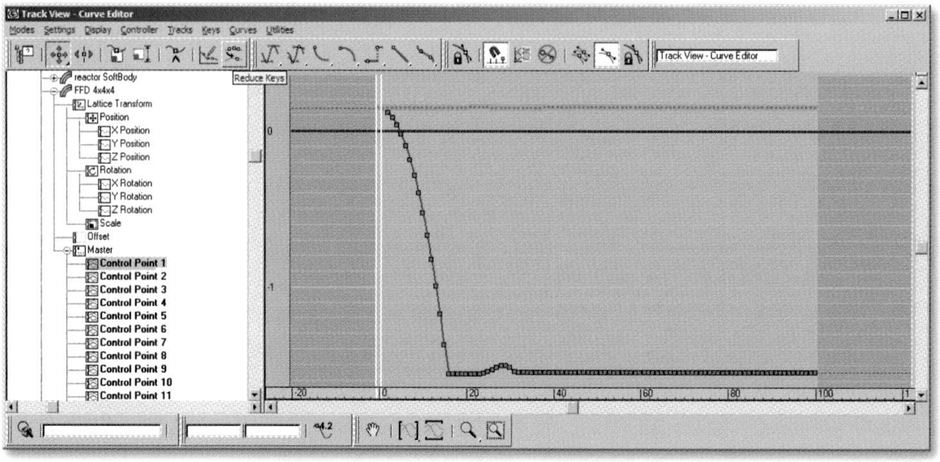

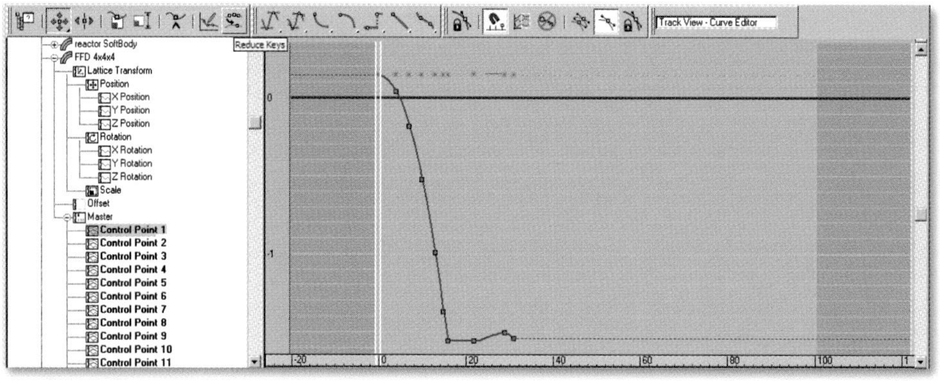

REACTOR: WHEN TO USE FFD-BASED OR MESH-BASED SOFT BODIES

The reactor provides two different methods of simulating soft bodies: FFD-based and mesh-based. FFD-based soft bodies use the control points of an FFD lattice for the simulation, whereas mesh-based soft bodies use the vertices of a mesh.

FFD-based soft bodies in the reactor provide an easier way of simulating soft bodies when the objects have a high number of vertices. (Those objects would be hard to simulate using a mesh-based approach.) FFD-based soft bodies also have a somewhat different behavior than mesh-based soft bodies. FFD-based soft bodies usually behave like jelly, whereas mesh-based soft bodies tend to behave more like objects filled with water or air.

Another main difference is that FFD soft bodies use the FFD lattice for collision detection. You can make the FFD lattice conform to the original mesh (see the "Use Conform to Shape in FFD-Based Soft Bodies in the Reactor" tip earlier in this chapter), but if, for example, your mesh has holes and you want to simulate them (you want objects to go through those holes), you need to use mesh-based soft bodies.

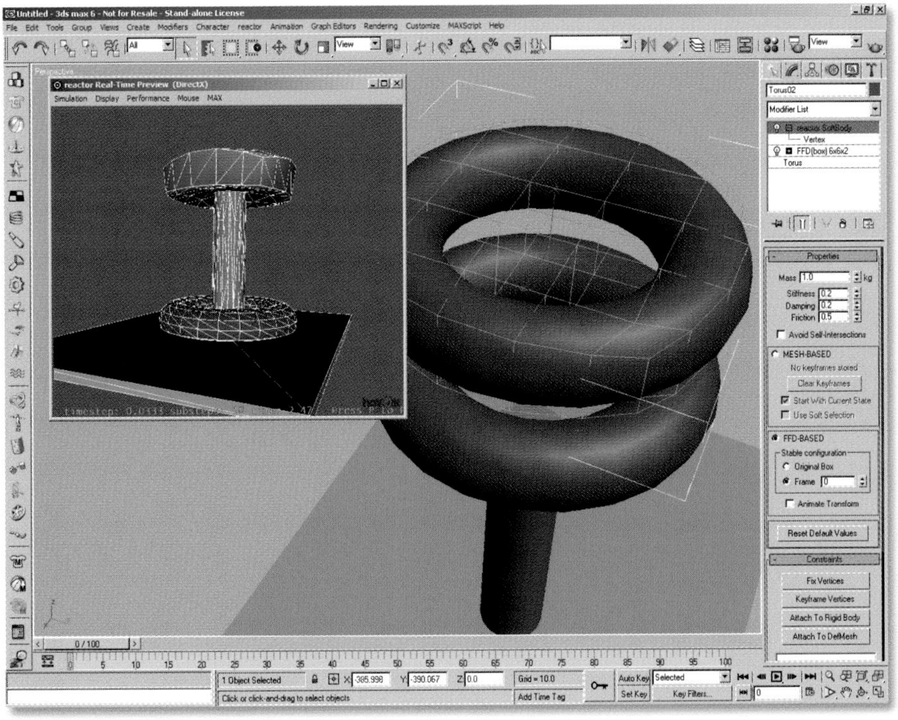

SIMULATE DISJOINTED GROUPS OF OBJECTS INDIVIDUALLY

Reactor allows you to group objects in collections, which can be enabled/disabled individually. If in a single scene you have sets of objects that don't interact with each other (let's say, the ponytail on a character and a group of rocks falling down a cliff beside him), it is usually a good idea to simulate each group individually (first the hair and then the rocks, or vice versa). This has two advantages: First, the reactor usually provides a faster simulation because it doesn't have to check for interactions between all groups of objects; second, it allows you to tweak each group individually, without having to recalculate the whole scene. In our example, the ponytail simulation is more complex, so it might require you to use a higher number of sub-steps, whereas the simpler simulation of rocks falling down can use just a few sub-steps. To simulate groups individually, group them in collections and disable all collections except those you are interested in on each simulation.

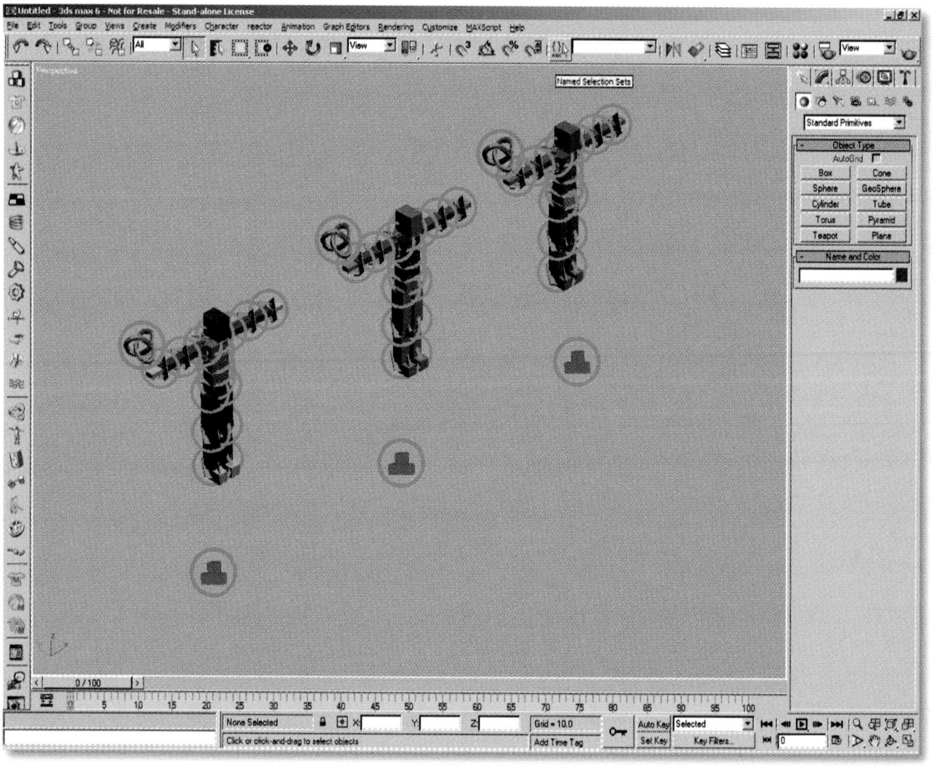

NAME YOUR DEFORMABLE CONSTRAINTS

The reactor modifiers for Cloth, Soft Body, and Rope store a list of *deformable constraints* (vertex attached to rigid bodies, fixed in space, and so on). Although those attachments are given a default name when they're created (such as "attach to rigid body"), it is always handy to provide a more meaningful name, particularly if you have more than one constraint on each modifier (such as "attach to neck," "attach to left arm"). You can rename a deformable constraint by clicking twice on its name on the list of constraints inside the modifier Constraints rollout.

HOW BONES WORK IN 3DS MAX: THE RULES

Every major 3D package has a bone system of some sort. Bones are usually parented into "chain" hierarchies, although in 3ds max this isn't strictly necessary. In the 3ds max program, a bone (Command Panel > Create tab > Systems > Bones) can be any object with its bone property turned on. So, what is a bone? Generally, a bone "chain" is a hierarchy of objects that obey two transformation rules:

- Any child bone must remain a fixed distance from its parent.
- Any parent bone must rotate to point at its child.

Most 3D packages permit a bone to have one—and only one—bone child. That's not so for 3ds max! Any bone can have multiple bones as children. So, to fulfill the second rule, parent bones point to *the average position of their child bones.* Note that this flexibility can cause some "screwiness" with branching bone chains, especially if you add or delete bone branches from bone hierarchies.

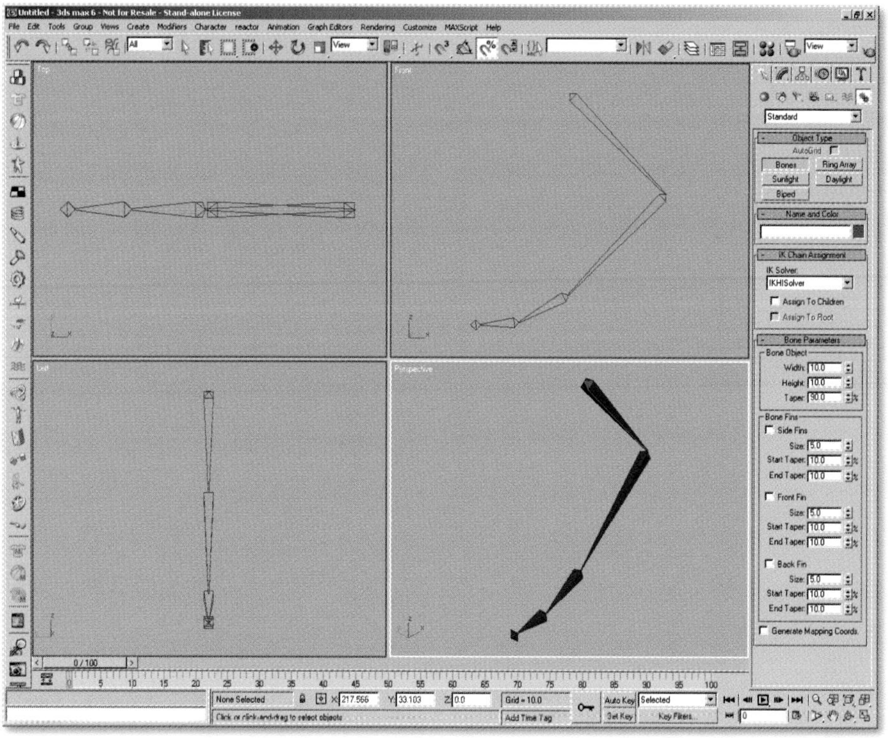

HOW BONES WORK: A COROLLARY

As the previous tip stated, you need to remember a couple of rules when working with the 3ds max program's bones. Here's a third bones rule to commit to your little gray cells:

- A bone only exhibits bone behavior if it has a bone child.

Ever notice the little bone "nub" at the end of 3ds max bone chains? This is why it's there: so that the bone *above* it will act like a bone. You can make your own nubs (after creating an initial bones setup) in the main toolbar > Character > Bone Tools (BT) > Bone Editing Tools rollout using the Create End button. The other reason for the nub is convenience when assigning IK to a chain. (Remember: The position of a bone is at the base, not the pointed end. Without the nub, the IK solver does not affect the bone above it.)

In 3ds max, *moving* a child bone rotates its parent bone. The child remains a fixed distance from the parent. (This distance is the parent's "length.") However, you can find an additional bone property called Freeze Length in the Bone Tools > Object Properties rollout. With a parent bone's Freeze Length off, a child bone can be dragged any distance from its parent. This causes the parent to stretch, which can be useful in character animation. In addition, the Skin modifier uses this stretch value for squashing effects.

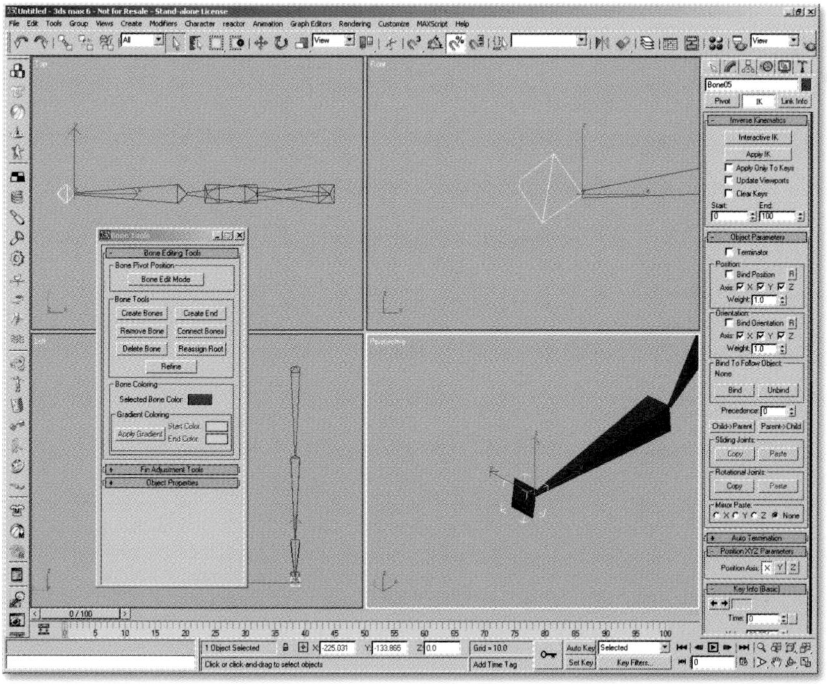

BONE STRETCH—AND HOW TO CONTROL IT

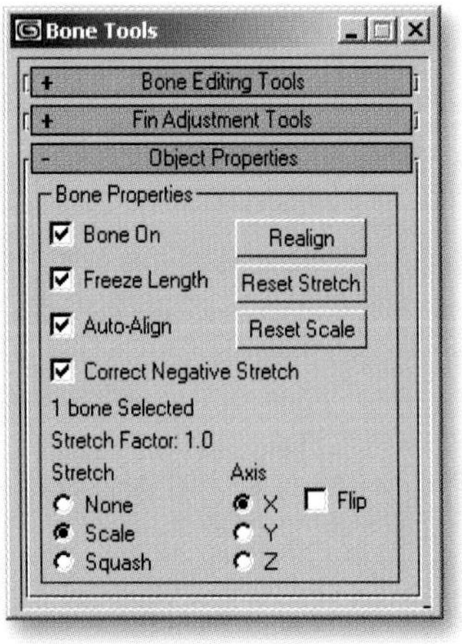

In 3ds max, a bone's stretch factor is set to unity (1.0) when it's created. The stretch is a derived value that is the ratio of the initial bone length to the current bone length. The length *can be changed only if Freeze Length is off!* You can then move the bone's child, thereby creating the stretch.

The Reset Stretch button in the Bone Tools > Object Properties rollout sets the currently selected bones back to unity stretch. Also (new for 3ds max 6), Bone Edit mode preserves the current bone stretch during bone chain editing.

ARE YOUR BONES SCALING NEGATIVELY WHEN YOU MIRROR THEM?

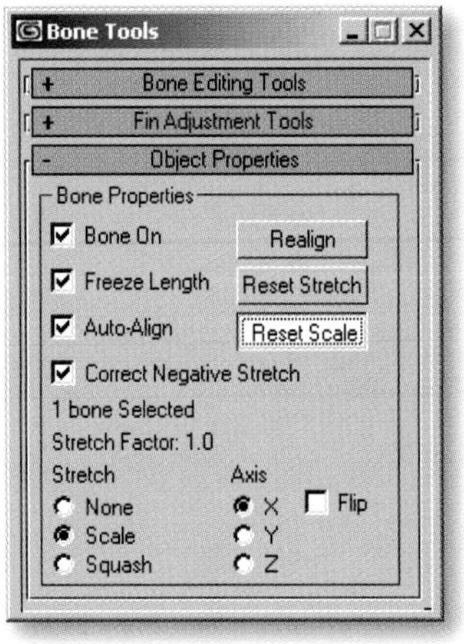

Nope, the title of this tip isn't a bad country and western song. A lot of systems (especially game engines) don't like negatively scaled bones. The Kaydara Filmbox .FBX file format doesn't like negative bones either. To fix this, go to the Character > Bone Tools > Object Properties rollout, and click on the Reset Scale button. This correctly strips off any naughty negative scaling. You can also reset negative stretch. (For more information on Kaydara, go to http://www.kaydara.com.)

BONES GONE TOTALLY WACKY?

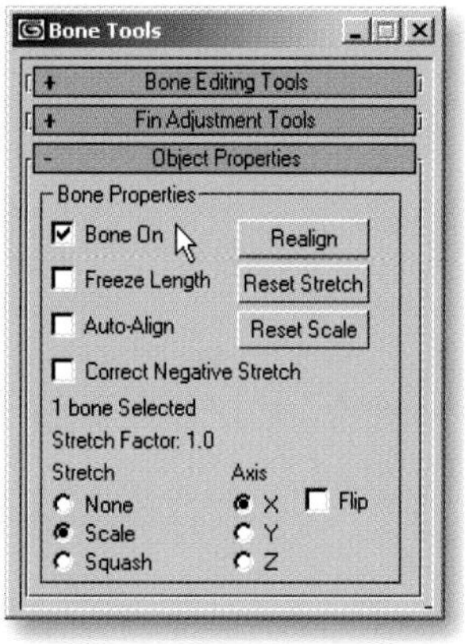

Because the 3ds max program's Bone system uses special bone primitives that are real 3D objects, not just icons, your 3ds max bones can sometimes get completely decoupled from the bone hierarchy links that control them. To realign bones, try clicking *all* the buttons in the Character > Bone Tools > Object Properties rollout, especially Bone On. Eventually, you can get your bone objects to realign and the stretches to reset.

BONES LOOK "STRETCHY"? BONE TOOLS WILL TELL

The stretch factor of a bone is a derived value. It isn't stored anywhere in 3ds max; it's merely a ratio. If you open Character > Bone Tools > Object Properties and select a single bone, you can see the bone's stretch.

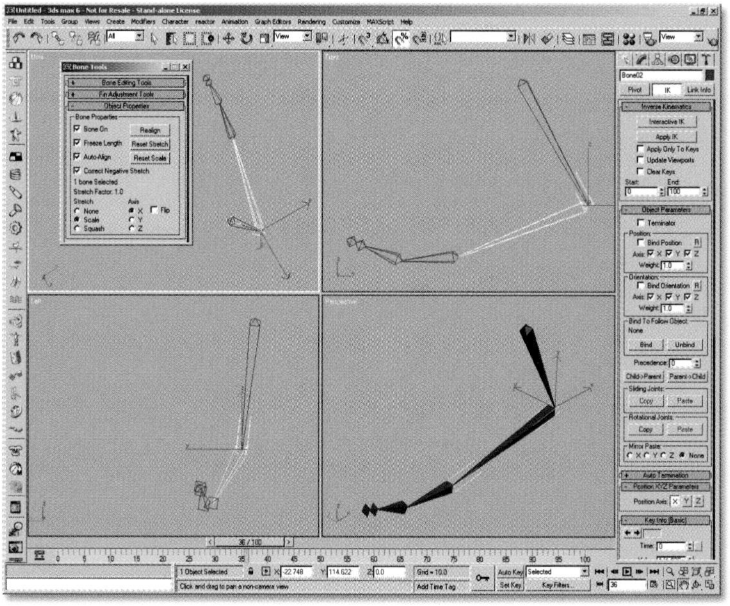

SWITCH TO SMOOTH INTERPOLATION FOR BONE ROTATIONS WHEN DOING "IK FOR FK POSE"

The IK for FK Pose (Inverse Kinematics for Forward Kinematics) option of history-independent (HI) IK is a powerful tool for character animation. (The HI IK Solver in 3ds max does not rely on IK solutions calculated in previous keyframes in the timeline.) Its operation as a one-step FK rotation keyframing tool is unique to 3ds max. It's best used for non-directed, freeform animation of limbs, such as character arms. Arms, when moving freely (for example, when they're not connected at the hand to other fixed or moving objects), generally look better and more believable when they move in arcs. IK for FK does this by converting IK handle moves directly into bone rotation keyframes that interpolate as nice arcs between keys. These "arc" limb movements look even better when the limb bone rotations use the Smooth interpolation, instead of the default Auto Tangent.

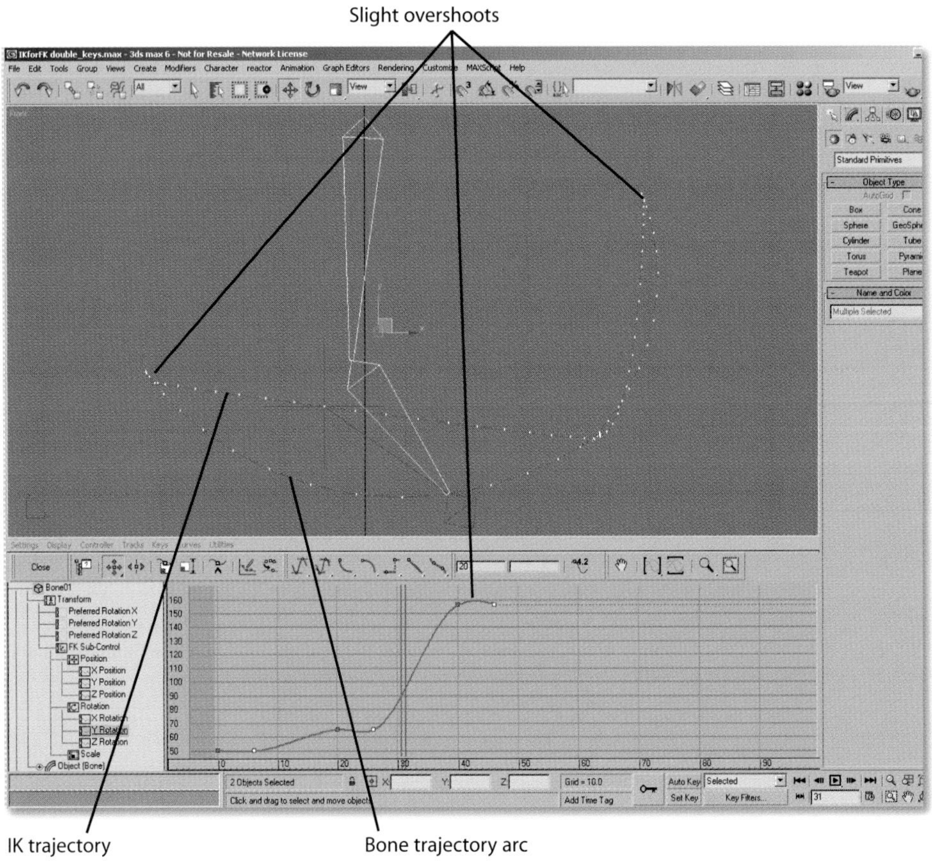

The Auto Tangent default Bezier interpolation in 3ds max is handy. It prevents the classic cubic curve "overshoot" problems found in Smooth. However, many character animators *prefer* Smooth Interp PRS (Position/Rotation/Scale). One of the oldest tricks in the book, when keyframing characters, is to set identical keyframes about 2 to 5 frames apart. Smooth interpolation automatically creates "overshoots" between the key pairs, thus giving the performance quick and easy anticipation and follow-through. This works particularly well with IK for FK. *Nice character animation really fast!*

With an HI IK Solver assigned to your bones, you set Motion Panel > Enabled off and IK for FK Pose on. Set the Euler rotation keys for your bones to Smooth to achieve the effect. You can do this in the TrackView Curve Editor by selecting keyframes for your bone rotations and clicking the Smooth icon. Alternatively, you can change the Customize > Preferences > Animation > Controller Defaults for Bezier controllers to Smooth, but doing so sets *all* Bezier controller interpolation to Smooth for new keyframes.

COPY SKIN WEIGHTS BETWEEN OBJECTS WITH SKINUTILITIES

A little-known tool called SkinUtilities (Command Panel > Utilities > More > SkinUtilities) is included in 3ds max 6. With a Skin object selected, SkinUtilities generates a new copy of the object with the weights stored in a special channel. The Skin weights can then be transferred off this new object and onto another Skinned object. SkinUtilities does this by detecting the proximity of the original bones and vertices within a set radius to the target object's bones and vertices, much the same way the Mirroring rollout tools do in Skin. The new "SkinData" object can be transformed just as any other object in 3ds max. (This includes scaling.) This makes it ideal for use as a Skin weight transfer tool between Mirrored objects. SkinUtilities also works well with "near-symmetrical" objects because it matches source to target bones and vertices based on proximity, and then weights the target vertices as nearly as possible by averaging the weights of nearby vertices.

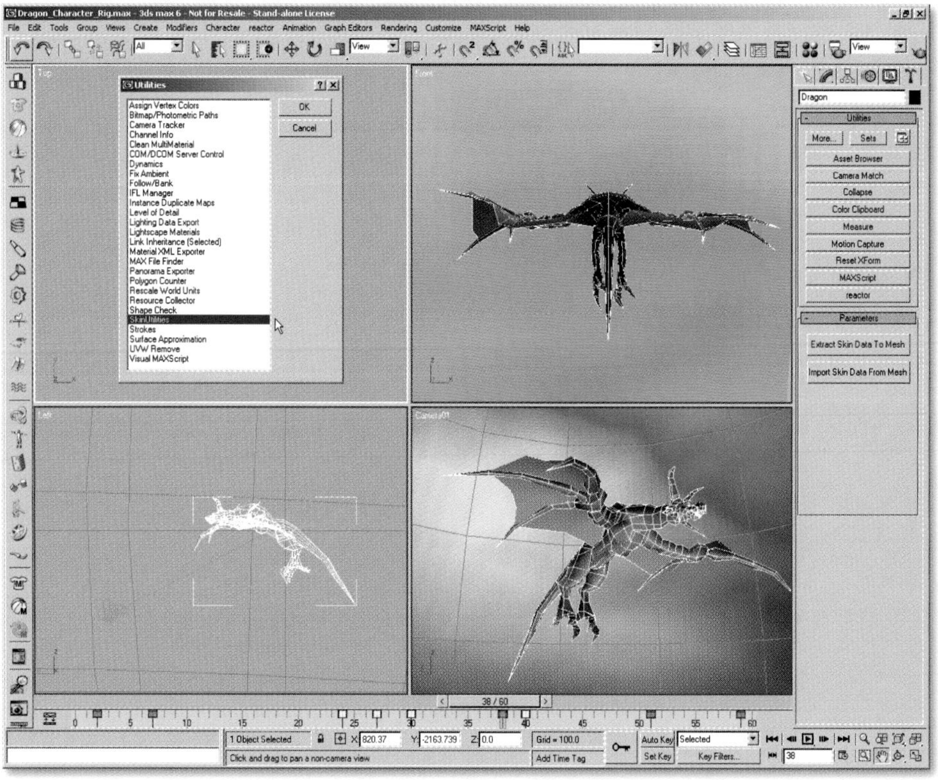

SIMPLE SWARMING WITH NOISE CONTROLLERS

Character Studio's Crowd Control feature enables you to produce "flocking" behavior for objects in your scene—everything from milling crowds of people to schools of fish and, yes, flocks of birds. You can also produce behavior like this through MAXScript, for example, by writing a MAXScript that adjusts "following objects" to move toward and away from a lead object.

However, if you don't have Character Studio or MAXScript expertise, and you want to do just a simple "swarm" effect, here's an easy trick: First, create a dummy object, and then link each object you want to "swarm" to the dummy. Animate the dummy object moving through your scene; the linked swarm objects are carried along with it. (Not very exciting.) However, open the Curve Editor, and change each "swarm object's" Position Controller type to Noise Position. This gives each object an erratic movement around the parent dummy object (like moths fluttering around a light bulb, or a swarm of gnats.) To "dampen" the frenetic movement, turn the frequency down from 0.5 to a lower level and turn off fractal noise. Alter the X, Y, and Z Strength values for each object as necessary to get the swarm objects' paths closer or further to the dummy object. Finally, make sure the Random Number seed values for each "swarm" object are different; that way, they won't all be moving on the same path.

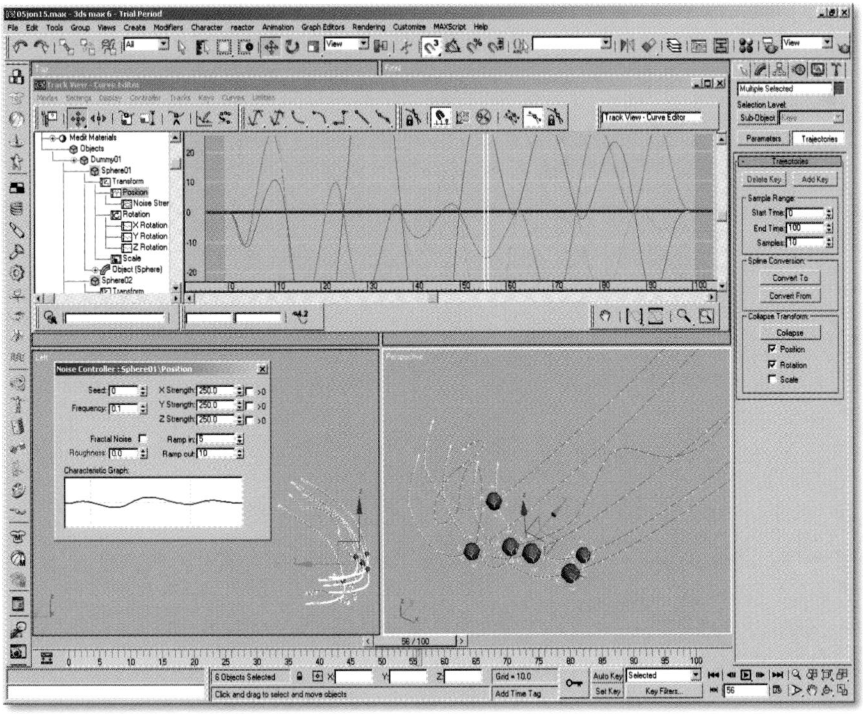

Making It Beautiful

Making It Beautiful

rendering tips

3ds max has always had one of the fastest renderers in the 3d industry. Its native scanline renderer has been the backbone of everything from cinematic special effects to architectural rendering to high-resolution print work. In short, it's a fast workhorse that gets most every rendering job done quickly. (People who want better control and more rendering options can also employ some excellent third-party renderers, such as the Brazil Rendering System [http://www.splutterfish.com/], Cebas's finalRender [http://www.finalrender.com] [http://www.cebas.com/], and The Chaos Group's V-Ray [http://www.chaosgroup.com].)

However, for those desiring more high-end render control within the core 3ds max package, fear not: With the release of 3ds max 6, the acclaimed mental images' mental ray 3.2 renderer is included. The mental ray 3.2 renderer brings fast raytracing, true sub-pixel displacement, advanced shaders and a complex shader language to adventurous 3ds max users.

In this chapter, I'll present several dozen tips on how to get the most out of your native 3ds max scanline renderer. In addition, contributor Aksel Karcher (a freelance designer and lighting technical director, at [http://www.akselkarcher.com/] weighs in with several mental ray tips for those 3ds max users who want to stay on the cutting edge.

RAY TRACING: SPEEDING UP THINGS (OBJECTS)

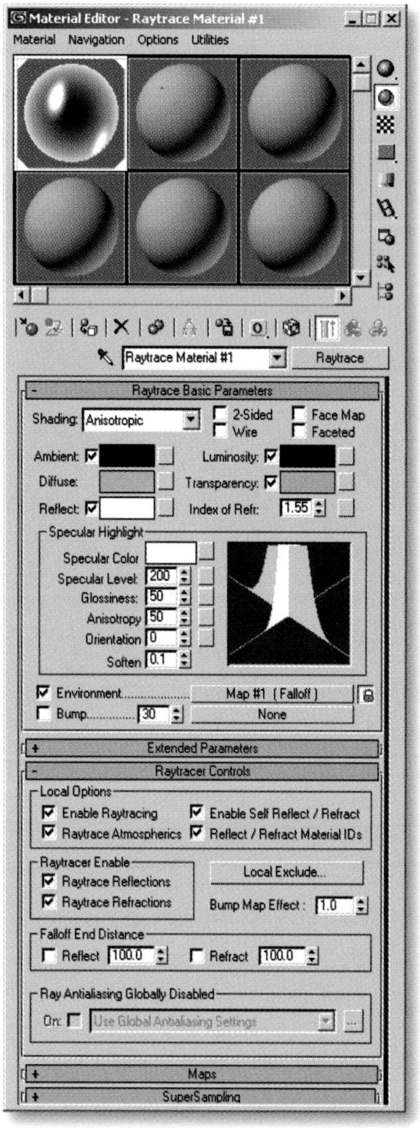

If you love the look of ray tracing in your scene (for glass and metallic surfaces) but you're not a fan of raytraced material rendering times when using the 3ds max scanline renderer, don't worry: You can speed up your renderings by doing a few simple things.

First, make sure antialiasing is unchecked in the Rendering > Raytracer Settings > Raytracer/ Global Ray Antialiaser menu when you're doing test renderings, then turn antialiasing back on when you're doing your final production rendering. (Note: You must be using the 3ds max default scanline renderer as your production renderer. If you have mental ray chosen instead, the Raytracer Settings and Raytrace Global Include/Exclude menu items are grayed out.) Second, check your scene object integrity: make sure you've welded the cores of Lathed objects, that objects have unified face normals, and that the objects aren't degenerate. (That is, they should not have missing or coincident faces, overlapping vertices, and so on.) Third, if you don't need to keep the modifier stacks active for some or all of your scene objects, then collapse them to the modifier stack results (preferably Editable Meshes). Fourth, keep your Raytrace material as one-sided instead of two-sided, unless it's absolutely necessary to represent surfaces such as thick glass.

RAY TRACING: SPEEDING UP THINGS (GLOBALS)

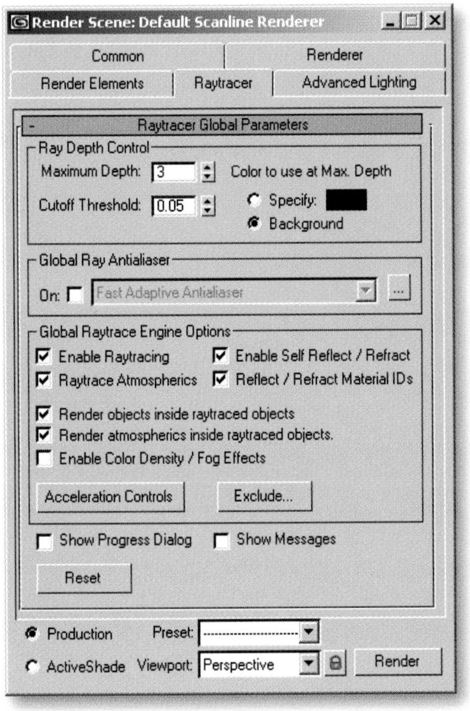

If you go to the Rendering > Raytracer Settings > Raytracer tab, you'll see that the default Ray Depth Control (Maximum Depth) is set to 9. This refers to how many times rays are "bounced" through the scene, and how many reflective objects will reflect in each another. ("Department of Redundancy Department here....") However, this is usually overkill for most basic scenes; unless you really need a "hall of mirrors" effect, try turning this setting down to 2 or 3; it will render much faster.

Note that the Raytracer Global Include/Exclude settings (in the Raytracer menu mentioned earlier) are for use with the 3ds max default scanline renderer only; changing these settings has no effect if you're using the mental ray renderer, which has its own ray tracing controls, under the mental ray rendering menu section Rendering Algorithms.

RAYTRACING: INDEX OF REFRACTION (IOR)

One of ray tracing's great strengths (besides creating physically realistic reflections for chrome surfaces and the like) is its capability to replicate the look of transparent materials. When light passes through a transparent surface, the light is typically bent or distorted. This distortion is known as refraction, and the amount of refraction is known as the *index of refraction* (IOR). The IOR results from the relative speed of light as it passes through a transparent medium relative to the medium that the viewer is in. Often, the more dense the object, the higher the IOR value will be.

Do you want to render realistic transparent objects using the 3ds max Raytrace material, but you can't find that convenient chart listing common substances and their IORs? Well, copy this down and put it in your pocket so that you can answer accurately the next time some stranger asks you, "Hey, dude, you gotta tell me—what's the IOR of table salt again?"

Material	IOR
Air	1.0003
Water	1.33
Ethyl alcohol	1.36
Glass	1.5–1.7
Lucite or Plexiglas	1.51
Crown glass	1.52
Sodium chloride (salt)	1.544
Quartz	1.544
Flint glass	1.58
Diamond	2.42

To use these values, just place them in the IOR spinner. (In the Raytrace material, the spinner is in the Raytrace Basic Parameters rollout; in the Standard material, it's in the Extended Parameters rollout.)

RENDERING: FILTERS FOR STILL IMAGES VERSUS VIDEO

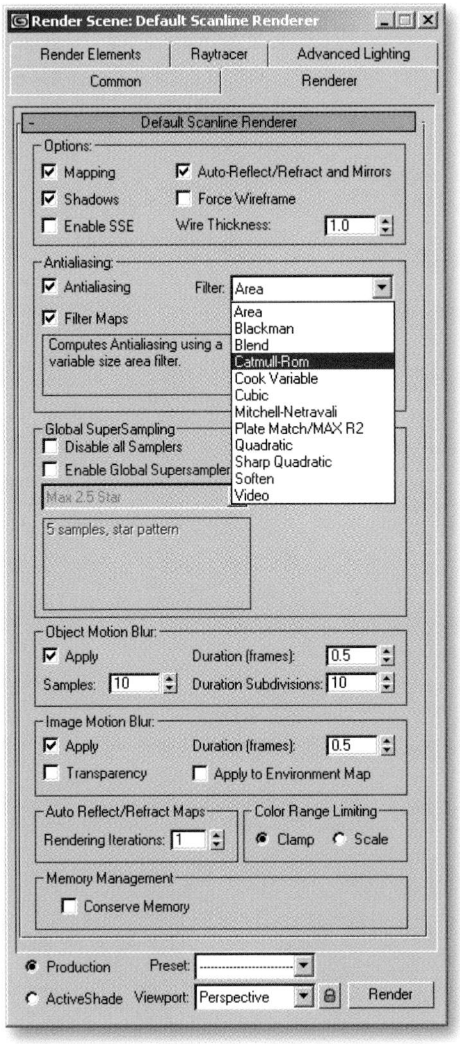

Rendering to video presents a different set of considerations than when you're simply rendering beautiful CG still images for print. If you're rendering to video, you should probably avoid using the 3ds max program's "sharpening" filters (in the default scanline renderer); those filters tend to add edge detail and might create aliasing problems on object edges, or texture scintillation (swimming) of both bitmap and procedural textures. The "sharpening" filters include Blackman, Mitchell-Netravali, and especially Catmull-Rom. They might look great for print, but be careful when using them for video; do extensive (animated) rendering tests first and preview your video work on a standard television before you commit to production rendering. (The scanline renderer video filter is designed specifically to mitigate aliasing on horizontal lines, so you should probably use that instead.)

RENDERING VIDEO: RENDER FRAMES, NOT FIELDS

Although many video production old-timers like rendering to fields, for a more realistic look, it's almost always preferable to render CG animation to individual frames and use motion blur (object, scene, or image) to smooth out fast movement in the frame. Frames are easier to deal with in paint and compositing programs (which many professionals use to tweak their results before committing to tape), and the end result looks much more like film than video. In addition, the filmic look helps to take off the inherent "CG look" of your renderings, whereas CG rendered to fields has a sharp "video" quality that many find undesirable. (However, if you want to show a CG representation of a "video" point of view in your 3D scenes, you might render those scenes in fields, and the rest in frames; the difference will be noticeable upon playback.)

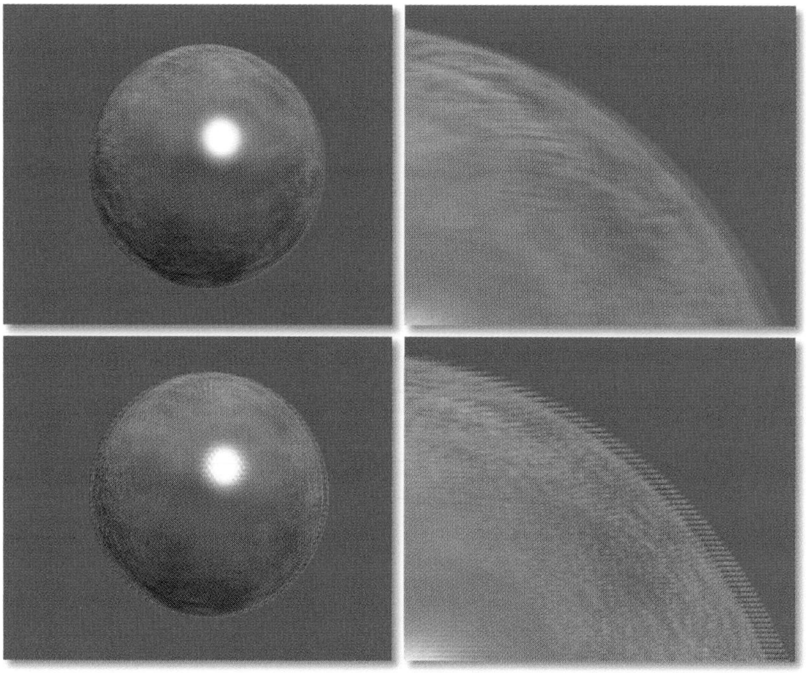

RENDERING VIDEO: MAKE SURE VIDEO COLOR CHECK IS ON

When you're rendering for video playback on a standard TV set (either NTSC or PAL), you need to make sure your renderings are color safe for video. Colors that are too bright or saturated smear or burn when broadcast on the average TV, making your work less impressive.

To address this problem, go to your Customize > Preferences > Rendering menu. Under Video Color Check, there are three options: Flag with Black (so you can do test renderings, see exactly where the offending colors are, and change them), Scale Luma (so you can bring down the brightness of the offending colors), and Scale Saturation (so you can bring down the offending Color value to acceptable limits). For peace of mind, I suggest selecting Scale Saturation by default; when you go to the Rendering > Render > Common menu, make sure that the Video Color Check box is checked under the Options area. Then, render away, safe in the knowledge that you're not going to offend your TV screen—or your viewers' eyesight.

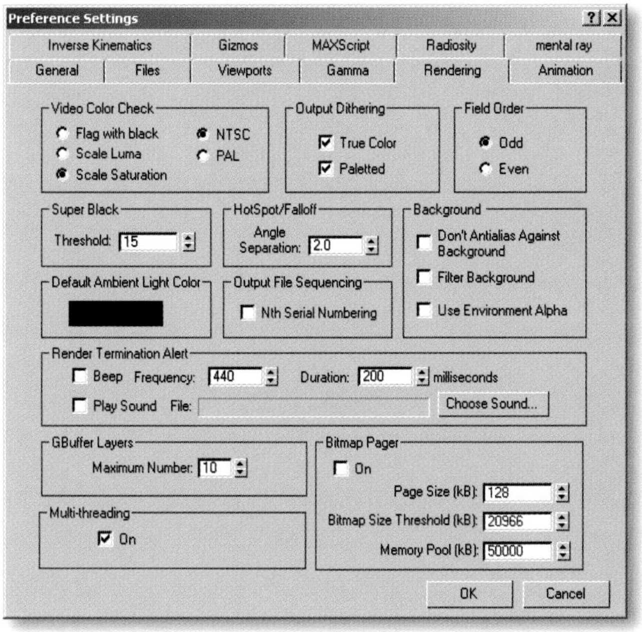

RENDERING VIDEO: CHECK YOUR GAMMA!

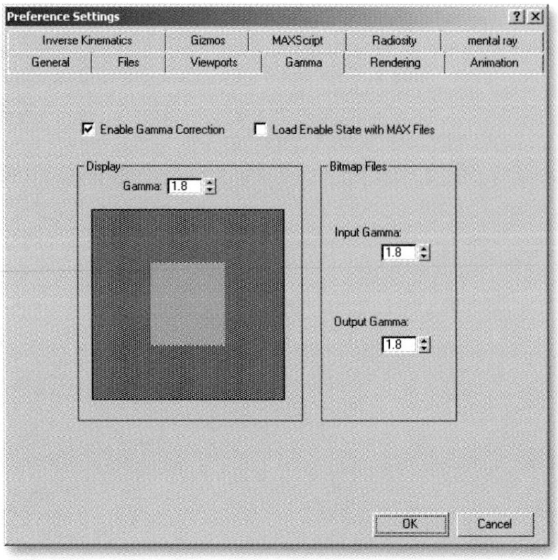

Changing your gamma settings before you render won't turn you into the Incredible Hulk, but it can improve your video renderings. By default, 3ds max has its gamma correction turned off, but if you're rendering to video, you should probably turn it on, or your renderings will appear extremely dark on broadcast video. To set this, go to Customize > Preferences > Gamma, check Enable Gamma Correction, and then adjust your display settings. For video, I usually leave my Display Gamma at 1.8, and I change my Bitmap Files' Input and Output Gamma to 1.8 as well. Note that if you have your Material Editor menu open when you change your gamma settings, clicking OK in the Preference Setting menu shows the change in luminance immediately on the sample spheres and their backgrounds in the Material Editor.

A disclaimer: Gamma correction changes your input, display, and rendered output results across the board, not only for video images. You should not make this decision lightly without understanding the algorithm and nature of the changes to your renderings. Certain bitmap formats do not store gamma values, and some 2D applications do not gamma-correct; therefore, tracking your bitmap assets when mapping or compositing in a multiuser production environment becomes a bit trickier than when gamma is off. If you're in such a production environment, instead of setting Display Gamma to 1.8, you should adjust this setting to match each artist's monitor. With gamma set correctly across all devices, your rendered output should look the same, regardless of your final medium.

RENDERING GREAT BIG, GIANT, HONKING, ENORMOUS IMAGES SUCCESSFULLY

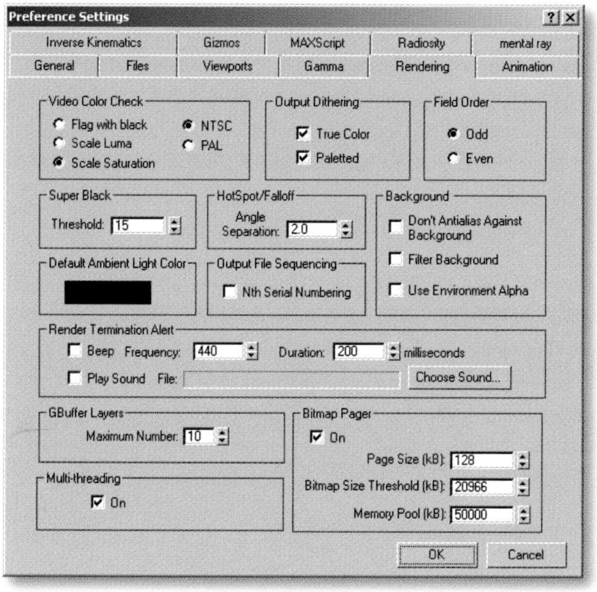

Sometimes you might be called upon to render an enormous, multi-thousand-pixel resolution image, such as for a poster, a billboard advertisement, or other large sign. Even though 3ds max can render images of up to 10,000 × 10,000 pixels, just processing an image like this can drain gigabytes of RAM right out of the fastest, best-equipped workstation. In these cases, if you simply can't get a giant image to render without your machine running out of RAM and dying a painful death, then you need some hard drive cache help. Just go to Customize > Preferences > Rendering, check the Bitmap Pager "On" box, and adjust the memory size parameters as necessary. (You'll have to close and restart 3ds max for this setting to take effect.) 3ds max pages the additional memory required to render the scene to your hard drive, and you get your "Burma Shave 3000" billboard rendered.

Also, in this same dialog: If you're running a dual-CPU system (or one of the new Intel Hyperthreaded CPUs), make sure that the Multi-Threading box is checked. You want both your CPUs to be working hard on your rendering!

DON'T RENDER MOVIES—RENDER FRAMES!

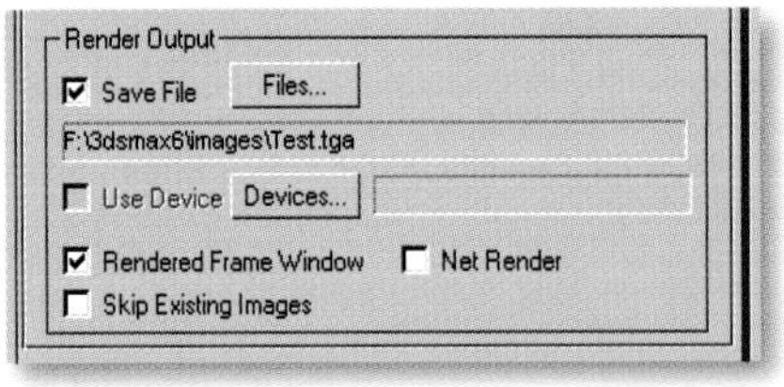

Unless you're rendering a small-format, quick-and-dirty test animation, get into the habit of always rendering image sequences (.TGA, .TIF, .PNG image formats; avoid using .JPG unless you simply don't have the hard drive space) rather than movie files (.AVI, .MOV, and so on). Image sequences have many advantages over straight movie formats.

First, unless you originally used a lossless codec for your sequence, you'll experience an ugly drop in image quality when playing back your animation. Second, if you render an enormous (that is, memory-hogging) animation, you have to load that entire file into RAM to play it, and if you have a slow graphics card, it will run like a turtle dipped in caramel. Third, it's tougher to do any kind of post-production manipulation, such as compositing, on a movie file—especially an .AVI that uses a lossy codec—than an image sequence. (You can't save an alpha channel for compositing in an .AVI file.) Fourth, if you encounter an error during the rendering, or 3ds max or your computer crashes, you'll lose only the unrendered frames, rather than your entire animation (which might get corrupted during the crash). Fifth, your mom said no, and she doesn't want to have to tell you again!

The bottom line is, don't render movies; render image sequences, and load them (or resize them as necessary, upon loading) into the RAM Player. (Choose Rendering > RAM Player from the main 3ds max toolbar.)

SPEAKING OF THE RAM PLAYER…

Now, despite all the previous warnings, what if you're just itching to create a movie file? (Maybe you want to distribute your animation over the web or on CD.) You can do this in several ways in 3ds max. You can create Windows Media Player .AVI or QuickTime .MOV files from an image sequence by loading the sequence in the RAM Player and then clicking on one of the Save Channel buttons. From there, you can choose to save to any other file type.

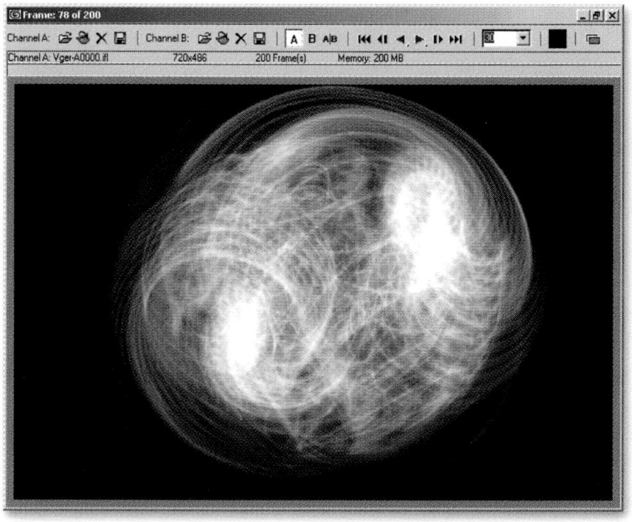

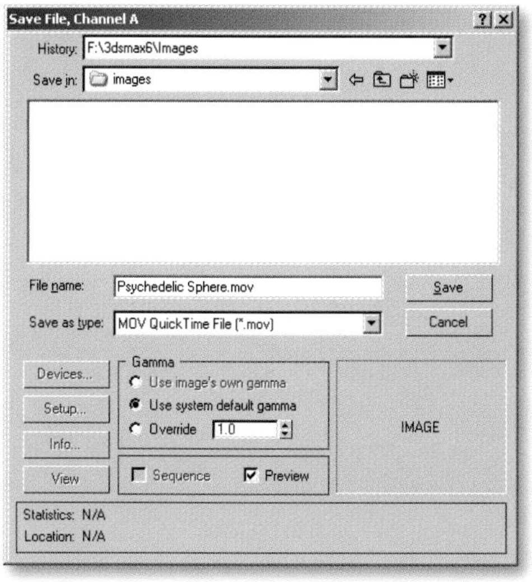

RERENDERING FROM THE ENVIRONMENT BACKGROUND

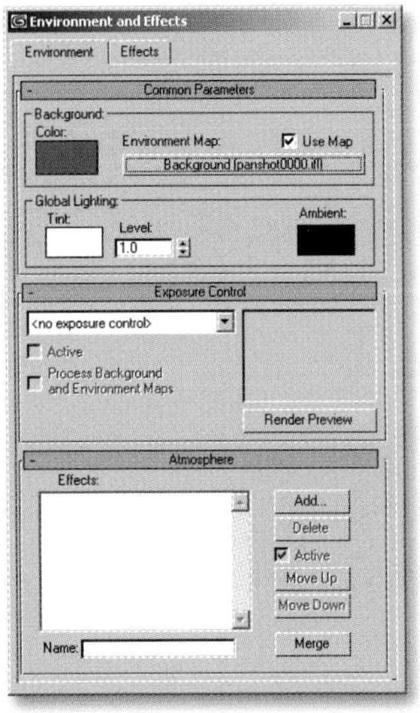

If using the RAM Player seems too easy, and you want to make your life more complicated (well, only a tiny bit), you can load an existing image sequence into the background of an empty 3ds max scene file (using Screen Coordinates, not Spherical Environment; otherwise, it will look wacky) and then render it out again from any viewport. Just choose a different format, and you're ready to go.

OKAY, SO YOU REALLY WANT TO RERENDER YOUR ANIMATION…

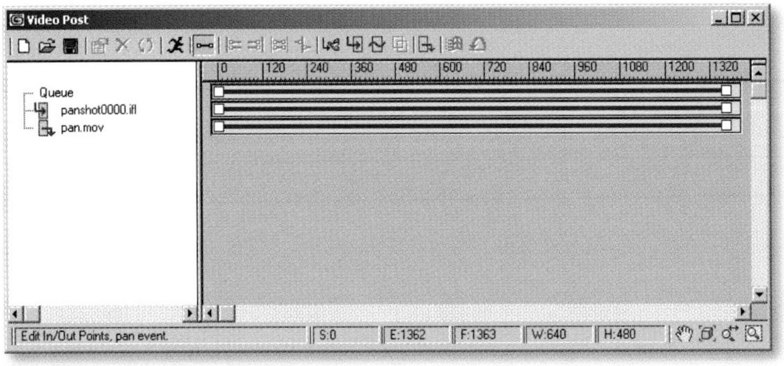

All right, continuing the previous discussions: Say that you've rendered an NTSC D-1 (video) video resolution (720 × 486) image sequence or animation, and you want to resize it for web playback (half-size, like 360 × 243).

In 3ds max, go to Render > Video Post, load the image sequence as an image input event, choose your new output size, and then add an image output event. Save the file in the format of your choosing.

Or, if you have Discreet's Combustion compositing program (or Adobe AfterEffects, or another compositing program), you can simply load the image sequence and rerender it (as done previously) to the size and format of your choosing.

IFL = IMAGE FILE LIST

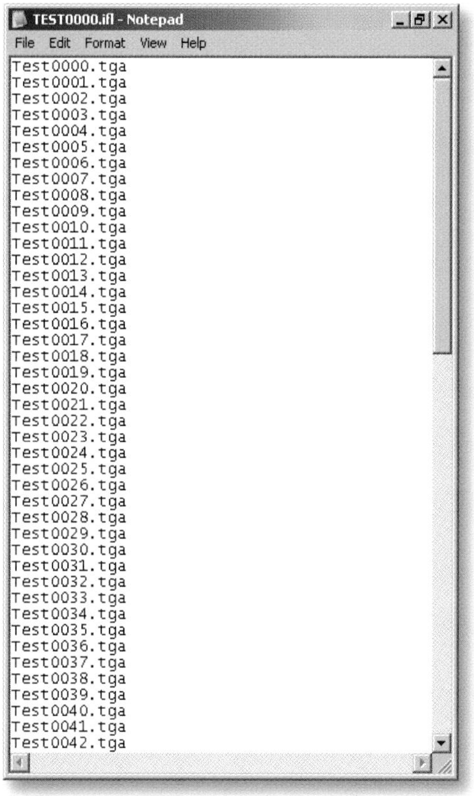

When you pick any frame of a sequentially numbered image sequence in the 3ds max program's File > View Image File, Video Post, an Environment background, the Material Editor, or elsewhere in the program, 3ds max automatically creates an image file list, or .IFL file. (You have to have the Sequence box checked in the relevant dialog; otherwise, you'll load only the individual frame you pick.) An .IFL is simply a text file that lists each frame of the sequence.

For example, if you had previously rendered a 100-frame sequence, starting on frame 0, called Test.tga, and you picked the first image to load as a sequence, then a file called something like TEST0000.ifl would be created in that same directory. If you opened this file in a text editor, it would simply be a listing like this:

Test0000.tga

Test0001.tga

Test0002.tga

Test0003.tga

... (and so on, until you get to the last frame, which follows)

Test0099.tga

(Note: You don't have to choose the first frame in the sequence; any frame in the sequence will do, as long as the Sequence check box is checked.)

YOU CAN'T CREATE .IFL FILES ON READ-ONLY MEDIA!

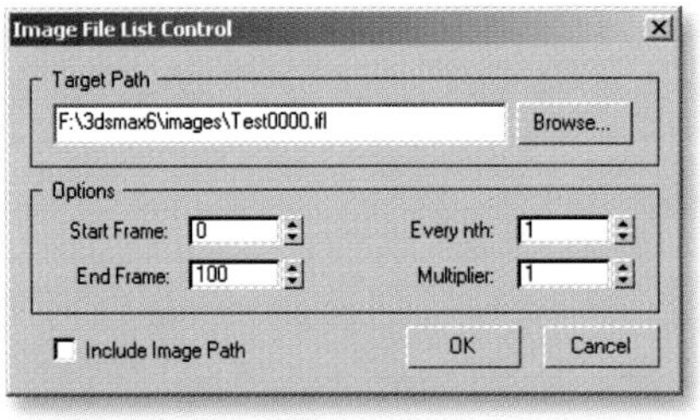

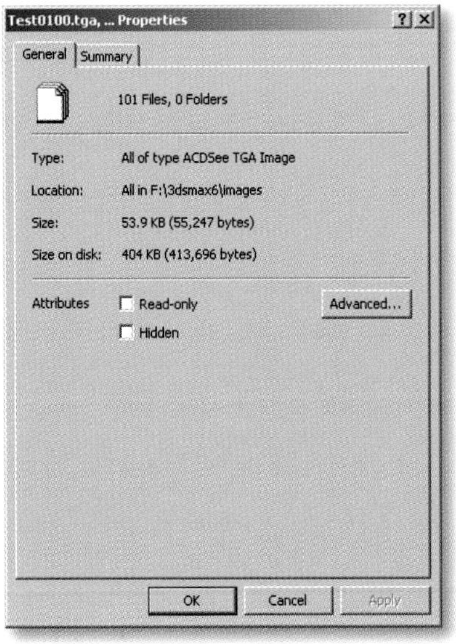

By default, the 3ds max program attempts to create .IFL files in the same directory in which you choose a frame of the image sequence. Consequently, you get an error message saying that the program can't create an .IFL file if you try to pick a frame from a CD-ROM folder, for example. (The program can't write the .IFL file to the CD.)

That's no problem. When you go to create the .IFL file, change the target path in the Image File List Control menu to a local hard drive path, and make sure that you check the Include Image Path box as well.

If you have sufficient hard drive space, you can also just copy the image sequence from the CD-ROM to a hard drive folder, and then create the .IFL file there. (Note: If you want to resave or overwrite the copied images after they're on your hard drive, you need to change their properties so that they're not still set to read-only. Just go into Windows Explorer, select all the files you need to modify, right-click and select Properties, and uncheck the Read-Only box.)

MANIPULATING IMAGE SEQUENCES USING .IFLS

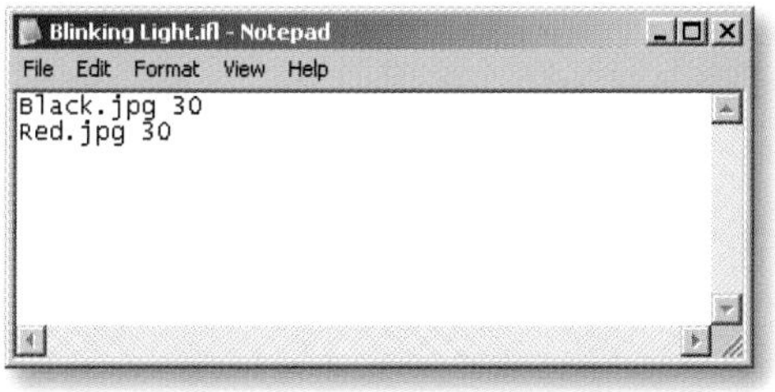

Image sequences and .IFL files are useful for many things in 3ds max: prerendered animated backgrounds, animated bitmap textures, and so on. They're also useful for allowing you to "time" events in a prerendered image sequence to something else happening in your scene.

For example, you could create a "blinking light" material that consists of, say, 30 frames of a black bitmap and 30 frames of a red bitmap, which would cycle on and off during the course of your animation. However, you could also simply use one frame each of black and red bitmaps by having your .IFL file include the duration (in frames) of each bitmap in the sequence, like this:

Black.jpg 30

Red.jpg 30

Placing the number 30 after the name of the bitmaps holds each bitmap for that number of frames in the sequence.

CREATE NESTED .IFL FILES

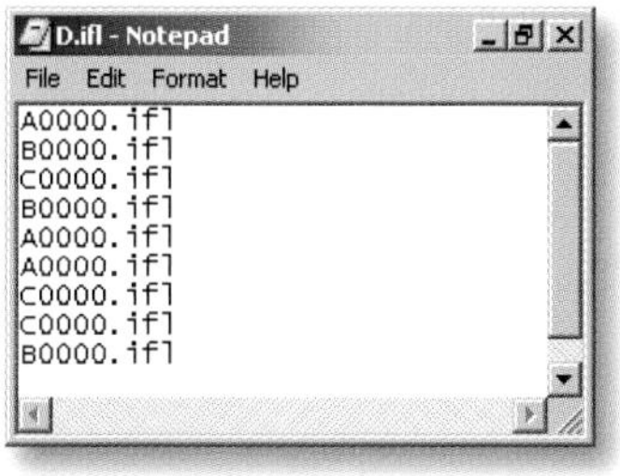

An .IFL file doesn't just have to be lists of bitmaps; it can also contain other .IFL files, for complex effects. For example, if you have multiple .IFL files for .JPG bitmap sequences A0000, B0000, and C0000, you don't have to have one giant .IFL file listing every frame of these sequences. If you've already created the individual A0000.ifl, B0000.ifl and C0000.ifl files, you could "gang" these together by creating a new .IFL (called D.ifl or whatever you want) that reads as follows:

A0000.ifl

B0000.ifl

C0000.ifl

This would then play each 100-frame sequence in turn. You could also randomize the order of nested .IFL files within the larger .IFL file, if necessary for your sequence.

A CHICKEN AND EGG PROBLEM: HOW DO YOU SET UP AN ANIMATED BACKGROUND FOR A SCENE IF YOU HAVEN'T RENDERED THE BACKGROUND YET?

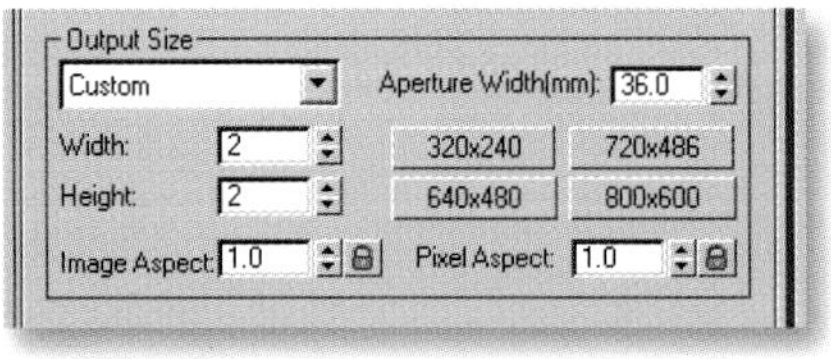

Here's a wacky scenario: Sometimes you might want to do a network rendering of several sequences in order, in which Scene A renders a .TGA bitmap sequence that you want (ultimately) loaded as an Environment background for the following Scene B. However, how do you load (or create) an .IFL list of an image sequence that you haven't rendered yet?

Well, one thing you could do is load an existing .IFL file (that has an equal or greater number of rendered frames as the new sequence you want to render) in a text editor such as Notepad or WordPad. Then just do a search and replace on the words/letters you need to replace with the new words/letters (to correspond with the Scene A rendered frame filenames), and resave the file with a different filename. You'll also have to make sure the frame count equals the frame count of your current sequences.

Here's a fast and dirty way to create the A bitmap sequence and its associated .IFL for the background of Scene B. First, reset 3ds max to an empty scene, set the frame count to be the exact amount as your A animation sequence, set your render resolution at 2 × 2 pixels (I'm not joking), and then render a series of blank (black) frames with the A sequence filename. The incredibly tiny frame size makes this black "proxy" sequence render incredibly fast. When you're finished, load Scene B, and load this proxy bitmap sequence as the background (which creates a properly named .IFL). Now, resave the Scene B file, and then load Scene A and render the "good," final A Background bitmap sequence, overwriting the tiny 2 × 2 pixel files you just rendered. If you're doing network rendering, you can then load Scene B and queue it up *after* Scene A; when Scene B renders, it renders with the new A Bitmap Environment background.

COULD YOU MAKE THINGS MORE COMPLICATED, PLEASE? (WHAT ABOUT USING A COMPOSITING PROGRAM?)

Yes, the previous example was pretty verbose and complicated for such a simple trick. And yes, most 3D professionals would say that ultimately you're probably better off rendering all your sequences as separate passes (with alpha channels) and then compositing them with a program such as Discreet's Combustion.

However, not all 3ds max artists can afford a full-blown compositing program (although Chapter 10, "Aftermarket Accessories," offers some inexpensive substitutes). Consequently, tricks such as those listed previously are necessary if you want to break down your scenes into more easily managed layers and use 3ds max as your final compositor. Just remember: You need to make sure you have your sequences and their respective (proxy) backgrounds set up properly in your network rendering before you commit it; otherwise, you'll get a "Missing External Files" warning, and that sequence will fail.

COMPOSITING USING VIDEO POST

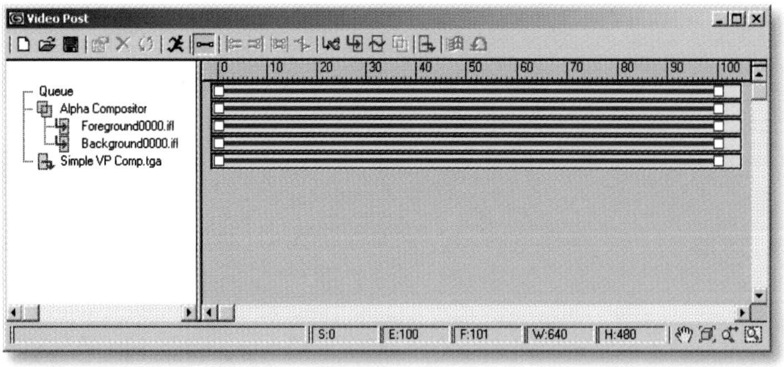

Okay, even if you don't have the cash for a commercial compositing program, you can still do simple alpha composites using the venerable 3ds max Video Post feature. (Discreet occasionally muses about removing this long-neglected feature from the program, yet there are still battle-hardened 3ds max veterans, as well as newbies, who scream "No! Over my dead body!")

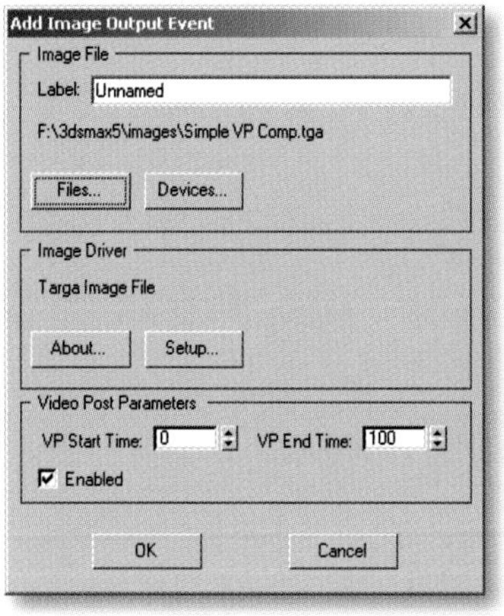

Here's how to do a simple alpha composite in Video Post: First, make sure you have your rendered elements (such as background and foreground elements) rendered with proper alpha channels. (You should have rendered them as .TGA, .TIF, .PNG, .RPF, or .RLA files.) Although the background images don't have to have an alpha channel, foreground elements most definitely *do*. Go to Rendering/Video Post, and click the Add Image Input Event button. Click the Files button, and then browse to the appropriate directory and load your background image sequence first. Then repeat the process with the foreground element. (Sorry. You can do only two elements at once with this technique.) When you have both elements loaded in the Video Post queue, Ctrl-click on each element to select both of them, and then click on the (now active) Add Image Layer Event button. Choose Alpha Compositor from the menu, click the Add Image Output Event button, set your final filename to the appropriate composite name, set your render resolution parameters, and then render. (Note that nothing can be selected in the queue if you want to choose the output event.) If you want to layer more elements on top of this composite, just repeat the process, and make sure you render your composite to an image format with an alpha channel, as above.

RENDERING WITH SCANLINE MOTION BLUR: MULTI-PASS AND IMAGE

Motion blur on fast-moving 3D objects, as well as depth of field (DOF), help increase the realism of your 3D renderings and give a sense of scale, if used appropriately. Image motion blur simply "smears" a fast-moving object's motion across the frame. Image motion blur is fast, but it works only on linear motion, so it's not effective for things like rotating propellers and fan blades. Object motion blur samples an object's motion through the frame, and then composites multiple "slices" of the object on a per-frame basis.

The 3ds max Camera Multi-Pass motion blur (set in the Modify panel of a selected camera) simulates what a real-world camera does and gives the best results if you're using the 3ds max scanline renderer. In the real world, a camera's shutter is open for a period of time, information at an infinite number of intervals is exposed onto your film, the shutter closes, and another photo is taken. Consequently, everything in your photo gets blurred, including shadows, hair, and other elements that tend to pose complex rendering problems in the 3D world. The disadvantage to this technique when done in the 3D realm is speed; the camera effectively has to do multiple renderings of a single frame, with a moving object's motion "sampled" during the course of the frame.

There are workarounds for this technique, however. If you don't mind compositing your scene elements, then render your scene in layers (as mentioned earlier), and use Multi-Pass motion blur just on the spinning objects in that element. Then use (fast) image motion blur on other object layers.

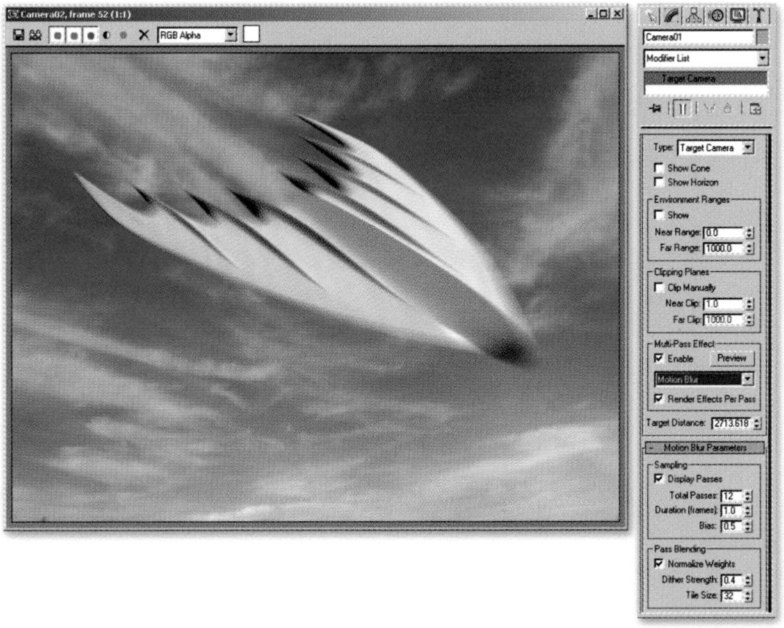

RENDERING WITH SCANLINE: MIX IMAGE AND MULTI-PASS MOTION BLUR

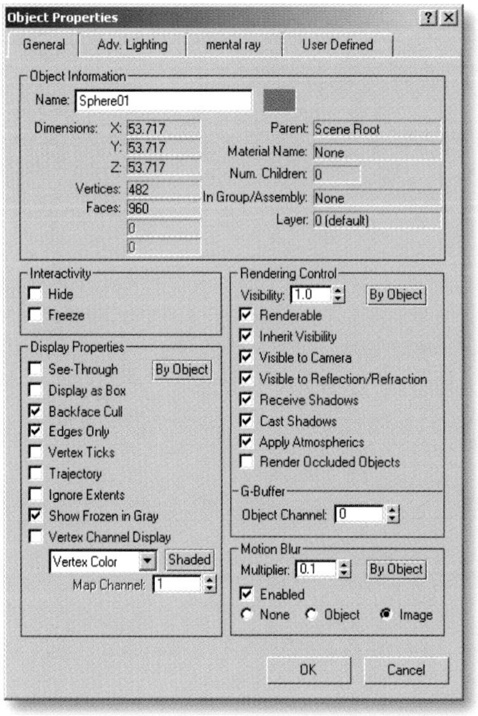

If you really want to improve your 3ds max scanline motion blur effect (and don't mind a hit on rendering time), then look into combining the different types of motion blur. You can combine Image and Camera Multi-Pass motion blur in the same render pass.

For example, if you want the camera shutter to be open for 0.5 (frames), set the Camera Motion Blur Parameters Duration to 0.5, and then set your desired object(s) Properties > Image Motion Blur Multiplier to 0.1. This gives you five sub-frames of accurate camera (or scene) motion blur, and then the Object Image motion blur with blur between those sub-frames.

RENDERING IMAGES FOR PRINT: TEACH THOSE PRINT FOLKS A LESSON (OR TWO…)

It never fails—I'll have someone in the print industry want me to supply him with a 3D rendered image for a magazine or a poster, and when I ask, "What resolution do you want it?" he responds, "Make it 300 DPI." If this happens to you, first, resist the urge to smack the person. Second, explain that DPI—dots per inch—is simply a way of subdividing (measuring) a fixed, final value (your 3D rendering), *not* the actual measurement itself. (It's like asking, "How far is it from here to the next town?" and the person responds, "55 miles per hour.") Arrghhh!

Instead, tell the client that you need to know both the DPI *and* the final print size. For instance, if that person is running an image that's going to be 8 inches × 9 inches, at 300 DPI, then (in general) you should render your 3D graphic at a figure of 1 pixel equals 1 dot. Multiply 300 DPI by this final print size, and you'll get a rendered image that's 2400 × 2700 pixels. That's what you should render and deliver to the client (along with your invoice asking for immediate payment).

RENDERING IMAGES FOR PRINT: OH YEAH, ANOTHER THING…

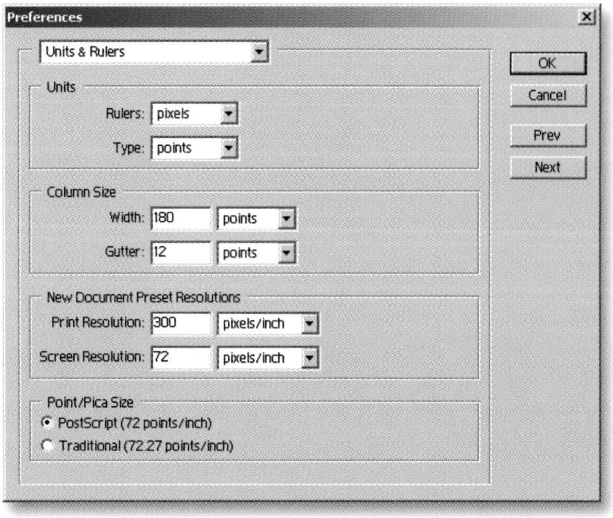

Adobe Photoshop, the *de facto* image-editing standard for all these print folks (and a lot of 3D artists as well) defaults to assigning a figure of 72 DPI (screen resolution) to any image it loads. This causes a lot of print people immediate heart attacks when they load your 3D image and discover it's not "300 DPI," and then they call you up saying, "It's the wrong size!"

Again, as in the previous tip, resist the urge to smack them, take a deep breath, and explain that they can change their screen DPI setting in Photoshop (release 7.x) to whatever their little heart desires by going to Edit > Preferences > Units & Rulers, and making sure that Screen Resolution is the same as Print Resolution. (In Photoshop 7.x, the default new document preset resolutions are 300 pixels/inch for print, and 72 pixels/inch for screen.)

"THOSE PRINT PEOPLE"—MAKE IT EASIER ON THEM WITH 3DS MAX 6

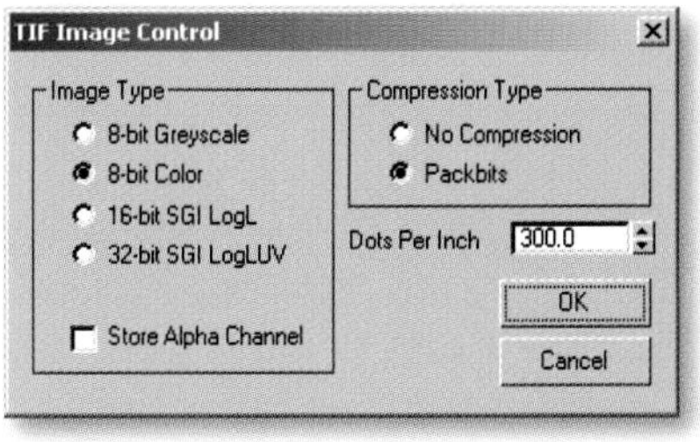

I'm going to beat this dead horse one more time: Most final render image formats that 3D artists use don't have a thing to do with DPI; they're just output to whatever pixel resolution you set them at (such as 720 × 486 for a standard NTSC video rendering).

However, that's not true of .TIF (Tagged Image File Format, or .TIFF for the Macintosh crowd) files; you can embed the actual DPI information in them, which will delight "those print people" mentioned earlier. In 3ds max 6, when you're rendering images for print, make sure a.) You render them as .TIF files, and b.) When you set the .TIF preferences, set the dots per inch to whatever the print clients want. Doing so embeds the correct DPI information in the rendering and warm the cockles, ventricles, and other parts of their hearts.

THE PRINT SIZE WIZARD (ENOUGH WITH THE PRINTING STUFF ALREADY!)

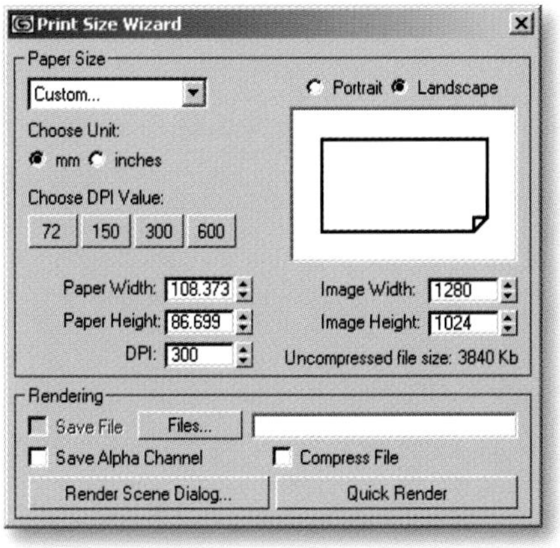

Okay, here's one final thought about outputting your 3D renders to print. 3ds max 6 comes with a dynamite new feature: the Print Size Wizard. Go to Rendering > Print Size Wizard, and a cute little dialog appears. Here, you can dial just about any render-to-print settings you want. Set your output to portrait or landscape, choose the unit measurements (millimeters or inches), choose DPI values, paper width and height, and image size. Simple, yes?

MENTAL RAY IS IN THE BUILDING!

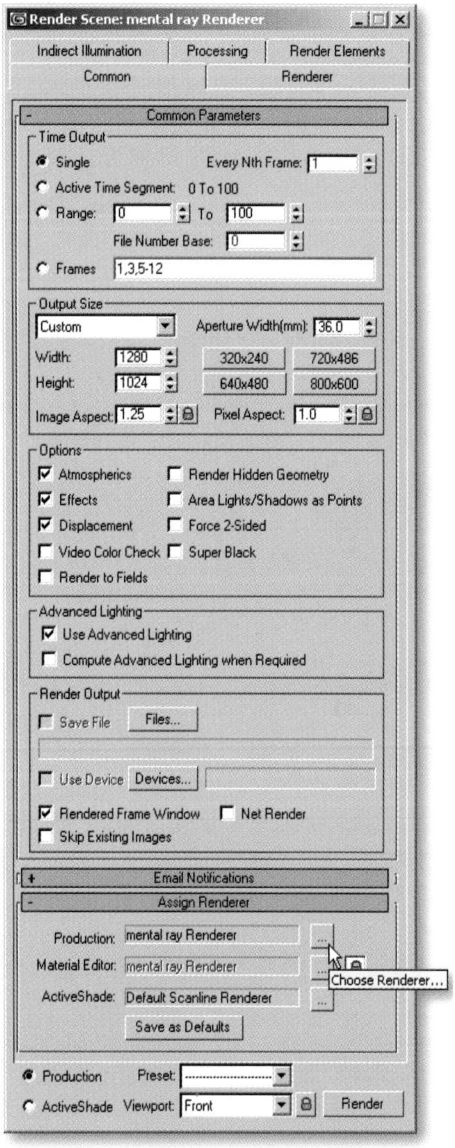

As of the release of 3ds max 6, a node-locked (single PC) version of mental images' acclaimed mental ray 3.2 renderer is included as an alternate to the 3ds max scanline renderer. (Chapter 3, "Waxing the Finish: Materials Tips," mentions this as well, but in case you're skipping around in this book, here you go!) Mental ray is noted for the quality of its global illumination and ray tracing. It's been used by a number of large special effects houses on cinematic visual effects for such films as *The City of Lost Children*, *Fight Club*, and *Star Wars Episode II: Attack of the Clones*.

To choose mental ray as your production renderer, just go to Rendering > Render > Common, and under the Assign Renderer section of the rollout, click the Choose Renderer button and select the mental ray renderer. Note that mental ray works with all core 3ds max materials, but it also includes its own material and shading types, which you can pick from the 3ds max 6 Material Editor.

MENTAL RAY IS ON THE COUCH!

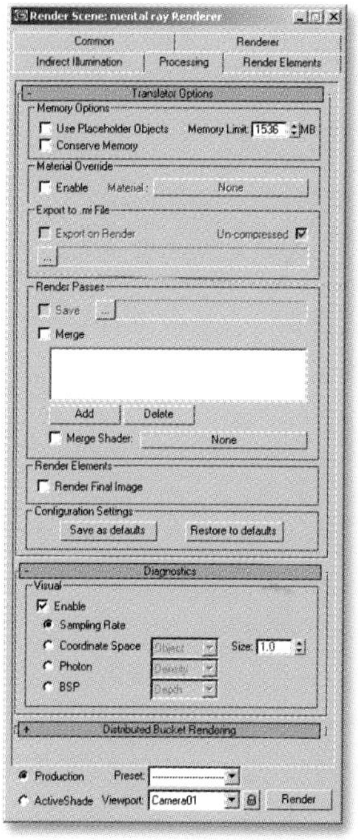

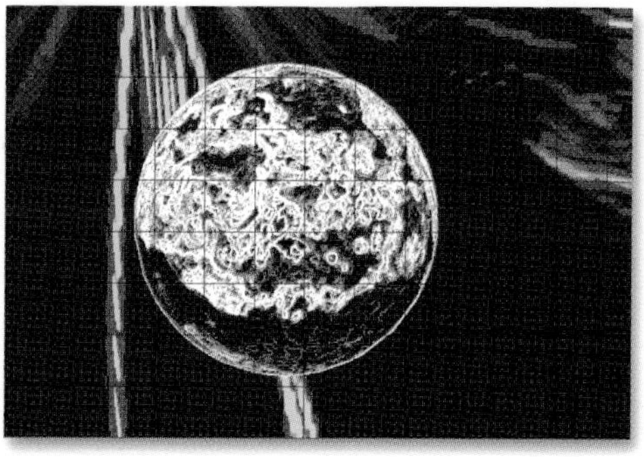

Do you get tired of tweaking your mental ray settings over and over again but not getting exactly the results you're looking for? You can help diagnose your problems by using the aptly named Diagnostics rollout. Just pick mental ray as your production renderer (see the previous tip); then, in the Render menu, click the Processing tab and under Diagnostics: Visual, check the Enable box.

Turning on Diagnostics: Visual gives you an invaluable tool to optimize and tweak your render. You can choose to diagnose your pixel sampling rate (for antialiasing problems), coordinate space, photon emission, or the BSP (Binary Space Partitioning) Tree—all the areas in which your rendering times can be short and sweet or be stretched out until the heat death of the universe.

As an example, to adjust your photon settings, open your scene, make sure you have mental ray as your assigned renderer, and then go to Rendering > Render > Indirect Illumination and make sure you have your photon generators set. (Check the Global Illumination Enable box.) Go to the Processing tab, and under the Diagnostics section, enable Visual and set it to Photon. Now when you render, you'll see a "false color" representation of your scene, showing areas with dense photons as red, and areas that are lacking photons as blue. You can then use this visual guide to tweak your photon count and photon radius until your diagnostic render shows a smoother range of color, with red in the most important areas of your scene. When you're ready to do your final render, turn off Diagnostics: Visual, and you're all set!

USE MENTAL RAY'S IMAGE SAMPLING WISELY

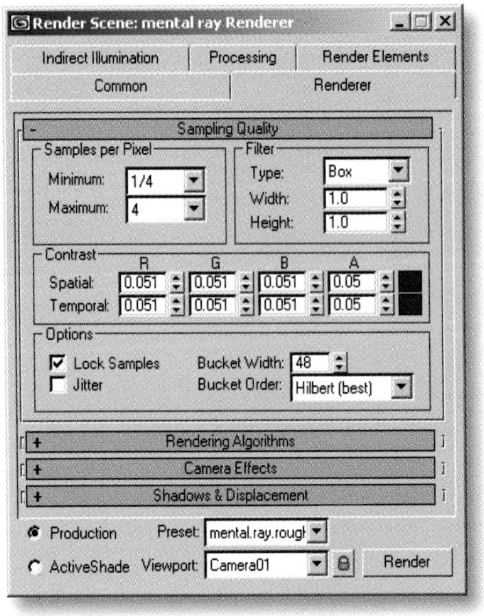

Scene sampling for antialiasing can be a complicated task for any renderer, even a sophisticated engine such as mental ray. If you're just doing preview renderings (to test your lighting, for example), you can speed up your workflow considerably by mental ray sampling only what you really need.

If you're simply working on your overall scene composition and lighting, leaving the mental ray Samples per Pixel Minimum/Maximum values at their defaults costs you unnecessary time. The default values (Minimum 1/4, Maximum 4) mean that mental ray will take 4 samples per 1 pixel in areas with many details, or 1 sample per 4 pixels in areas with fewer details.

If you set both Minimum and Maximum Samples per Pixel to 1/64, mental ray is forced to only take 1 sample for each "bucket" of 64 pixels. This creates a coarse rendering, but it renders at incredible speed and might be just what you need to get your overall look correct before you commit to production-level sampling settings. Just save this setup as Render Preset (on the Rendering > Renderer tab, at the bottom of the dialog box). Call it "Rough Preview" and keep it handy for future use.

IN MENTAL RAY, CONTRAST CAN SAVE YOUR DAY!

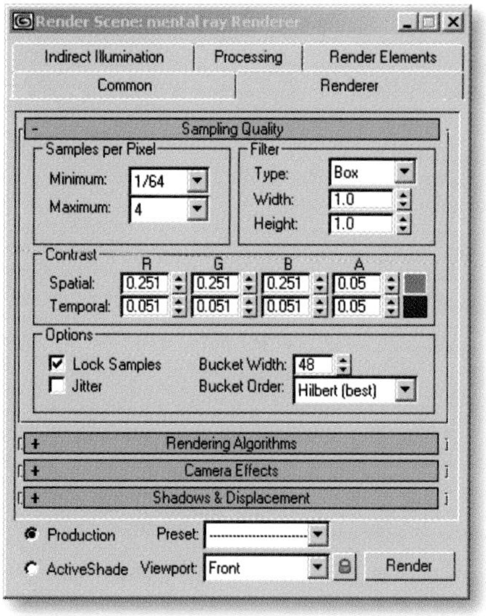

Have you tweaked your mental ray pixel sampling and noticed that you still seem to lose important details, even with a high Maximum Sampling per Pixel setting? You notice that you're losing fine details (such as wispy cables or antennas in an architectural rendering), but at the same time, your render times seem to be going through the roof—and you don't want either of those to happen!

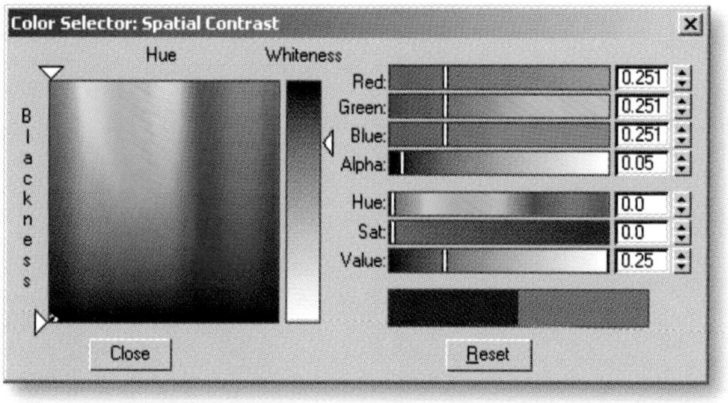

You can fix this and render even highly detailed scenes without too much hassle by memorizing two words: Contrast settings. (Actually, you shouldn't just memorize them, you should use them.) The Contrast settings are located on the mental ray Renderer > Renderer tab, right below the Samples per Pixel values, and their defaults are set 0.05. Contrast settings determine how to "weight" the Samples per Pixel values—toward the Minimum or the Maximum values you have set. If your fine scene details get chewed away in the rendering, it's usually not because your Maximum sampling rate is too low, but because your Contrast settings are too low.

To fix this, keep your existing Samples per Pixel Min/Max values within reasonable limits. (There's no need to go above Minimum 1/64, Maximum 4 for very detailed scenes; for most scenes, even Minimum 1/16, Maximum 1 should work fine with finals.) However, if your scene details show rendering artifacts with these settings, increase your Contrast values slowly, working toward a lighter gray. This triggers the Maximum Sampling values earlier and should fill out those fine details. (Note: The Contrast Spatial settings are primarily for still renderings; adjust the Temporal settings if you need to tweak fine details during an animation.)

HIDDEN LINE RENDERING: RENDER TO VECTORS IN MENTAL RAY

So, your client wants her 3D model rendered as a hidden-line rendering (in Vector format, no less) for print reproduction, or for the web? (And she wants it today!) No problem. Just go to mental ray's Rendering > Render > Renderer menu, and under Camera Effects, enable the Contours switch. (Note that you'll have to reassign your scene materials using one of mental ray's Contour shaders, but that shouldn't be a big deal. Just adjust your line width and color settings until you get the effect you want.)

Then, in the Camera Effects rollout, click on the Shader button in the Contour Output slot and choose Contour PS as the new shader. Click-drag this slot into an unused sample slot in your Material Editor, and make it an instance. In the Material Editor, you will now be able to adjust your output settings, and then you can just type in your final render path for the vector output, with the Adobe Illustrator .EPS format as the suffix (for example, C:\3dsmax6\images\test.eps). Click on Render again, and you'll produce an .EPS vector file that you can open in Adobe Illustrator or Macromedia Flash without problems. (Note: You might not see rendered results in your 3ds max Rendered Frame window, but you can load the final .EPS file into a program such as Adobe Illustrator or Photoshop, and adjust it there.)

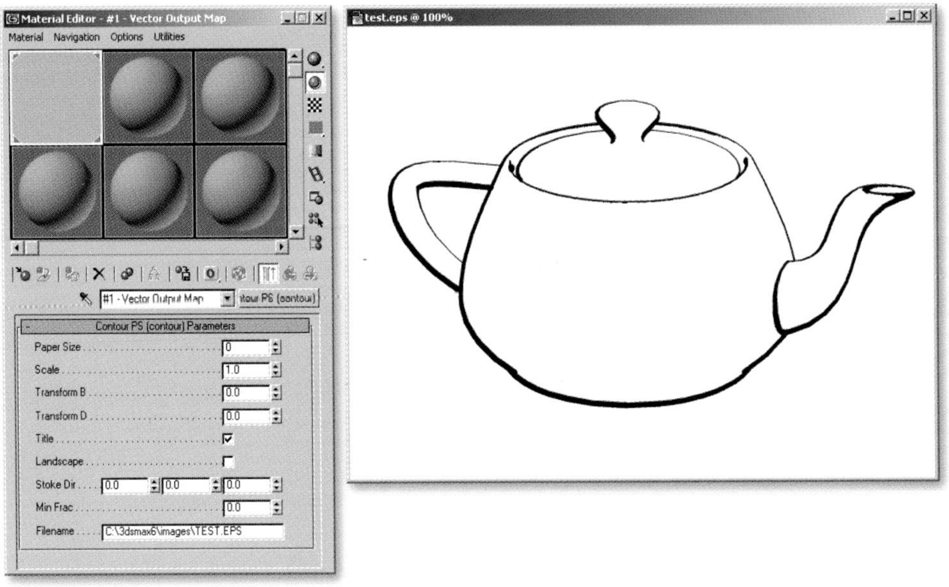

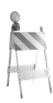

TRIM YOUR (BSP) TREE IN MENTAL RAY

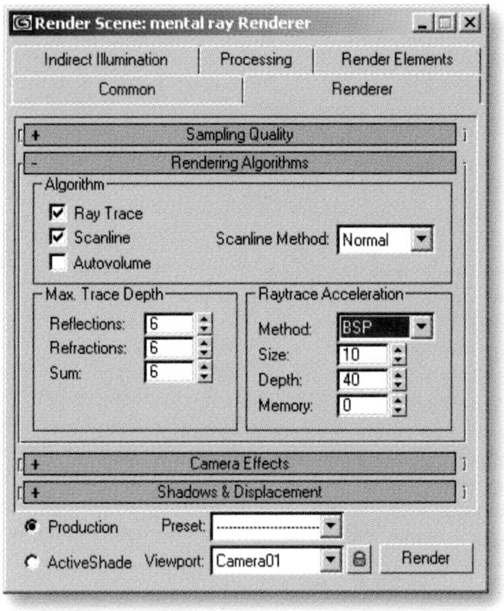

In mental ray's Rendering > Render > Renderer tab, look at the Rendering Algorithms section. Under Raytrace Acceleration: Method, there's a drop-down menu where the default is set to BSP. A BSP (binary space partition) "tree" basically is a method of categorizing your whole scene with the help of an imaginary sub-divided bounding box encompassing your scene. This is necessary because it helps mental ray cast rays much faster in this structure than without.

The subdivision cells of this bounding box are called voxels, and the creation of those is what you control with the two settings Size and Depth. Size is the number of cells along one side, so the default would divide your whole scene into a maximum of 10 × 10 × 10 cells. Depth is the parameter that tells mental ray how many subdivisions of one cell should be allowed. The default of 40 allows a maximum of 40 subdivisions in voxels, with a lot of faces.

That's the theory. In practice, you're looking for a good balance between the creation of your BSP tree (the "idle" time before the actual render starts, when the grid is built and subdivided) and the render time of your image. Increased BSP values can cause a long scene render preparation time but result in a lightning-fast render; conversely, decreased settings result in the preparation/render time equation being reversed. The time difference might not be seconds; it might be much longer.

Depending on the complexity of your scene, pay attention to your BSP settings and experiment with different Size and Depth subdivision values. Due to the nature of the default "bounding box" effect, you might be better off tweaking these settings from scene to scene until you get the results you want (or at least, the results that you can live with).

MENTAL RAY PREFERENCES: PLEASE LEAVE ME A MESSAGE

You can both display and save your 3ds max 6 mental ray rendering information (in an exhaustively verbose format) by going to Customize > Preferences, clicking on the Mental Ray tab, and then checking pretty much every box in that menu. (Save your .LOG file to your 3ds max 6 \scenes folder and call it something like mr-renders.log.) Then go to Rendering and click on the mental ray Message Window item. You'll get a window that displays a whole heap of rendering information (useful for diagnosing potential problems) when you then render with mental ray.

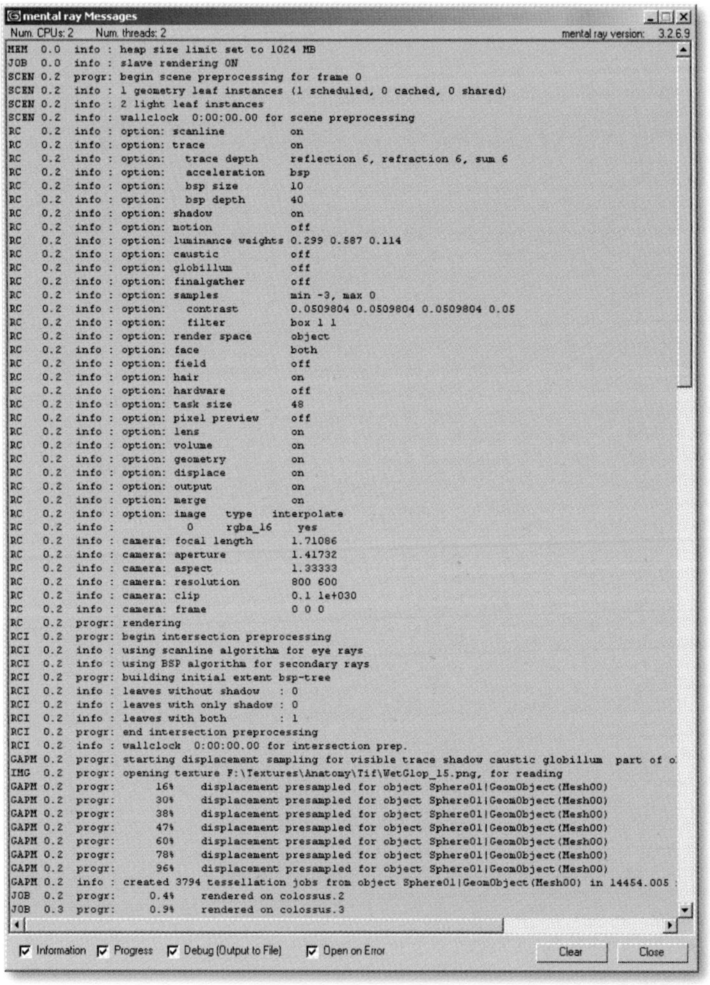

mental ray Messages
Num. CPUs: 2 Num. threads: 2
mental ray version: 3.2.6.9
MEM 0.0 info : heap size limit set to 1024 MB
JOB 0.0 info : slave rendering ON
SCEN 0.2 progr: begin scene preprocessing for frame 0
SCEN 0.2 info : 1 geometry leaf instances (1 scheduled, 0 cached, 0 shared)
SCEN 0.2 info : 2 light leaf instances
SCEN 0.2 info : wallclock 0:00:00.00 for scene preprocessing
RC 0.2 info : option: scanline on
RC 0.2 info : option: trace on
RC 0.2 info : option: trace depth reflection 6, refraction 6, sum 6
RC 0.2 info : option: acceleration bsp
RC 0.2 info : option: bsp size 10
RC 0.2 info : option: bsp depth 40
RC 0.2 info : option: shadow on
RC 0.2 info : option: motion off
RC 0.2 info : option: luminance weights 0.299 0.587 0.114
RC 0.2 info : option: caustic off
RC 0.2 info : option: globillum off
RC 0.2 info : option: finalgather off
RC 0.2 info : option: samples min -3, max 0
RC 0.2 info : option: contrast 0.0509804 0.0509804 0.0509804 0.05
RC 0.2 info : option: filter box 1 1
RC 0.2 info : option: render space object
RC 0.2 info : option: face both
RC 0.2 info : option: field off
RC 0.2 info : option: hair on
RC 0.2 info : option: hardware off
RC 0.2 info : option: task size 48
RC 0.2 info : option: pixel preview off
RC 0.2 info : option: lens on
RC 0.2 info : option: volume on
RC 0.2 info : option: geometry on
RC 0.2 info : option: displace on
RC 0.2 info : option: output on
RC 0.2 info : option: merge on
RC 0.2 info : option: image type interpolate
RC 0.2 info : 0 rgba_16 yes
RC 0.2 info : camera: focal length 1.71086
RC 0.2 info : camera: aperture 1.41732
RC 0.2 info : camera: aspect 1.33333
RC 0.2 info : camera: resolution 800 600
RC 0.2 info : camera: clip 0.1 1e+030
RC 0.2 info : camera: frame 0 0 0
RC 0.2 progr: rendering
RCI 0.2 progr: begin intersection preprocessing
RCI 0.2 info : using scanline algorithm for eye rays
RCI 0.2 info : using BSP algorithm for secondary rays
RCI 0.2 progr: building initial extent bsp-tree
RCI 0.2 info : leaves without shadow : 0
RCI 0.2 info : leaves with only shadow : 0
RCI 0.2 info : leaves with both : 1
RCI 0.2 progr: end intersection preprocessing
RCI 0.2 info : wallclock 0:00:00.00 for intersection prep.
GAPM 0.2 progr: starting displacement sampling for visible trace shadow caustic globillum part of o
IMG 0.2 progr: opening texture F:\Textures\Anatomy\Tif\WetGlop_15.png, for reading
GAPM 0.2 progr: 16% displacement presampled for object Sphere01|GeomObject(Mesh00)
GAPM 0.2 progr: 30% displacement presampled for object Sphere01|GeomObject(Mesh00)
GAPM 0.2 progr: 38% displacement presampled for object Sphere01|GeomObject(Mesh00)
GAPM 0.2 progr: 47% displacement presampled for object Sphere01|GeomObject(Mesh00)
GAPM 0.2 progr: 60% displacement presampled for object Sphere01|GeomObject(Mesh00)
GAPM 0.2 progr: 78% displacement presampled for object Sphere01|GeomObject(Mesh00)
GAPM 0.2 progr: 96% displacement presampled for object Sphere01|GeomObject(Mesh00)
GAPM 0.2 info : created 3794 tessellation jobs from object Sphere01|GeomObject(Mesh00) in 14454.005
JOB 0.2 progr: 0.4% rendered on colossus.2
JOB 0.3 progr: 0.9% rendered on colossus.3
Information
Progress
Debug (Output to File)
Open on Error
Clear
Close

RENDERING AESTHETICS: OUTER SPACE SCENES

Although multiple combinations of lights (key light, fill light, and "kickers," or edge lights) might work in most 3D scenes, sometimes harsh, unidirectional light (which 3D programs excel at creating) is actually the aesthetic you want. Moody, film noir-ish lighting is one, but the most common unidirectional lighting scheme for 3D artists/science fiction fans (let's face it, there's a lot of overlap there) is when you're rendering outer space scenes. Generally, you'll light a spacecraft model with a single spot or directional light, and little or no fill light, unless it's passing by a planet, an illuminated space station, or a nebula. For increased realism, you could use a colorful nebula background in your scene as the rationale for tinted fill light on your spacecraft models. Other details, such as self-illuminated windows and "practical" lights on the model (making it look as if it has beacons illuminating its surface, like the refitted Enterprise from *Star Trek: The Motion Picture*), increase the realism and scale of your scene.

RENDERING AESTHETICS: UNDERWATER SCENES

To render realistic underwater scenes, you should duplicate the murkiness and light qualities that are inherent in the environment. To mimic these atmospheric conditions, go to Rendering > Environment > Atmosphere, and add fog, volume fog, or volume light to your scene. You should determine the scale of your scene (are you in the ocean, or just in a swimming pool?), adjust your camera's Environment Ranges settings, and then your Fog settings to match the amount of murkiness you need. To create the illusion of depth drop-off in the ocean, apply a Gradient Environment Color Map (such as light cyan to darker blue to navy or black) to tint the fog as well.

RENDERING AESTHETICS: DISTANT LANDSCAPES

For more realistic outdoor scenes, especially if you're seeing a distant horizon, you should always add a slight amount of atmospheric haze (Rendering > Environment > Atmosphere > Add > Fog). If you look at a distant mountain range (or if you don't have one right outside your window, just grab a travel magazine or pretend), you'll notice how colors become muted and washed out with distance. You can use just a slight amount of atmospheric fog (it depends on the scale of your scene), and the colors will determine the clarity or quality of your "atmosphere." For clear outdoor settings, using a slight bit of white fog is desirable; for sunset or urban settings (where the air might be more polluted), a slight yellowish or reddish cast makes your horizons look better.

Finally, experiment with adding a Gradient Environment Color Map to your fog so that your skies are more realistic. Make your skies darker at the top and lighter on the horizon, as if the sun is rising or setting.

RENDERING AESTHETICS: STILL LIFE AND MACROPHOTOGRAPHY

The smaller the scale of your scene, the more you should use a shallow depth of field (DOF). In real-world photography, a tiny camera tends to have a correspondingly small ability to capture "distant" objects in a scene—and if you're simulating microphotography, "distant" might be only a fraction of an inch away. The more objects in your scene go in and out of focus relative to their nearness/distance to the camera, the smaller the scene will look. (If you use shallow depth of field in a room interior, it will resemble a dollhouse shot with a snorkel camera.)

Both the 3ds max scanline renderer (through the Camera Depth of Field Parameters rollout) and the 3ds max 6 mental ray renderer offer DOF options; use them carefully when you're rendering your scene, especially because this is a computationally intensive effect. (Also, be forewarned: If you combine depth of field effects with atmospheric effects, raytracing, or global illumination and caustics in mental ray, your render times will go through the roof.)

Note that if you do have a compositing program, such as Discreet's Combustion, you're probably better off rendering your scene to different render layers, and then adding animated Blurring effects (to simulate DOF) as a post-process. (That's how the cinematic special effects experts do it, so you should, too!)

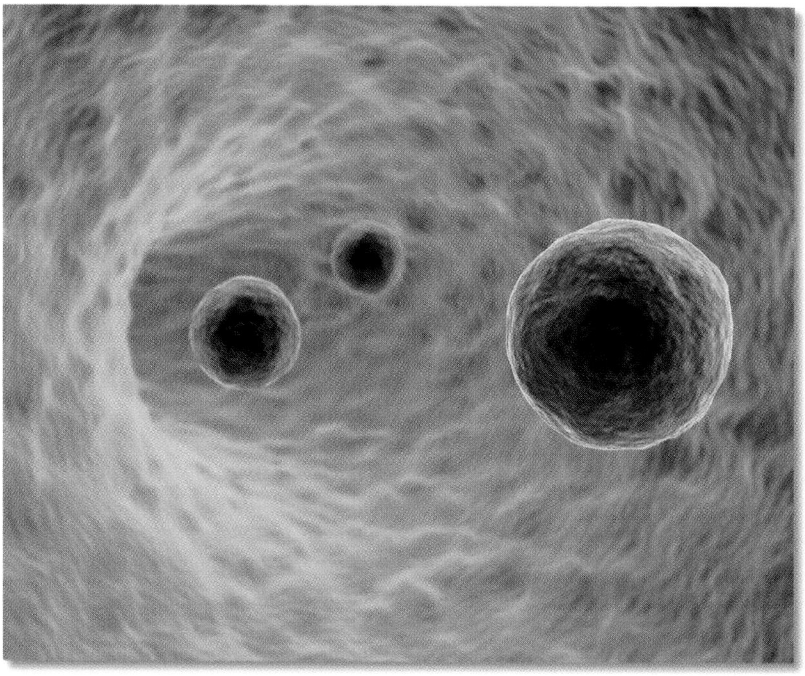

"HELLO… YOU'VE GOT RENDER!"

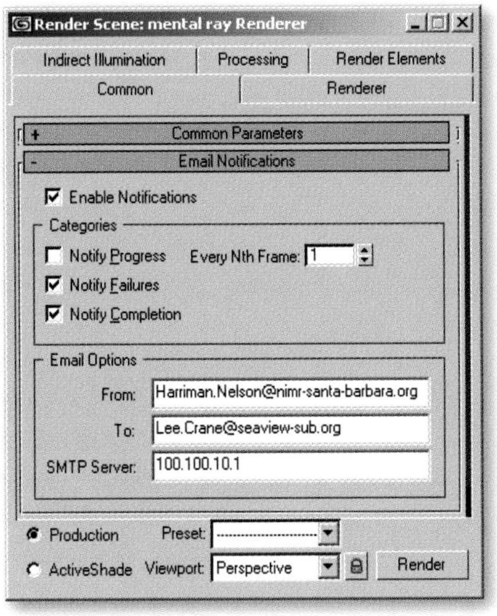

Okay, so you've set up several 3D sequences to render, and you're going to walk away from your computer (or render farm) for a while. If you can't resist the urge to check on your renders (even while you're away from home), and you have an always-on Internet connection, you can have 3ds max actually contact you to let you know what's up. Just go to the Rendering > Render Scene > Common panel, and open the Email Notifications rollout. There, you can enable Notifications and set up various categories of email alerts detailing general frame progress, failures, and/or completion of the job. All you have to do is put in the correct From and To email addresses and the address of your SMTP server, and you're good to go. If you have a cell phone or a personal digital assistant (PDA) such as a Palm Pilot or Blackberry that receives email, you can get the status of your renders while you're on the road, in a restaurant, or even in the middle of a romantic interlude.

"Honey, you have the most beautiful…."

BEEP, BEEP!

"Whoops, gotta go—my rendering of the Enterprise attacking the Death Star just finished!"

Custom Features

Custom Features

special effects tips

I'm a child of the 1960s. (Yep, that's how stinkin' old I am.) I grew up watching the original Star Trek, Voyage to the Bottom of the Sea, Batman, Land of the Giants, Time Tunnel, Lost in Space, The Invaders, *and so on. If a show had cool vehicles, monsters, dinosaurs, explosions, laser beams, or costumed crime fighters, I'd watch it. In short, if a show had cool special effects, I'd be parked in front of the TV set.*

These days, I don't just sit in front of the TV or in a movie theater watching special effects; I also sit in front of a computer, and work to create special effects of my own using 3ds max. And, chances are, if you're reading this book, you're doing the same—figuring out new ways to create cool effects to dazzle your clients, your boss, your spouse/significant other, your pets, or yourself.

In this chapter, I present a range of techniques to help augment your 3ds max effects—from rendering animations backward to speeding up your particle systems rendering. And speaking of particles, contributor Dan Meblin chimes in with some cool techniques for getting the most out of Particle Flow, the event-driven particle system introduced (via subscription) to users after the release of 3ds max 5, and now included in 3ds max 6.

HEAD OVER HEELS: RENDERING BACKWARD USING VIDEO POST

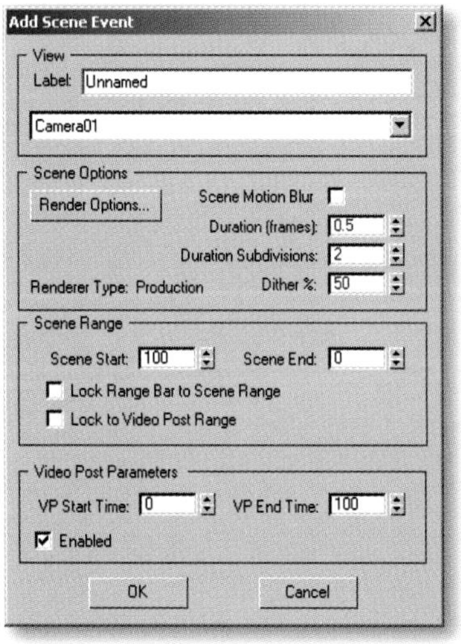

An often-heard wish of many 3ds max users is to be able to render a sequence backward. Of course, you could render normally and then list the frames in reverse order in an .IFL (image file list), or load the sequence in a non-linear editing (NLE) package such as Adobe Premiere, and reverse the animation there.

But there's an out-of-the-box way to do this directly in 3ds max. Go to Rendering > Video Post, and click on the Add Scene Event button. Under Scene Range, uncheck the Lock to Video Post Range check box. Also uncheck the Lock Range Bar to Scene Range check box. In the Scene Start box, enter your current last frame, and in the Scene End box, put your current first frame as the End frame. Close the Add Scene Event dialog to return to Video Post, and click on the Add Image Output Event button. Choose your output format (either sequential images or a movie file), and then execute the Video Post queue to render.

MERGE ATMOSPHERIC EFFECTS

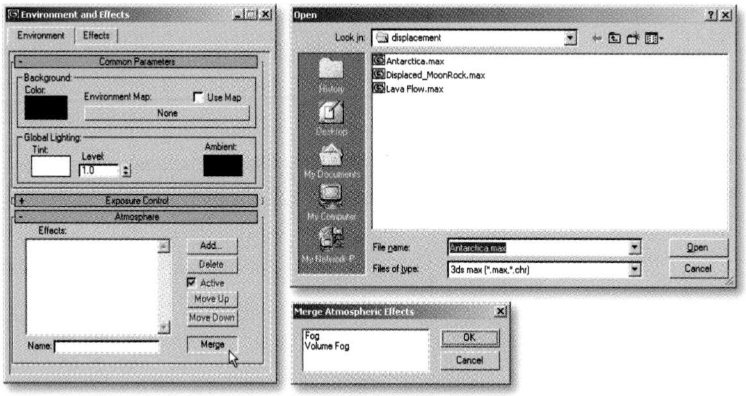

If you've created an atmospheric effect that you like and saved it in a .MAX scene file, remember that you can import these settings from this scene into your current scene by using the Rendering > Environment > Atmosphere > Merge button, and browsing to the 3ds max scene that contains your atmosphere settings. (Note that if the merged scene contains animated parameters, you might have to change these settings to match the length of your current scene; otherwise, the new effects might simply appear to "stop" in the middle of your rendering, while the rest of the scene animation continues.)

COMBINING THE NOISE MODIFIER AND THE FIRE EFFECT

Although it's been superseded by more complex third-party volumetric effects (such as AfterBurn), the 3ds max Fire Effect (formerly called "Combustion" until Discreet used that name for its desktop compositing package) still has some use left in it. Introduced originally with 3D Studio MAX Release 1, the Fire Effect (found in the Rendering > Environment > Atmosphere > Add > Fire Effect menu) produces simple fire and gaseous explosions, and it renders fairly quickly.

You apply the Fire Effect to an atmospheric gizmo (found in the Command Panel > Create tab > Helpers > Atmospheric Apparatus), which then determines the Fire Effect shape: box-like, cylindrical, or spherical. However, here's something nifty: You can vary the shape of the gizmo during the animation by putting a Noise modifier on the gizmo, and then animating the Noise parameters. Doing this distorts the gizmo's overall shape during the animation, and results in a more flickering, uneven fire, or even a "fluidic-looking" explosion. (It's great for underwater effects.) Experiment with it and see!

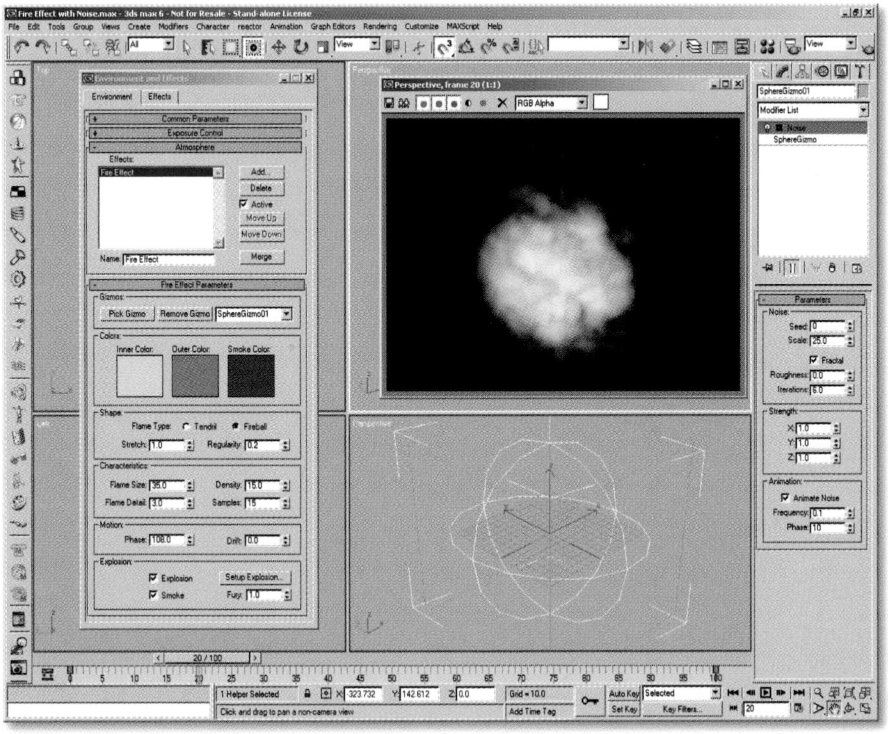

BIG BANGS AND LITTLE FIRECRACKERS: PLACE EXPLOSIONS WHERE YOU WANT THEM

There's still some life left in the old 3ds max Bomb Space Warp (found in the Command panel > Create tab > Space Warps > Geometric/Deformable drop-down). If you bind it to meshes in your scene, it'll blow them apart into polygonal faces (which isn't altogether realistic because most real-world objects aren't composed of eggshell-thin exteriors and hollow interiors). However, you can use the Bomb Space Warp to blow up pieces of geometry that are parented to your base object—the "skin" of a spaceship mesh, for example—and produce realistic results. In addition, by parenting dense meshes (such as spheres, bound to Bomb space warps) to your base object, applying self-illuminated materials to the spheres, and then setting Track View Visibility keys to hide/unhide them at the appropriate times during your animation, you can create the illusion of "impact" explosions on the surface of your object. Finally, add Noise modifiers to the spheres (under the Bomb pace warps on the object stack; this jumbles the spheres' surfaces, making the "pieces" more jagged) apply glow effects to the sphere materials, and you're good to go.

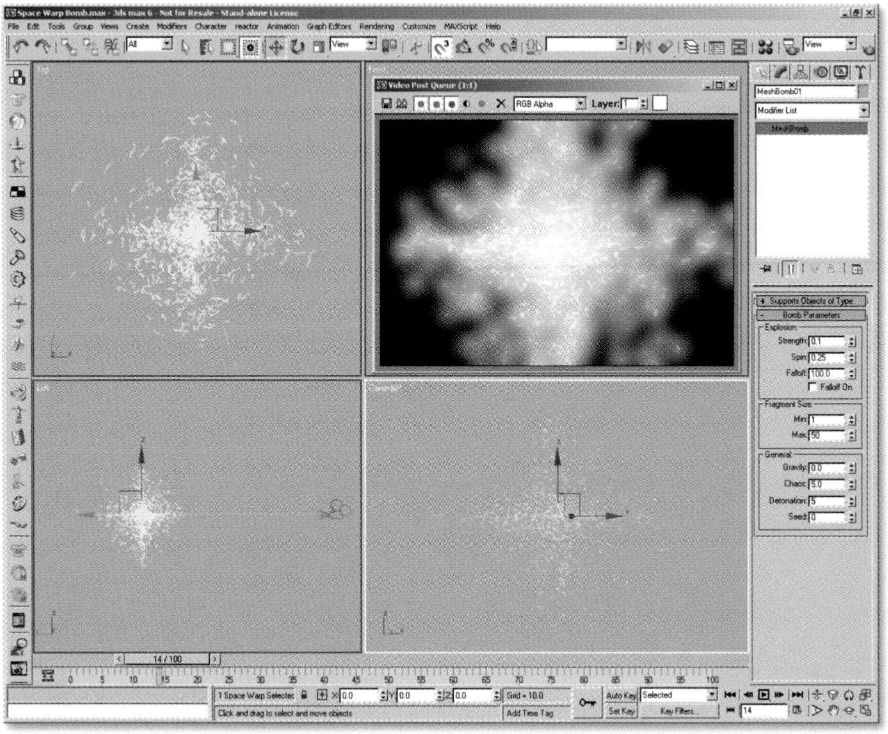

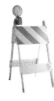

USE PRERENDERED EXPLOSIONS IN YOUR SCENES

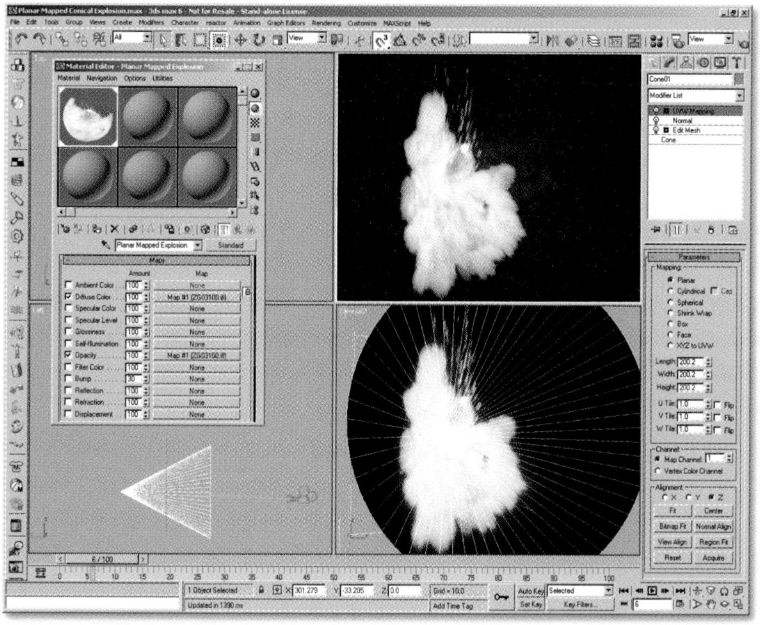

Okay, so let's say you don't want to have "live" explosion effects in your scene, such as Fire Effects or parented spheres/Bomb space warps on your meshes, as outlined in the previous two tips. You can use "canned," prerendered explosion effects, mapped onto 2D "cards" (quad patches or open-ended cone geometry, with Planar UVW mapping coordinates) instead. Just place the quad patches or cones in your scene where you want the explosion effect to occur, apply two-sided, self-illuminated materials with Additive Transparency to the objects, set all Specular and Glossiness settings to 0, and load the explosion image sequence(s) in both the Diffuse and Opacity map slots of the materials. (You should point the cone "base," with its bottom faces deleted, toward the camera, and leave the cone tip embedded in the object; it should serve as the origin point for the explosion, if the original imagery was centered in the frame.) In addition, right-click on each explosion object, choose Properties, and uncheck the Cast Shadows and Receive Shadows boxes so these objects won't be affected by your scene lighting.

By using prerendered frames of elaborate explosive effects, you can create the illusion of massive destruction in your 3D scene. These techniques usually require less render horsepower than using actual volumetric or particle effects in your scene, although multiple opacity-mapped objects in your scene tend to render less quickly than completely opaque geometry. Where do you get such imagery? You can produce it with the 3ds max Fire Effect, particle systems, geometry and Bomb space warps, the Video Post Lens Effects Glow filter, third-party plug-ins such as AfterBurn, or actual filmed pyrotechnic imagery available from Visual Concepts Engineering (http://www.vce.com) or Artbeats (http://www.artbeats.com.)

INTERACTIVE LIGHTING WITH EXPLOSIONS

In the last thrill-packed tip, you (I hope) created a cool explosion effect by taking prerendered imagery, mapping it onto geometry in your scene, and then letting it rip.

Here's another way to tie this effect into the scene: Add interactive lighting (seemingly created by the explosion) onto the objects that are supposed to be blowing up. For each explosion effect, create a Spotlight (Command panel > Create > Lights > Target Spot), and have it pointing perpendicularly to the explosion object. Select the Spotlight, go to the Modify panel, and under the Advanced Effects rollout, you'll see the Projector Map button. (Actually, it's a slot that displays a loaded map.) Open your Material Editor and click-drag the bitmap for the explosion object to the Spotlight Projector Map slot; make it a copy, not an instance. Then click-drag this map from the Projector Map slot *back* to an empty Material Editor slot, and make it an instance. The projected explosion bitmap sequence matches the timing of the original explosion object material, but by adjusting the Blur and Blur offset of the new Instanced Explosion Projector map, you can soften the lighting effect on the surface of your object.

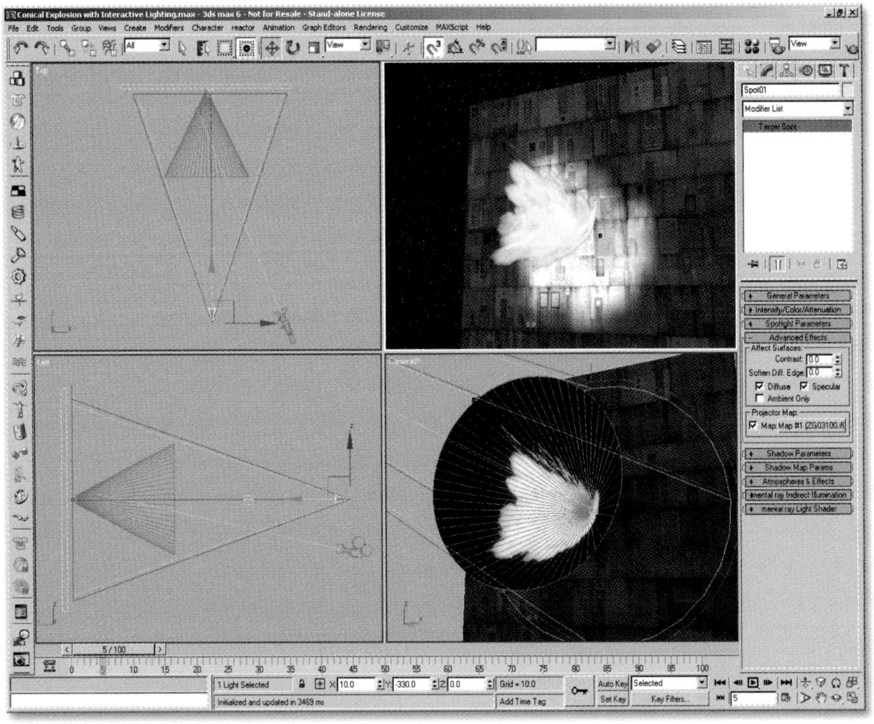

SPEAKING OF PROJECTOR LIGHTS… CREATE ANIMATED WATER CAUSTIC PATTERNS

Okay, so you're doing an underwater scene, and you want to simulate the effects of dappling light patterns (called *caustics*) on the bottom of your ocean floor or swimming pool geometry. That's easy: You just use a variation of the Spotlight Projector Map techniques described in the previous tip.

In the Spotlight that's lighting your underwater surface, click on the Projector Map slot, and from the Material/Map Browser, choose Noise. Open your Material Editor, and then click-drag a copy (make it an instance) of the Spotlight Projector Noise map to an empty slot in the Material Editor. Under the Noise Parameters rollout, change the Noise Type to Turbulence, and click the Swap button next to the Color #1 and Color #2 (Black and White) swatches to reverse their order. You can then animate the caustic patterns by clicking on the Auto Key button, going to the end frame of your sequence, and changing the Phase parameter of the noise. (Use the Make Preview feature in the Material Editor to check the speed of the phase; the larger the scale of your scene, the slower the phase effect should be.)

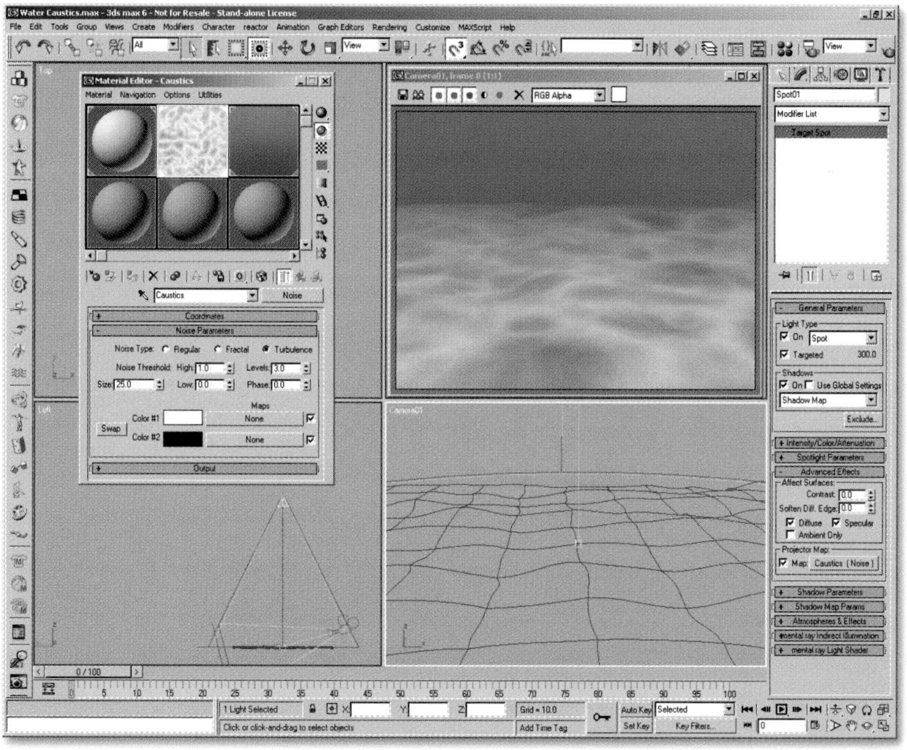

ABOVE THE WATER: WET SURFACES

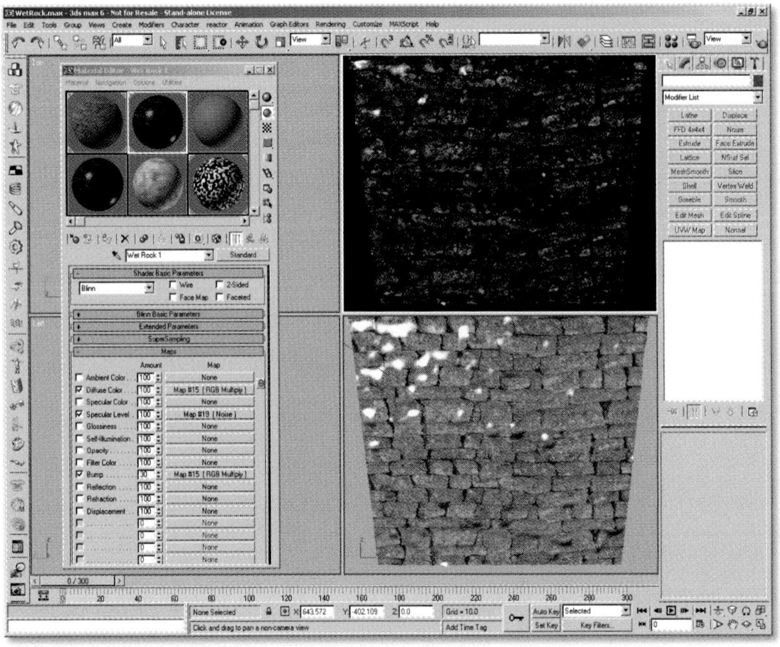

Although the 3ds max 6 mental ray renderer includes various "wet" shader effects (such as the Wet-Dry Mixer material), you can duplicate some of these effects just by using the core 3ds max material settings and the native scanline renderer.

To produce a wet-looking surface—say, the rocks under a particle-systems waterfall—you should make your rock material Diffuse maps darker and more saturated than they would appear if they were dry. (You can load your rock bitmap textures into an image editing program such as Adobe Photoshop, and use the Image > Adjustments > Brightness/Contrast and Hue/Saturation tools to make the image darker and more saturated. Alternatively, you can load the same bitmap into both slots of an RGB Multiply map, and place that in the Diffuse Color map slot of your rock material.) To produce extremely bright specular highlights, crank up the Specular Level to well above 100, and increase the Glossiness setting to 50 or above. (You also should have some bright lights in your scene to pick out the specular highlights.)

Want to improve this effect even more? Then use a Composite map or a Shellac material in a Multi-Layer shader to layer additional specular highlights on top of your original rocky surfaces. (See Chapter 3, "Waxing the Finish: Materials Tips," and note the tips on the Multi-Layer Shader at the end of that chapter.)

RUNNING WATER?

In the previous tip, you saw how to create wet-looking surfaces. If you want to suggest running water flowing over your rocky meshes, open your rock material in the Material Editor, go to the Maps rollout, click on the Glossiness slot, and from the Material/Map Browser, pick the Noise map. By adjusting the Noise Size parameters, turning on Auto Key, and animating the X, Y, or Z Offset values, you can make the specular highlights appear to "flow" a specific direction.

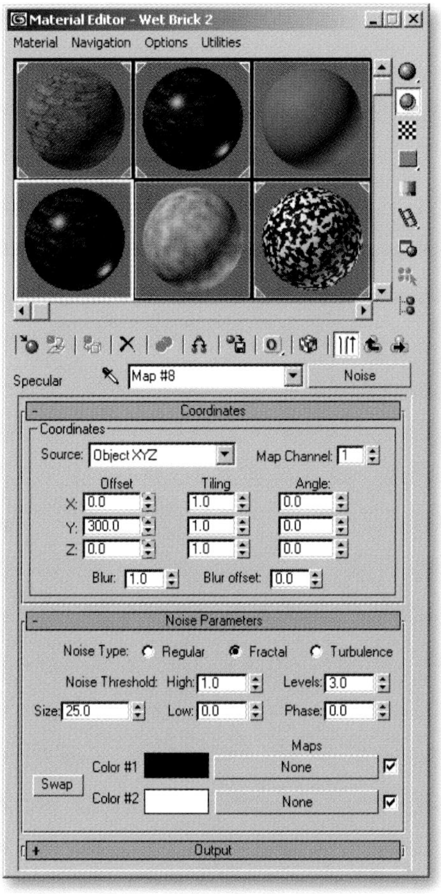

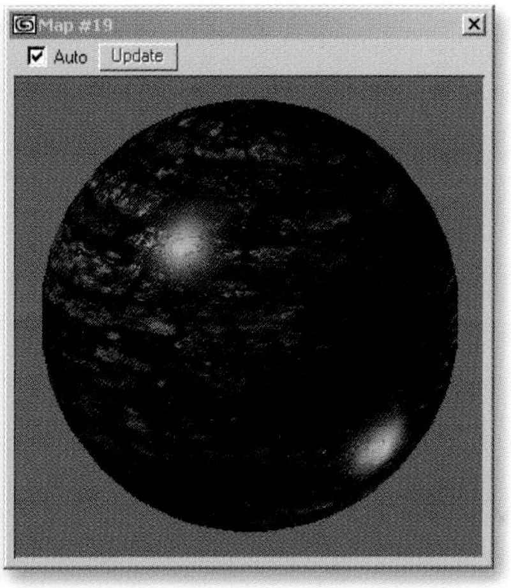

MAKE MINE "DRY"

Okay, enough with the soggy surfaces tips. If you want to create "dry" surfaces, such as objects that have a matte or chalky finish, then don't just reach automatically for the 3ds max Standard material shading types Blinn or Phong. Instead, use the Oren-Nayar-Blinn (ONB) shader, located in the Material Editor under the Shader Basic Parameters drop-down. The ONB shading type produces what's known as non-Lambertian shading, which is well-suited for rough, dry surfaces, such as rock, stucco, brick, chalkboards, and so on. The effect of this shader is to "spread out" or diffuse the light that plays across the surface of your object. Rough surfaces, such as brick walls, tend to absorb or scatter light with little falloff across their surface. For many rough, matte, or satin materials, this type of finish is more realistic than the standard light response you get with Phong- or Blinn-shaded materials, even if you've cranked down the specular highlights on the material. For best results, adjust the Diffuse Level and Roughness settings (under the ONB Basic Parameters rollout) to get the effect you want.

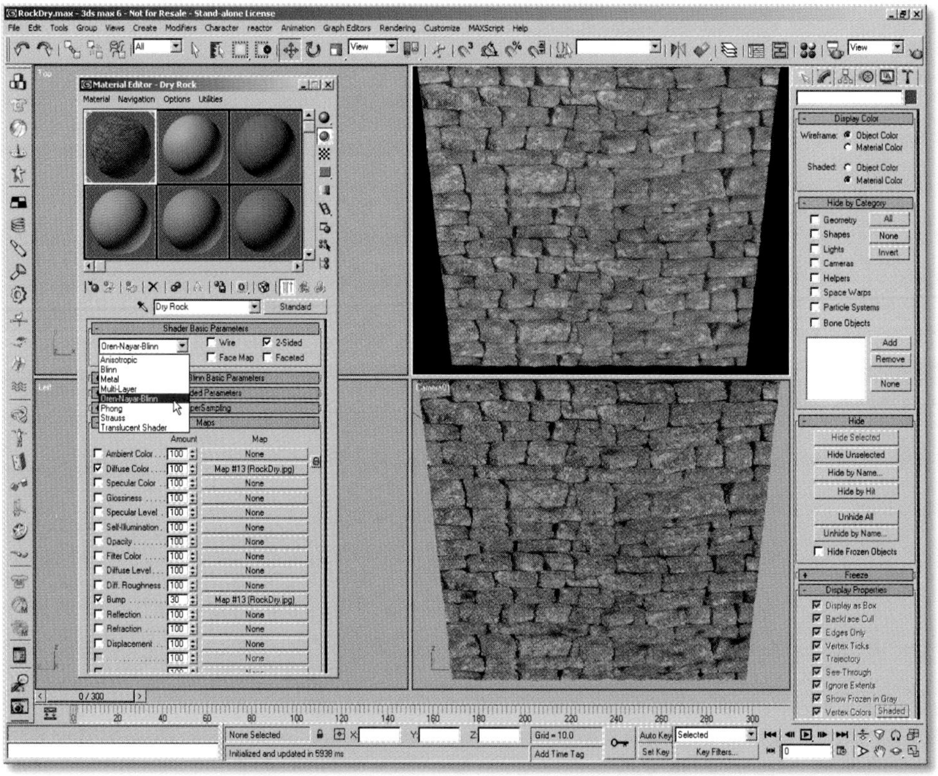

DON'T FORGET SPECIAL EFFECTS PLUG-IN SCRIPTS!

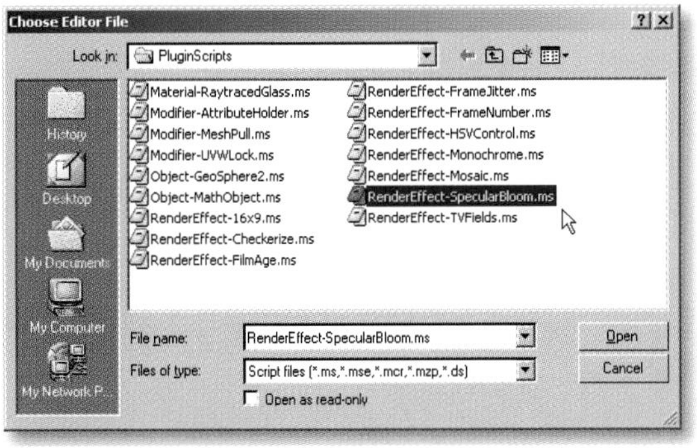

3ds max has a number of hidden features, written in MAXScript, designed specifically to produce cool special effects.

To find (and load) them, go to the Command panel > Utilities tab, click on the MAXScript button, and then click on Run Script. When the Choose Editor File menu appears, go to your 3dsmax6\scripts\PluginScripts folder. There, you'll see a multitude of special effects scripts. When you run a particular script, it loads a new feature into 3ds max that you can access by going to the relevant menu—the Material Editor's Material/Map Browser for custom materials; the Rendering > Effects menu for Render Effects scripts, and so on.

PARTICLE FLOW: HOT, HOT KEYS!

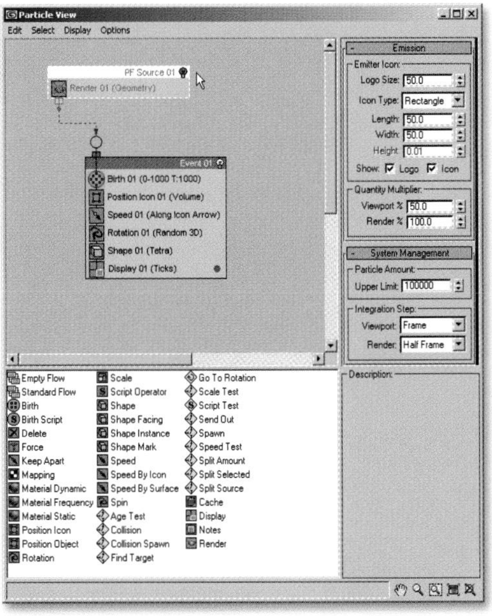

Particle Flow has some essential hotkeys specially designed to make your life a lot easier.

6 key—Since the Particle Flow window is not "dockable," it covers up your workspace behind it while it resides on your screen. The "6" key toggles the Particle View window on and off, remembering the exact position and size it was the last time it was visible.

Middle Mouse Button/Wheel—You can use the Middle Mouse Button/Wheel to pan quickly inside the Particle View window. This comes in handy when you're creating complex particle systems with many events and complex wiring.

Esc Key—Escape interrupts Particle Flow from calculating the system. When pressed, the Escape key disables the PF Source event at the top of the flow. The light bulb icon in the PF Source event turns dark, and the Render operator within it has a red "X" thru it. To re-enable the PF Source event and start calculating again, simply click on the grayed-out "light bulb" icon.

SPEAK OF THE DEVIL: THE SPECULAR BLOOM SCRIPT

I mentioned the cool special effects plug-ins you can load into 3ds max via MAXScript. Here's one of the most useful: Frank Delise's specular bloom script. Specular "bloom" is the effect of extremely bright highlights appearing "blown out" on film or video; essentially, the light kicking off a shiny surface is so bright that it appears to "glow" the area around the specular highlight. (Basically, it's an additive blur effect.)

Adding specular bloom to your renderings can impart a more realistic quality (if you're rendering shiny car bodies under bright lights, or sunlight), or it can actually produce an ethereal, "fantasy" look as well. To use this effect, go to the Command Panel > Utilities tab, click on the MAXScript button, and then click on Run Script. When the Choose Editor File menu appears, go to your 3dsmax6\scripts\PluginScripts folder, click RenderEffect-SpecularBloom.ms, and click the Open button. Then go to the Rendering > Effects menu and click the Add button. You'll see the new specular bloom effect, which you can pick and then apply to the specular highlights in your scene.

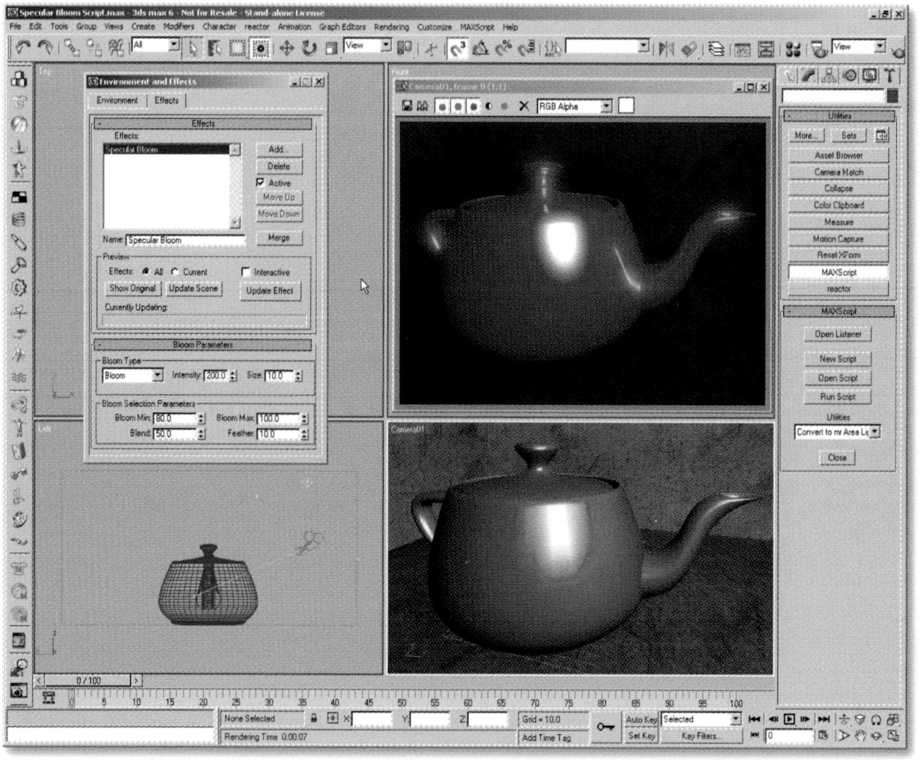

PARTICLE FLOW: "CACHE" IN YOUR POCKET

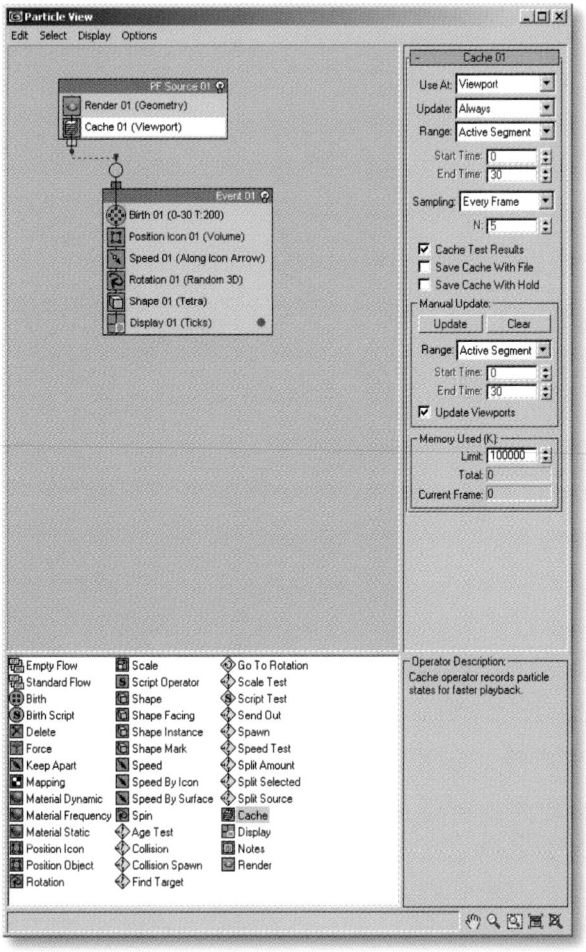

When you're creating large complex systems, Particle Flow can become extremely sluggish. This is because every time a change is made to the flow (changing Operator parameters, adding new operators, and so on), the entire system needs to recalculate. Sometimes even moving the Time Slider to a new frame can turn into a painfully long wait.

The best way to combat this issue is with the Cache operator. This nifty device allows you to precalculate the states of every particle in the system, or just the particles in a specific event to RAM. Using this, the Cache operator can also speed up your real-time previews. Cache information can even be saved into your .MAX file so the system won't have to recalculate if you close and reopen the file.

In the Particle View window (main toolbar > Graph Editors > Particle view), drag a Cache operator from the Operator Depot and place it under the Render operator in the PF Source 01 event. By placing it there, it will serve as a cache for all the events that are wired to that source. Select the newly installed Cache operator and set Update to Manually. Now, no matter what changes you make to the system or to the objects in the world that interact with the system, particle flow will not update. If you click the Update button, Particle Flow recalculates the entire system. This allows you to freely make multiple changes without having to wait for a recalculation after each change. During the update, a large progress bar displays at the bottom of the 3ds max window.

You can also put a Cache operator into a separate event. Doing this caches the data in that particular event.

PARTICLE FLOW: SEND IN THE CLONES

Sometimes a Particle Flow operator needs to reside in multiple events. Particle Flow allows you to easily "drag-copy" these operators from event to event, or even make a new event (if you drag into the open space of the Particle View window.)

To do this, first hold the Shift key, and then place your mouse over an operator. The cursor adds a "+" to it. Begin to drag the operator to a new event. When you let go of the mouse, the Clone Options dialog appears asking if you want to create a copy or an instance. Choosing Copy creates an independent operator (just as if you had dragged a fresh one from the depot below). Choosing Instance creates an instanced operator that reflects the same parameters as the original operator it was cloned from. An instanced operator's name is displayed in *italic*.

You can have an unlimited number of instances of a single operator. Making a change to any instanced operator propagates that change to all the other instances. If you want to convert an instanced operator to a normal copy, simply right-click on it and choose Make Unique.

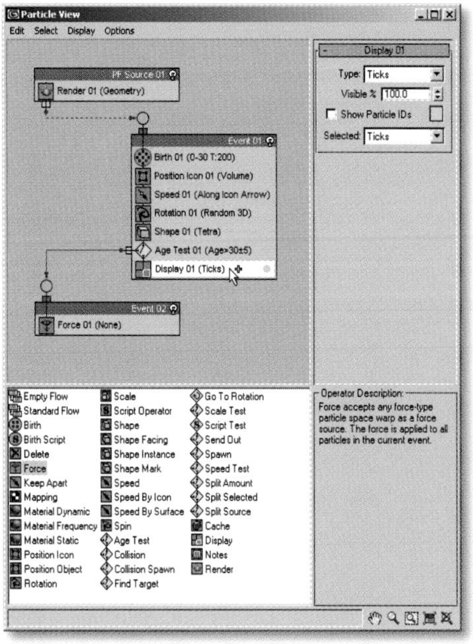

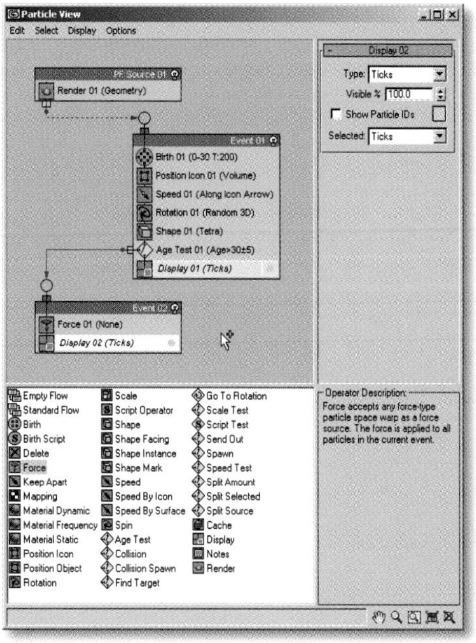

PARTICLE FLOW: ADD A LITTLE VARIATION!

The Shape Instance operator allows you to use any piece of geometry (animated or static geometry) as a particle. Making anything from leaves, asteroids, or even flocking birds is a snap! But did you know that you can instance an entire library of unique objects as particles? For instance, you can create 20 slightly different shaped asteroids and instance them all using a single Shape Instance operator.

To do this, group all the objects you plan to instance as particles and then, in the Shape Instance operator, click the Particle Geometry Object button, and then click on the group in a viewport. Check the Group Members check box. This randomly chooses from all members of the instanced group and uses a different group member each time a particle is born. Checking the Acquire Material check box allows each particle to retain the material originally assigned to it.

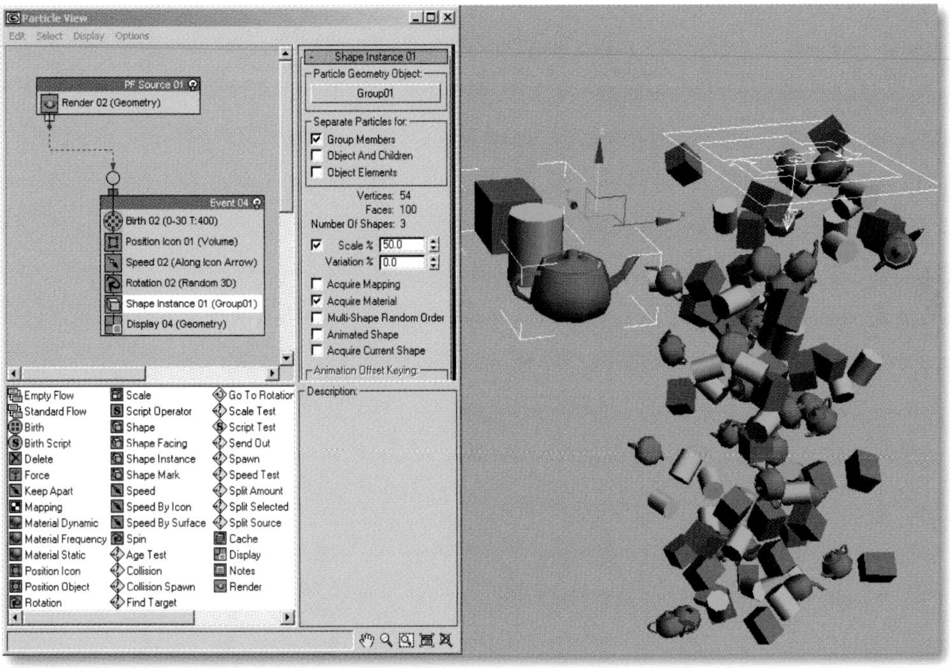

Detailing the Chassis

Detailing the Chassis

MAXScript tips

Jon A. Bell here with a brief introduction…

One of the biggest "names" in the 3ds max world is Bulgarian-born Borislav "Bobo" Petrov, a programmer and 3D graphics artist who's known as "The King of MAXScripts. Bobo" is famous for seeing a 3ds max feature request posted online from a fellow user, and then writing and posting a script that will address that user's problem, sometimes only an hour or so after the original posting. Needless to say, Bobo's work has earned him the undying gratitude of thousands of 3ds max users.

Over the years, Bobo has written literally hundreds of MAXScripts and made many of them publicly available on his website (http://www.scriptspot.com/bobo/). If you're looking for a way to get something accomplished in 3ds max, and you don't know how to do it in the program's native tools, then there's probably a MAXScript that could fix the problem—and in all probability, Bobo has already written it. Check it out, and while you're at it, check out this chapter for some of Bobo's best MAXScript suggestions.

Note: This chapter assumes that you already have some familiarity with MAXScript and with creating new toolbar buttons by using the Customize > Customize User Interface > Toolbar > New feature. If not, you should definitely brush up on this information from the 3ds max manuals and Online Help before you tackle some of these tips.

Okay, that's enough talk from me. Take it away, Bobo!

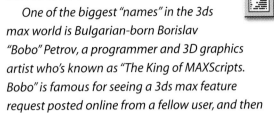

THE MACRO RECORDER AS PROGRAMMING AID

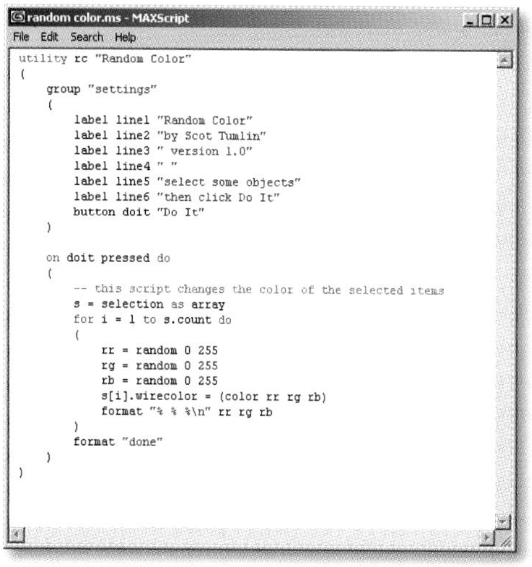

You can use the 3ds max Macro Recorder (located in MAXScript > Macro Recorder) to help understand how MAXScript works. Not sure how to write code for a given task? Use the Macro Recorder to record the tasks. The Macro Recorder then converts your actions into MAXScript. Paste the code created by the Macro Recorder into your own scripts and then examine the results. (To open the MAXScript Listener window, just go to MAXScript > MAXScript Listener or press the F11 key.)

MAXSCRIPT: GOOD FOR YOUR TIRED EYES

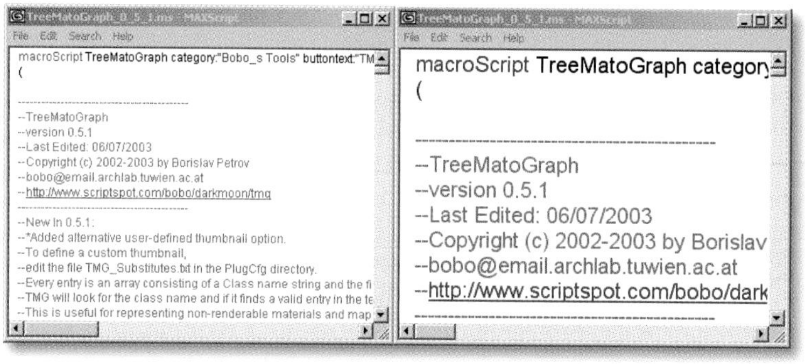

Almost everyone knows that you can change the size of the MAXScript Editor text (as well as the font type) from the Customize > Preferences > MAXScript menu. However, a hidden feature is inherited from the RichEditor code that the MAXScript editor is based on. If you hold down the Ctrl key and roll your mouse wheel, the size of the font changes interactively. That feature is great for examining parts of complex code, or when demonstrating scripting when you're projecting the 3ds max user interface (UI) on a screen in front of an audience!

Don't have a wheel-equipped mouse? Well, you should get one—it's cheaper to use this trick than to buy new contact lenses when using MAXScript!

SINGLE QUOTES MAKE MAXSCRIPT NAMES HAPPY!

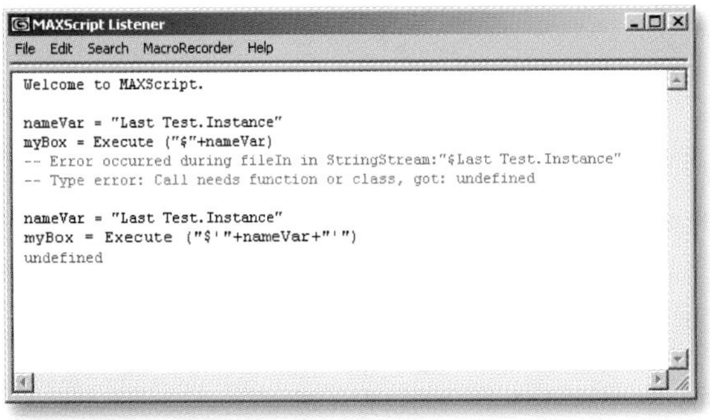
MAXScript Listener
File Edit Search MacroRecorder Help
Welcome to MAXScript.
nameVar = "Last Test.Instance"
myBox = Execute ("$"+nameVar)
-- Error occurred during fileIn in StringStream:"$Last Test.Instance"
-- Type error: Call needs function or class, got: undefined
nameVar = "Last Test.Instance"
myBox = Execute ("$'"+nameVar+"'")
undefined

In general, an object path name in MAXScript (the "address" of a 3ds max object) is given a dollar sign ($) and the name of the object as it appears in the 3ds max user interface. A couple special characters (such as a period and a blank space) cannot be part of a MAXScript name but are legal and can appear in the 3ds max UI. If you try to use a name containing such special characters in MAXScript, you are asking for trouble!

For example,

```
myBox = $Box01.NewestCopy Last Revision
```

is an invalid object name in MAXScript, but it's completely legal in 3ds max.

MAXScript is nice enough to provide you with a way around this problem, though. Any characters that are enclosed inside a pair of single quotes are read as a single string of symbols; special characters are then accepted and do not generate an error!

The previous name enclosed in single quotes works without problems:

```
myBox=$'Box01.NewestCopy Last Revision'
```

You should keep this in mind, especially when using string variables to build filenames dynamically; you can never be sure what crazy names other users might have given to their objects. For example,

```
nameVar = "Last Test.Instance"
myBox = Execute ("$"+nameVar)
```

puts the dollar sign and the string stored in the `nameVar` variable into a single string and then tries to convert it via the Execute function to an actual MAXScript object path. This causes an error because the name contains special characters.

Do this and everything will be peachy:

```
nameVar = "Last Test.Instance"
myBox = Execute ("$'"+nameVar+"'")
```

APROPOS QUOTES: DON'T LET MICROSOFT WORD BE "SMART!"

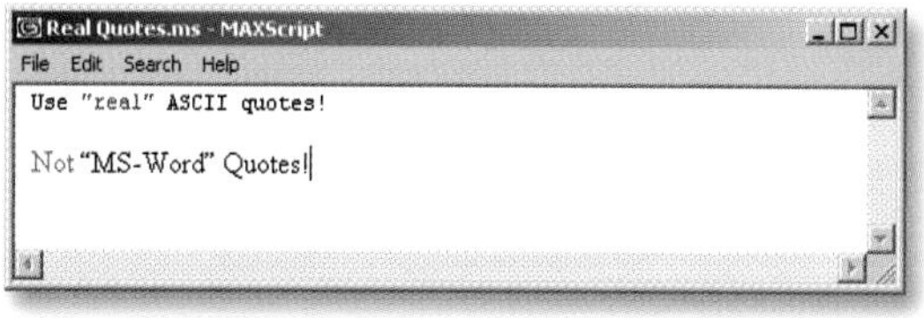
Real Quotes.ms - MAXScript
File Edit Search Help
Use "real" ASCII quotes!
Not "MS-Word" Quotes!

MAXScript accepts only regular quotes. Some word processors, such as Microsoft Word, have an AutoFormat function that turns regular quotes into so-called "smart quotes"—opening and closing quote characters with a different ASCII code. MAXScript prints an error if you try to write your code in Microsoft Word and copy and paste it to a MAXScript Editor. Be sure you use pure ASCII text to avoid any problems.

THE PROPERTIES, THEY ARE A-CHANGING…

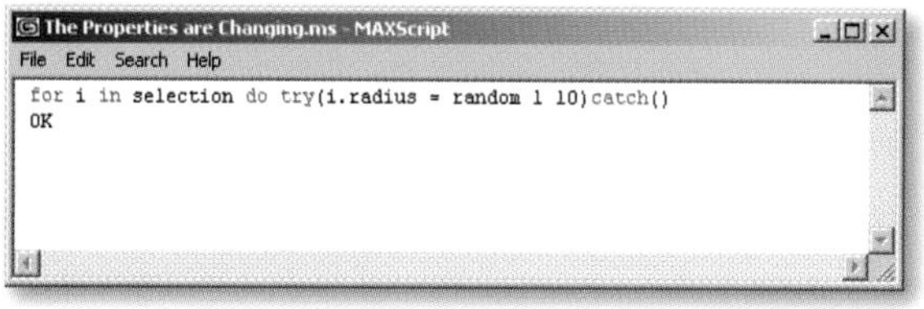
The Properties are Changing.ms - MAXScript
File Edit Search Help
for i in selection do try(i.radius = random 1 10)catch()
OK

MAXScript is a great tool for changing properties among multiple objects. A single line of code could modify a complete scene in fractions of a second without mouse clicks, your having to search through UI rollouts, and so forth.

For example, if you have a number of objects in the scene with the same property—let's say a large number of sphere primitives—you could change their radius to the same value using this:

```
for i in geometry where classof i == Sphere do i.radius = 10
```

If you want to randomize the values between 1 and 10 units, you could just say

```
for i in geometry where classof i == Sphere do i.radius = random 1 10
```

You could affect any selected objects by changing the code to this:

```
for i in selection do try(i.radius = random 1 10)catch()
```

In this case, any selected object with a radius property—including GeoSpheres and Teapots—is affected. Learning these simple tricks can speed up your workflow tremendously!

SUPER-DUPER EXPERT MODE

Have you ever dreamed of a max UI that shows only the four viewports, allowing you to navigate by the quad menu or keyboard shortcuts alone? The current 3ds max Expert mode does remove most UI elements, but it still leaves the Time slider, main toolbar, and Track Bar visible.

The following short script brings you a step closer to your dream. Unfortunately, the disabling of the main menu has been blocked since 3ds max 4, but you can disable every other UI element with the following code:

```
macroScript SuperExpert category:"Killer Tips"
(
  state = not(timeslider.isVisible())
  trackbar.visible = state
  timeSlider.setVisible state
  if state then cui.expertModeOff() else cui.expertModeOn()
  statusPanel.visible = state
)
```

Type the code into an empty MAXScript Editor window, and press Ctrl+E to evaluate the code. Then go to Customize > Customize User Interface > Keyboard, locate the Killer Tips category, and assign a shortcut (such as Shift+X) to the SuperExpert item. Pressing the keys toggles the complete 3ds max UI on and off.

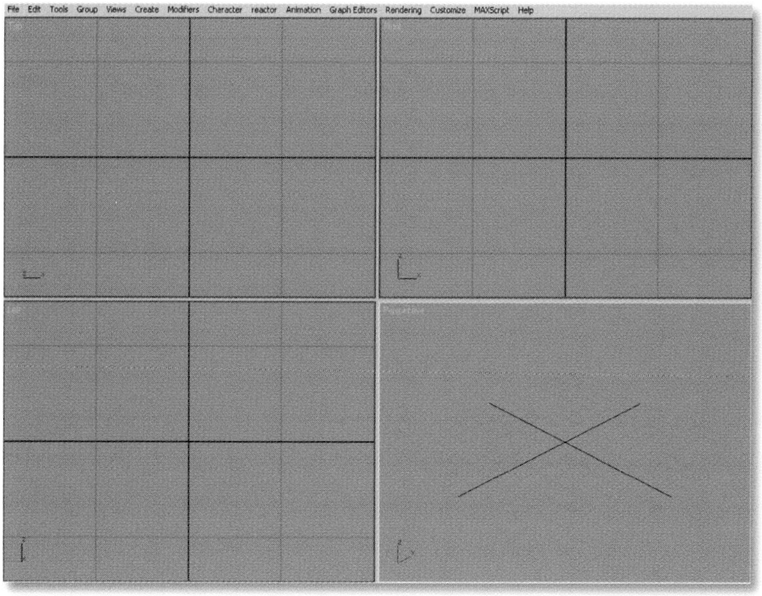

CHASING SHADOWS: ACCESSING THE .SHADOWCASTING PROPERTY OF LIGHTS

Although this tip is documented in the MAXScript online Reference guide, many users overlook it. That's a shame; this tip can save you hours of production time!

A couple of properties in MAXScript have duplicate names at base object and node level, which makes accessing only one property a difficult task. One of these properties is the `.castShadows` property of Lights. Because every node also has a `.castShadows` property that controls whether a geometric object will be seen by a light's shadow generator, then typing just this

```
$Omni01.castShadows = true
```

does not turn on the Omni light's Shadows On check box but enables the Cast Shadows check box in the Object Properties dialog instead!

To force the light to do what you really want, you have to tell its base object to cast shadows, like this:

```
$Omni01.baseObject.castShadows = true
```

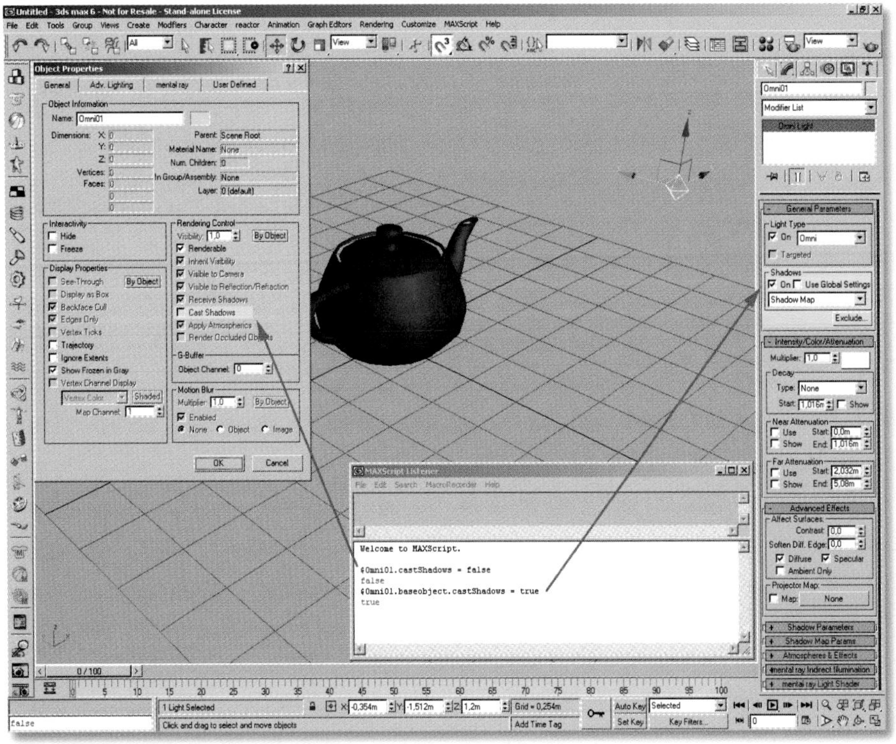
Welcome to MAXScript.
$Omni01.castShadows = false
false
$Omni01.baseobject.castShadows = true
true

TRUE NAMES

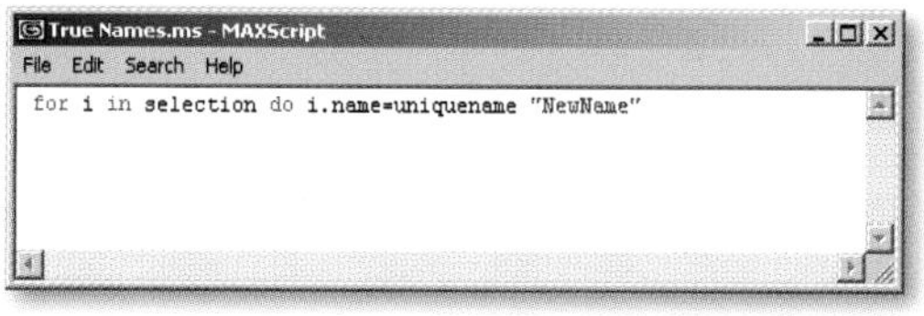
True Names.ms - MAXScript
File Edit Search Help
for i in selection do i.name=uniquename "NewName"

Multiple renaming utilities are available online for 3ds max, and one has even shipped with 3ds max since Release 5. Still, it's convenient to know how to rename objects quickly with MAXScript. The following line of code renames all selected objects to the name "NewName" and adds trailing numbers as required thanks to the MAXScript `uniquename` function:

```
for i in selection do i.name = uniquename "NewName"
```

A HELPFUL PHOTOSHOP GENIE

3ds max remembers the last rendered image it produced, and it can show it to you inside the application in the Rendered Frame window (formerly known as the Virtual Frame Buffer, or VFB). However, to open this image in another application, you have to either render to a file or use the Save Bitmap button in the RFW.

MAXScript also has access to this image. Using the following short piece of code, you can save the bitmap to a temporary file on disk and then open your preferred paint application, say, Adobe Photoshop, to edit it:

```
macroScript OpenLastImage category:"Killer Tips"
(
temp = getLastRenderedImage()
thePath = (GetDir #image)+"/temp.tga"
temp.filename = thePath
save temp
shelllaunch "photoshop.exe" thePath
)
```

Changing the last line of the script to another application name opens the image in that program.

If you want to open the image in the default application that is registered with the Windows operating system (such as an image viewer like ACDSee), you can simply use the following line

```
shelllaunch thePath ""
```

as the last line of the script. Windows opens the file in whatever application you have registered for viewing .TGA files.

THE MATERIAL EDITOR: 24 CLEAR SAMPLES

The following short but useful script reloads the Material Editor defaults from the MEDIT.MAT library and resets the 24 sample slots:

```
macroScript GetMEditDefaults
buttontext:"Get Default MEdit State" category:"Killer Tips"
(
  max mtledit
  loadMaterialLibrary (getDir #defaults+"/medit.mat")
  for i = 1 to 24 do meditmaterials[ i] = currentMaterialLibrary[ i]
  loadMaterialLibrary (getDir #matlib+"/3dsmax.mat")
)--end script
```

Note that in the past, the MEDIT.MAT file was located in the \Matlibs folder. In 3ds max 6, it is located under the Defaults\MAX folder.

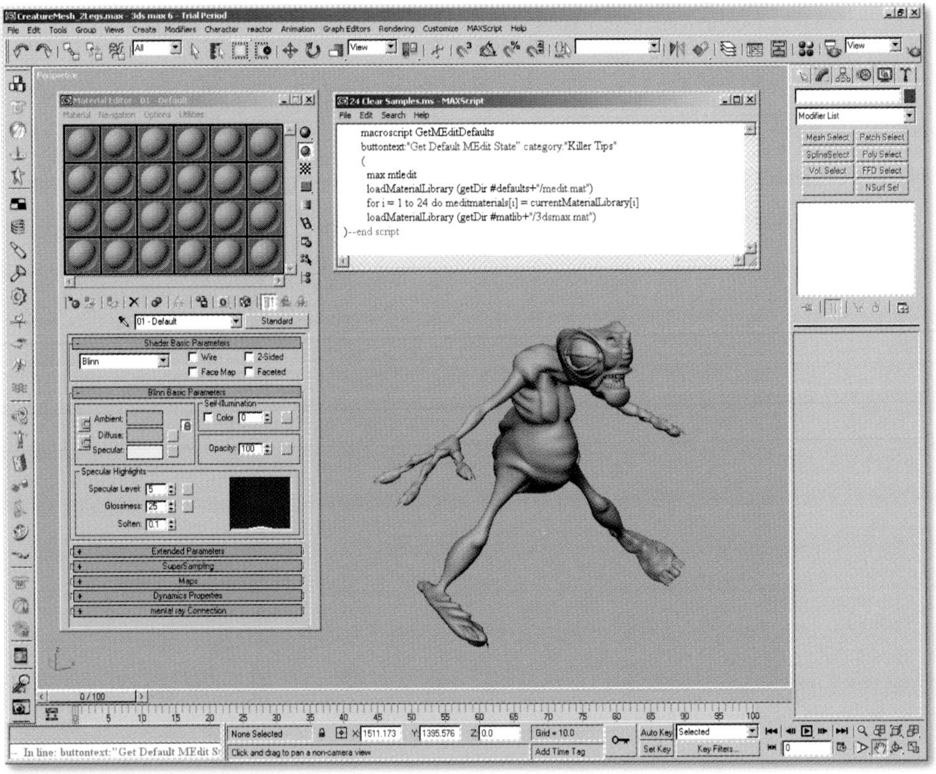

THE MATERIAL EDITOR: 24 *NEW* SAMPLES

Here's yet another script related to the Material Editor defaults. This one creates a new MEDIT.MAT library out of the 24 current samples in the Editor:

```
macroScript SetMEditDefaults
buttontext:"Set Default MEdit State" category:"Killer Tips"
(
  max mtledit
  default_lib = (getDir #defaults+"/medit.mat")
  loadMaterialLibrary default_lib
  for i = 1 to 24 do currentMaterialLibrary[ i] = meditmaterials[ i]
  copyfile default_lib (getDir #defaults+"/medit.bak")
  saveMaterialLibrary default_lib
  loadMaterialLibrary (getDir #matlib+"/3dsmax.mat")
)--end script
```

Note: This script creates a backup of your original MEDIT.MAT by copying it to the filename MEDIT.BAK, in case you get into trouble. (And we all know you want to stay out of trouble!)

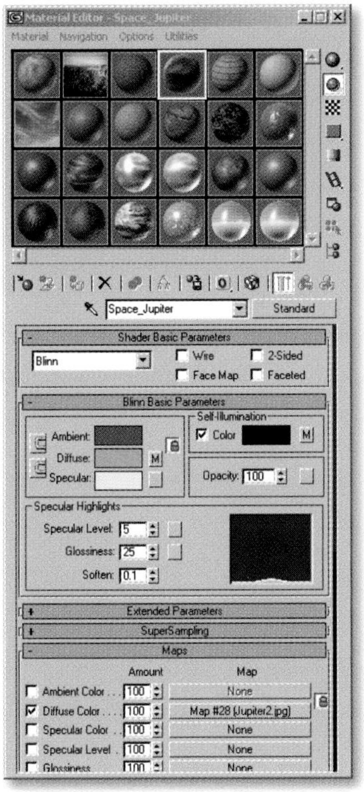

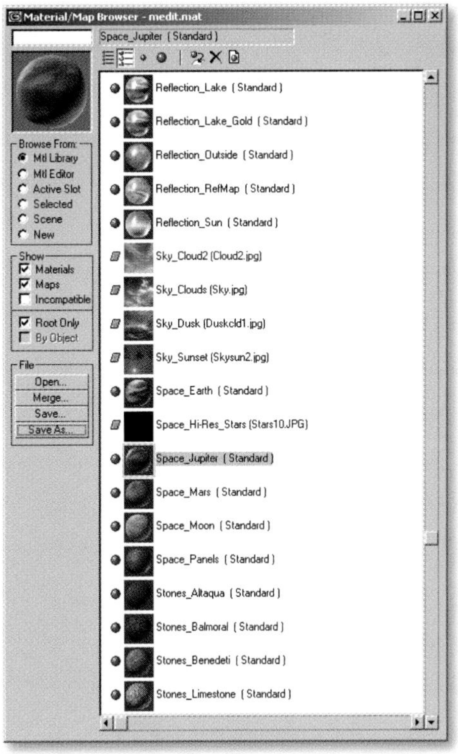

PAINT YOUR WORLD: ASSIGNING RANDOM MATERIALS

Imagine this: You've modeled a Lego brick piece and built a 3D house model out of these pieces. (Don't laugh; I've seen people do it!) Typically, Lego building block pieces are pretty colorful. You could assign a couple of materials to the bricks manually, but why don't you let Mr. Random Chance (actually, another MAXScript command) play the painter?

The following code lets you assign a random material from the 24 (viewable) Material Editor slots to all currently selected objects in your scene:

```
for i in selection do i.material = meditmaterials[ random 1 24]
```

Randomness is often a good thing when you're working with computer graphics. It can also be a nice way to experiment quickly with different random variations, or just have fun with crazy material assignments. (Imagine assigning random materials to an architectural model and getting grass on the roof, stone on the windows, and concrete on the doors. Thrill your clients with your wild imagination!)

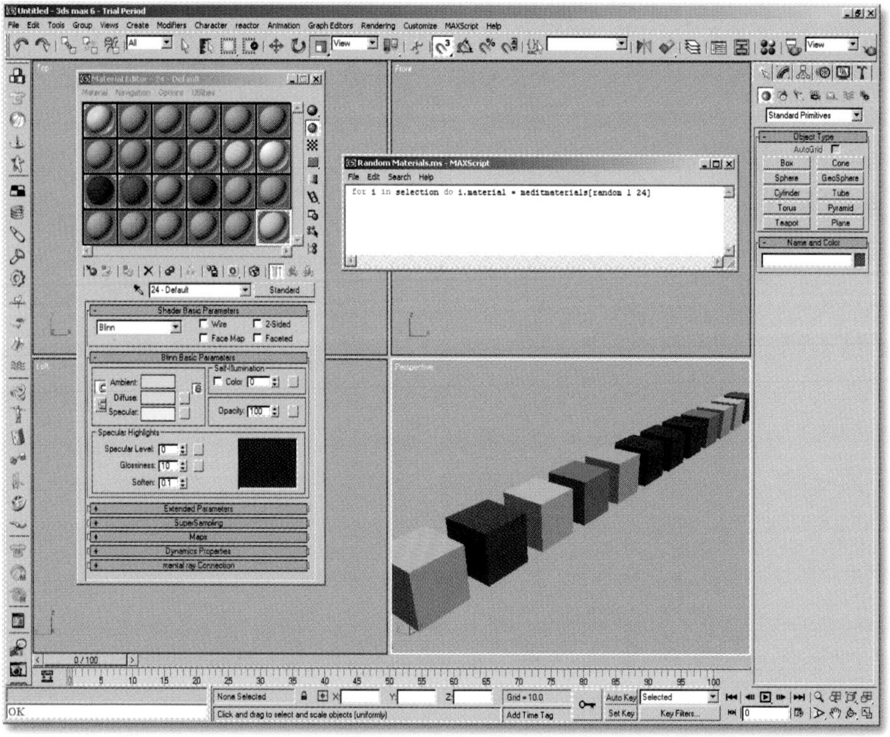

THE CASE OF THE NON-EXTRUDED EXTRUSION

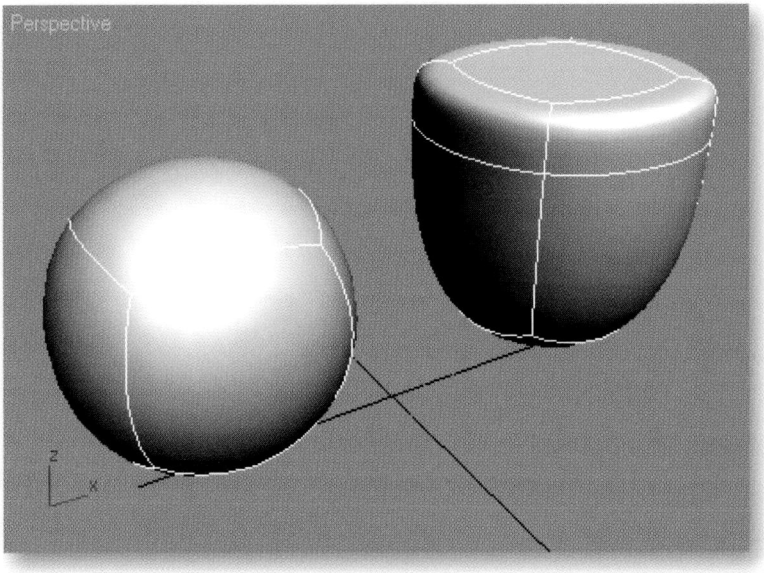

The Editable Poly feature in 3ds max provides several modeling tools for users, and it has strong integration within MAXScript. You can do some modeling operations quickly with 3ds max's integrated tools, but once again, you can always use MAXScript to accelerate your modeling steps, especially with poly modeling.

For instance, doing a "zero face extrusion" can be a useful operation when working with editable polys. Obviously, creating an extrusion with a height of 0.0 is not impossible using the existing Extrude feature, but being able to do this allows you to add even sharper face details to a MeshSmoothed object. (It's even more helpful if you can assign said action to a keyboard shortcut.)

The short script that follows creates a MacroScript ActionItem, which you can assign to a key, and which will do a Zero Extrusion operation in just milliseconds (instead of your spending actual seconds going over to the Modify panel).

```
macroScript ZeroExtrude category:"Killer Tips"
(
  on isEnabled return
    selection.count == 1 and classof selection[ 1] .baseobject  == Editable_Poly
  on execute do
    polyop.ExtrudeFaces $.baseobject (polyop.GetFaceSelection $.baseobject) 0.0
)
```

The accompanying illustration shows a box without segments that has been cloned and converted to an editable poly object. Both boxes have a MeshSmooth modifier added, but the second box has a zero extrusion on the top face.

MACROSCRIPT REMINDER

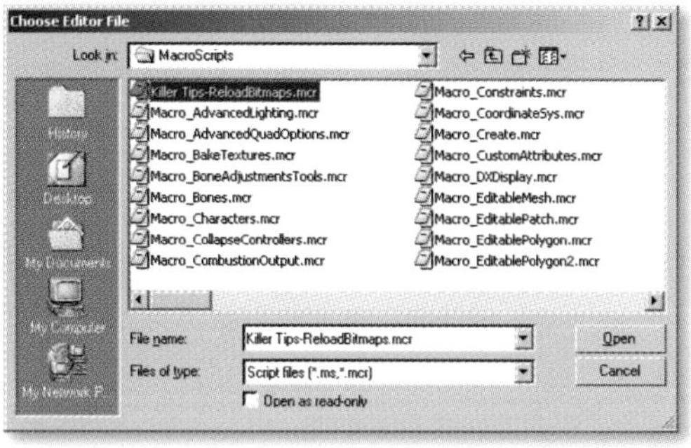

Here's something to remember when you're using 3ds max 6: When you execute a MacroScript, it's saved in the 3dsmax6\UI\MacroScripts folder. This ensures that your MacroScripts are always available if you assign them to toolbars, menus, or keyboard shortcuts.

STARTING WITH NOTHING: GENERATING LEADING ZEROES…

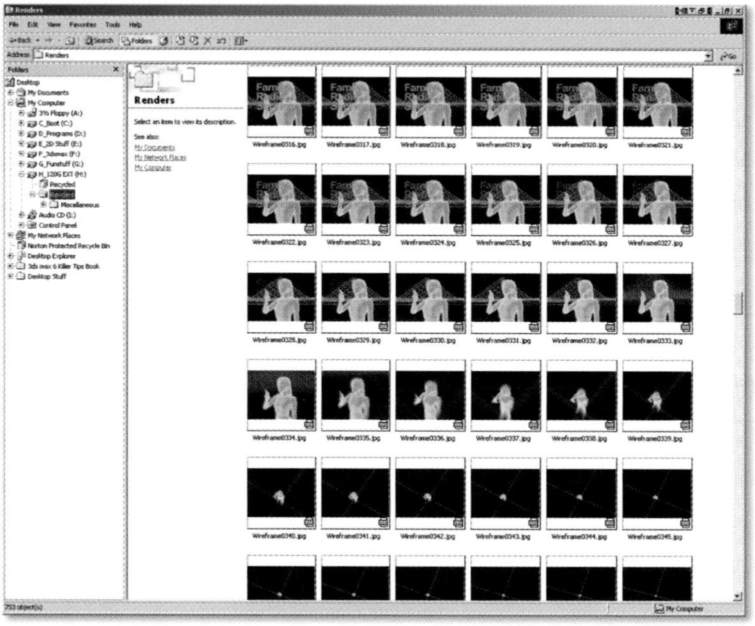

In some cases, it's necessary to render single frames by calling the `render()` method in MAXScript. Unfortunately, this method generates automatic filenames with leading zeros only when rendering a range of frames, but not when rendering single images in a MAXScript loop. Obviously, you have to do the job yourself. There are a couple of ways to get the zeroes. Here's one of the shorter ones:

```
fn getLeadingZeros num = (substring "0000" 1 (4-(num as string).count) )
```

We will use this function later in this chapter, in a longer script called "The MaxTrix Reloaded." (Remember: These tips are from real-world production and are actually useful!)

SMART MESH OPTIMIZATION: PRESERVE YOUR MAPPING COORDINATES

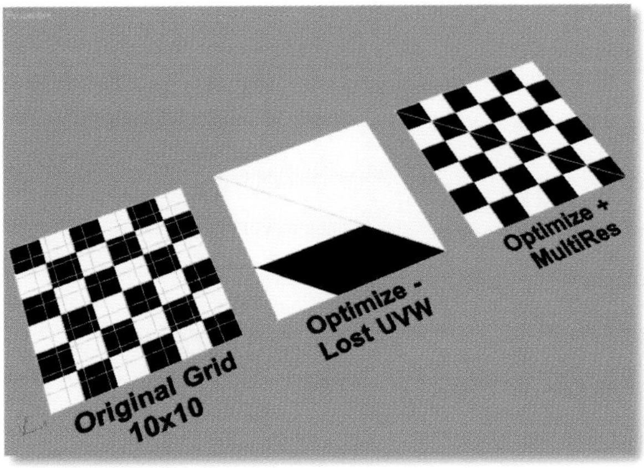

3ds max provides two different mesh optimization modifiers (available from the Command panel > Modify tab > Modifier list drop-down menu) for selected objects. Both have different features, and both have positive—and negative—aspects. The Optimize modifier is angle based, letting you specify the angle between two faces to determine the optimization of the mesh. On the flip side, Optimize does not preserve UV mapping coordinates. The MultiRes modifier lets you specify the exact number of vertices of the final mesh, but it does not let you specify an angle between faces; it selects the angle automatically to reach the desired vertex count. Consequently, you can't remove additional tessellation from an object automatically; you have to "dial in" vertex values until you reach the desired result. However, unlike Optimize, MultiRes preserves all your UV mapping channels!

It would be cool to marry the positive features of these two modifiers and avoid the negatives ones. Well, what MAXScript has joined together, let no man put asunder!

```
sel = selection as array
max modify mode
for obj in sel do
(
  addmodifier obj (optimize facethreshold1:0.0001 )
  select obj
  numverts = obj.numverts
  deletemodifier obj 1
  addmodifier obj (multires())
  obj.multires.reqGenerate = true
  select obj
  obj.multires.vertexCount= numverts
)
select sel
```

This is how it works: One modifier is applied to your object, the resulting vertex count is stored to a variable, and then the modifier is deleted. Then a second modifier is added, using the stored vertex count as the target result. Note that this technique works best with mostly planar (and highly tessellated) objects. Some complex objects might lead to different results when applying Optimize and MultiRes.

BAKING FRESH AND TASTY OBJECTS: EXPORTING MESH ANIMATION

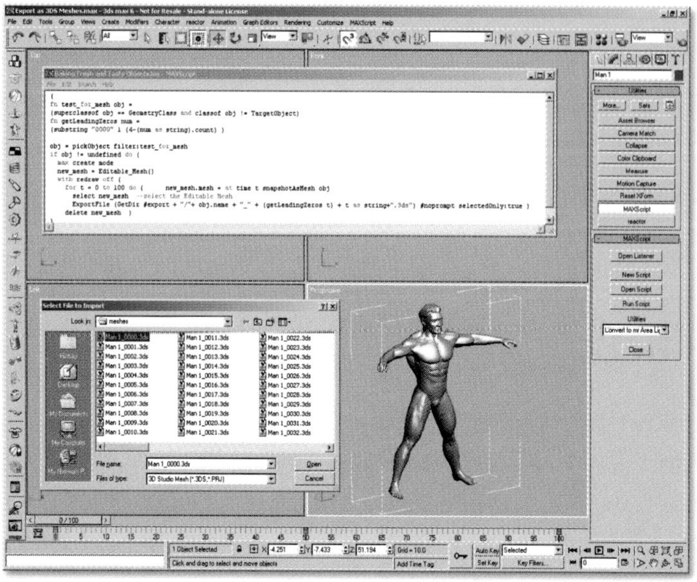

The following scripted function lets you capture the mesh of an animated geometry object on a per-frame basis and save single frames to the venerable old .3DS file format. The script bakes both deformations and object transformations, keeping the pivot point at the world origin. (In addition, you can change the format extension to .OBJ or any other supported format to export to other 3D applications.)

```
(
fn test_for_mesh obj =
(superclassof obj ==
GeometryClass and classof
obj != TargetObject)
fn getLeadingZeros num =
(substring "0000" 1 (4-(num as string).count) )

obj = pickObject filter:test_for_mesh
if obj != undefined do (
  max create mode
  new_mesh = Editable_Mesh()
  with redraw off (
    for t = 0 to 100 do (      new_mesh.mesh = at time t snapshotAsMesh obj
      select new_mesh  --select the Editable Mesh
      ExportFile (GetDir #export + "/"+ obj.name + "_" + (getLeadingZeros t) + t
      ➥as string+".3ds") #noprompt selectedOnly:true )
    delete new_mesh  )
)
)
```

Type the code into a new editor and press Ctrl+E to evaluate. The script expects you to pick an object with the mouse in the viewport, or by using the Select by Name dialog. Then the script exports .3DS files into your 3dsmax6\meshes folder, one for each frame between 0 and 100. After running the script on your selected object, go to File > Import and browse to your 3dsmax6\meshes folder. You should see the saved objects there.

Want to import these meshes back into 3ds max? Just stay tuned for the next tip!

EATING TASTY BAKED OBJECTS: IMPORT YOUR SINGLE-FRAME MESH ANIMATION FILES

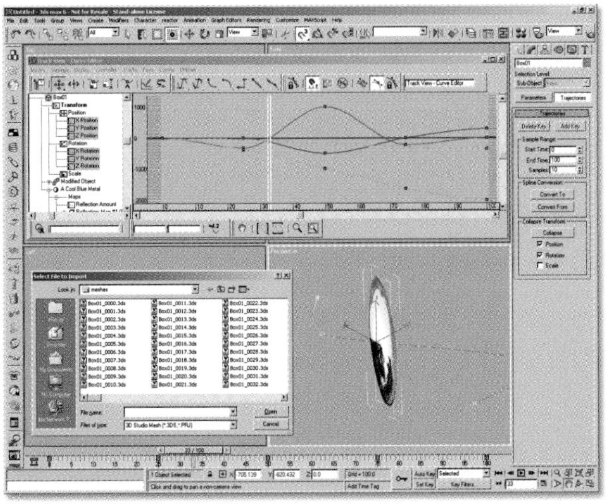

You can use the following function to convert multiple single-frame meshes stored in any supported format (such as .3DS, .OBJ, .DXF, and so on) to a single editable mesh with vertex animation.

```
fn importMeshAnimation inName ext=
(
inFiles = getFiles (GetDir #export
+ "/"+ inName + "_*" +"."+ext)
if inFiles.count > 0 do
(
  sort inFiles
  max create mode
  with redraw off
  (
    importFile inFiles[ 1] #noprompt
    baseObj = selection[ 1]
    baseObj.name = uniquename (inName+"_Base")
    vertCount = baseObj.numverts
    animateVertex baseObj #all
    filesCount = inFiles.count
    for f = 2 to filesCount do
    (
      max select none  --deselect everything
      pushPrompt ("Importing Mesh "+f as string+" of "+filesCount as string )
      importFile inFiles[ f] #noprompt
      currentObj = selection[ 1]
      for v = 1 to vertCount do
        animate on at time (f-1)
          baseObj[ 4][ 1][ v] .value = getVert currentObj v
      delete currentObj
    )
    pushPrompt "Import Finished"
  )
)
)
--call the function for file called "Box01" and
-- import from 3DS format:
importMeshAnimation "Box01" "3ds"
```

Note that the top portion of this script defines the function, and the last line executes it. The filename "Box01" should be replaced by your exported object name; if this parameter doesn't match, the script does nothing. Likewise, the parameter for the extension (".3DS") must match.

KA-BOOM! EXPLODE AN OBJECT TO ELEMENTS

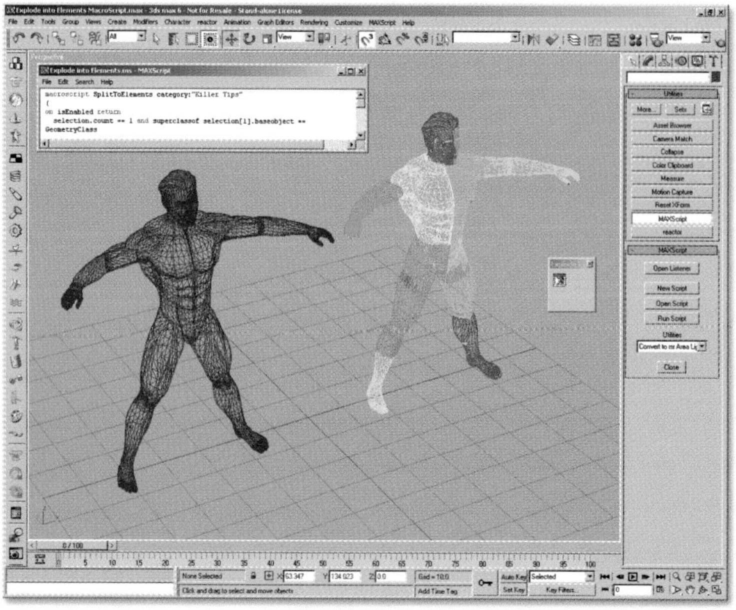

Okay, here's a Zen koan: How can you blow something up but leave it intact? Simple: Just run a MAXScript that splits a complex object to its individual elements but preserves the original object.

```
macroscript
➥SplitToElements
➥category:"Killer
Tips"
(
on isEnabled return
   selection.count ==
   ➥1 and super-
   ➥classof selec-
   ➥tion[ 1] .base-
   ➥object ==
GeometryClass

on execute do
(
  obj = copy selection[ 1]
  convertToMesh obj
  while obj.numfaces > 0 do
  (
    tmesh = meshop.detachFaces obj (meshop.getElementsUsingFace obj #{ 1} )
asmesh:true
      newObj = Editable_Mesh()
      newObj.transform = obj.transform
      newObj.mesh = tmesh
      update newObj
  )
  delete obj
))
```

Now, the next time a mystical guru on top of a fog-shrouded mountain asks you how one can blow up something while leaving it intact, you can answer him. Better yet, just show him the previous piece of code (and then ask him for a MAXScript that plays the sound of one hand clapping).

CONVERTING SELECTIONS BETWEEN SUB-OBJECT LEVELS

You know all about the editable poly selection conversion feature, right? (It was in all the newspapers.) Although this feature is somewhat hidden, it's also quite powerful and fun to use. Just select a couple of sub-object elements, such as vertices, hold down the Ctrl key, and click a different sub-object level, such as for the Polygon level. Zap! Look, Ma! The respective faces using the selected vertices have become selected, too!

The Mesh Select modifier also features a similar option under Get from Other Levels. But what about editable meshes? Isn't it a darn shame that this sort of functionality isn't built into the venerable editable mesh?

But look, up in the sky! Is it a bird? Is it a plane? No, it's MAXScript, once again, coming to the rescue. It provides built-in functions for converting editable mesh selections, but because most people don't have time to write a lot of MAXScripts, it's easier for 3ds max users to use scripts that someone else has written.

You can find a set of selection-converting MacroScripts in the new MAXScript Online Reference shipping with 3ds max 6 under the topic "Online Help Script Examples" in the area "Locating Information in this Help File." Just copy and evaluate these scripts, assign them to keyboard shortcuts, or add them to a toolbar or your quad menu, and up, up, and away you go. Oh yes—an additional Select Open Edges macro is included for your enjoyment!

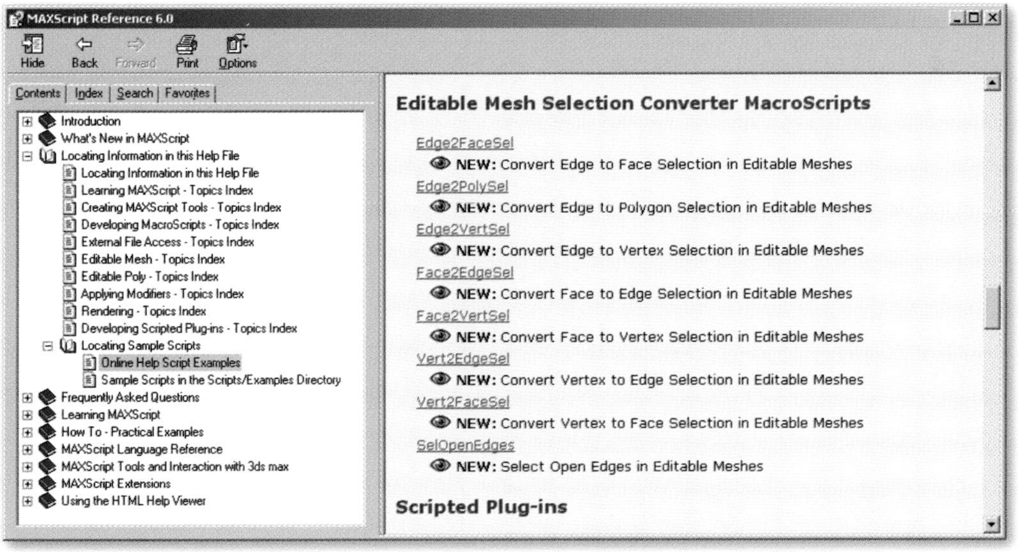

WHEN WORLDS COLLIDE: COLLISION DETECTION USING MESH INTERSECTION

The following scripted function demonstrates a possible way to detect collisions between two objects, called here "Box01" and "Sphere01." Although it's not as powerful as the collision detection provided by Havok's reactor 2 feature in 3ds max 6, it's still a cool hack that you might find useful.

The function calculates the intersection between two supplied objects. The trick: multiplying two meshes in MAXScript returns their intersection, adding them returns their union, and subtracting them returns (surprise!) their subtraction. If the resulting intersection mesh has vertices, the two objects collide. The function prints the result and the position of an eventual intersection to the Listener and also creates a Point helper at the center of the common volume.

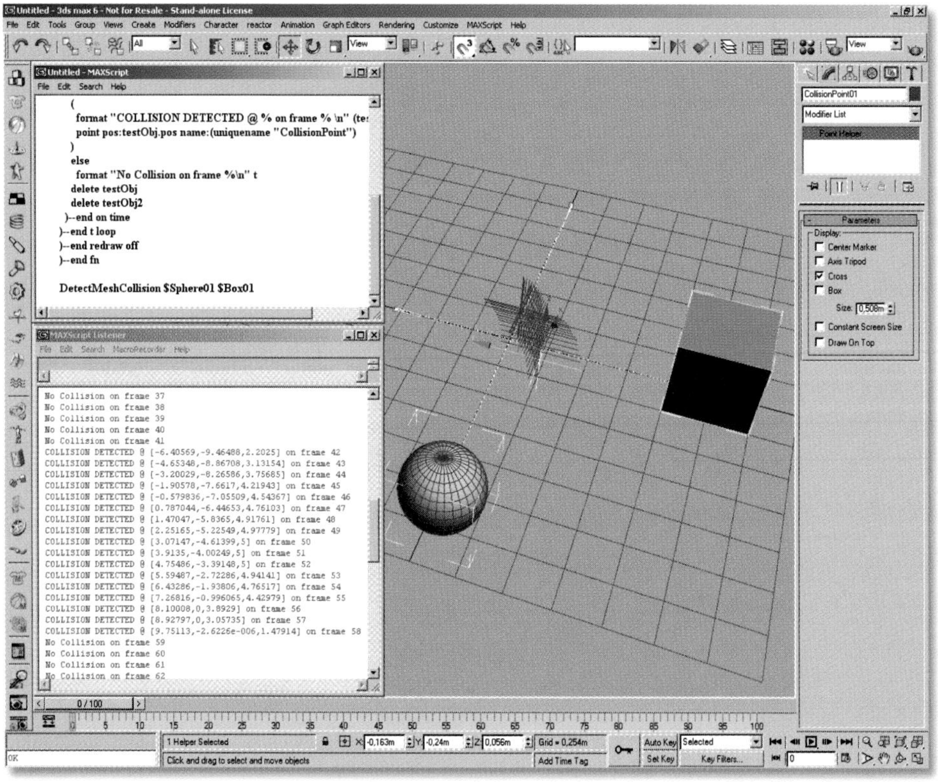
Untitled - 3ds max 6 - Not for Resale - Stand-alone License
Untitled - MAXScript
format "COLLISION DETECTED @ % on frame % \n" (te:
point pos:testObj.pos name:(uniquename "CollisionPoint")
else
format "No Collision on frame %\n" t
delete testObj
delete testObj2
)--end on time
)--end t loop
)--end redraw off
)--end fn
DetectMeshCollision $Sphere01 $Box01
MAXScript Listener
No Collision on frame 37
No Collision on frame 38
No Collision on frame 39
No Collision on frame 40
No Collision on frame 41
COLLISION DETECTED @ [-6.40569,-9.46488,2.2025] on frame 42
No Collision on frame 59
No Collision on frame 60
No Collision on frame 61
No Collision on frame 62
CollisionPoint01
Modifier List
Parameters
Display:
Center Marker
Axis Tripod
Cross
Box
Constant Screen Size
Draw On Top
1 Helper Selected
Click and drag to select and move objects
Auto Key
Set Key
Key Filters...
Add Time Tag

```
fn DetectMeshCollision obj1 obj2 =
(
with redraw off
(
for t = 0 to 100 do
(
  at time t
  (
    testObj2 = copy obj2
    testObj = (copy obj1 * testObj2)
    centerPivot testObj
    resetXForm testObj
    if testObj.numverts > 0 then
    (
      format "COLLISION DETECTED @ % on frame % \n" (testObj.pos) t
      point pos:testObj.pos name:(uniquename "CollisionPoint")
    )
    else
      format "No Collision on frame %\n" t
    delete testObj
    delete testObj2
  )--end on time
)--end t loop
)--end redraw off
)--end fn

DetectMeshCollision $Sphere01 $Box01
```

Note that the collision function is defined by most of this code, but the last line is the actual execution of the function:

```
DetectMeshCollision $[ object 1 name]   $[ object 2 name]
```

Also, note that the reported collision point is not the exact point of intersection, but rather the pivot center of the intersection set. This distinction is important if you're expecting something incredibly accurate, rather than a close approximation. For more details on how to access collision data generated by reactor 2, see the MAXScript documentation that ships with 3ds max 6.

WE BELONG TOGETHER! (THAT IS, COPLANAR FACES IN EDITABLE POLY)

A missing feature from the editable poly object is the option to select polygons based on the angle between them. In the editable mesh, this feature is called Ignore Visible Edges. The following short script performs the same operation on editable poly objects:

```
macroScript SelectCoplanarPoly
buttonText:"CoplanarPoly" category:"Killer Tips"
(
fn selectCoplanarPolys angleThreshold = (
  poly = selection[ 1]
  currentSelection = (polyOp.getFaceSelection poly) as array
  threshold = cos angleThreshold
  cnt = 0
  while cnt < currentSelection.count do (
    cnt +=1
    currentFace = currentSelection[ cnt]
    currentFaceNormal = polyOp.getFaceNormal poly currentFace
    currentEdges = polyOp.getEdgesUsingFace poly #(currentFace)
    facesOfTheEdge = (polyOp.getFacesUsingEdge poly currentEdges) as
    ➥array
    for f in facesOfTheEdge do (
      compareFaceNormal = polyOp.getFaceNormal poly f
      if findItem currentSelection f == 0 and dot currentFaceNormal
compareFaceNormal >= threshold do
        append currentSelection f )
  )
  polyOp.setFaceSelection poly currentSelection
  redrawViews()
)
rollout SelectCoplanarPoly_Rollout "CoplanarPoly" (
  spinner angle_threshold "Angle: " range:[ 0,180,0.1] scale:0.1 field-
width:45
  button select_them "SELECT" width:100 height:30
  on select_them pressed do
    if subObjectLevel == 4 and classof selection[ 1] .baseobject ==
Editable_Poly do
      selectCoplanarPolys angle_threshold.value
)
destroyDialog SelectCoplanarPoly_Rollout
createDialog SelectCoplanarPoly_Rollout 130 60
)
```

This saves you the trouble of converting your objects to editable meshes and back just to select coplanar faces. (Note that you must have at least one polygon selected before running this tool; a dialog box appears allowing you to set the planar threshold for selection.)

KEEP THE HELP UP!

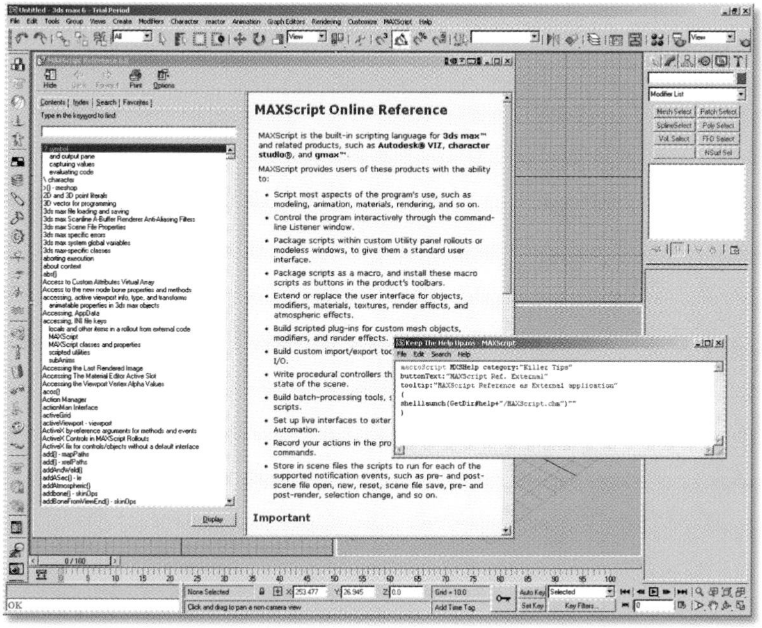

The 3ds max Help files (in .CHM format, naturally) that are included with the program are managed as "children" of the main application. If you minimize the 3ds max UI, the .CHM viewer goes away, too. If you close 3ds max, the Help files close with it. You don't like this? You're not alone!

Once again, MAXScript offers a solution. The example that follows launches the MAXScript Reference as an external application. If you close 3ds max, the Help file is still open, and it won't minimize with the main application. You can do the same with the other Help files by replacing the string "/MAXScript.chm" with the name of the respective file, such as "3dsmax.chm," "3dsmax_t.chm," and so on.

```
macroScript MXSHelp category:"Killer Tips"
buttonText:"MAXScript Ref. External"
tooltip:"MAXScript Reference as External application"
(
shelllaunch(GetDir#help+"/MAXScript.chm")""
)
```

To use this script, open a new MAXScript editor and type in the code, press Ctrl+E to evaluate the script, go to Customize > Customize User Interface > Menus, and then open the Category drop-down list. Drag the action item from the "Killer Tips" category to the expanded menu entry. Save the changes to the menu. Then say, "Thanks, MAXScript!"

IFL, BE MY GUIDE!

You've probably lain awake at night, tossing and turning, wondering, "How do I replace the content of the images listed by an image file list (.IFL) file without changing the .IFL file itself? Although .IFL is a valid input file format in 3ds max, it's not an "output" format. Obviously, if the filenames listed in the IFL file are regular base names with unique trailing numbers, you could set up the renderer to output exactly these names.

But (and it's a big "but!"), if the content of the .IFL is more obscure, non-standard, or even hand-written with a text editor, chances are you cannot replicate the filenames directly. However, take a look at the code that follows. (And if you're feeling ambitious, type it and save it!)

```
macroScript RenameByIFL category:"Killer Tips"
(
  theIfl = getOpenFileName types:"IFL (*.ifl)|*.ifl" caption:"Select
  ➥Reference IFL"
  if theIfl != undefined then
  (
    source_dir = getSavePath caption:"Select Folder with Files to Rename
    ➥based on IFL"
    if source_dir != undefined then
    (
      rendered_files = sort(getFiles (source_dir + "\\*.tga"))
      rendered_count = rendered_files.count
      if rendered_count > 0 then
      (
        read_ifl = openFile theIfl
        line_counter = 0
        while not eof read_ifl do
        (
          line_counter += 1
          theLine = readline read_ifl
          if line_counter <= rendered_count then
          (
            format "Renaming % to %\n" rendered_files[ line_counter]
            ➥theLine
```

```
            if (renameFile rendered_files[ line_counter]
            ➥(source_dir+"\\"+theLine)) then
              format "Success!\n"
            else
              format "FAILED!\n"
          )
          else
            format "No image found for IFL entry %\n" theLine
        )
      close read_ifl
      )
      else
        format "No images found in the specified folder %\n" source_dir
    )
    else
      format "No path selected!"
  )
  else
    format "No IFL File Selected."
)
```

Note: The script shown uses .TGA as the default filename. If you use any other file format, you'll have to adjust the "rendered_files" line. As shown earlier, one solution is for you to render to some proxy filename first, and then use this small MAXScript to read the names from the .IFL and rename the newly rendered animation files to these names. It's as easy as apple pie, but with fewer calories.

SHADES OF GRAY: USING RENDEREFFECTS FOR CUSTOM RENDERING

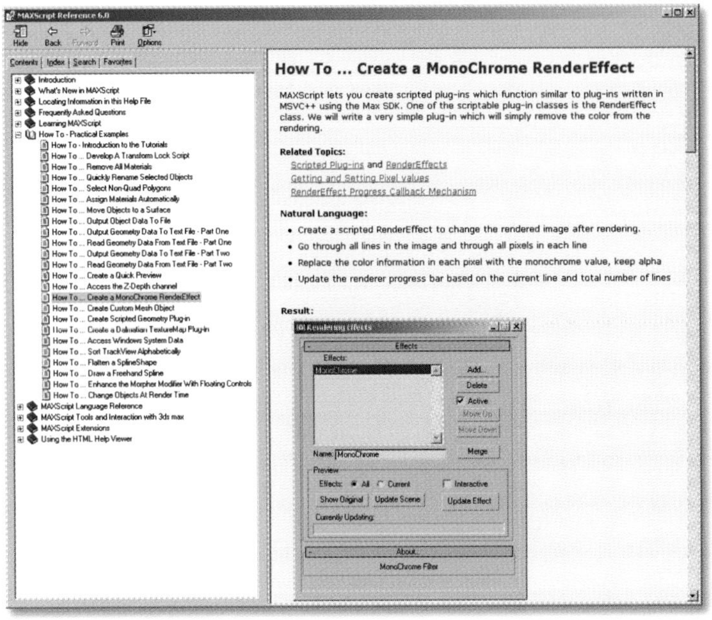
MAXScript Reference 6.0
How To ... Create a MonoChrome RenderEffect
MAXScript lets you create scripted plug-ins which function similar to plug-ins written in MSVC++ using the Max SDK. One of the scriptable plug-in classes is the RenderEffect class. We will write a very simple plug-in which will simply remove the color from the rendering.
Related Topics:
Scripted Plug-ins and RenderEffects
Getting and Setting Pixel values
RenderEffect Progress Callback Mechanism
Natural Language:
Create a scripted RenderEffect to change the rendered image after rendering.
Go through all lines in the image and through all pixels in each line
Replace the color information in each pixel with the monochrome value, keep alpha
Update the renderer progress bar based on the current line and total number of lines
Result:
Effects
Add...
Delete
Active
Merge
Show Original
Update Scene
Update Effect
About...
MonoChrome Filter

The MAXScript online documentation shipping with 3ds max contains useful examples that you can modify for your own enjoyment. For instance, the following code is based on the "How to Create a MonoChrome RenderEffect" tutorial shipping with 3ds max. By adding just a couple of lines, this simple RenderEffect is transformed into a much more powerful filter, allowing you to specify the exact number of gray shades in your final rendering!

```
plugin RenderEffect MonoChromeShaded name:"MonoChrome Shaded"
classID:#(0x9e6e9e78, 0xbe815df6)
(
parameters main rollout:params (
color_count type:#integer default:16 ui:color_count )
rollout params " MonoChrome Shades Filter" (
spinner color_count "Number Of Shades" type:#integer range:[ 2,256,16] field-
width:60 )
on apply r_image progressCB: do (
  progressCB.setTitle "MonoChrome Effect"
  local oldEscapeEnable = escapeEnable
  escapeEnable = false
  bmp_w = r_image.width
  bmp_h = r_image.height
  gradient_colors = 256.0/color_count
  for y = 0 to bmp_h-1 do
```

```
    (
      if progressCB.progress y (bmp_h-1) then exit
      pixel_line = getPixels r_image [ 0,y] bmp_w
      for x = 1 to bmp_w do (
        p_v = gradient_colors  * floor (pixel_line[ x] .value / gradient_colors
 )
        pixel_line[ x]  = color p_v p_v p_v pixel_line[ x] .alpha
      )
      setPixels r_image [ 0,y] pixel_line
    )
    escapeEnable = oldEscapeEnable
  )--end on apply
  )--end plugin
```

To use this, just type the previous code in a MAXScript Editor, and save it to your 3dsmax6\ plugins folder as "monoChromeShaded.ms". Then restart 3ds max, open the Environment and Effects RenderEffect dialog, and on the Effects tab, add "MonoChrome Shaded" to the queue. Set it to the number of grayscale values you need, and off you go!

FOUR TIPS FOR THE PRICE OF ONE, OR, CONVERTING FILE FORMATS

3ds max is like the proverbial Swiss army knife: You can often use it to perform actions that you would employ another application to do. For example, there are many different ways you can convert a set of single images to a different format (and some of them are listed in Chapter 6, "Making It Beautiful: Rendering Tips," earlier in this book.) But, just to recap:

- You can create an .IFL sequence from the single files, load it as input event in Video Post, and add an output event to write to a different format.
- You can load the .IFL as background animation and render the empty scene to the new format.
- Probably the most elegant way (provided you have enough RAM): You can load the sequence in the RAM Player, press the Save Channel button, and select a new file type.

Or, you can take a gander at this:

```
(
 theFiles = getFiles ((GetDir #image) + "/test*.rpf")
 theImage = openbitmap theFiles[ 1]
 local new_image  = bitmap theImage.width theImage.height
 close theImage
 for i in theFiles do
 (
   theImage = openbitmap i
   new_image.filename = ((GetDir #image) + "/" + getfilenamefile i  +
".tga")
   print (new_image.filename)
   copy theImage new_image
   save new_image
 )
 close new_image
 new_image = undefined
 gc light:true
)
```

Again, please note the lines specifying the source and destination filenames and extensions; you'll have to change the relevant lines if you want to switch to a different folder or image format (.TGA, .TIF, and so on). As indicated earlier, you can also write a script to convert between the formats, but this is hard-core stuff for geeks only, especially when compared to the other methods listed previously. (Not that I know of any 3D or programming geeks associated with this book, mind you….)

LET THE INK FLOW (WITH GLOBAL CONTROL)

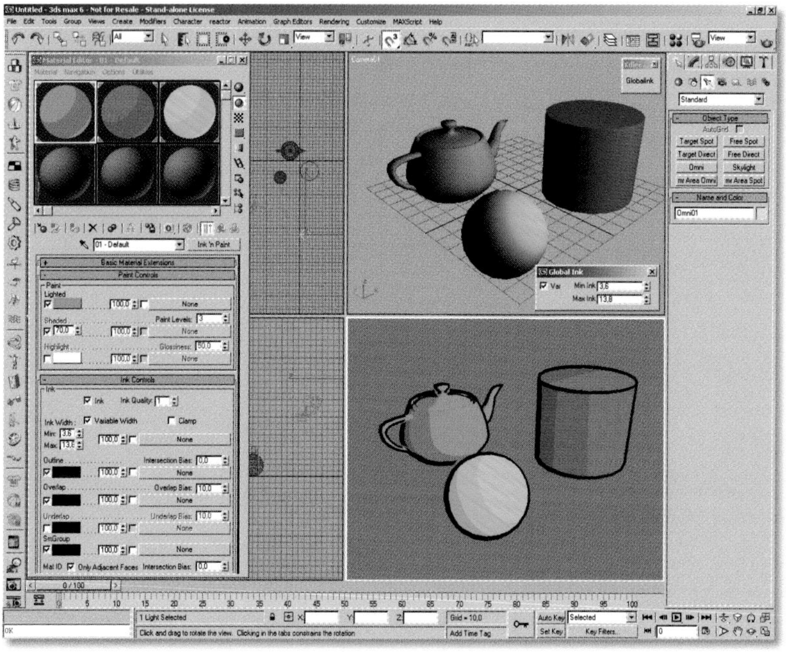

The ink width of the Ink 'n Paint material is controlled per material. This script gives you a global control that changed all Ink 'n Paint materials in the scene at once:

```
macroScript
➥GlobalInk
➥category:"Killer
➥Tips"
(
rollout
➥GlobalInk_
➥rollout "Global
➥Ink"
(
  spinner
  ➥min_ink_width
  ➥"Min Ink"
  ➥range:
  ➥[ 0,100,2]
  spinner max_ink_width "Max Ink" range:[ 0,100,4]
  checkbox var_width "Var" checked:false pos:[ 5,5]
  fn updateAllInks = (
    for m in sceneMaterials where classof m == InkNPaint do (
      m.ink_auto_vary_on = var_width.state
      m.min_ink_width = min_ink_width.value
      m.max_ink_width = max_ink_width.value )
    )
    on var_width changed state do updateAllInks ()
    on min_ink_width changed val do updateAllInks ()
    on max_ink_width changed val do updateAllInks ()
  )
  try(destroyDialog GlobalInk_rollout)catch()
  createDialog GlobalInk_rollout 200 50
  for m in sceneMaterials where classof m == InkNPaint do (
    GlobalInk_rollout.min_ink_width.value = m.min_ink_width
    GlobalInk_rollout.max_ink_width.value = m.max_ink_width
    GlobalInk_rollout.var_width.state = m.ink_auto_vary_on
  )
)
```

Now you can modify your Ink 'n Paint line easily to create different results.

THE MAXTRIX RELOADED: CREATING BULLET TIME WITH SUB-FRAME RENDERING

A cool (but not widely known) MAXScript feature of the 3ds max scanline renderer is its ability to render sub-frames. Simply passing a floating point time value to the frame: parameter of the `render()` method gives you the power to slow down an animation without even touching the time properties of the scene, or (you guessed it) create "Matrix-style" "bullet time" effects in just a few lines of code!

```
(
fn getLeadingZeros num = ( substring "0000" 1 (4-(num as string).count) )
out_bmp = bitmap 320 240
originalCamera = $Camera01
newCamera = FreeCamera()
TheTime = 0.0; TheNumber = 0; TheTimeStep = 1.0; TheTimeDelta = -0.01
While TheNumber < 100 do (
       TheTimeStep += TheTimeDelta
    If TheTimeStep < 0.01 do TheTimeDelta = -TheTimeDelta
    TheTime += TheTimeStep
       TheNumber += 1
       newCamera.transform = at time TheNumber originalCamera.transform
       render frame:TheTime to:out_bmp
       out_bmp.filename = GetDir #image +"/testframe_"+ (getLeadingZeros
TheNumber) + TheNumber as string +".tga"
       save out_bmp
)
delete new_camera
close out_bmp
out_bmp = undefined
gc light:true
)
```

This simple script takes a camera called Camera01 and renders to single frames by slowing down the time to a crawl and then increasing it back again. For example, if you create an exploding object using a PArray set to object fragments, you could watch the explosion slowing down and speeding up again. If you animate the camera moving normally around the exploding object, the script takes its animation and uses its values "through" the slowed-down animation to render a second temporary camera that respects the sub-frame rendering settings.

THE IMAGE WITHIN: READING THUMBNAILS

I'll warn you right up front: This is a hack. It's not how scripting was meant to be, but it works! The following code opens a .MAX file for binary input and reads the thumbnail bitmap stored in it. Bluntly, the function does some black magic. Don't ask why it works; just be happy that it does.

```
fn ReadMaxThumbNail file_path = (
local bs = Fopen file_path "rb"
fseek bs (-50000) #seek_end
local s = 0, counter = 0
local readBmp = bitmap 132 132 color:(color 127 127 127)
while s != 185729024 and counter < 20000 do (
  s = ReadLong bs #signed
  counter += 1
)
if s == 185729024 then (
  fseek bs (-34) #seek_cur
  local b_height = ReadByte bs #unsigned
  ReadByte bs #unsigned
  b_width= ReadByte bs #unsigned
  for i = 1 to 45 do r = ReadByte bs #unsigned
  for v = 0 to (b_height-2) do (
    pix = #()
    for h = 0 to (b_width-1) do (
      r = ReadByte bs #unsigned
      g = ReadByte bs #unsigned
      b = ReadByte bs #unsigned
      try ( col = color b g r ) catch (Fclose bs; return readBmp)
      append pix col
    )--end h loop
    setpixels readBmp [ 2,132-((132-b_height)/2)-v] pix
  )--end h loop
)
Fclose bs
readBmp
)
```

Just type this code in a new script and save it in your 3dsmax6\StdPlugs\StdScripts folder. That way, the function is globally accessible each time you start 3ds max. In the next tip, you'll see how you can use the function to create a small thumbnail gallery of your 3ds max files.

I KNOW WHAT YOU RENDERED LAST SUMMER

A Render History system stores copies of your test renders in a Preview folder and lets you quickly compare variations in modeling, lighting, and texturing. It also manages the file saving for you, even when you render to the Virtual Frame Buffer (oops—Rendered Frame Window in 3ds max 6) only.

The following MacroScripts implement a simple Render History system. The first script defines a PostRender callback that is executed every time a rendering has finished. It captures the last rendered image and saves it under a unique name.

```
macroScript RHOn category:"Killer Tips"
(
callbacks.removeScripts #postRender id:#KillerTipsRenderHistory
txt = "renderHistoryBmp = getLastRenderedImage()\n"
txt +="FileCount = (getFiles ( (GetDir #preview)+
\"/RenderHistory_*.tga\")).count \n"
txt += "TheFileName = (GetDir #preview) + \"/renderHistory_\"+ (substring
\"0000\" 1 (4-(FileCount as string).count) ) + (FileCount+1) as string +
\".tga\" \n"
txt +="renderHistoryBmp.filename = TheFileName\n"
txt +="save renderHistoryBmp\n"
txt +="renderHistoryBmp = undefined\n"
callbacks.addScript #postRender txt id:#KillerTipsRenderHistory
)
```

This MacroScript removes the PostRender callback and disables the saving of Render History images:

```
macroScript RHOff category:"Killer Tips" (
callbacks.removeScripts #postRender id:#KillerTipsRenderHistory )
```

This MacroScript deletes all Render History images from the previews folder:

```
macroScript RHClear category:"Killer Tips" (
q = querybox "Are you sure you want to clear all Render History Files?"
if q then (
IflList = getFiles ((GetDir #preview)+"/renderHistory_*.tga")
for f in IflList do deleteFile f )
)
```

This MacroScript collects all Render History images from the previews folder, creates a new IFL file listing all the files, and opens it in the RAM Player as long as there are any images to show:

```
macroScript RHShow category:"Killer Tips" (
IflList = sort (getFiles ((GetDir #preview)+"/renderHistory_*.tga"))
IflPath = (GetDir #preview)+"/renderHistoryView.ifl"
IflOut = createFile IflPath
for f in IflList do (format "%\n" f to:IflOut)
close IflOut
if IflList.count > 0 then RAMplayer IflPath "" else messagebox "No Render
History Files Found!"
)
```

Evaluate these scripts and place them on a toolbar by dragging them from the "Killer Tips" category in the Customize > Customize User Interface > Toolbars dialog.

To use, click the RHOn button. If you render any views now, the resulting images are written to the previews folder. You can click RHOff anytime to disable the saving, and then click RHOn again to enable it and so on. To view the collected images and compare them, click the RHShow button.

A BUNCH OF COLORFUL WIRES

When your viewport display is set to Edged Faces, an unselected shaded mesh displays the material color, while a wireframe mesh uses the object color. And, if you enable the Show Map in Viewport button (in the Material Editor), the shaded mesh displays the texture.

Here's an alternative approach: What if you copy the Diffuse color of the material to the object color? The resultant wireframe display gives you a hint of your final result when the Diffuse map and Diffuse color are mixed together.

```
macroScript DiffuseToWire
  category:"Killer Tips"
  buttontext:"Copy Diffuse To Wireframe Color"
(
  for o in geometry do
    if o.material != undefined and classof o.material == Standard do
      o.wirecolor = o.material.diffusecolor
)
```

This script copies the Diffuse color to the object color of all geometry objects that have a Standard material assigned. You can customize the Material Editor menu to add this script to the Utilities menu.

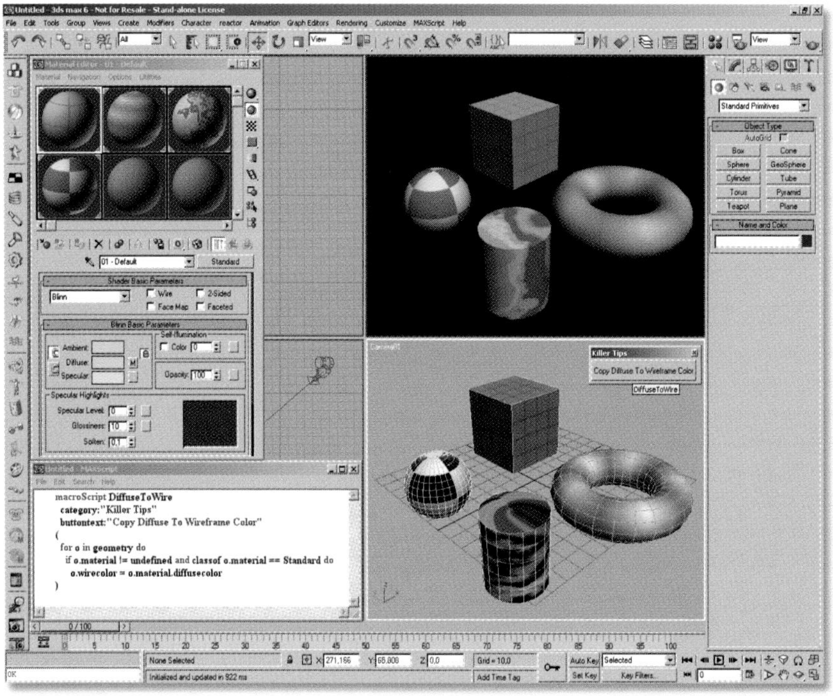

A KNOTTY PROBLEM: CREATING AUTOCAD-STYLE COORDINATE INPUT

Many users coming to 3ds max from Autodesk's AutoCAD ask for a relative and polar coordinate input, such as when creating splines. Following is a simple script that lets you create a spline by typing in absolute, relative, and polar coordinates.

```
macroScript TypeInSpline category:"Killer Tips" (
  new_spline = SplineShape()
  addNewSpline new_spline
  endOfInput = False
  while not endOfInput do   (
    a = pickPoint terminators:#("e","c") prompt:"Enter New Point
Coordinates:\n"
    if a[ 2] == "e" do endOfInput = true
    if a[ 2] == "c" do (
      close new_spline 1
      endOfInput = true
      format "\nShape Closed\n"
    )
    if a[ 1] != undefined and a[ 1] != #rightClick do (
      addKnot new_spline 1 #corner #line a[ 1]
      if NumKnots new_spline 1 > 1 then updateShape new_spline
      format "%\n" (getKnotPoint  new_spline 1 (NumKnots new_spline 1))
    )
  )
  if NumKnots new_spline 1< 2 then (
    delete new_spline
    format "Not Enough Points, Shape Deleted.\n" )
  else (
    updateShape new_spline
    format "Shape Input End \n"
  )
)
```

Note: Use the MAXScript Listener to enter knot coordinates. You can use C to close the spline and finish, or E to end without closing.

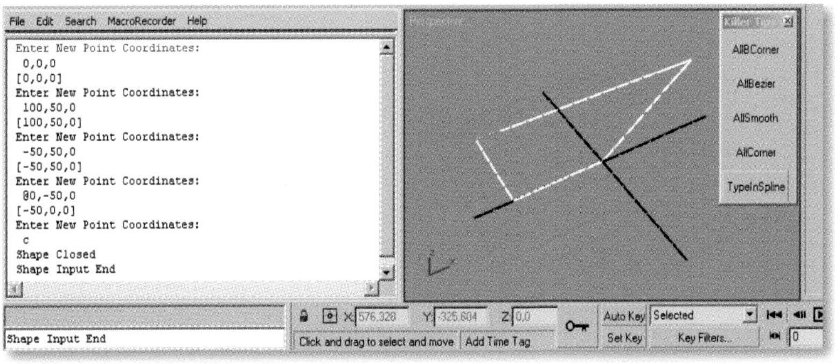

THIS KNOT IS NOT WHAT I THOUGHT: CHANGING SPLINE VERTEX TYPES

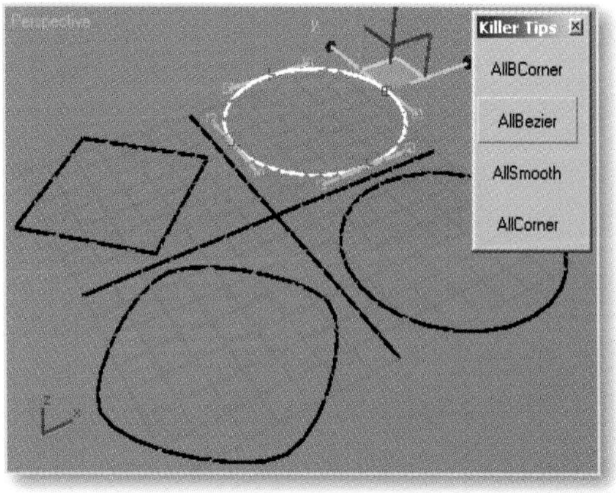

Are you importing hundreds of AutoCAD spline models (via the .DWG format) into 3ds max, and having to change the corner types of every shape? Do you enjoy the hours you spend doing this? (I thought not.) Well, a judicious use of MAXScript can save you from this drudgery.

```
global changeAllKnots
fn changeAllKnots spline type =
(
try
(
      for s = 1 to (numsplines spline) do
              for k = 1 to numKnots spline s do
                     setKnotType spline s k type
      updateshape spline
)catch()
)

macroScript AllBezier category:"Killer Tips" (
  for i in selection where superclassof i == shape do changeAllKnots i
#bezier
)
macroScript AllCorner category:"Killer Tips" (
  for i in selection where superclassof i == shape do changeAllKnots i
#corner
)
macroScript AllBCorner category:"Killer Tips" (
   for i in selection where superclassof i == shape do changeAllKnots i
#beziercorner
)
macroScript AllSmooth category:"Killer Tips" (
   for i in selection where superclassof i == shape do changeAllKnots i
#smooth
)
```

The previous simple script goes through selected objects, finds the editable splines, and switches all your vertices to the desired corner type. (You must assign the four MacroScripts to a toolbar or the quad menus; this gives you quick access when you're working with lots of splines.)

NEXT VIEWPORT, PLEASE!

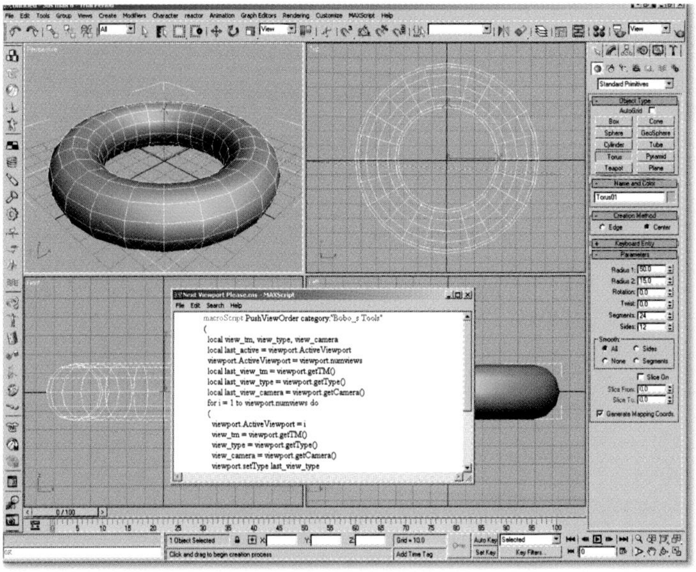

The following MacroScript switches the order of viewports, as you desire.

In the case of the default 3ds max four-viewports layout, the bottom-right Perspective viewport moves to the upper-left viewport, the Top viewport moves from the upper-left to the upper-right quadrant, the upper right (Front view) moves down left, and the lower left (Left view) moves to the lower-right viewport.

```
macroScript
PushViewOrder category:
➥"Killer Tips"
(
  local view_tm, view_type, view_camera
  local last_active = viewport.ActiveViewport
  viewport.ActiveViewport = viewport.numviews
  local last_view_tm = viewport.getTM()
  local last_view_type = viewport.getType()
  local last_view_camera = viewport.getCamera()
  for i = 1 to viewport.numviews do
  (
    viewport.ActiveViewport = i
    view_tm = viewport.getTM()
    view_type = viewport.getType()
    view_camera = viewport.getCamera()
    viewport.setType last_view_type
    viewport.setTM last_view_tm
    try(viewport.setCamera last_view_camera)catch()
    last_view_tm = view_tm
    last_view_type = view_type
    last_view_camera = view_camera
  )
  try(viewport.ActiveViewport = last_active)catch()
)
```

If you click the script's button again, the viewport "places" rotation continues, until you're back where you started.

COUNTING CAMERAS (TO FALL ASLEEP?)

The following simple MAXScript function returns a list of all cameras currently displayed in the four viewports.

```
fn getViewCameras =
(
  cam_array = #()
  original_view = viewport.activeViewport
  for i = 1 to viewport.numViews do
  (
    viewport.activeViewport = i
    append cam_array (viewport.getCamera() )
  )
  try(viewport.activeViewport = original_view)catch()
  cam_array
)getViewCameras()
```

Note: The script returns the value "undefined," where no camera is assigned to a viewport.

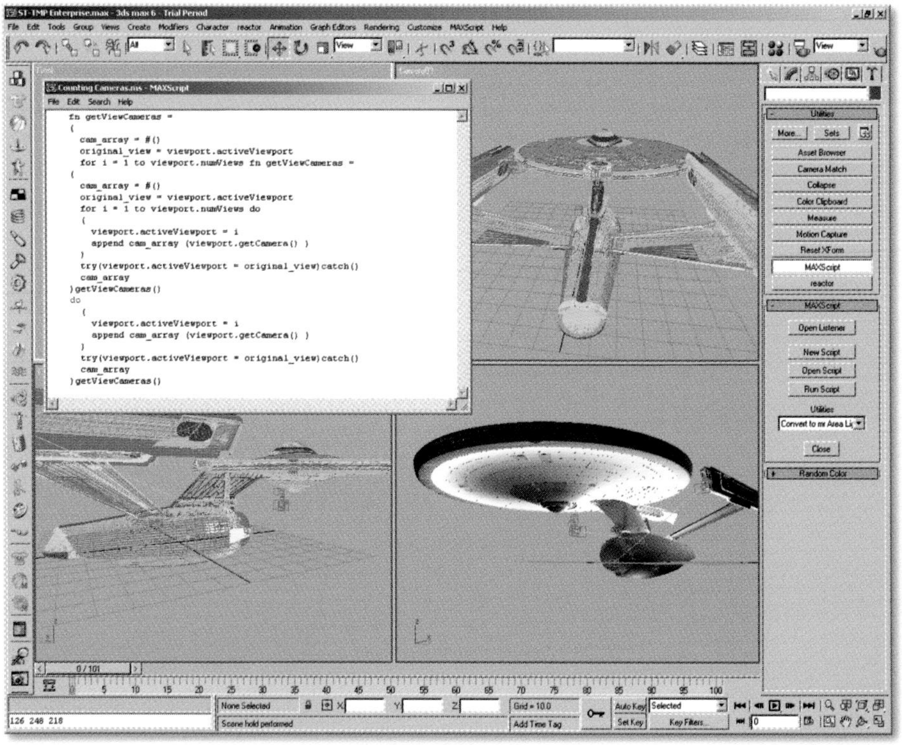

THE EYE IN THE SKY: RECORDING YOUR VIEWPORTS WHILE WORKING

There are some rather expensive screen capture applications available that let you record every action you perform on your computer desktop. (This software is useful for people doing software training CDs, videotapes, and DVDs.) But what if you had a simple MAXScript that would let you do the same thing, and save some money in the process?

The following script snapshots your 3ds max desktop viewports, using a timer set to record a frame every n seconds. (In this sense, it works similarly to the 3ds max 6 Animation > Make Preview feature, which snaps a single viewport image to create a file showing your scene animation.)

```
macroScript RecordViewport category:"Killer Tips"
(
  local preview_name, view_size, anim_bmp
  rollout RecordViewportRollout "Record Viewport" (
    edittext RecordName "AVI Name:" text:"RecordViewport"
    spinner FramesPerSecond "Frames Per Second" range:[ 0.01,60.0,10.0]
    ➥fieldwidth:40
    checkbox OpenAfterRecord "Open AVI After Record" checked:false
    checkbutton startRecord "START RECORDING" width:180
    timer clock "recordClock" active:false
    on startRecord changed state do (
      clock.active = state
      if state then (
        clock.interval = 1000.0/FramesPerSecond.value
        preview_name = (getDir #preview)+ "/"+RecordName.text + ".avi"
        view_size = getViewSize()
        anim_bmp = bitmap view_size.x view_size.y filename:preview_name
      )
      else (
        close anim_bmp
        gc light:true
        if OpenAfterRecord.checked then ramplayer preview_name ""
      )
    )
    on clock tick do (
      dib = gw.getViewportDib()
      copy dib anim_bmp
      save anim_bmp
    )
  )--end roll
  destroyDialog RecordViewportRollout
  createDialog RecordViewportRollout 200 100
)
```

Note: This utility lets you record multiple frames per second, but you could also set it up to record just one frame every 100 seconds and thus create a time-lapse animation of your viewport work.

CATCH THE RAINBOW: ANIMATING VERTEX COLORS USING UNWRAP UVW

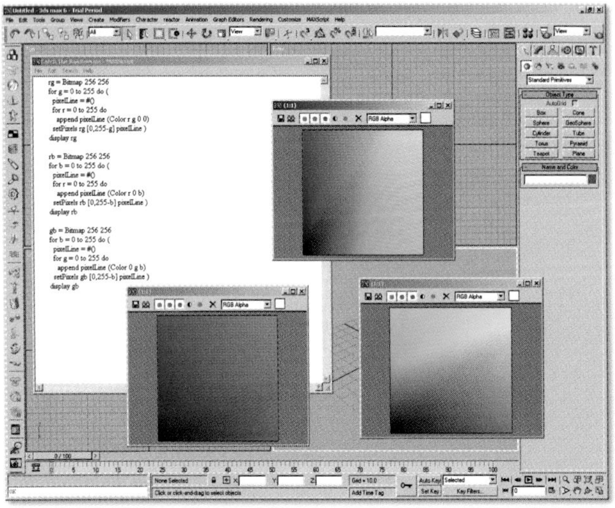

3ds max 6 lets you animate the opacity of vertex paint layers—but did you know that you can actually animate the position of every vertex color in color space using the Unwrap UVW modifier? To make your life easier, you could create three bitmaps representing the RG, RB, and GB color combinations corresponding to the UV, UW, and VW coordinates. The following MAXScript code creates the bitmaps for you. You can then save them to your 3dsmax\Images folder manually:

```
rg = Bitmap 256 256
for g = 0 to 255 do (
  pixelLine = #()
  for r = 0 to 255 do
    append pixelLine (Color r g 0 0)
  setPixels rg [ 0,255-g] pixelLine )
display rg

rb = Bitmap 256 256
for b = 0 to 255 do (
  pixelLine = #()
  for r = 0 to 255 do
    append pixelLine (Color r 0 b)
  setPixels rb [ 0,255-b] pixelLine )
display rb

gb = Bitmap 256 256
for b = 0 to 255 do (
  pixelLine = #()
  for g = 0 to 255 do
    append pixelLine (Color 0 g b)
  setPixels gb [ 0,255-b] pixelLine )
display gb
```

Load these images as the background in the Unwrap UVW Editor and enable Auto Key. Then go to a different frame and move the color vertices by hand to the desired color locations in UV, UW, and VW views corresponding to the sides of the color picker "cube."

PAINT OVER EVERYTHING: CLEAR ALL MATERIALS

Want to clear all the material assignments from your scene without affecting anything else? Then just type the following line in the MAXScript Listener window:

```
Geometry.material = undefined
```

Zap! Your materials are cleared, and you're ready to start reassigning materials from scratch.

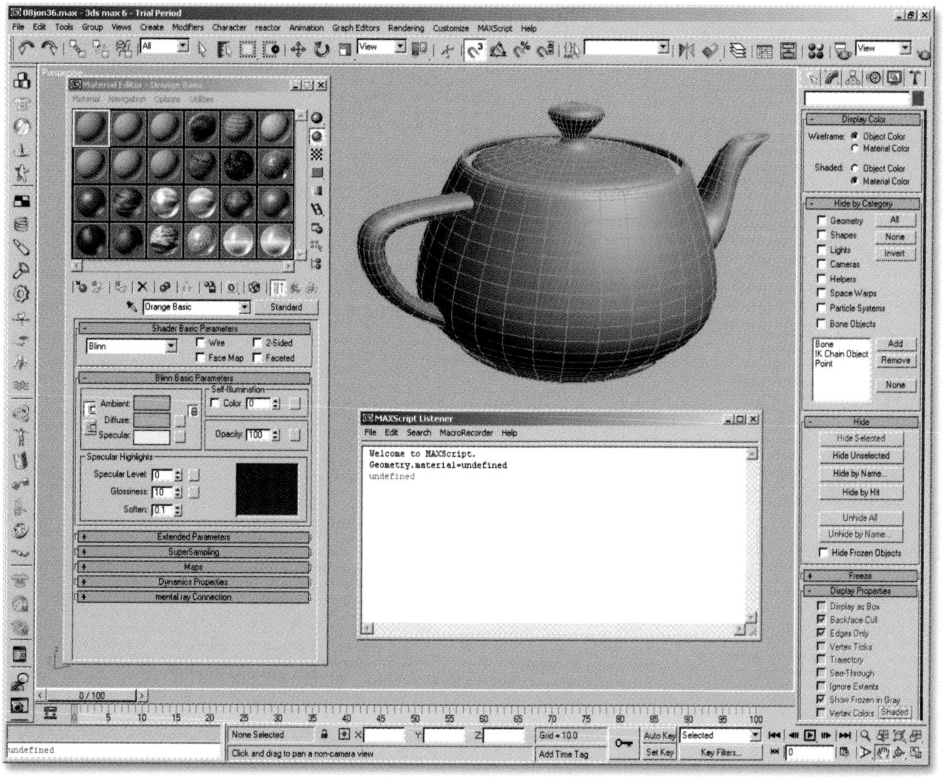

THUMBNAIL PICTURES AT AN EXHIBITION

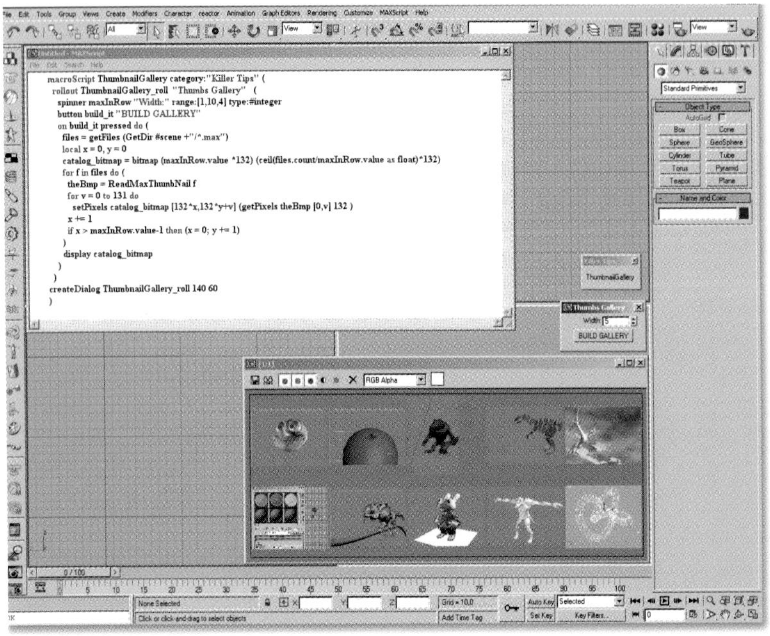

In our last tip, you should have typed the "Thumbnails" code and saved it to your 3dsmax6\StdPlugs\StdScripts folder. Now, check out the following code:

```
macroScript
➥ThumbnailGallery
➥category:"Killer
➥Tips" (
  rollout
  ➥Thumbnail
  ➥Gallery_roll
  ➥" Thumbs
  ➥Gallery"    (
    spinner
    ➥maxInRow
    ➥" Width:"
    ➥range:
    ➥[ 1,10,4] type:#integer
    button build_it "BUILD GALLERY"
    on build_it pressed do (
      files = getFiles (GetDir #scene +"/*.max")
      local x = 0, y = 0
      catalog_bitmap = bitmap (maxInRow.value *132)
(ceil(files.count/maxInRow.value as float)*132)
      for f in files do (
        theBmp = ReadMaxThumbNail f
        for v = 0 to 131 do
          setPixels catalog_bitmap [ 132*x,132*y+v] (getPixels theBmp [ 0,v] 132 )
        x += 1
        if x > maxInRow.value-1 then (x = 0; y += 1)
      )
      display catalog_bitmap
    )
  )
createDialog ThumbnailGallery_roll 140 60
)
```

The previous script provides you with a small rollout containing a spinner to define the width of your thumbnail gallery and includes a simple button to generate the gallery.

MAXSCRIPT KNOWS YOUR CODE!

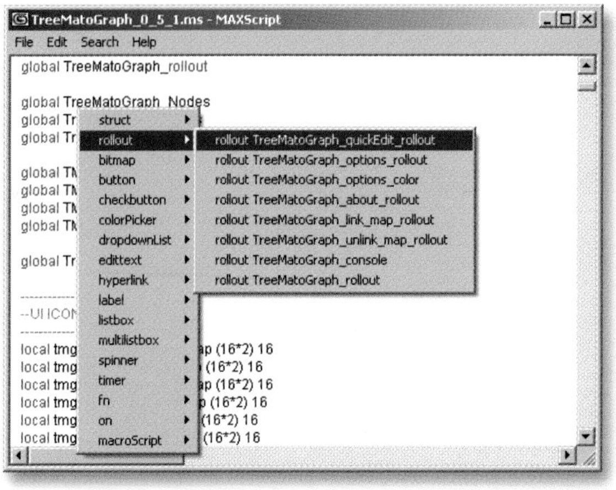

Many scripts fit on a single page, but some people don't stop there; as their code grows larger, even with well-written comments, locating specific parts of the script can become difficult.

However, MAXScript knows what you are doing. Just hold down the Ctrl key and press the right mouse button. A context menu appears, listing categories such as structures, rollouts, functions, user interface elements, event handlers, and macroscript definitions. Selecting any of their sub-items jumps you instantly to the relevant position in the script. Zap, and you're there!

STEP RIGHT UP—FREE BITMAP MEMORY!

There is a magic MAXScript command that does a lot of housekeeping work. It releases unused bitmap memory, consolidates fragmented memory, and reloads all bitmaps that your current 3ds max scene uses.

This function is

```
freeSceneBitmaps()
```

You can quickly type this in the MAXScript Listener and press the numeric Enter key, or, if you are either lazy or smart (or both), add the command as a button to your toolbars or assign it to a shortcut for easy access.

Select the text `freeSceneBitmaps()` in the MAXScript Listener and drag it to a toolbar. A new MacroScript is created with the command in its code.

If you are slightly more experienced with scripting, you could write the MacroScript yourself, evaluate it, and customize the UI. The script would look like the following:

```
MacroScript ReloadBitmaps category:"Killer Tips" (freeSceneBitmaps())
```

Consulting the Manual

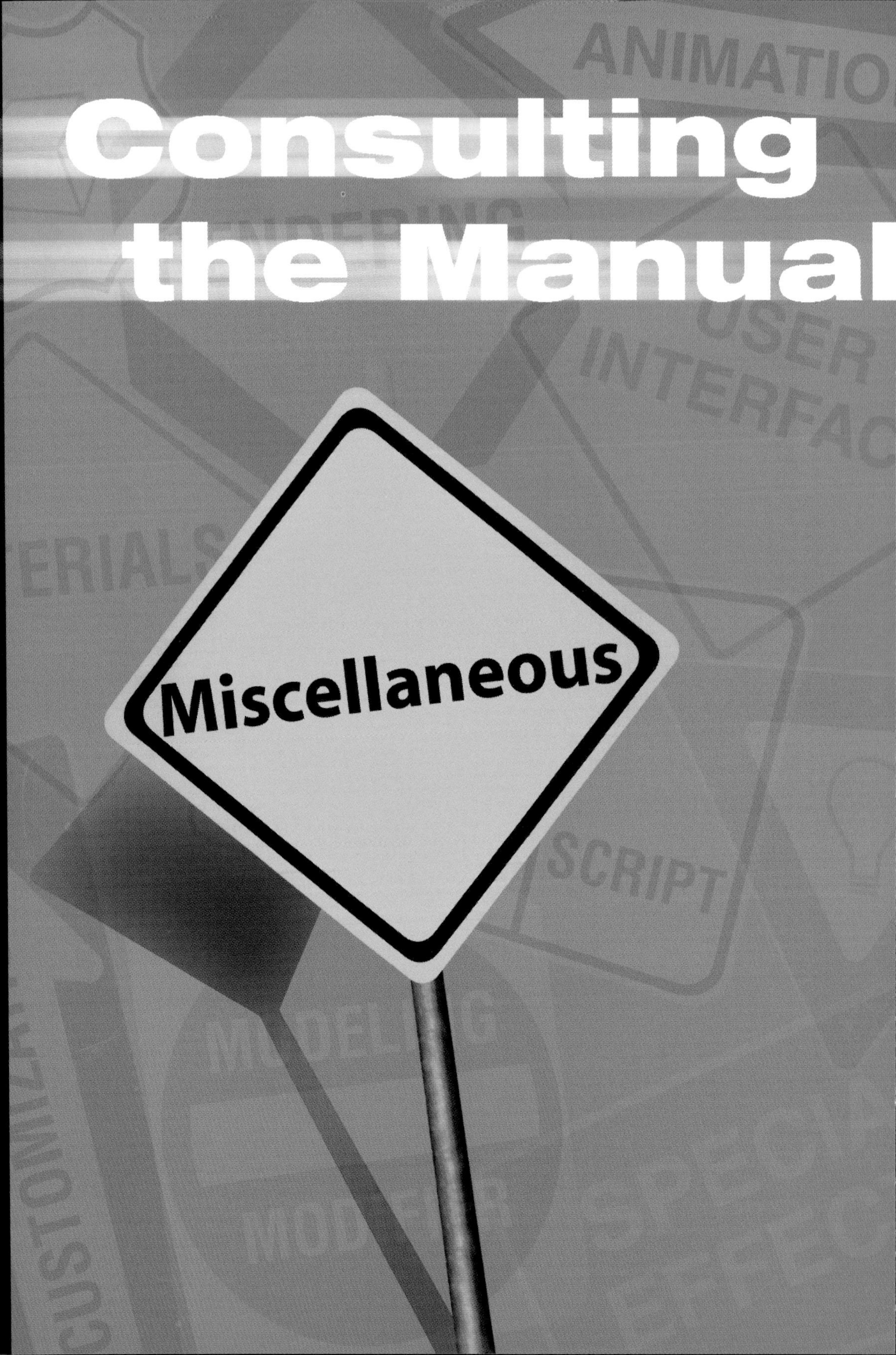

Consulting the Manual

tips on miscellaneous features

What are "miscellaneous" features of 3ds max? Well, one could say that they're features that aren't directly related to the acts of creating models, texturing them, lighting them, and animating them. Instead, they're "housekeeping" features—tools you use to manage your scenes and your overall 3ds max installation.

(One could also say that "miscellaneous features" is a category for "stuff that the author of this book couldn't figure out where it went in the other chapters, so he put it here." And you know what? That's just as accurate!)

In this chapter, I present various tips on how to work with the overall 3ds max program more efficiently and manage your 3D assets better—including troubleshooting problem files. In addition, Ben Lipman (Anatomical Travelogue, at http://www.anatomicaltravel.com), Cy Shuster (software developer and a member of Autodesk's Technical Support team), and Mark Gerhard of Discreet present a wealth of tips on how to deal with the Portable License Utility and use the 3ds max Asset Browser.

ZIP INSIDE! "COMPRESS ON SAVE" REDUCES FILE SIZE FOR FREE

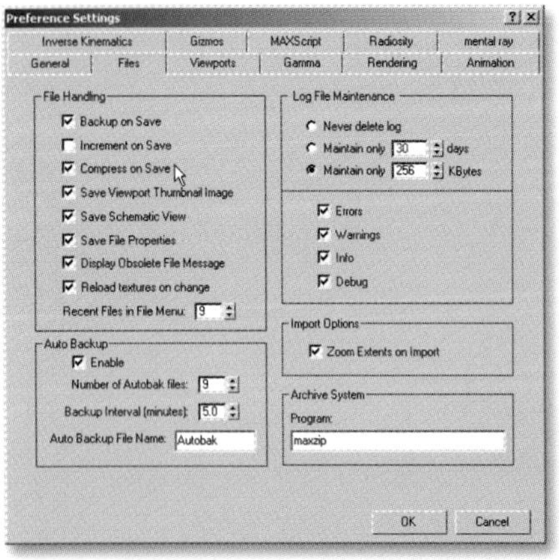

Need to free up some space for your 3ds max scene files? Well, there're two things you can do.

First, get rid of all those pirated .mp3 and questionable .jpg files cluttering your hard drive before the RIAA and the vice squad, respectively, come after you. Second, remember that 3ds max has a compression algorithm built into its file saving system. Go to Customize > Preferences > Files and check Compress on Save. Any files saved with this mode on are reduced in size. Only file properties and thumbnail data remain uncompressed so you can access them via Windows Explorer and the 3ds max Asset Browser. A file containing 100 default parametric mesh spheres saved without compression takes 4.566K. The same file saved with file compression takes 1.349K. The uncompressed file can be compressed using WinZip to 1.307K. So why waste time compressing manually to save disk space when 3ds max can do it for you? Just check the option and enjoy!

PUT THE PLU SHORTCUT IN THE 3DS MAX 6 STARTUP MENU

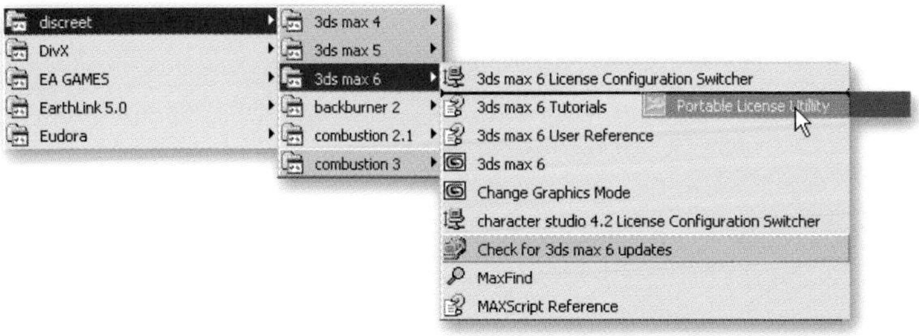

Where's the Startup menu shortcut for the PLU? Starting with 3ds max 6, the PLU Version 2 is a common component for many Discreet and Autodesk products, so it's now in the startup group called Autodesk.

Click on that group to open it, and then click and drag the PLU shortcut to the Discreet startup group. Hover on the PLU shortcut a moment (still dragging) until it opens, and then hover over the 3ds max 6 group, and drop it in that list anywhere you like.

This shortcut causes the PLU to open with "3ds max 6" as the current product. If you have more than one product installed using PLU version 2, their shortcuts select a different product. Before you export, make sure that the right product is selected in the Product drop-down list!

KILLING ME SOFTLY WITH YOUR 16-BIT PROCESSES

The 3ds max 4 and 5 C-Dilla licensing utility can cause your computer to slow down because it runs two services: CDilla64.exe and CDilla10.exe. Because CDilla10.exe is a 16-bit application, it has to run the NTVDM and wowexec.exe processes (actually, the ancient Microsoft Windows 3.1, under modern Windows emulation).

To remedy this, simply rename CDilla10.exe from your \WINNT folder (if you're using Windows 2000) or from the \WINDOWS folder (if you're using Windows XP). Rename it something like CDilla10.exe.BAK, so it wears a mask of 16-bit shame hanging around in that folder with all its 32-bit program compadres. (Don't worry; this isn't a "warez crack technique." The other CDilla utilities are still doing their jobs… and you free up some clock cycles doing this.)

Note: This tip is suggested for 3ds max releases 4 and 5 only. If you use the Portable License Utility (PLU) to transfer your 3ds max license to another computer, you might want to change this file back to its original name before using the utility, just to be on the safe side.

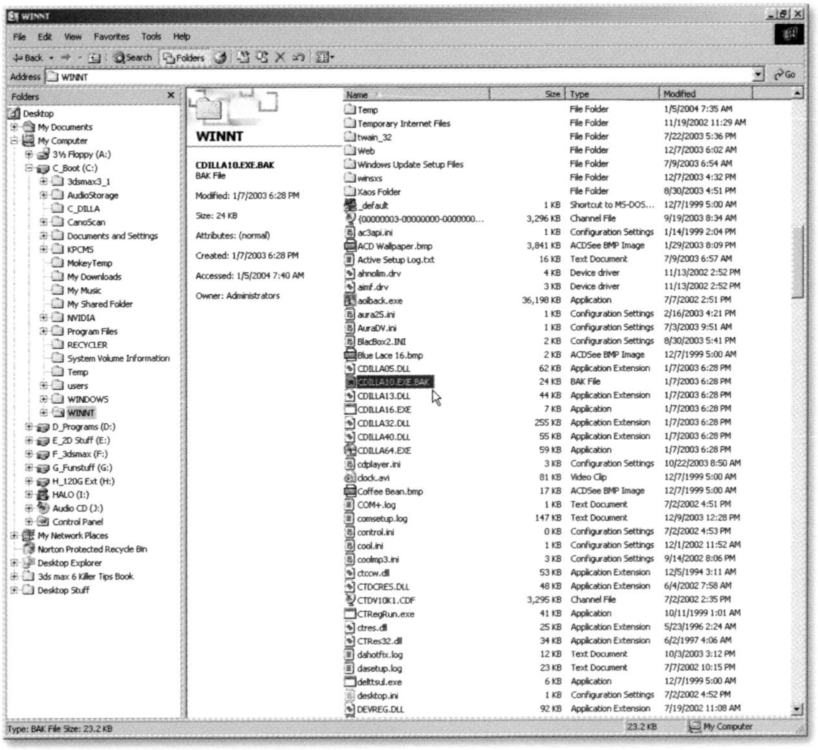

PLU QUICK START, WITH ONE COMPUTER

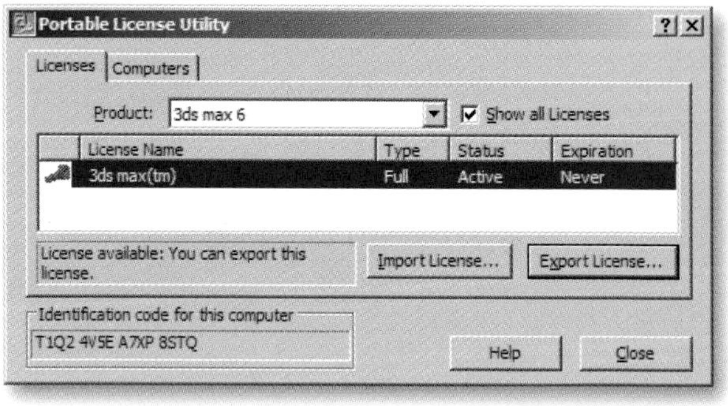

Are you nervous about trying the Portable License Utility (PLU)? Here's an easy way to get started, using just one PC. You can export your 3ds max license to yourself, and then import right back. Exporting removes the license from use on this PC and packages it into a portable form. Importing "unpackages" it. You just need a valid, authorized license (not a trial). For 3ds max 6, do this:

1. Exit all sessions of 3ds max.
2. Start the PLU from the Windows Start menu (in the Autodesk group; see the previous tip). Make sure the current product is 3ds max 6 in the drop-down list.
3. Select the license, and click Export License.
4. Under Export To, select this PC, and choose Use Transfer File.
5. Click Transfer License, and click OK on the Export to Current Computer warning dialog. That's it!

Now let's bring the license that was just exported back:

1. On the Licenses tab, click Import License and pick the Use Transfer File option.
2. Browse to the file you just created and click Import. You're done!

The PLU needs the unique identification code of the target PC, which it generates, in advance. It's like finding out someone's email address before you can send him email. (The computer name is ignored; that's a comment field for you.)

To move the license to another PC, you first have to install 3ds max there, to get its ID code. Before step 3, add this other PC under the Computers tab. (The PLU added this PC for you.) The benefit you get for this hassle is that if you lose the license file, or it becomes corrupt, you can re-create it any time by running Export again on the source PC.

Also, remember that the PLU has its own Help file, and there's a Help button on every dialog. The steps are similar for 3ds max 5, except you must manually add this PC to the computer list (Pool). Try it!

AUTOMATING THE PLU: NOW, THAT'S A SHORTCUT!

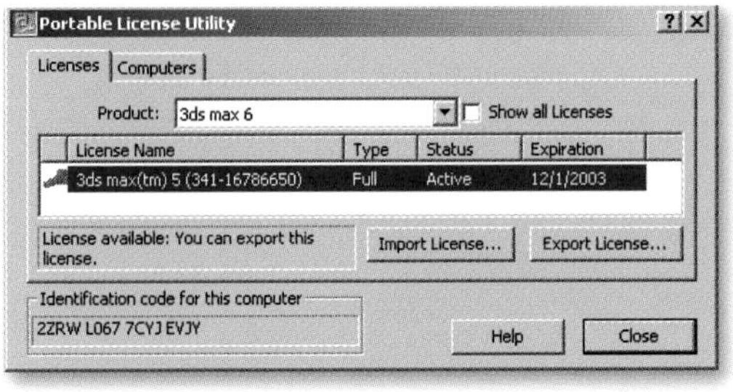

Although the PLU has many options, most people just move their license regularly between work and home. Here's how to make this routine. You need to know the "ID code" of the destination PC; running the PLU on that PC tells you.

1. Click Start and navigate to the Autodesk startup group.
2. Hold down the Ctrl key, left-click on Portable License Utility, and drag it to the desktop. (Ctrl makes a copy.)
3. Right-click on the new shortcut, and select Properties.
4. Click the General tab, and in the top edit box, type something more descriptive, such as PLU Max 6 To Home.
5. Click the Shortcut tab, click in the Target field, and press the End key. We'll add switches to what's there, which is like this (the language "enu" might differ):

   ```
   C:\Program Files\Common Files\Autodesk Shared\PLU.exe" /p:B1EC9000
   ➥/l:enu
   ```

6. Get the ID code of the PC you want to export to, removing any embedded spaces. Decide what filename you want to use. Carefully replace the underlined values in the following text, and add it to the end of the "Target" field. Be sure to start with a space.

   `/q /e:`*`A1A2B1B2C1C2D1D2`*` /o:`*`A:\Max6-To-Home.plu`*

   The italicized values in the previous line are just examples. The text after `/e:` is the ID code of the PC to export to. The text after `/o:` is the full path and filename of the transfer file (to a floppy, in this example). `/q` says to run in "quiet mode," without alerts. Remove this switch to see errors if the transfer doesn't work.

7. Click OK. You're done!

Now, any time you double-click on this desktop shortcut, your license is exported, creating the given transfer file—almost too easily! There won't be a single prompt, so be sure! Go back over these steps and double-check the values. I suggest naming the transfer file with the name of the target PC, to avoid confusion.

This is documented in the PLU's Help file under "command line switches."

WHICH PLU DO I USE?

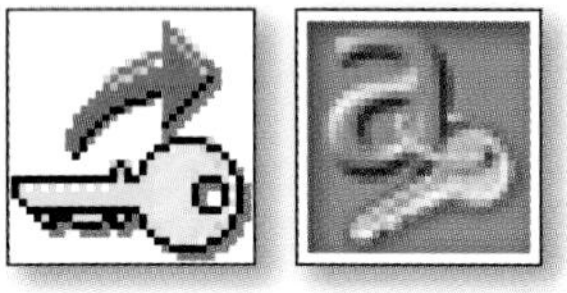

3ds max 4 and 3ds max 5 have their own unique versions of the Portable License Utility (PLU), installed in the same folder as the 3dsmax.exe. Those versions work only on their respective licenses, even though they use the same PLU software (the left icon in the figure). It's version 1.33D of the PLU. (See the Options tab in the PLU.)

3ds max 6 uses the new version 2 of the PLU (the right icon in the figure), which is a common component of many Discreet and Autodesk products (such as AutoCAD 2004). Version 2 doesn't work for earlier versions of 3ds max. Right-click on its window's title bar for the About box.

THE PLU: EASY MIGRATION FROM PRIOR RELEASES

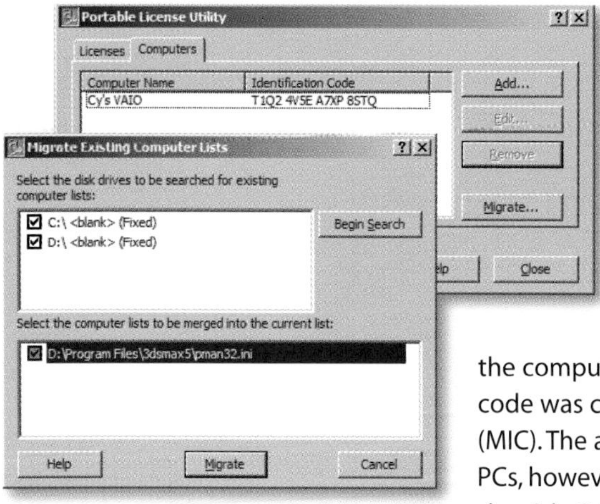

If you've used the PLU in 3ds max 5 or other Autodesk/Discreet products, you know that you must find out the unique identification code of the destination PC before you can export a license, and you must enter that code in the source PC's computer list.

In older products (PLU version 1), the computer list was called the pool, and the ID code was called the Machine Identification Code (MIC). The actual values of ID codes assigned to PCs, however, haven't changed with the PLU version 2 in 3ds max 6, so 3ds max includes a built-in utility to find your previous PLU pools and migrate them. This is a huge time-saver.

Simply click the Migrate button on the Computers tab, and check the drives to be searched. You can check any or all of the old pman32.ini files that the search finds, and then click Migrate on this dialog to merge them. It's safe to check all the files the search finds: if there are conflicts, such as duplicate entries for the same ID code, you are be prompted to resolve them.

Because the PLU version 2 is now a common component for Discreet and Autodesk products, these computer lists are shared across all products using it, so you'll never have to maintain multiple lists for multiple products again.

QUICK LICENSE IMPORTING

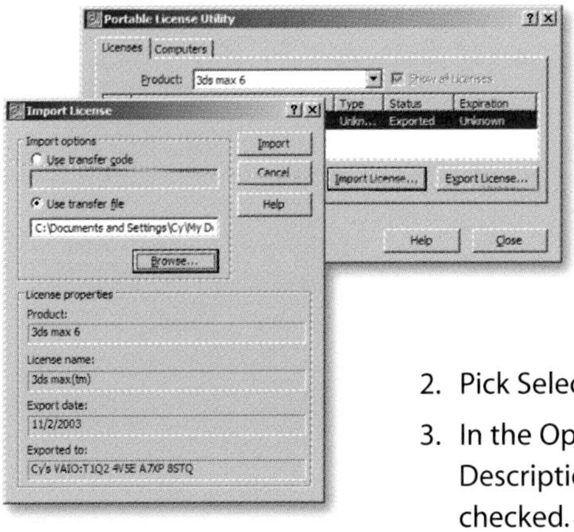

After you've exported a license, use the Transfer File method to create a .PLU file. You can use any method you like to get it to the other PC: floppy disk, email attachment, or shared network drive. After the .PLU file is on the destination PC, here's how to make importing quick (and relatively painless):

1. In Windows Explorer, double-click on the .PLU file. Windows will say it can't open this file.
2. Pick Select the Program from a List and click OK.
3. In the Open With dialog, type "PLU Transfer File" in the Type a Description field. Leave Always Use the Selected Program checked.
4. Click Browse and select C:\Program Files\Common Files\Autodesk Shared\PLU.exe.

Now (and on future double-clicks) the Portable License Utility runs automatically, selects the correct product, and even displays information about when this transfer file was created, and which PC was the target. This applies to 3ds max 6 only.

A TOOL, A UTILITY, AND AN EASTER EGG: FINDING FILES

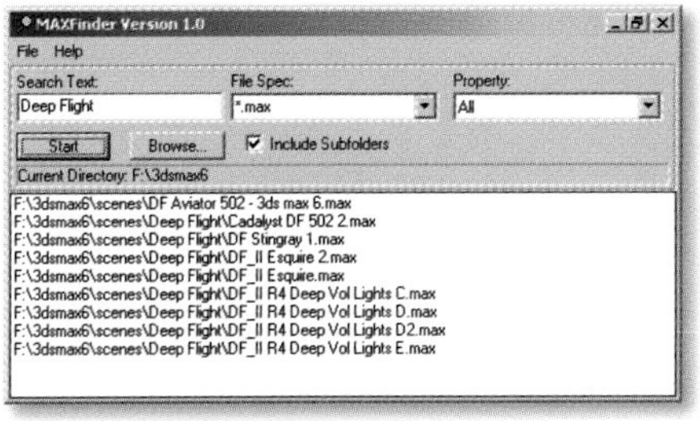

The MAX (File) Finder utility is a special beast. It's the only utility that is available not only in the Command Panel > Utilities tab > More drop-down menu > MAX File Finder, but also as a stand-alone tool that you can use without launching the application. See MaxFind.exe in your root 3dsmax folder. In addition, it's the only place in 3ds max you can find an Easter Egg—a non-feature addition to the software for just having fun. Open the Help > About dialog and see for yourself!

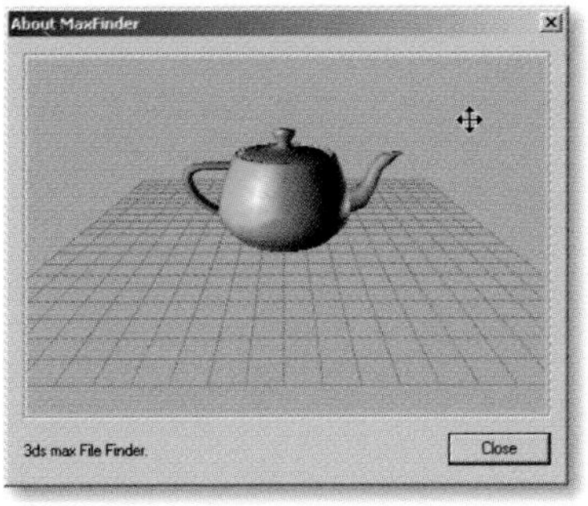

Although the Easter Egg is cute, the main function of this tool/utility isn't bad either. It will let you locate .max scene files by various criteria. For example, if you remember working on an object called "Deep Flight" but have no idea what scene it has been saved to, you could let the MAX File Finder search for files containing that object without even opening 3ds max!

RENDER PROBLEMS: FIX FACES BY TURNING EDGES

The bane of 3d rendering for polygonal models (such as 3ds max Editable Meshes) is when you have a cluster of long, thin triangular faces in part of your model. These might be caused by a bad boolean, importing (and converting) a model from a spline format, such as .IGEs, into an editable mesh, or simply sloppy model making. When you have a group of long triangular faces like this, you often get rendering errors (the faces "flicker") during animation, and applying a Smooth Modifier often doesn't completely fix the problem.

If you encounter a model like this, select the object, go into Sub-Object: Edge mode, and see if you can fix the problem by using the Turn tool (under the Edit Geometry rollout). Wherever possible, try to turn edges so that they're more evenly spaced and emanate from multiple surrounding vertices—a "radial fan" of edges/faces surrounding one vertex presents one of the most egregious problems to fix.

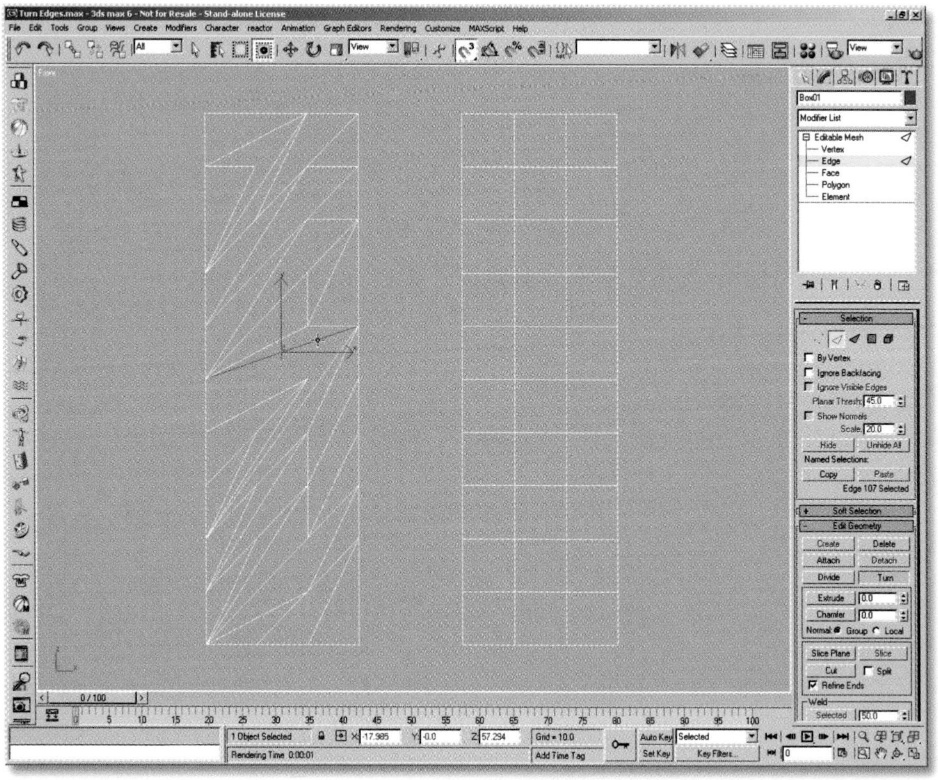

RENDER PROBLEMS: DIVIDE EDGES TO FIX FACES

In the previous tip, I mentioned how you could attempt to fix rendering problems in editable meshes by using the Turn feature in Sub-Object: Edges mode. If you can't seem to completely fix your rendering problems by turning the *existing* edges in your model, then use the Sub-Object: Edge > Edit Geometry > Divide tool. By selecting this button and then clicking in the middle of problem edges, you will add additional faces around a new vertex created at that point. By alternating between the Turn and Divide tools, you can usually create enough well-ordered faces to fix any rendering problems that might occur.

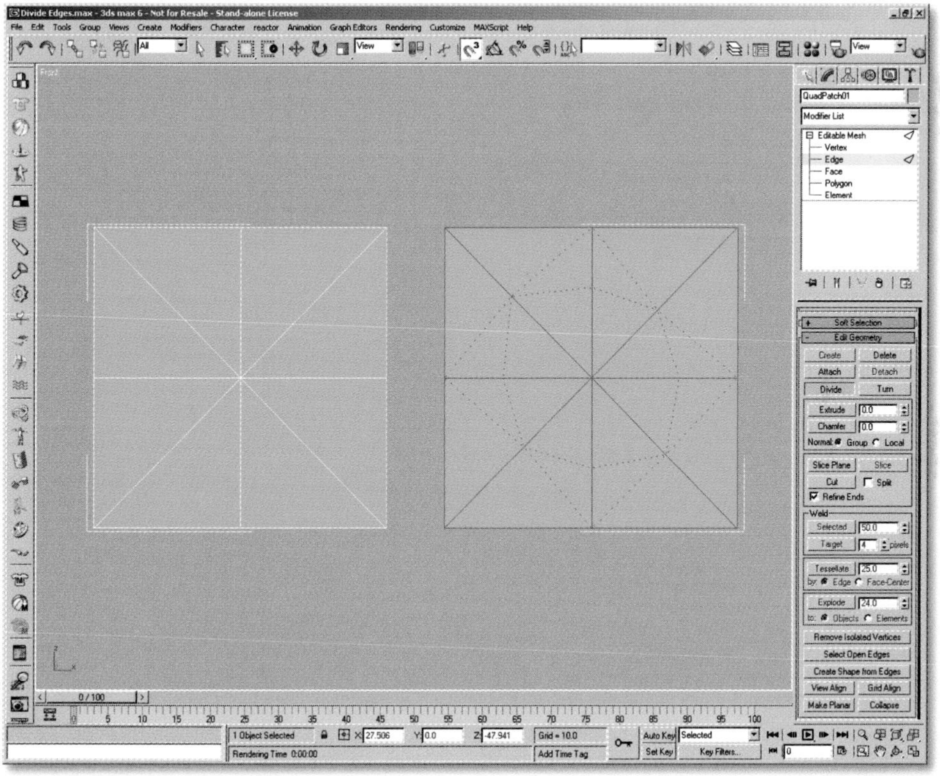

RENDER PROBLEMS: USE THE SLICE MODIFIER

Long cylindrical meshes (like the engine nacelles on a 3D model of the original Star Trek Enterprise, for example) are notorious for causing rendering problems. Once again, this often results from—you guessed it—long, triangular faces stretching down the length of the model. However, faces like these can't often be fixed by going into Sub-Object: Edge mode and turning the edges, because this sometimes changes the curvature of the cylindrical object.

If you can't turn the edges, and using the Divide tool seems like a hassle, see if you can use the Slice modifier (Command Panel > Modify > Modifier List > Slice), set to Refine Mesh, to sub-divide the cylinder. By applying several Slice modifiers spaced evenly down the length of your cylinder, you can often break up the thin triangular faces into polygons whose edges have more equal proportions.

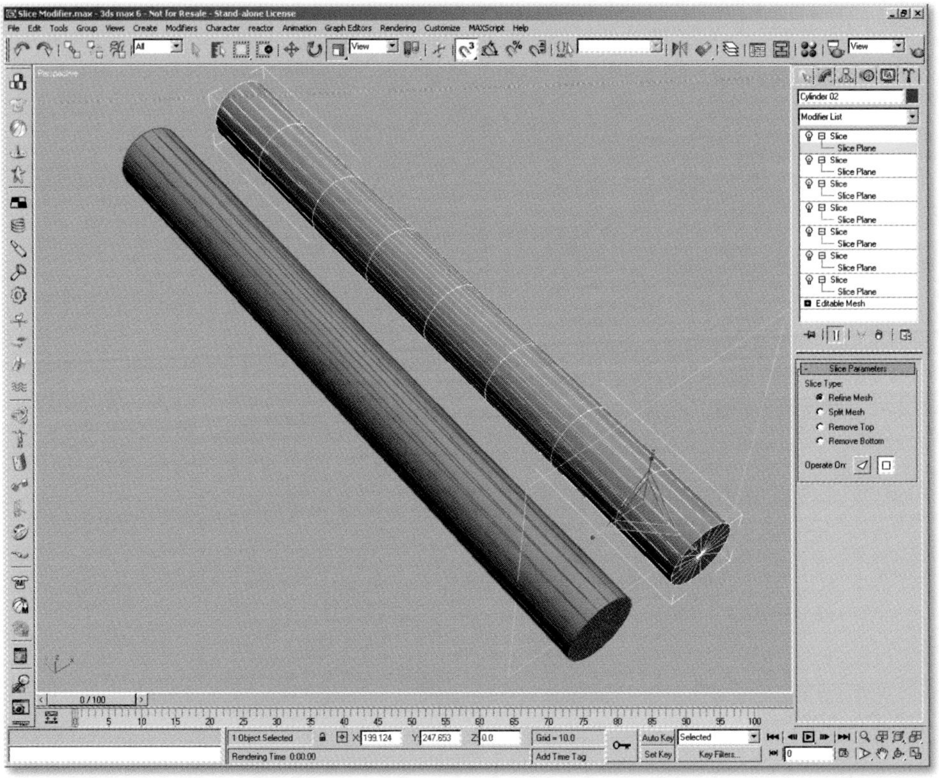

RENDER PROBLEMS: MAKE PLANAR

Okay, so you've followed the previous tips to fix polygonal rendering problems, and you're still getting flickering faces? The problem might be that you have non-planar triangular faces (caused sometimes by moving their adjacent vertices from their original positions).

If you have a group of triangular faces comprising a surface on your model that can be completely *flat* (a tabletop, for example), then you might be able to fix the problem by selecting your object, going into Sub-Object: Polygon mode, selecting the "problem cluster" of faces, and then clicking on the Make Planar button (at the bottom of the Edit Geometry rollout). This flattens the selected polygon to the summed average of the surrounding vertices. However, because this moves those surrounding vertices as well, make sure that you do render tests to ensure the new vertex positions don't cause rendering errors with faces or polygons around your "newly fixed" area.

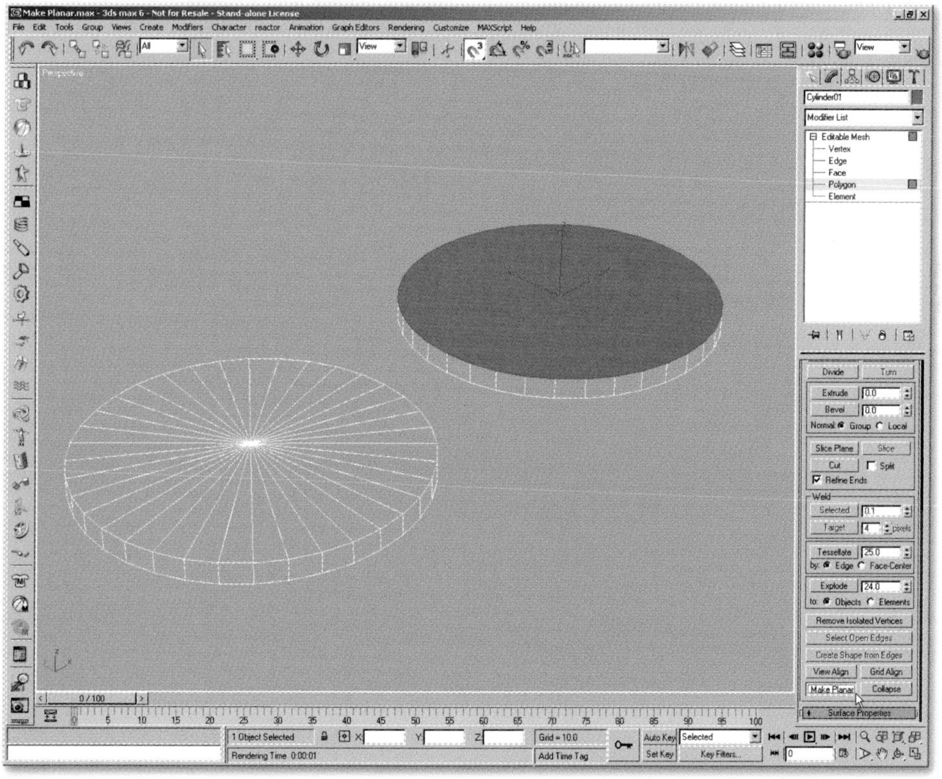

RENDER PROBLEMS: DON'T FORGET THE SMOOTH MODIFIER!

Okay, so you've followed all the previous "Fix my editable mesh!" tips, and things are looking pretty good… but still not perfect. Well, your final step should be to apply a Smooth modifier (Command Panel > Modify > Modifier List > Smooth) to your entire model (not just to the previously problematic faces). Check the Auto Smooth and Prevent Indirect Smoothing boxes, and then render your model again.

Still having problems? Then you should probably consider just biting the bullet and rebuilding the part of your model that's causing you trouble.

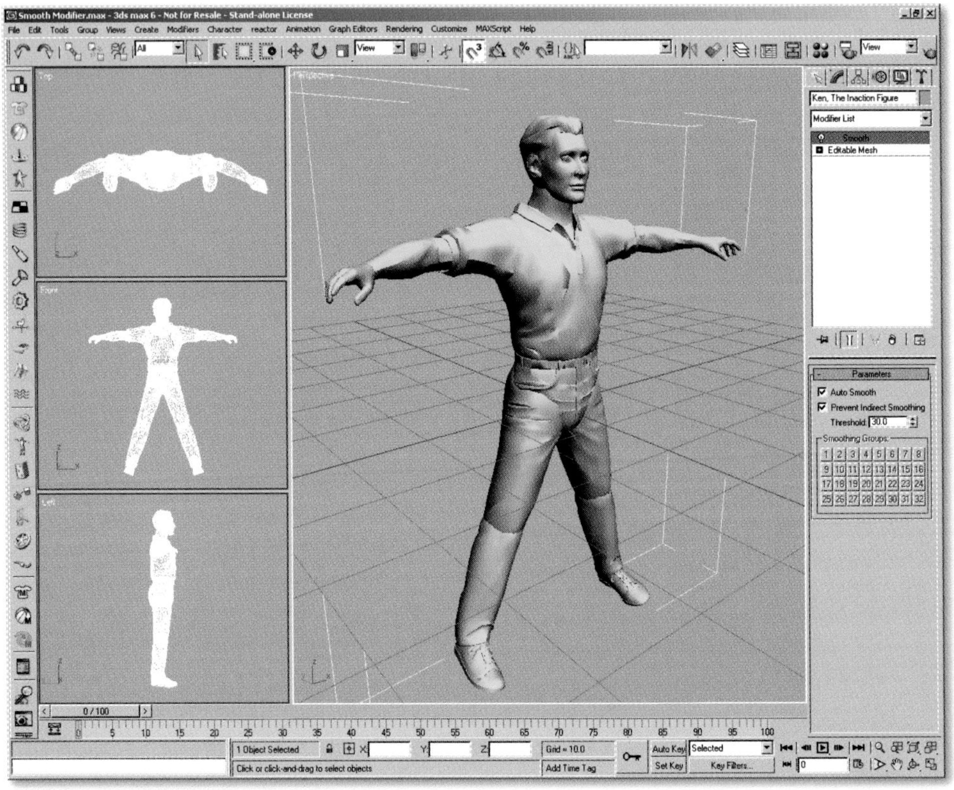

RESCUING YOUR WORK: PREVENTATIVE MEDICINE

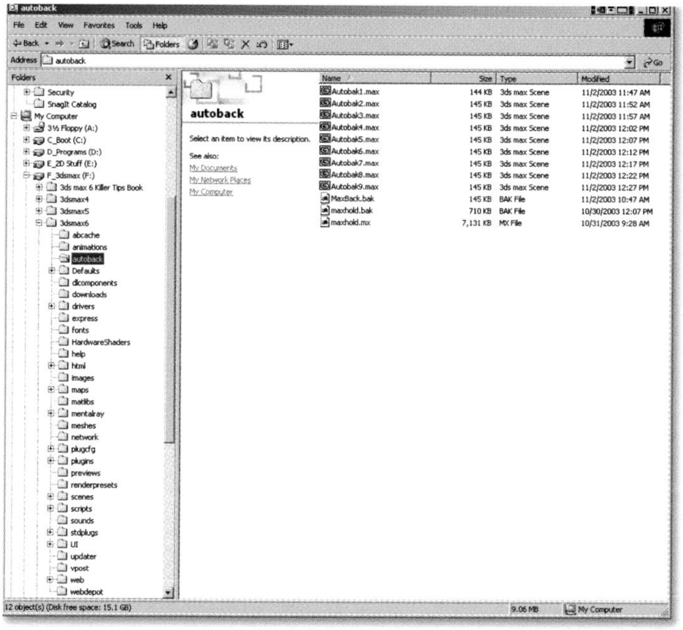

It's one of the scariest things you can face after you've spent an enormous amount of time working on a model or a scene: Your computer crashes as you're saving your scene, or 3ds max has a problem in the middle of a Save operation, and when you relaunch 3ds max and try to reload your file, it won't load; it's been corrupted.

Okay, don't panic. First, do the following:

1. Did you select Edit > Hold on your scene file before the problem occurred? If so, click Edit > Fetch and see if you can retrieve a version of your scene. If you can, and it's recent enough for you to continue your work without too much hassle, then save this scene under a new filename. (Don't overwrite your original scene, even if you think it's corrupted!)
2. Are you running with the Autoback feature enabled? (Go to the main toolbar > Customize > Preferences > Files tab > Auto Backup area; you should have this set to 9, the maximum number of files.) If you are, then—quickly—open a Windows Explorer window, go to your 3dsmax6\autoback folder, and check the creation dates on the files. The most recent one should be the one you want; you can click-hold and drag this file directly into a new 3ds max session. (Or, within 3ds max, select File > Open, go to the \autoback folder, and load this Autoback file.) If you wait too long within 3ds max (or simply use the program to load and examine each autoback.max file), your open 3ds max program might resave the current scene file and overwrite the very autoback.max file you need!
3. In the Customize > Preferences > Files tab, under File Handling, make sure Backup on Save is checked. If it is, then your original file would be saved to 3dsmax6\autoback\MaxBack.bak; you can rename this file and load it directly into 3ds max.

If these tips don't work, proceed to the next tips—and don't panic yet. There are still ways to (potentially) salvage your work.

TROUBLESHOOTING CORRUPTED FILES: MERGE HALF-AND-HALF

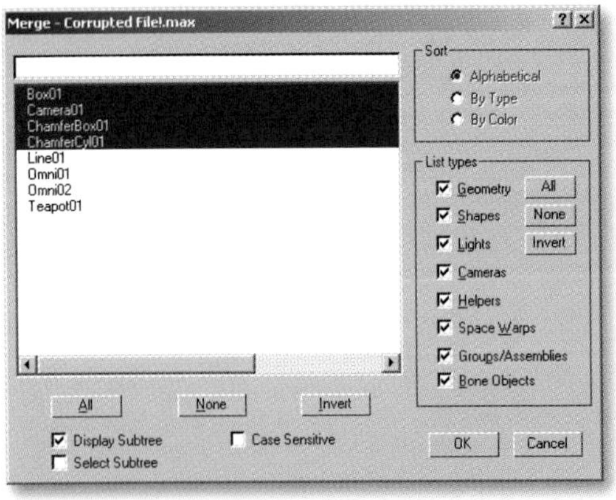

Okay, so you've determined that you don't have a good backup of your previously saved scene, and the only thing you have to work with is a single, seemingly corrupted .MAX file. The file either won't load into 3ds max, or after it does load, you can't work with it without 3ds max crashing again.

The problem might be a corrupted element within the scene file, not the entire file. Here's one of the best ways to isolate a problem in a scene file. (This is standard operating procedure for 3ds max testers to identify crash bugs in a scene.)

1. Open 3ds max, select File > Merge, and pick the corrupted scene file. When the Merge dialog opens, select half of the elements (geometry, lights, cameras, and so on) in the scene, and try to merge them. If the elements merge successfully, save the resultant scene with a new filename, and then try to merge the second half into a clean 3ds max scene.
2. If these elements load successfully, save the scene with a new filename, and then try to merge both scenes. Sometimes doing a merge of all scene elements into a new scene fixes a problem with the original scene file, and you're on your way.
3. If the second group of elements won't merge, select half of *those* elements, and keep repeating the process. Sometimes a single bad mesh can be the culprit; if you can merge everything from your original .MAX scene into a clean 3ds max scene, you only have to worry about replacing the one bad element that won't load.

This technique is considered a "binary search." By doing this, you can usually cut the scene down to a small subset containing the error. After you identify the bad elements, you can be fairly certain the remainder will merge correctly into a new scene.

TROUBLESHOOTING: SOLITARY CONFINEMENT FOR PLUG-INS

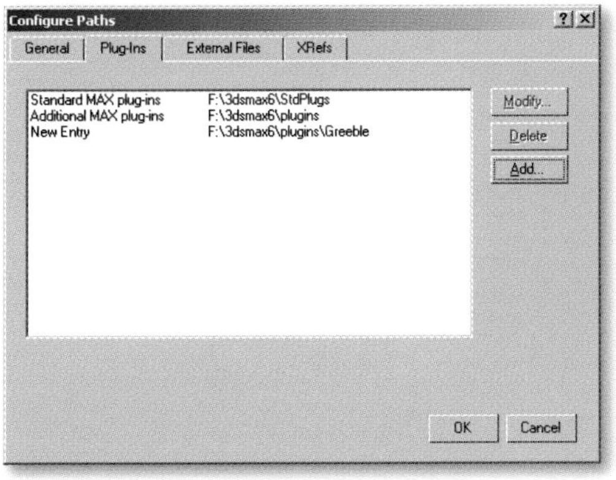

Sometimes scenes are corrupted by incompatible (that is, conflicting) plug-ins, either freeware/shareware that you've downloaded from the web, or commercial plug-ins.

To lessen the chances of bad plug-ins corrupting your scenes, before you install any freeware/shareware plug-ins, create new folders within your 3dsmax\plugins folder, and name the folder with the plug-in name or the name of the author or plug-in category so you can remember it. Install your plug-ins in their own specific folders, and then in 3ds max, go to Customize > Configure Paths > Plug-Ins, and add the specific folders you want 3ds max to load when you launch it.

If you suspect a plug-in is causing corruption in your files, you can eliminate the plug-in path easily in this menu by using the Delete button. Note that the Delete button won't eliminate the plug-in itself; it will just eliminate the folder path for the offending code when you relaunch 3ds max.

WHERE'S THE EXTRAS TOOLBAR?

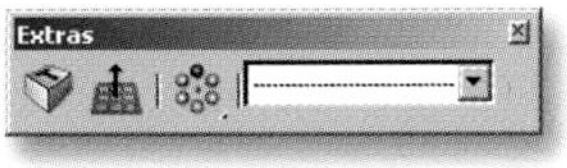

Okay, so there's an Extras toolbar. Where is it? Ordinarily, this toolbar is hidden, but you can open it by right-clicking on an open area of the main toolbar and choosing Extras from the drop-down menu. The Extras toolbar contains buttons for the Keyboard Shortcut Override Toggle, the AutoGrid feature, the Array/Snapshot/Spacing Tool flyout menu, and a Render Presets drop-down list.

OTHER TROUBLESHOOTING OPTIONS: RENAME YOUR .INI FILE

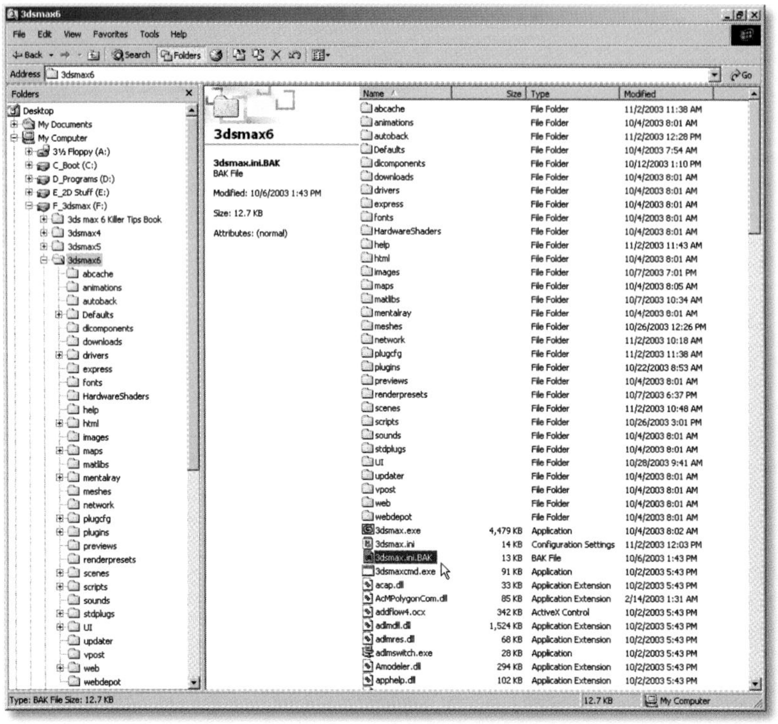

If 3ds max is causing you problems of any kind—especially creating corrupted files—and you can't isolate the culprit quickly (or you're just lazy and don't want to go through all the previous trouble-shooting steps), here's something to try.

Open your Windows Explorer window, go to your 3dsmax \root folder, and rename your 3dsmax.ini file to 3dsmax.ini.BAK. Then relaunch 3ds max. When you do, the 3ds max program creates a new, "plain vanilla" .INI file, which eliminates any settings that you had in the previous .INI file. Your old .INI file might contain flags for corrupt plug-in settings, paths to folders of ill-repute, or it might even be haunted. Either way, having a clean .INI file enables you to more quickly determine if old .INI settings were causing your problems.

Note that doing this also resets your desktop configuration, modifier button layouts, and various other features, so you might have to rearrange your 3ds max desktop elements to get them back the way you want. If the .INI file isn't the problem, you can always delete the new .INI file you just created and rename the .BAK file to 3dsmax.ini.

THE ASSET BROWSER: DRAG AND PLACE

The 3ds max Asset Browser, found in the Utilities Panel (Command Panel > Utilities tab > Asset Browser), is a great tool. You can use it to browse .MAX scene files, images, and other digital assets.

However, did you know that in the Asset Browser, you can click-hold and drag a .MAX scene into your current scene, and have it snap to its correct location in space by holding down the Ctrl key before you drag? In addition, if you turn on the AutoGrid button on the Extras toolbar (mentioned in an earlier tip), you can drag geometry into the scene and position it on mesh faces as well. This feature makes mechanical assembly animation "a snap!"

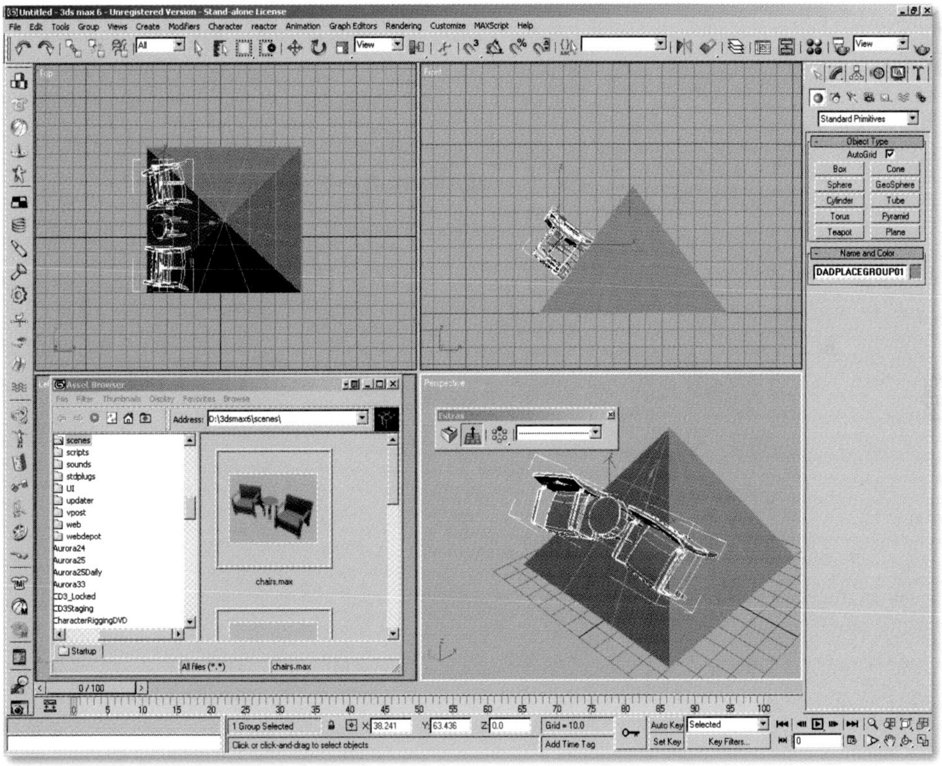

Aftermarket Accessories

Aftermarket Accessories

tips for using other programs with 3ds max

John Donne (1572–1631), English metaphysical poet and preacher, is often cited as coining the phrase, "No man is an island." Well, ol' John could have also been speaking of 3D graphics artists and their tools, some 350-plus years in the future. It's tough to do great 3D art with a 3D package alone—it's much more helpful to have a set of good 2D applications to supplement your 3D package of choice. For texture maps, you need a paint or image-retouching program. For complex compositing, you need a compositing package. A non-linear editing (NLE) package is helpful for cutting your rendered 3D material together for demo reels and your own animated films. Media players, sound creation, sampling and editing programs, scanning software, and video capture software are also useful for 3D artists who are deeply immersed in creating full-blown video or film productions that use 3D elements or are entirely 3D generated.

In this chapter, I present some of the more useful tips and tricks for using programs such as Adobe Photoshop (a mainstay of most 2D and 3D artists) and Discreet's combustion compositing software in conjunction with 3ds max. Don't have the extra dough to shell out for these programs, you say? No problem. I'll show you where you can find inexpensive—or even free*—paint and compositing packages to supplement your work. You can't get a better deal than that, can you?*

DON'T PAINT YOUR TEXTURE MAPS: PHOTOGRAPH THEM!

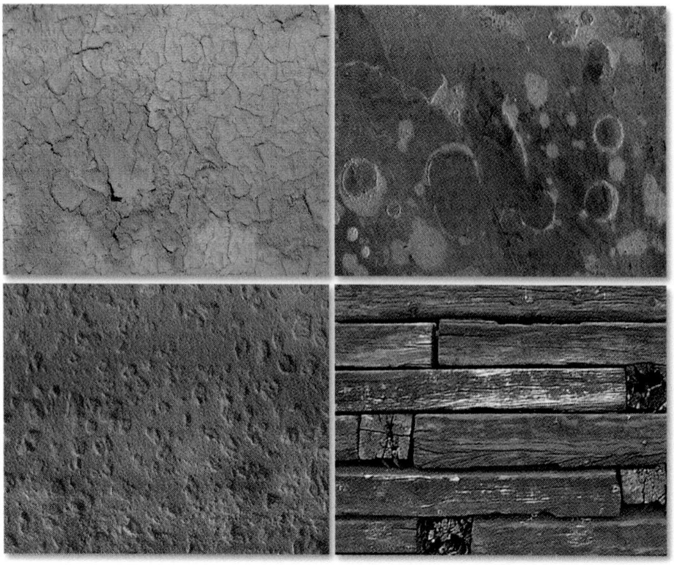

First, here's a piece of "texturing advice": Too many 3D artists think that the way to create a basic diffuse color map for their 3D objects is to simply paint it in Adobe Photoshop or Corel Painter, and then slap it on their 3D meshes. Although this might work fine for doing computer game textures, or non-photorealistic renderings, unless you're an utterly incredible artist, you're usually better off starting with a photo of something *real*. If you have a digital camera, take snapshots of everything you can think of—asphalt, bricks, concrete, wood surfaces, painted walls—and use those images as a starting point for your textures. (If you have a 35mm SLR film camera, then just scan your printed photos on a desktop scanner, or have the developer put them on a photo CD for you.) Try to take your pictures when the subjects are as flat-lit as possible, and take them perpendicular to the object surface. You want to minimize distortion when you apply the textures onto your objects. Need realistic skin textures? Stick your hand (or, um, other body parts) right onto your scanner, hold it still, scan it, and use *that* as a starting point for your epidermal textures.

If you don't have the time to capture your own real-world texture maps, you can find many freely available textures on the web, or available as texture collections from a variety of companies. (See the Appendix, "3ds max Resources" for a listing of some texture sources.)

PHOTOSHOP: ADD NOISE TO YOUR BITMAP TEXTURES

Regardless of the previous tip, you sometimes have to paint an original texture completely from scratch or cobble one together from existing digitized sources and retouch it substantially.

Here's a trick to help take the too-crisp "digital" look off your painted bitmaps: When you're satisfied with the overall bitmap, add a bit of noise to it. In Adobe Photoshop 7, load your image, and then go to Filter > Noise > Add Noise. Depending on the size of your bitmap and the final effect you want, add a small amount of Gaussian noise—say, 2–6 percent—to your image. The noise tends to break up the pure shading and lines on your bitmap, and even suggests an airbrushed or "painted" texture on your object.

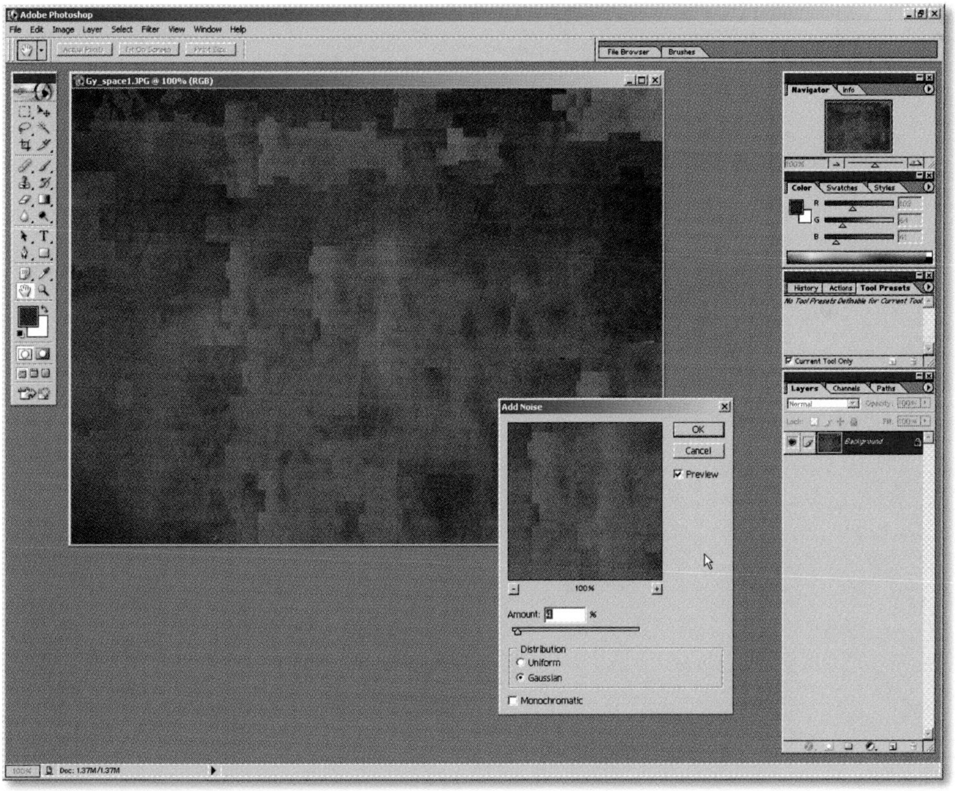

PHOTOSHOP: ADD PAINT OR RUST STREAKS WITH THE WIND FILTER

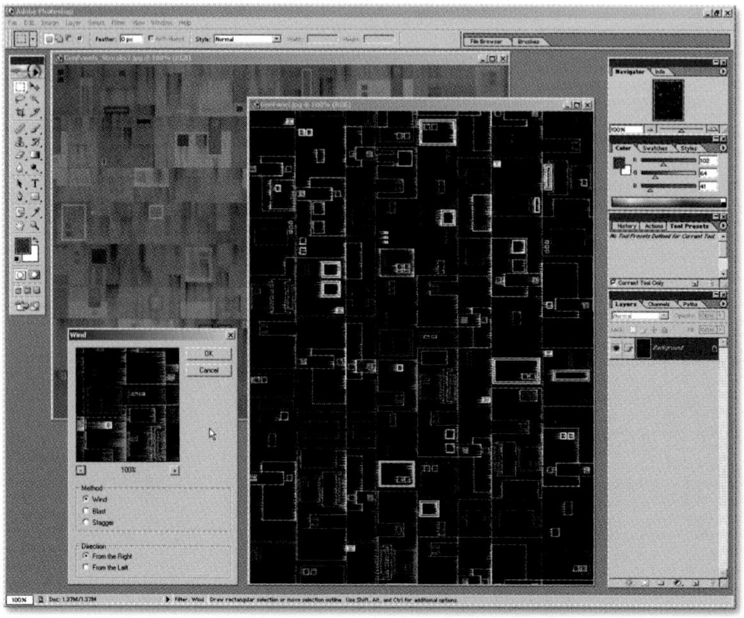

Want to add water streaks, rust smears, or carbon scoring to your bitmaps? You can paint these details by using the Airbrush tools in Photoshop or Painter, but here's another trick: Use the Photoshop Wind filter on a separate map (or layer), and then overlay it onto your existing bitmap.

If you have a bitmap representing metal plating, and you want to add rust streaks to it, in Photoshop, select the bitmap, select Layer > New > Layer, and add a layer on top of the existing bitmap. Then fill this layer with black, change your brush color to white, set the Layer type to Difference, and, using Photoshop's various painting tools, begin drawing. Create panel lines or rust along the contours of your underlying bitmap, concentrating on the areas in which you want the majority of "streaks."

When you're finished, go to Image > Rotate Canvas > 90° CW, and turn the entire bitmap on its side. Then go to Filter > Stylize > Wind. Under Method, leave Wind selected, and leave the Direction set to From the Right. Click OK, and you'll see the Wind filter streak the painted layer you just created. Go back to Image > Rotate Canvas, and rotate the canvas back 90 degrees counterclockwise. Now you can flatten the image, change the layer options, create a new layer, add color to the streaks, or otherwise modify the smeared lines as necessary. (Note that the preceding technique assumes you want the "streaks" to run down the bitmap; if your bitmap is going to be oriented differently on the final model, you might have to modify this technique.)

PHOTOSHOP: GENERATE CHROME REFLECTION MAPS (GUESS HOW?)

Although 3ds max comes with a wide variety of reflection maps, you might want to create your own chrome maps in Photoshop, just to impart a new "look" to your renderings, instead of relying on the stock bitmap textures.

Here's a way to do it. In Photoshop, select File > New, and create a tiny bitmap that's only 10 pixels wide by 5 pixels high. Click OK, and then go to Filter > Noise > Add Noise, and set the Amount to 400 percent. Click OK, and then go to Image > Image Size, and set the Width to 1024 and the Height to 512. (For reflection bitmaps, you're usually going to be using Spherical Environmental mapping coordinates, so it's best to have the bitmap be twice as wide as it is tall.) When you finish scaling up the image, you'll see a soft swirl of pixels. Select Filter > Sketch > Chrome, set Detail and Smoothness to 10, and then click OK. When you do, you should see a soft, chrome-like texture applied to your new bitmap. Save this in your 3dsmax6 \maps directory, and use it later when you need a grayscale chrome reflection map.

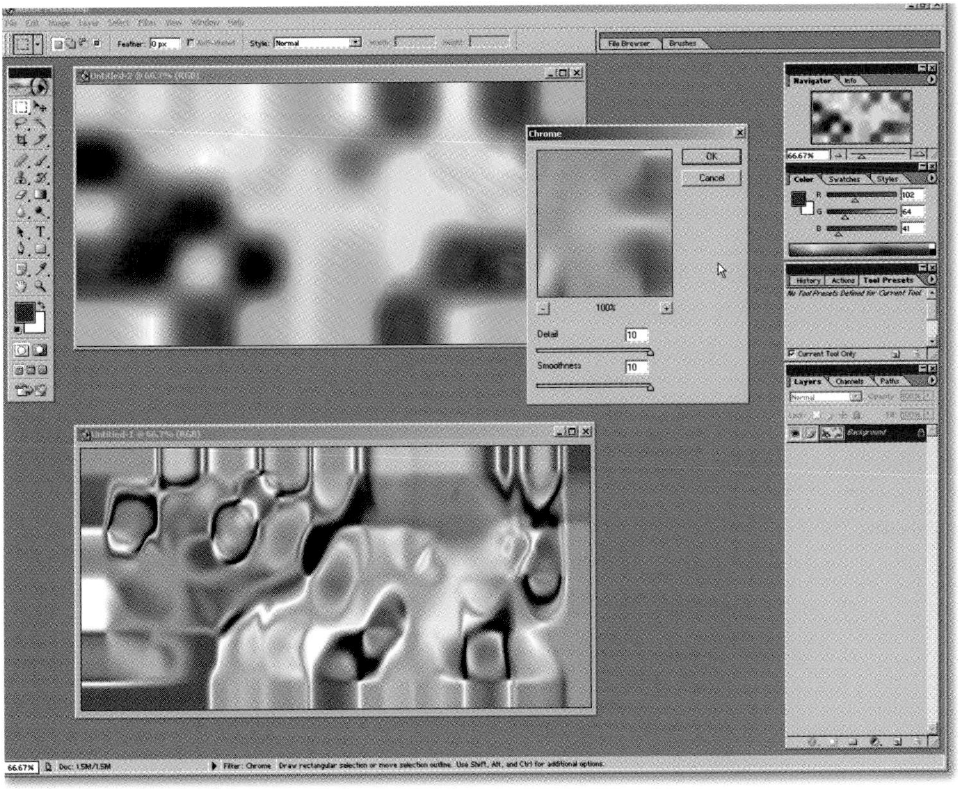

PHOTOSHOP: MAKE BITMAPS SEAMLESS USING THE OFFSET FILTER

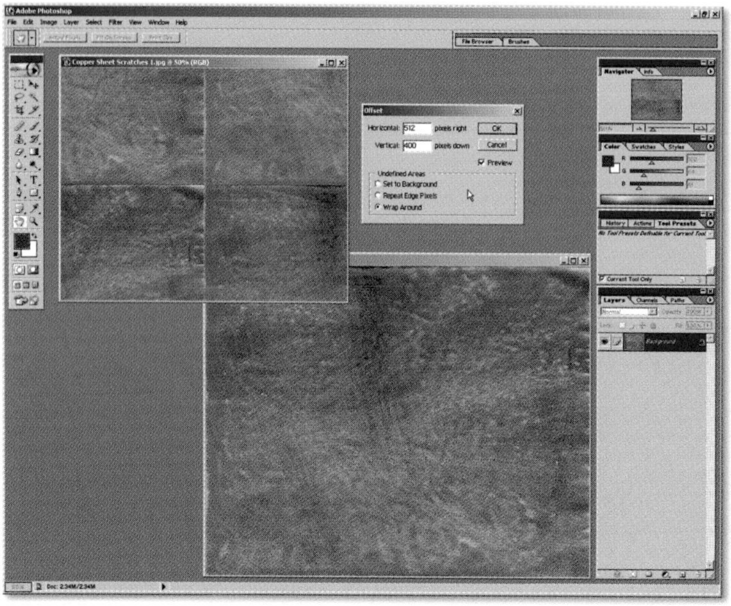

If you're using scanned photos or digital pictures as texture maps, you'll probably want to make them tile seamlessly in your scene. They're more versatile that way.

The best way to do this in Photoshop is to load the relevant bitmap, select Image > Image Size, and look at the Width and Height settings. Let's say that your bitmap is 1024 pixels wide by 800 pixels high. Note these dimensions (write them down or memorize them), and then click Cancel and go to Filter > Other > Offset. For the Horizontal setting, set this to half the width, or 512 pixels, and then set the Vertical dimension to 400 pixels down (half the current 800 pixel bitmap Height setting). Under the Undefined Areas section, make sure Wrap Around is selected, and then click OK. You'll see your bitmap offset into equally sized quadrants, with an obvious seam—the original edges of your bitmap—bisecting the image.

Now you can use Photoshop's tools—the Clone Stamp tool, Lasso (Copy), or Blur/Smudge—to retouch the edges of the seam using pieces of the surrounding image. When you're finished, use the Offset filter again with the same settings as before; this wraps the image around the way it was, but with the retouched edges. If you retouched the edges properly, the bitmap should tile seamlessly across the surface of your 3D objects when you use it as a texture map.

PHOTOSHOP: USE LAYERS TO CREATE "TEXTURE KITS"

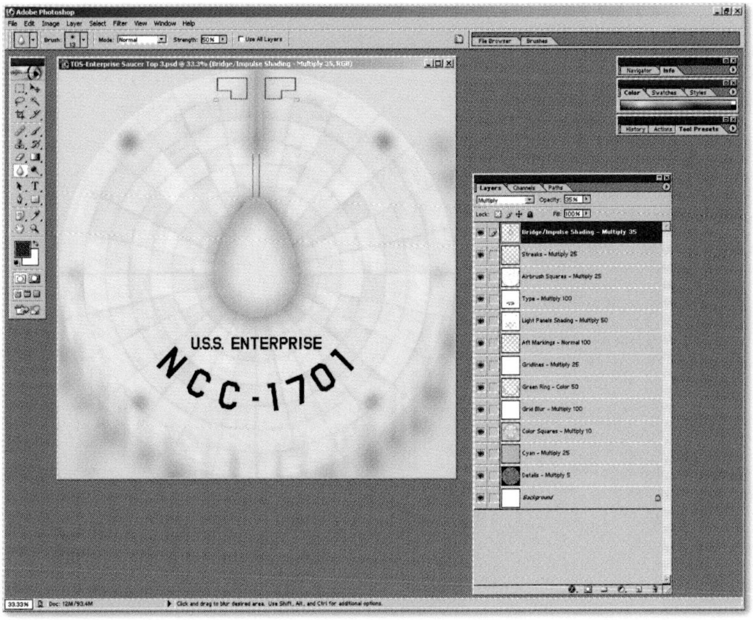

If you're creating complex textures in Photoshop, you should get into the habit of creating bitmap texture "kits" using the Photoshop Layers feature. For example, if you're creating a complex texture consisting of multiple effects (color overlays, text, Gaussian blurred panel lines, multiplied rust streaks, decals, noise/paint grain, and so on), then you're better off keeping each of these effects as separate layers in a Photoshop .PSD file. (Label each layer so that you can remember its specific contribution to the final image.) Although the .PSD file might be quite large, you can "flatten" the layers, save the flattened bitmap as a .TIF, .TGA, or .JPG file, and use that smaller single bitmap in 3ds max. If, after rendering, you want to make changes to the texture map, you can usually tweak just the relevant layer in the original .PSD file, and then reflatten and resave the image.

Also, remember that 3ds max can use native Photoshop .PSD files as bitmap textures, although you can't modify the layer information from within 3ds max as you can from within Photoshop—and again, those layers add up to pretty large files, which can devour your texture memory unnecessarily.

THE TEXPORTER PLUG-IN

There's a great free plug-in for 3ds max that helps you unwrap an object's UVW mapping coordinates into a flat wireframe map, which you can save as a bitmap "guide" to painting your textures. Mosey over to http://www.cuneytozdas.com, and download the nifty Texporter plug-in, written by Cuneyt Ozdas. (Currently, Cuneyt is a programmer working for Splutterfish on the Brazil Rendering System; you can find out more information on Brazil at http://www.splutterfish.com.) After installing the Texporter plug-in (in its own 3dsmax6\plugins\Texporter subfolder) and pointing your 3ds max plug-in paths to it, you'll find the utility in the Command Panel > Utilities tab > More > Texporter. You can use this plug-in to create a reference bitmap showing a wireframe version of your selected object's texture coordinates. You can utilize this bitmap as the bottom reference layer for your Photoshop texture "kit," as described in the previous tip.

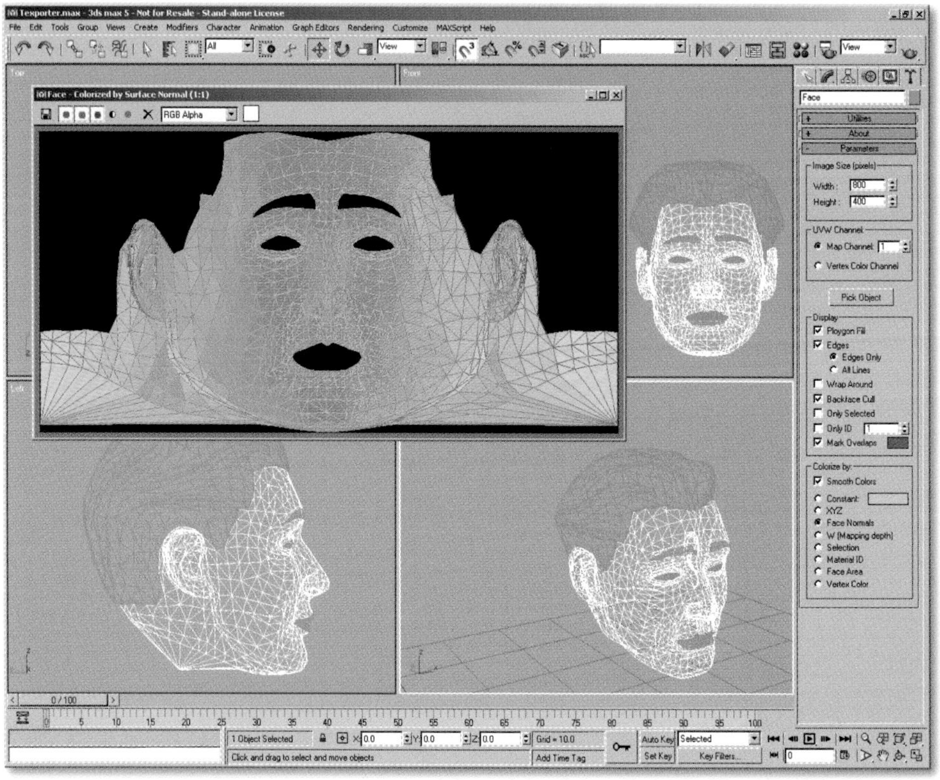

AUTOMATIC BITMAP UPDATES

Did you know that 3ds max 6 updates loaded bitmaps automatically, as the program is running? Assume that you have a bitmap called Sailing Ship Hull.jpg loaded into the Diffuse Color slot of a 3ds max material; the material is applied to an object in the scene, and you have the Show Map in Viewport button selected in the Diffuse Color map level of the Material Editor. If you're displaying your object in a shaded viewport, you should see the bitmap on the surface of the object.

Now, let's say that you have this same Sailing Ship Hull.jpg image loaded into Photoshop or another paint program, and you're making changes to it. When you press Ctrl+S to save the image, you'll see this same bitmap update automatically in your 3ds max Shaded viewport, with the changes you just made. If you have two monitors, you could open 3ds max on one and Photoshop on the other, and then go to town. This even works over a network; you can run 3ds max on one computer (pointing to the saved bitmap) and your paint program on another. The bitmap still updates when needed!

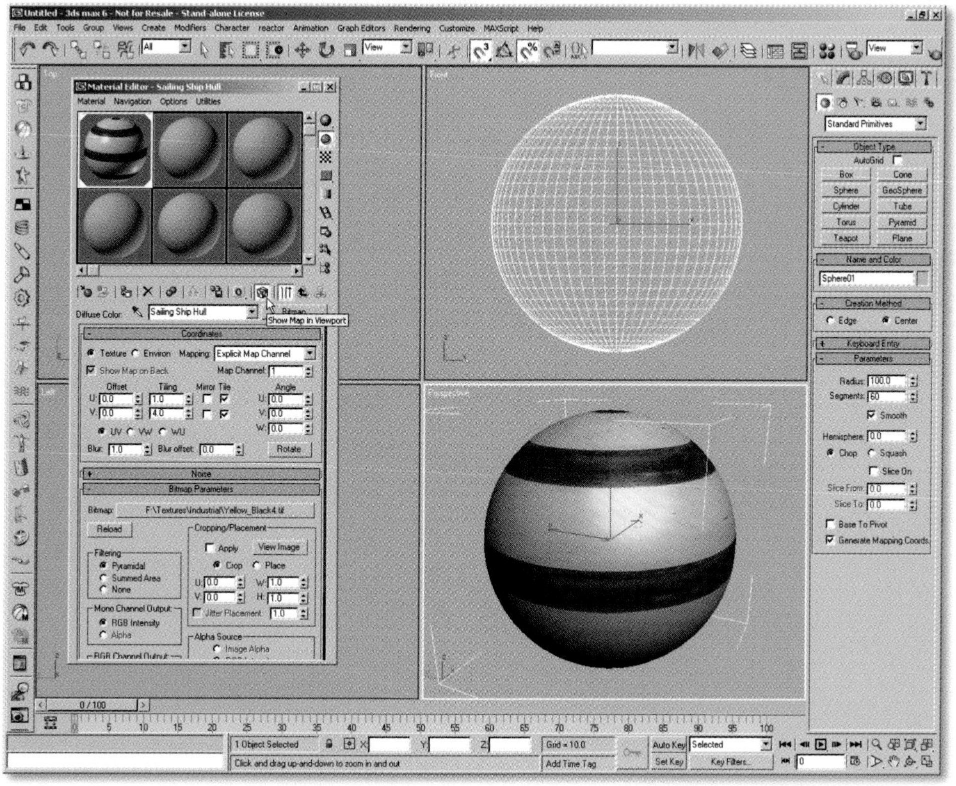

RENDER BOX SELECTED FOR PAINTING TEMPLATES

If you're painting texture maps for objects that are going to be mapped with UVW: Planar mapping coordinates, you should acquaint yourself with the 3ds max Box Selected render option, found in the main toolbar > Render Type drop-down menu. To use this feature, choose it from the Render Type drop-down menu, select an object to render, and then go to an orthographic viewport (such as the Top view). Select Rendering > Render, and then click the Render button. When you do, a Render Bounding Box/Selected menu appears, where you can enter the Width and Height resolution settings of the selected object. (Because you're probably going to use "fitted" UVW Planar mapping on your object, you should always keep the Constrain Aspect Ratio box checked.) When you click Render, 3ds max renders an image of the selected object that fits perfectly within the bounding box resolution. You can then save this image to disk, load it into your favorite paint program, and use it as a template to paint your texture details.

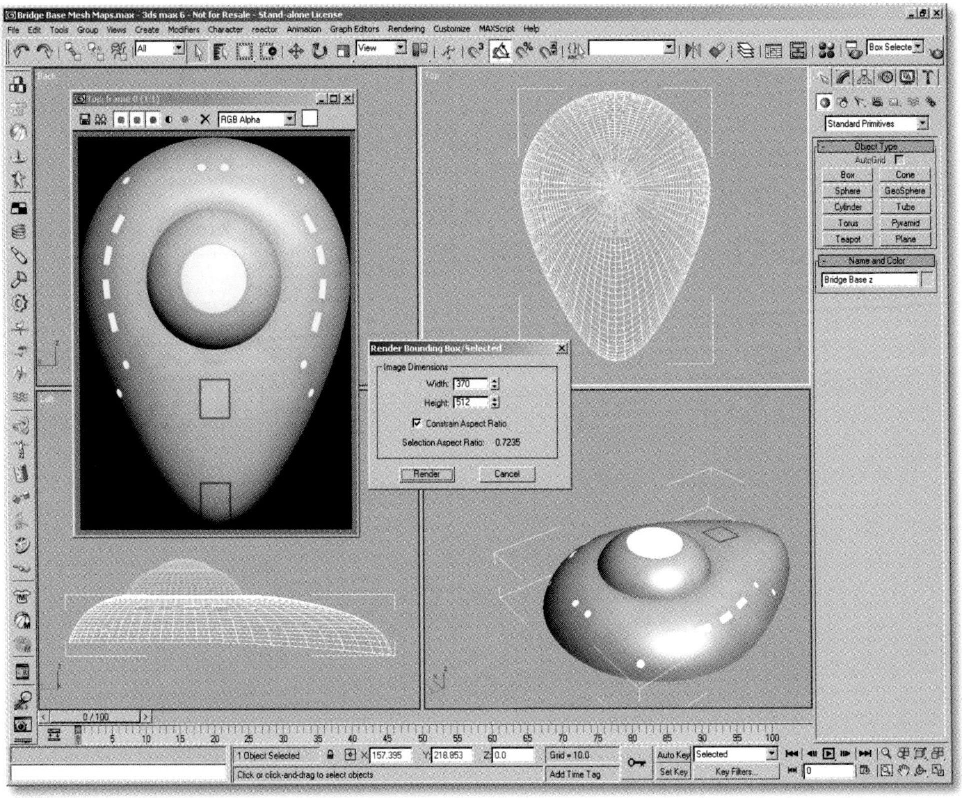

DISCREET'S COMBUSTION: WHITE-HOT AFTERIMAGES

Okay, here's a weird effect to try: Let's say you want to produce an intense impact effect of, say, a lightning bolt hitting an object, or a laser beam impacting a spaceship's shields. At the point of impact, you want to have the screen "white out" for a frame, to make the effect more jolting. So, you load your rendered sequence into Discreet's combustion (as a 2D sequence), shuttle to the relevant "impact" frame, go to Operators > Paint, and, using Toolbar > Flood Fill tool (with Tolerance set to 100 percent), you fill the frame with white.

Want to make this effect even "more" jolting (especially when projected on video)? Don't just create one opaque, white frame; on the frame after that, switch your Fill color to pure red (RGB 255, 0, 0) and fill that frame, with Paint Controls > Opacity set to 50 percent. This creates a red "wash" over your composite. Then go to the next frame, change your Fill color to purple (RGB 128, 0, 255), and repeat the process, adding a purple, 50 percent Opacity-value "wash" over this frame. When you're finished, render your composite. The resulting flash mimics the natural reddish-purple afterimage that the human eye sees after a bright light. (This trick was used throughout the film *Altered States* to heighten the impact of its effects.)

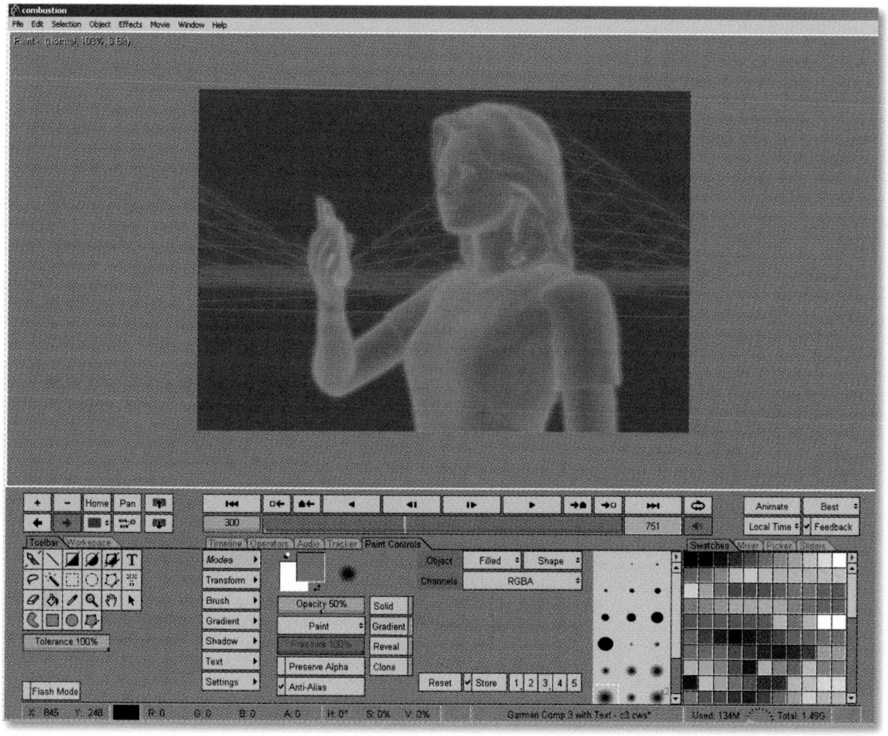

DISCREET'S COMBUSTION: MAKE TEXT MORE READABLE WITH "NEGATIVE GLOW"

You can employ several tricks to make text "read" more easily against a busy composited background. You can make the text colors brighter than the background, add Glow operators or Sharpen operators, or use other tricks (such as drop shadows) to make a text overlay pop out.

However, if you're compositing bright text (or other foreground elements that use an alpha channel) over a light background, and you can't use a drop shadow effect, then you can actually add a "dark halo"—basically, a "negative glow"—around the text. To do this, open your composite, go to the Workspace tab, and select your Text layer. Right-click, and from the menu, select Copy. Click on your Composite and paste a second layer of text right above the first layer. Select the first (bottom) text layer, and then go to the main toolbar > Operators > Blur/Sharpen > Gaussian Blur to blur this layer. In the Gaussian blur controls, set Radius to, say, 5.00, and then select the bottom text layer again. Under Composite Controls, set Transfer Mode to Difference. When you do, you should see a soft, dark "halo" appear around the edges of the second text layer, making it easier to read against a light background.

Note: Be careful when using this technique. You don't want the final effect to look like an old-fashioned "matte line," seen in a lot of bluescreen optical composites before the days of digital technology.

DISCREET'S COMBUSTION: A REMINDER ABOUT GLOW EFFECTS

One of the most-used techniques in digital compositing is adding glow effects to 3D elements. Whether it's creating brighter specular highlights on flying logo animation, or making the windows of a 3D ocean liner shine more brightly at night, you'll almost certainly need to make things glow to give your effects added "oomph." (It's a hard-to-measure quality, but you'll know it when you see it.)

In Discreet's combustion, remember that if you want to add a Glow operator to a layer, first check to make sure the original layer has an alpha channel. (If not, make sure that the Transfer mode—under Composite Controls > Layer—is set to Add or Lighten.) Then copy and paste the layer (see the instructions in the previous tip) on top of the original Layer #1. Go to Operators > Stylize > Glow and add a Glow operator to the new Layer #2; in Glow Controls, set the Radius, Minimum Luminance, and Strength parameters to whatever looks good. Now, if you view the composite, it might appear that the Glow operator is adding a glow to the Layer #2's alpha channel, instead of just the "bright areas" of the layer. To fix this, make sure Layer #2 is selected, and then in Composite Controls > Layer, click on the None button under Stencil Layer and pick the original Layer #1. Set it to use alpha (if appropriate); if the layer image(s) lack an alpha channel, or if the entire layer still seems to glow, click the Luma button instead. This should create a proper glow effect.

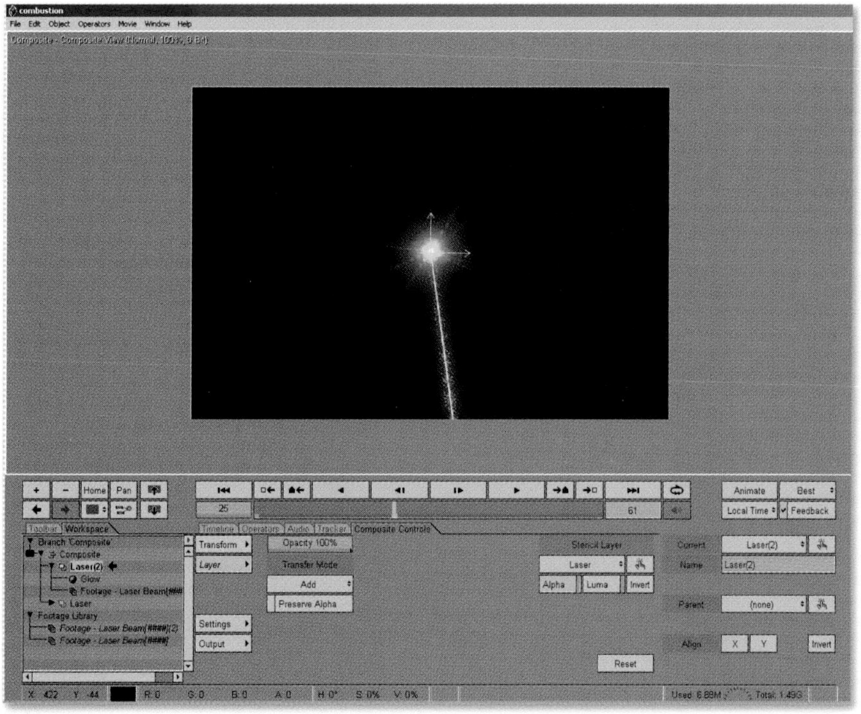

DISCREET'S COMBUSTION: REMEMBER RENDER ELEMENTS IN 3DS MAX!

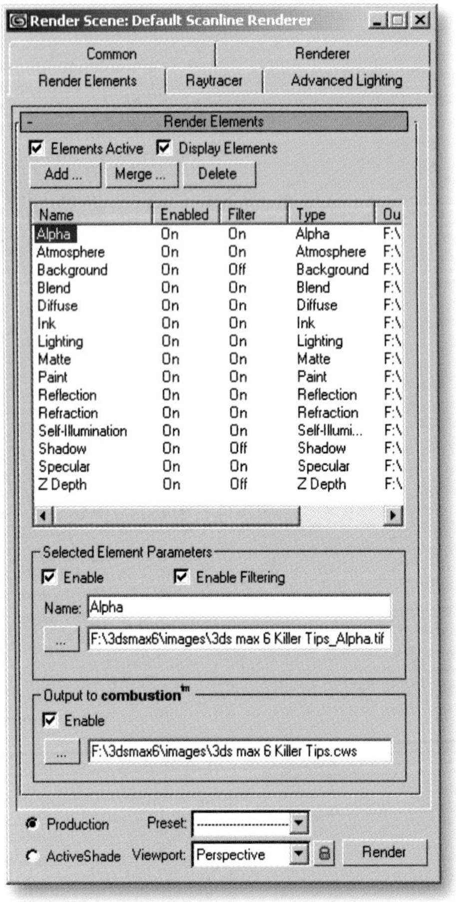

Don't forget: If you own both 3ds max (beginning with 3ds max 4) and combustion, you can output separate elements from your rendering—called, appropriately enough, Render Elements. If you go the main toolbar > Rendering > Render > Render Elements tab, you can click the Add button and output the following separate channels, or elements: Alpha, Atmosphere, Background, Blend (a combination of elements that you can determine), Diffuse, Ink, Lighting, Matte, Paint, Reflection, Refraction, Self-Illumination, Shadow, Specular, and Z Depth. (Whew!)

In addition, if you've already picked your output filename and drive path, by checking the Enable box under the Output to Combustion area, 3ds max saves a combustion .CWS file automatically, in the same folder as your original rendered images and elements. All you have to do when your 3ds max rendering is finished is launch combustion, go to File > Open Workspace, and then pick the .CWS file created at the conclusion of the rendering. The rendered elements load into combustion with the appropriate Layer > Transfer Mode properties already set. Just tweak each layer as necessary in your composite (adding glow effects to the Self-Illumination element, for example), and then rerender from combustion!

CONVERTING THE MASSES: POLYTRANS

Okay, it's not a paint or animation tool, but it's certainly useful for 3d artists. Need help in converting 3D model files that you've gotten from the web or from people not using 3ds max? Then check out PolyTrans, available from http://www.okino.com. PolyTrans both imports and exports a huge variety of 3D file formats, including 3D Studio .3DS, Alias Triangle files, the Atari ST CAD 3D .3D2, AutoCAD .DXF ASCII/Binary files, Imagine .IOB, LightWave .LWO, Stereo Lithography (.STL), trueSpace .COB, Wavefront and Rhino .OBJ, and more. If you swap a lot of 3D data in a multi-3D-software platform production environment, then PolyTrans is an indispensable piece of software to add to your digital toolkit. (Note that a feature-limited demo version of PolyTrans Release 4.1 is included on the 3ds max 6 Partners CD.)

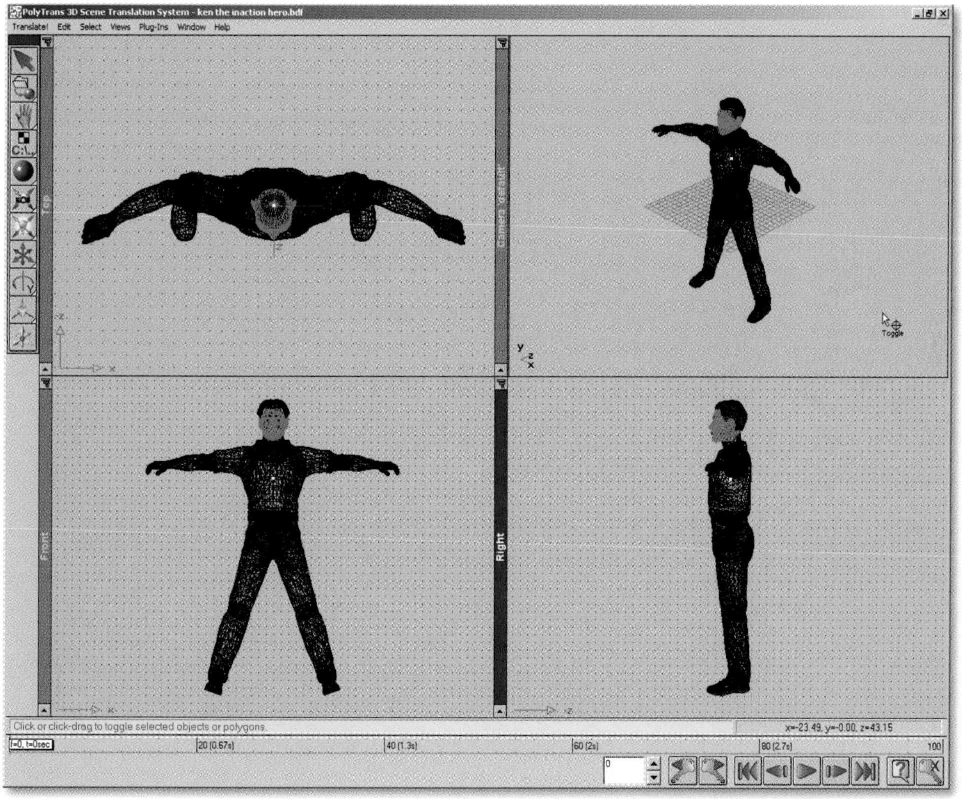

PREPARING IMAGES FOR MOTION TRACKING

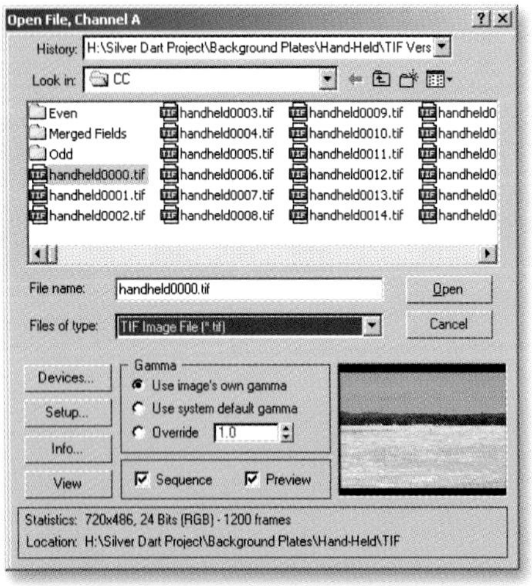

If you've shot live-action video, and you want to later digitize it and motion-track it (using such programs as 2d3's Boujou, Autonomous Effects' Scene Genie, the RealViz MatchMover Corsica, or Andersson Technologies' SynthEyes), here's an important rule: Don't save the digitized video to a lossy image format, such as .JPG. The .JPG image format (even when saved with "lossless" compression) may still introduce image artifacts which change randomly in every frame, which can cause problems with the previously mentioned motion tracking software. Play it safe—save your digitized footage in a lossless format (.TIF or .TGA are fine), and use those images for your motion tracking. You may eat more hard drive space, but you'll save yourself from tearing out your hair when you can't get a good motion track on a particularly difficult .JPG image sequence.

For more information on Boujou, Scene Genie, MatchMover and SynthEyes, go to their respective manufacturer's websites at http://www.2d3.com, http://www.afx.com, http://www.realviz.com, and http://www.ssontech.com.

FREE STUFF: THE GIMP

The GIMP stands for the GNU Image Manipulation Program. (GNU is a recursive acronym that means "Gnu's Not Unix." It's part of the Open Source Software (OSS) movement, which largely sprang up around Linus Torvald's Linux operating system, and it's a world much too large for me to summarize here. If you want more information on Linux and the OSS community, just do a search on the web, and you'll be inundated with information.)

Anyway, the GIMP is a freely distributed piece of software that is suitable for such tasks as photo retouching, image composition, and image authoring, and it contains many of the same features as Adobe's Photoshop program. The GIMP is fast, elegant, has a great deal of support, and need I emphasize again, it's free. All you have to do is download it and install it.

For more information, go to http://www.gimp.org. This is the primary distribution point for the latest GIMP releases, patches, plug-ins, and scripts, and it's updated regularly.

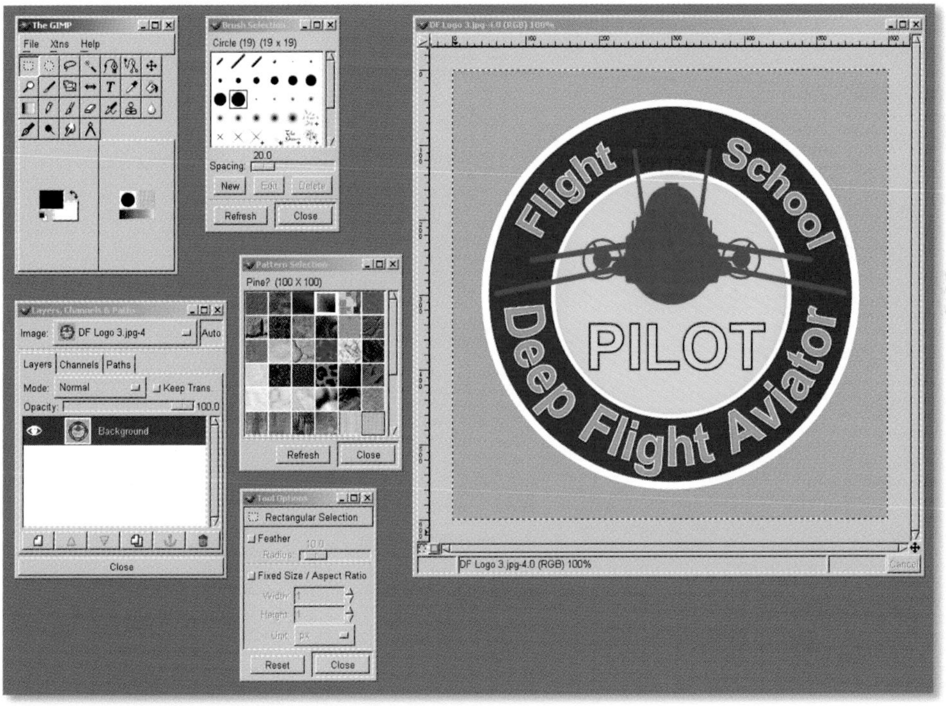

FREE STUFF: THE CINEPAINT PAINTING AND IMAGE RETOUCHING PROGRAM

CinePaint (formerly FilmGIMP) is a free Open Source Software (OSS) painting and image-retouching program that is designed to work with 35mm film and other high-resolution high dynamic range images. It's the most popular Open Source tool in the motion picture industry—used in the films *2 Fast 2 Furious, Scooby-Doo, Harry Potter, Stuart Little*, and others. CinePaint is used for painting of background mattes and for frame-by-frame retouching of movie frames. CinePaint is available for Linux, Macintosh OS X, Windows, and other popular operating systems.

The 32-bit per channel color range of CinePaint appeals to 35mm cinematographers and professional still photographers because film scanners are capable of greater color bit-depth than can be displayed on an 8-bit per channel monitor or can be manipulated in typical programs. However, CinePaint is a general-purpose tool that is useful for working on images for motion pictures, print, and the web. CinePaint supports many file formats—both conventional formats such as JPEG, PNG, TIFF, and TGA images—and more exotic cinema formats such as Cineon and OpenEXR.

To download CinePaint, go to http://cinepaint.sourceforge.net/.

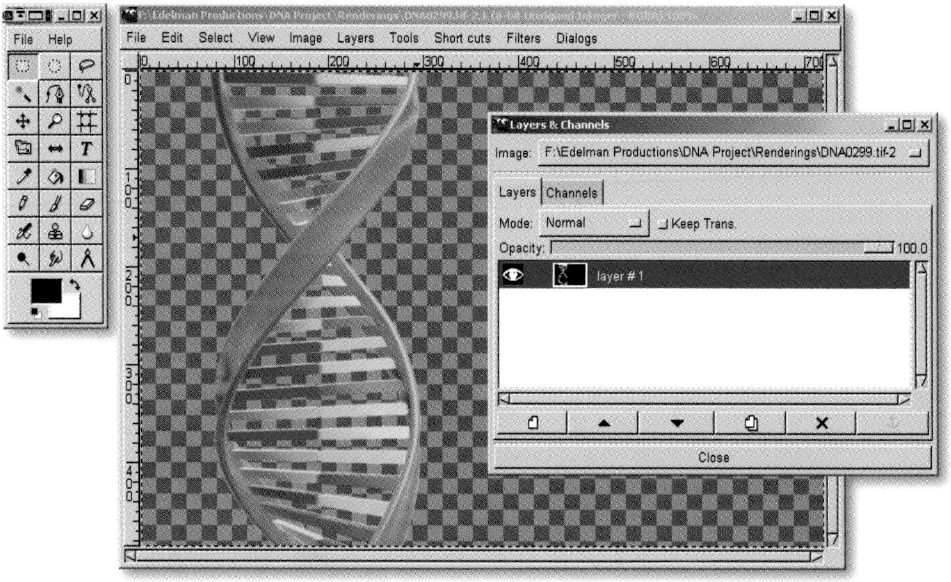

SUPPORT FOR THE GIMP

Okay, so you've downloaded and installed The GIMP, and you need even more support? Fear not. Lots of resources are available on the web for the software, including a dedicated Internet newsgroup.

Have a question about the software? Then get help directly from The GIMP-lovin', GIMP-using community. Just point your newsreader to comp.graphics.apps.gimp, and ask away!

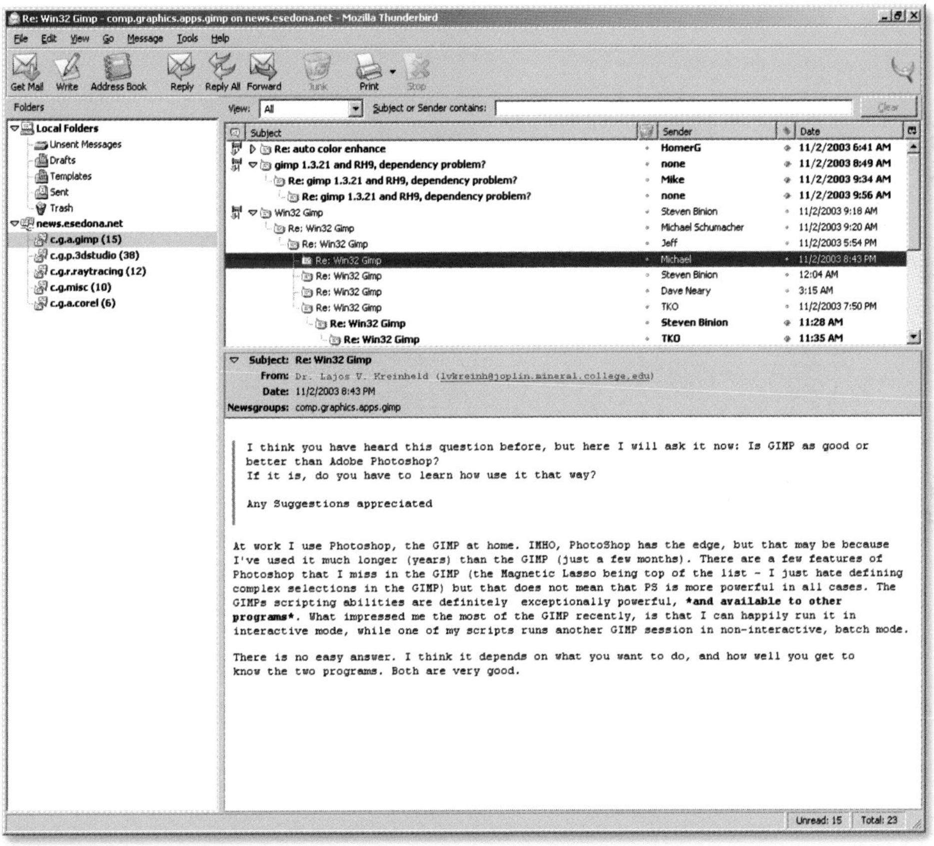
Re: Win32 Gimp - comp.graphics.apps.gimp on news.esedona.net - Mozilla Thunderbird
File Edit View Go Message Tools Help
Get Mail Write Address Book Reply Reply All Forward Junk Print Stop
Folders
View: All
Subject or Sender contains:
Local Folders
Unsent Messages
Drafts
Templates
Sent
Trash
news.esedona.net
c.g.a.gimp (15)
c.g.p.3dstudio (38)
c.g.r.raytracing (12)
c.g.misc (10)
c.g.a.corel (6)
Subject
Sender
Date
Re: auto color enhance
HomerG
11/2/2003 6:41 AM
gimp 1.3.21 and RH9, dependency problem?
none
11/2/2003 8:49 AM
Re: gimp 1.3.21 and RH9, dependency problem?
Mike
11/2/2003 9:34 AM
Re: gimp 1.3.21 and RH9, dependency problem?
none
11/2/2003 9:56 AM
Win32 Gimp
Steven Binion
11/2/2003 9:18 AM
Re: Win32 Gimp
Michael Schumacher
11/2/2003 9:20 AM
Re: Win32 Gimp
Jeff
11/2/2003 5:54 PM
Re: Win32 Gimp
Michael
11/2/2003 8:43 PM
Re: Win32 Gimp
Steven Binion
12:04 AM
Re: Win32 Gimp
Dave Neary
3:15 AM
Re: Win32 Gimp
TKO
11/2/2003 7:50 PM
Re: Win32 Gimp
Steven Binion
11:28 AM
Re: Win32 Gimp
TKO
11:35 AM
Subject: Re: Win32 Gimp
From: Dr. Lajos V. Kreinheld (lvkreinh@joplin.mineral.college.edu)
Date: 11/2/2003 8:43 PM
Newsgroups: comp.graphics.apps.gimp
I think you have heard this question before, but here I will ask it now: Is GIMP as good or better than Adobe Photoshop?
If it is, do you have to learn how use it that way?
Any Suggestions appreciated
At work I use Photoshop, the GIMP at home. IMHO, PhotoShop has the edge, but that may be because I've used it much longer (years) than the GIMP (just a few months). There are a few features of Photoshop that I miss in the GIMP (the Magnetic Lasso being top of the list - I just hate defining complex selections in the GIMP) but that does not mean that PS is more powerful in all cases. The GIMPs scripting abilities are definitely exceptionally powerful, *and available to other programs*. What impressed me the most of the GIMP recently, is that I can happily run it in interactive mode, while one of my scripts runs another GIMP session in non-interactive, batch mode.
There is no easy answer. I think it depends on what you want to do, and how well you get to know the two programs. Both are very good.
Unread: 15
Total: 23

appendix

3ds max Resources

Since the release of (what was then called) 3D Studio MAX in April 1996, the 3ds max world has been blessed with a huge amount of third-party support—reference, tutorial, and tips books, plug-ins (both commercial and freeware/shareware), training CDs, videotapes and DVDs, 3ds max-compliant hardware and software drivers, online tutorials, texture map and stock footage collections… the list goes on.

The best way for you to find 3ds max resources, of course, is by searching the web. Type "3ds max resources" in almost any search engine, and you'll be inundated with links, web rings, and more links.

However, to spare you some search time, I've listed some of the top sources for 3ds max information in this appendix. By following only a few of the URLs listed here, you can link to dozens—perhaps hundreds—of websites that offer a wealth of 3ds max information. In addition, the various 3D newsgroups can offer answers to some of your tech questions.

Note: This is by no means a comprehensive list because web resources change regularly. However, the following are some of my favorite spots to visit when I need information about the 2D/3D world.

WEB SITES

There are lots of relevant websites, so I've organized them into categories to make them a little more accessible.

3DS MAX-SPECIFIC SITES

- **http://www.discreet.com**—The home page of Discreet, the multimedia division of Autodesk.
- **http://support.discreet.com**—The best source for Discreet software support. If you have a question about 3ds max, combustion, or any other Discreet software, this should be your first stop.
- **http://sparks.discreet.com**—The Discreet website portal for 3ds max developers, both commercial and non-commercial.

  http://ssontech.com—Andersson Technologies, LLC, developers of SynthEyes, a camera/motion tracking program

MAJOR 3DS MAX DEVELOPERS AND PLUG-IN DEALERS

- **http://www.2d3.com**—Developers of the Boujou camera/motion tracking system.
- **http://www.afx.com**—Developers of Scene Genie, a camera and motion tracking package that works well with 3ds max.
- **http://www.cgcharacter.com**—Developers of Absolute Character Tools (ACT), an advanced muscle and skin system for character animation.
- **http://www.charanitech.com**—Developers of Character Animation Technologies (CAT), a complex character animation rigging system for 3ds max.
- **http://www.cebas.com**—One of the oldest and most noteworthy 3ds max plug-in developers, with a wide variety of plug-ins, including finalRender Stage-1, Thinking Particles, Ghostpaint, RealLensFlare, and more.
- **http://www.chaosgroup.com**—Developers of the acclaimed V-Ray renderer for 3ds max; go to this site to download a demo version of V-Ray.
- **http://www.deespona.com**—Home of the Deespona model library, an extraordinary collection of 5,000 high-resolution 3D models, all with textures, in 3ds max format.
- **http://www.digimation.com**—The original 3D Studio DOS/max plug-in developer and distributor has branched out into offering 3D models (including the entire Viewpoint catalog) and a variety of other digital services.
- **http://www.ghost3d.com**—Developers of the Surf-It, ResErect, and Scribe-It plug-ins for 3ds max, which allow users to digitize physical objects using the Faro or Immersion Microscribe digitizing arms. (See http://www.faro.com and http://www.immersion.com.)

- **http://www.id8media.com**—A large West Coast (U.S.) dealer and distributor of 3ds max plug-ins and other programs; it also carries a large variety of 3D training materials.
- **http://www.npowersoftware.com**—Developers of Power Booleans, Power Solids, and other modeling plug-ins for 3ds max.
- **http://www.realviz.com**—Developers of various packages, including the MatchMover camera/motion tracker.
- **http://www.splutterfish.com**—Developers of the acclaimed Brazil Rendering System; go to this site to download a demo version of Brazil.
- **http://www.trinity3d.com**—A large Midwest U.S.-based dealer and distributor of 3ds max plug-ins and other programs; also carries a large variety of 3D training materials.
- **http://www.turbosquid.com**—Distributor for the Discreet Certified Plug-ins Program, and of a huge number of digital assets for 3D artists, including meshes, shaders, texture maps, and more.

3DS MAX AND 3D NEWS SITES

- **http://www.3dcafe.com**—3D industry news, reviews, and tutorials, with loads of free stuff, such as 3D models, plug-ins, and standalone software.
- **http://www.3dluvr.com**—3D industry news, reviews, and tutorials; the Techzone area hosted by hardware guru Greg Hess is especially informative.
- **http://www.cgchannel.com**—3D industry news, reviews, and interviews with noted artists.
- **http://www.cgtalk.com**—Includes various discussion forums covering news, general 3D topics, hardware, and artists' work.
- **http://www.highend3d.com**—Includes discussion forums for general 3D topics, a 3ds max-specific area, job listings, and more.
- **http://www.maxunderground.com**—3ds max-specific news, updated as often as possible (usually daily.)
- **http://www.scriptspot.com**—"The most comprehensive site for 3ds max scripts on the web." This is Borislav "Bobo" Petrov's site, featuring some of the most useful MAXScripts you've ever seen. (See Chapter 8, "Detailing the Chassis: MAXScript Tips," some of Bobo's best scripts and tips.)

TECHNOLOGY AND GENERAL GEEKINESS

- **http://www.2cpu.com**—One of my personal favorite technology sites, devoted to people running multi-CPU systems (which includes a lot of 3ds max users). Its forums—particularly the Motherboard forum—have some of the most helpful hardware gurus around. If you build your own dual-CPU computers, you should bookmark this site.
- **http://www.slashdot.com**—The premiere technology/computer geek website, updated daily (often hourly) with cool tech news (although it's strongly biased toward anything that's *not* Microsoft.)
- **http://www.theregister.co.uk**—The *National Inquirer* of online PC technology websites, this British site is full of techno-gossip, although you might have to take some of their speculations and rumors with a grain of salt.

VISUAL EFFECTS, FILMMAKING, AND FUN STUFF

- **http://www.aintitcool.com**—The original movie geek website. Still lots of fun, although webmaster Harry Knowles needs to learn that a.) "no one" is always two words and b.) *The Matrix Reloaded* would *not* have been a better movie had it featured vampires and werewolves.
- **http://www.blur.com**—The home of Blur Studio, one of the most famous special effects houses in the 3ds max community because of their 3D software of choice and because of the excellent quality of their work.
- **http://www.cinescape.com**—A good complementary site to Cinescape Magazine; this site offers movie, TV, animation, and comics gossip, updated daily.
- **http://www.darkhorizons.com/news.htm**—This Australian site features lots of good movie gossip, updated several times a week, with a leaning toward genre films.
- **http://www.filmscoremonthly.com**—A website, a magazine, and a CD label devoted exclusively to movie soundtracks. Much of the soundtrack music I listened to while writing and editing this book came from Film Score Monthly.
- **http://www.intrada.com**—The largest (and best!) purveyor of movie soundtracks online, Intrada is both a soundtrack store and a music label, and it features staff members who can give you the lowdown on just about any film score ever recorded. (I've spent thousands of dollars at this store over the past 15 years or so.)
- **http://www.vfxpro.com**—A website that covers visual effects news, with an emphasis on digital effects technology.
- **http://www.vfxtalk.com**—A discussion site for visual effects; also offers a gallery, industry news, and tutorials.

BOOKS

http://www.amazon.com: I don't really need to say much about this site, do I? Amazon.com features millions of books, CDs, videos, DVDs, software, electronic hardware, and other stuff to delight your heart. Do a search on "3ds max," "3d character animation," "digital lighting and texturing" or any other subject, and if there's a book on it, you'll probably find it here.

Here is a list (admittedly incomplete) of some non-3ds max-specific titles you should search for; these books are indispensable for 2D/3D animators, filmmakers, and digital artists:

- *Acting for Animators* by Ed Hooks (Heinemann Publishing, 2001)
- *Animals in Motion* by Eadweard Muybridge (Dover Pubns., 1957)
- *The Animator's Survival Kit* by Richard Williams (Faber & Faber, 2002)
- *The Animator's Workbook* by Tony White (Watson-Guptill Pubns., 1988)
- *The Art of the Storyboard: Storyboarding for Film, TV, and Animation* by John Hart (Focal Press, 1998)
- *The Artist's Complete Guide to Facial Expression* by Gary Faigin (Watson-Guptill Pubns., 1990)
- *Cartoon Animation* by Preston Blair (Walter Foster Pub., 1995)
- *Character Animation in Depth* by Doug Kelly (The Coriolis Group, 1998)
- *Digital Character Animation* by George Maestri (New Riders Publishing, 1996)
- *Digital Character Animation 2, Volume 1* by George Maestri (New Riders Publishing, 1999)
- *Digital Cinematography and Directing* by Dan Ablan (New Riders Publishing, 2002)
- *Digital Lighting & Rendering* by Jeremy Birn (New Riders Publishing, 2000)
- *Digital Texturing & Painting* by Owen Demers (New Riders Publishing, 2001)
- *Film Directing, Cinematic Motion: A Workshop for Staging Scenes* by Steven D. Katz (Michael Wiese Productions, 1998)
- *Film Directing Shot by Shot: Visualizing from Concept to Screen* by Steven D. Katz Michael Wiese Productions, 1991)
- *The Filmmaker's Handbook: A Comprehensive Guide for the Digital Age* by Steven Ascher (Plume, 1999)
- *The Five C's of Cinematography: Motion Picture Filming Techniques* by Joseph V. Mascelli (Silman-James Press, 1998)
- *How Not to Write a Screenplay: 101 Common Mistakes Most Screenwriters Make* by Denny Martin Flinn (Lone Eagle Publishing Company, 1999)

- *The Illusion of Life: Disney Animation* by Ollie Frank/Johnson Thomas (Hyperion Press, 1995)
- *The Male and Female Figure in Motion: 60 Classic Photographic Sequences* by Eadweard Muybridge (Dover Pubns., 1984)
- *Screenplay: The Foundations of Screenwriting* by Syd Field (DTP, 1984)
- *Setting Up Your Shots: Great Camera Moves Every Filmmaker Should Know* by Jeremy Vineyard and Jose Cruz (Michael Wiese Productions, 2000)
- *Shot by Shot: A Practical Guide to Filmmaking* by John Cantine (Pittsburgh Filmmakers, 1995)
- *Story: Substance, Structure, Style, and the Principles of Screenwriting* by Robert McKee (Regan Books, 1997)
- *Timing for Animation* by Harold Whitaker and John Halas (Focal Press, 2002)

MAGAZINES

- *American Cinematographer* (http://www.theasc.com/magazine) often has articles on special effects for both film and TV.
- *Animation Magazine* (http://www.animationmagazine.net) covers the world of animation, both traditional cel work and digital productions.
- *Cinefantastique Magazine* (http://www.cfq.com) has been published for almost 30 years, and it often features articles on special effects for film and TV.
- *Cinefex* (http://www.cinefex.com) is a quarterly magazine that covers cinematic (and occasionally, television) special effects. Although the magazine is expensive, it's worth every penny. When I get my copy in the mail, I read it cover-to-cover. If you're interested in special effects techniques, you should be reading this!
- *Starlog* (http://www.starlog.com) is a science fiction media magazine that occasionally covers special effects and computer graphics.

INDEX

SYMBOLS

A

B

C

F

G

N

S

V

W-Z

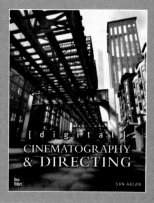

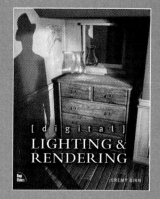

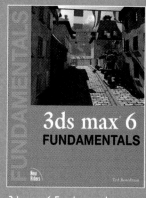

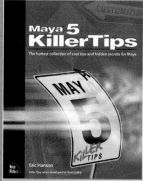

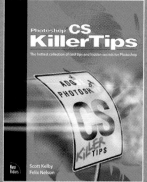

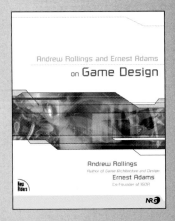

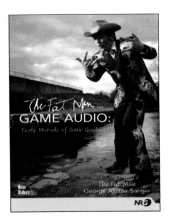

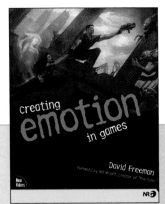

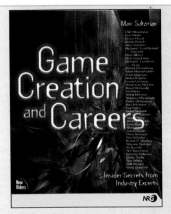

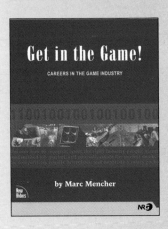